Theory and History of Folklore

Theory and History of Literature
Edited by Wlad Godzich and Jochen Schulte-Sasse

Vladimir Propp

Theory

and History

of Folklore

Vladimir Propp

Translated by
Ariadna Y. Martin and Richard P. Martin
and several others

Edited, with an Introduction and Notes,
by Anatoly Liberman

Theory and History of Literature, Volume 5

University of Minnesota Press, Minneapolis

The University of Minnesota Press
gratefully acknowledges Robert B. Ridder's financial
assistance in the preparation of this book.

Published by the University of Minnesota Press,
2037 University Avenue Southeast, Minneapolis, MN 55414
Printed in the United States of America

Library of Congress Cataloging in Publication Data

Propp, V. IA (Vladimir IAkovlevich), 1895-1970.
  Theory and history of folklore.

  (Theory and history of literature ; v. 5)
  Bibliography: p. 213
  Includes indexes.
  1. Folk literature, Russian—History and criticism—Addresses,
essays, lectures. 2. Tales—Soviet Union—History and criticism—
Addresses, essays, lectures. 3. Tales—History and criticism—
Addresses, essays, lectures. 4. Folklore—Methodology—Addresses,
essays, lectures. I. Liberman, Anatoly. II. Title. III. Series.
GR202.P7513 1984   398.2'0947   83-14840
ISBN 0-8166-1180-7
ISBN 0-8166-1182-3 (pbk.)

Contents

Editor's Note

The present volume is a miscellany by Vladimir Propp, a famous Russian folklorist, the author of the book *Morphology of the Folktale*. It contains seven articles, two chapters from the book *Historical Roots of the Wondertale*, and the introduction to the book *Russian Heroic Epic Poetry*. Chapters 1-4, 9, and 10 were translated by Ariadna and Richard Martin. Chapter 5, translated by Laurence Scott, was published earlier in *Dispositio*, and Chapter 6, translated by C. H. Severens, in Matejka and Pomorska (see Propp 1971). Chapters 7 and 8 were translated by Maxine L. Bronstein and Lee Haring. Chapter 6 was revised, and Chapters 5, 7, and 8 extensively revised, by Anatoly Liberman.

Since Chapter 5 is Propp's rejoinder to Lévi-Strauss, Lévi-Strauss's critique of *Morphology of the Folktale* was added to this book in the form of a special supplement. Its source is *Structural Anthropology 2,* Chapter 8; the article was translated by Monique Layton and revised by the editor.

We wish to thank the editor-in-chief of *Dispositio* Professor Walter Mignola, Professor Ladislav Matejka, Professor Krystyna Pomorska, and Basic Books, Inc. for their permisssion to reproduce the materials first published by them.

This book is the outcome of a collaboration between Ariadna and Richard Martin and Anatoly Liberman. The translation is faithful to the original, but a certain number of abridgments have been made, none exceeding a sentence or two. Richard Martin checked the quotations in German and French and either translated them from the original or found their published English versions. He also checked all Propp's references, which are imperfect in the Russian text, and prepared the entire manuscript for print.

In the system of transliteration adopted for the present edition, c=ts, č=ch, ij=y, š=sh, x=kh, ž=zh, and ë (after š, č)=o, so Žirmunskij=Zhirmunsky, Uxov=Ukhov, etc. Apostrophe stands for palatalization and can be disregarded when it is word final or interconsonantal (in this way *Rus'* and *Vol'ga* will become *Rus* and *Volga*), but before a vowel apostrophe designates *y*; e.g., *Afanas'ev=Afanasyev*. Only the best known names, such as Pushkin, Gogol, and Chekhov, appear below in their more or less traditional spelling. We have also retained O. M. Freudenberg's own transliteration of her name. The only Russian word used in the text without any explanation is *bylína* 'an epic lay'; the other words worth noting are *bogatýr'* 'an epic hero' and *knjaz'* 'prince, Grand Duke.'

Everyone interested in oral literature, in the history of literature, in comparative literature, in Russian folklore, in structuralism, in the impact of Marxist ideas on the humanities, and in the state of the art in the Soviet Union, will find a great deal of invaluable information in this book, and since it should inevitably appeal to a broad range of specialists and students, the notes were written for those who have had minimal or no exposure to old literatures, Russian history, and Russian folklore. But the introductory article has a sophisticated reader in view and takes the knowledge of many things for granted.

Translation of this miscellany often amounted to repeating Propp's research. The difficult and painstaking work with Propp's sources would have been impossible without the constant help of two Interlibrary Loan Divisions: those of the Pennsylvania State University and the University of Minnesota. It is also our pleasant duty to express our gratitude to Professor Alan Dundes for his comments on the manuscript and to Mr. Robert B. Ridder for his financial assistance to the University of Minnesota Press, when *Theory and History of Folklore* was only a project.

Introduction

1. Life and a General Overview

Vladímir Jákovlevič Propp was born on April 17 (29), 1895, in St. Petersburg to a family of German extraction. He spent the tempestuous years 1913-1918 as a student at the University of St. Petersburg, where he majored in Russian and German philology. He started his career as a teacher of these languages in secondary school but soon became a college instructor of German; in the list of his publications are three textbooks for Russian students of German and one article on German grammar. In 1932 he joined the faculty of Leningrad University and worked there until his death. During the first years at the University he also taught languages, but after 1938 he concentrated on folklore and never returned to linguistics or language pedagogy. He chaired the Department of Folklore until folklore was incorporated into the Department of Russian Literature. Like many university professors, he had close ties with the Academy of Sciences of the USSR (Levin 1967, Breymayer 1972a).

In 1928 Propp brought out his first book (actually his first published work) *Morphology of the Folktale*. Much later he recollected, "I called it *Morphology of the Wondertale*. To make the book more attractive, the editor replaced the word *wondertale* and in this way led everybody . . . to believe that the book would concern itself with the general laws of the folktale. . . . But my intention was not to study all the various and complex types of the folktale; I examined only one strikingly distinctive type, viz., the folk wondertale" (p. 70, below). Abroad, the book was noticed and praised only by Jan de Vries (1930, 336-39). In the USSR three friendly reviews (by R. Šor, D. K. Zelénin, and V. N. Peretc), of which Peretc's is the most detailed, welcomed its appearance. Zelenin (1929, 287) finished his review with the prophetic words, "I have no doubt that his method has a great future''; but that future was still a long way off. It came after thirty years of relative obscurity, when the book was translated into English.''One wonders,'' remarked Melville Jacobs (1959, 195), ''what its influence might have been upon a generation of non-Russian folklorists if it had been translated at once,'' and added, ''unfortunately, the 1958 translation is too late to render Propp a stimulating example of what can be done by his method.'' Now that another quarter of a century has elapsed, two things can be said about Jacobs's statement. First, Jacobs probably thought that the book had made a great stir in the Soviet Union. In this he was mistaken, because the 1928 edition of *Morphology* passed practically unnoticed in its own country. Second, as we know now, it did render Propp a stimulating example, especially after Claude Lévi-Strauss reviewed it in 1960 (Lévi-Strauss 1960; pp. 167-89, below). One of the first to accept Propp's principles and apply them to a new body of material was Alan Dundes (Dundes 1962 and 1964). If in France Propp became known through Lévi-Strauss's critique, in the United States it was Dundes who made Propp famous. The terms of the acceptance and dissemination of Propp's heritage were also determined by these two scholars. The most active French structuralists (Roland Barthes, Algirdas Greimas, Tzvetan Todorov, Claude Bremond) discussed *Morphology* in terms of semiotics and, following Lévi-Strauss's cue, kept improving Propp's scheme, whereas Dundes and those who learned about Propp from him were interested in the practical application of the new method, rather than in the criticism of Propp's epistemological foundations. Most of Propp's early readers admired his book even when they disagreed with the author's procedures and conclusions. His profound knowledge of Russian folklore combined with the attainment of a structuralist appealed on both sides of the Atlantic. Irritated pronouncements like the following by Melville Jacobs (1966, 415-16) were rare.

> It is easy to exaggerate the merits of Propp's work. Indeed, the flattery belatedly granted him has gone out of bounds. Propp made no significant advance in field methods. He offered no advance in method of analysis or theory about expressive content. What he did was to present one content-centered facet of a corpus of oral literature materials for purposes of exposing one aspect, an architectural one, of its literary style. In doing that he was enabled to perceive the inutility of motif and tale-type concepts.

However, critical remarks and important counterproposals were not uncommon. These will be discussed in the next section. Here I would like only to enumerate a few works that aimed at popularizing Propp, elucidating the positions of Lévi-Strauss, Greimas, and Bremond, and taking sides in the polemics between Propp and French structuralism. The list is not complete, because by 1970 Propp's name acquired a classical ring, to use de Meijer's phrase, and by the mid Seventies it became a ''household word'' among folklorists, so it is hardly possible to take into account every work in which *Morphology* is mentioned. Nor have I cited works in which tales of different peoples are analyzed with reference to Propp, including even such significant analyses as Marie-Louise Tenèze's articles and book, for such can fill a volume (see Holbek 1978 and de Meijer 1982a and b). By now the Proppian wave has partly retreated, and *Morphology*, together with the controversy it aroused, occupies a place of honor among the best known contributions to the science of folklore. All the works mentioned below are later than Lévi-Strauss's review and Dundes's pioneering essay. Arranged chronologically, they will allow the interested reader to trace the migration of Propp's ideas in the West: Bravo 1967 (a detailed discussion of *Morphology* with some sections on *Historical Roots* and structuralism as a trend; Bravo is the editor of the Italian translation of *Morphology*); Avalle 1970 (a survey of the polemics between Lévi-Strauss and Propp; pp. 71-74 are devoted to a comparison of Propp's and Trubetzkoy's ideas); Hendricks 1970 (pp. 89-99: Propp, Barthes, and Todorov; see also Hendricks 1975, in which the ideas of Propp, Greimas, and Bremond are compared in detail and nontrivially); de Meijer 1970 (Lévi-Strauss versus Propp); Vehvilainen 1970 (the author's 1967 presentation at a linguistic congress; no one in the audience seems to have heard about Propp, and Vehvilainen's idea that he approaches the folktale from a linguistic point of view caused a few surprised comments); Hansen 1971 (one chapter, pp. 28-54, centers on Propp, Greimas, and Bremond; the criticism, p. 34, is insignificant); Régnier 1971 (a useful discussion of Propp's functions; see also Régnier 1974, Chapter 8, "La notion de système préinterpretatif," and Chapter 12, "Les commentateurs français de Propp," in which the author sides with Propp against Greimas and Bremond); Todorov 1971 (a collection of papers written between 1964 and 1969; pp. 15-18 contain a brief discussion of Propp's method); Eimermacher 1972 (Propp and the general theory of genre; the main emphasis is on the constant elements of the literary text); Holbek 1972 (a critical review of Hansen 1971; pp. 54-55 are about Propp); Guépin 1972, 1973; Larivaille 1974 (a logical reorganization of Propp's functions, somewhat in the spirit of Greimas); Borillo 1975 (Propp and linguistic structuralism; Borillo and Borillo 1976 is a different work but on the same subject); Oppitz 1975 (pp. 201-4 are devoted to Propp and a defense of Lévi-Strauss's position); and Güttgemanns 1977 (at present, Güttgemanns is the main advocate of Propp in Germany).

Long before Propp became famous, two authors working in the United States had accorded him some attention in their manuals: Gleb Struve, in the context of postwar Soviet life (1951, 342; the same in 1971, 362-63), and Victor Erlich (1955, 217-18; the same in 1965, 249-51; 1981, stereotyped edition).

In his survey of 1969, Meletinskij examines the reaction of French structuralism to Propp and mentions many other works on *Morphology*. Thus, he discusses the Rumanian publications, which, except for Pop's articles in international journals, are little known outside their country of origin (the Romanian translation of *Morphology* appeared in 1970: see Propp 1970 and Bărbulescu 1971).

Meletinskij's survey has been translated into several languages (the English version is in *Genre* 4, 1971; the second English version in Maranda 1974, 19-51, is better avoided, because the translation was made from the German). Special mention should be made of Breymayer 1972a and b. His works are very informative, and he gives references to a number of Biblical studies whose inspiration has been Propp's book. These references are all the more interesting because, if one can judge by the programmatic issue of *Interpretation* (vol. 28, No. 2, April 1974) devoted to literary structuralism, in the United States even the invited authors from the area of theological studies did not know anything about Propp in 1974 and equated structuralism only with the French school.

The appearance of *Morphology* in English turned out to be such a success that a second Russian edition of the book (1969) was published three years after the Italian edition (which contained Propp's rejoinder to Lévi-Strauss), a year after its Polish and second American edition, and shortly before Propp's death. In 1965, Leningrad University celebrated Propp's seventieth birthday with considerable pomp. Meletinskij gave a paper on *Morphology*, and Žirmunskij and P. N. Berkov added their laudatory comments. In the wake of *Morphology's* triumph, several more works by Propp were published in the United States (1971 a and b, the latter with helpful notes; 1975b; 1976c).

The basic idea of *Morphology* is that the tremendous diversity of details in Russian wondertales is reducible to one single plot, that the elements of this plot (thirty-one in number) are always the same and always follow one another in the same order and, finally, that only seven different characters should be taken into consideration. In 1934 Propp published an article entitled "On the Origin of the Wondertale (A Magic Tree on the Grave)," which gave the first glimpse of his theory of origins hinted at in the last lines of *Morphology* but at that time unknown to the public. Two more articles ("Men's House in the Russian Wondertale" and "Ritual Laughter in Folklore") came out in 1939, and that same year, on June 15, Propp defended his work *The Genesis of the Wondertale* as his doctoral dissertation (corresponding to the German *Habilitationsschrift*). His readers were D. K. Zelénin and I. I. Tolstoj (Zelenin 1940, 54). The war prevented the publication of the work when it was written, and *Historical Roots of the Wondertale* appeared only in 1946. In *Historical Roots*, Propp attempted to prove that the structure of the wondertale, as it is described in *Morphology*, is traceable to the initiation and funeral rites.

Meanwhile, the political situation in the Soviet Union deteriorated rapidly, and the ax fell on both of Propp's books. The early Thirties witnessed a fierce fight against formalism, which was understood as any deviation from socialist realism in poetry, painting, and music, as something vaguely synonymous with "bourgeois modernism," and as any novelty in general; even professional studies of rhyme, meter, etc., were proclaimed formalistic. *Morphology*, with its interest in the structure of the tale, easily fitted the all-embracing definition (see, e.g., Petróv

1936, 40, 43, 44, 47; a relatively courteous article). Ju. M. Sokolóv mentioned Propp four times in his compendium. He said a few words about Propp's formalistic mistakes, added that Propp had already returned to the fold (as evidenced by Propp 1934), and two hundred pages later retold *Morphology* with unconcealed approval (Sokolov 1941, 109, 115 and note 5 to it, 320, 327; in the English translation of 1950 see pp. 139, 147 and note 172, 419 and 428-29).

Soon after the war another campaign was launched, this time against "rootless cosmopolitans." The enemy was identified with Jewish scholars and in addition with everyone guilty of sycophancy or kowtowing to the West, as the phrase went. The motto of the campaign became *Russian priority*. Every discovery in the arts and sciences was shown to have been made by Russians, and a passing reference to the most innocent foreign authority from Jacob Grimm onward or a biography of Pushkin mentioning Byron's influence on Russian Romanticism could undo a well established scholar (see a detailed account in Struve 1951, 358-72; 1971, 336-52). *Historical Roots* was used as a flagrant example of "sycophancy" (owing to its predominantly foreign bibliographical apparatus), and neither the fact that Propp's main texts were Russian tales nor the Marxist protestations scattered generously in the introductory chapter saved him from condemnation.

As early as July 1947 *Literaturnaja gazeta* [*The Literary Gazette*], the main political overseer of Soviet literature, published a bitter invective against *Historical Roots* (Lazutin 1947). According to the critic, Propp had dissociated the genesis of folklore from its history and espoused idealism and formalism, because instead of tracing folklore to objective reality he deduced later forms of folklore from earlier ones. A still more virulent attack was launched by *Novyj mir* [*The New World*]; Propp's *Historical Roots* was likened to a London or Berlin telephone directory (Tarasenkov 1948, 134-36). The Institute of Ethnography of the Academy of Sciences of the USSR arranged a public meeting for branding this and several other "unpatriotic" books (see Kuznecov and Dmitrakov 1948 and a report in Sokolova 1948). But this pogrom was only the beginning.

The political vortex suddenly sucked in the great Russian literary scholar Aleksandr Veselóvskij, by that time long dead. V. F. Šismarjóv, V. A. Desníckij, V. M. Žirmúnskij, V. Ja.Propp, M. I. Steblín-Kaménskij (the latter still little known in the Forties), and even N. Ja. Marr (1864-1934), the onetime dictator of Soviet linguistics, considered themselves Veselovskij's pupils or at least recognized his achievement (as was the case with Marr). These people attempted to defend their teacher in special mongraphs and in journal polemics (in those days *Oktjábr'* [*October*], which later became the standard-bearer of obscurantism, offered its pages to Veselovskij's school, and *Novyj mir*, which for several years after Stalin's death symbolized the spirit of the thaw, was among the most vociferous organs of the blackest reaction; however, between 1948 and 1952, the two journals became indistinguishable). Veselovskij's fate was probably decided in the Central Committee before the beginning of the polemics (this was the usual pattern of "discussions" under Stalin). In any case, the exchange of opinions came to an abrupt end on March 11, 1948, when the newspaper *Kul'tura i Žizn'* [*Culture and Life*] (an official party organ) published an article that castigated Veselovskij as a bourgeois liberal (a very ominous accusation), enemy of the revolutionary democrats (that is, Černyšévskij and Dobroljúbov) and cosmopolitan. Propp's name was not mentioned, but the destruction of Veselovskij's school could not pass him by. On April 1 (it had to be April 1!) a new meeting was convened, this time at Leningrad University. A. G. Demént'ev (later a commissar in Tvardóvskij's post-Stalin *Novyj mir*) gave the keynote speech, in which he repeated everything said by *Kul'tura i žizn'* and added a few derogatory remarks about Propp, who "had uncritically based himself on the works of foreign folklorists and ethnographers and deprived the Russian fairy tale (so dear to us) of all national, ideological, and artistic peculiarities, and it became like the fairy tale not only of other European peoples, but of the Australians, Polynesians, etc. The Russian tale has been bled white and robbed of its soul by Professor Propp, let alone the fact that under his pen the fairy tale has lost its historical and class features, because he reduces all its images and motifs to prehistory" (Dement'ev 1948, 84).

Propp was the first to participate in the "discussion." Both *Vestnik Leningradskogo universiteta* [*The Herald of Leningrad University*] and *Literaturnaja gazeta* published reports of that meeting (see I. V. 1948 and Anonymous 1948/2). The report in *Vestnik* is much more detailed. Propp's answer is typical of those given during such campaigns and purges. Since neither Gleb Struve (1949) nor Felix Oinas (1971a) reproduces this answer, I will give it here in full, though the printed Russian text is itself condensed. This is what Propp said (I. V. 1948, 132).

> I consider the article "Against Bourgeois Liberalism in the Study of Literature" to be a most important document, which determines a decisive stage in the development of our science. It is not fortuitous that the article concerns itself with Veselovskij. Aleksandr Veselovskij was the last undethroned idol of bourgeois prerevolutionary science. This idol, the greatest of them all and therefore the most dangerous, has fallen and fallen irrevocably. No attempts at rehabilitation will save him from the verdict pronounced by history. No compromises, no hesitations of any sort in our assessment of him, that is, of the entire science he represented, can now be entertained. . . . The history of our science is the history of the development of our national and class self-awareness. Everything in our science that has conduced to the forging of this awareness and all our modern social, material and spiritual culture (sometimes in a hard and bloody struggle) is our science. Everything that was in the way of this process is a science alien and inimical to us.
>
> Our modern science (I mean mainly folkloristics) lags behind the general upsurge of our socialist construction. I am grieved to admit

this fact, but I cannot smooth it over. We lag behind, because, among other things, we have not yet rooted out the old science. Tradition is strong and it drags us down. We often rely not on the works of the great revolutionary democrats, not on the classics of Marxist-Leninist-Stalinist science but on bourgeois scholars.

While I was writing and when I finished my latest book *Historical Roots of the Wondertale,* I was happily convinced that I had created a genuine Marxist work, because I explain spiritual phenomena by referring to the social-economic base. But disappointment came soon. My book lacks the chief element, namely, the people. The question of the people, their ideology and struggle is not as much as posed in it, though Belinskij, Dobroljubov, Gorky, and Lenin insisted just on such an approach. Like the Mythologists, I turn the fairy tale back into the remote prehistorical past. Like the Historical school, I ignore the message and the artistic organism of the fairy tale and treat it as only an archaeological document. I did not look upon myself as a comparativist, but I interpret the Russian fairy tale in light of the creative output of other peoples, that stand at earlier stages of human culture. Hence my critics' imputations of harmful cosmopolitanism, which, indeed, I cannot counter. All the charges brought against me by Comrade Dement'ev are fair.

There can be only one conclusion: we should work and work unremittingly. If we once and for all sever ties with the tradition that drags us down, we shall create works worthy of our great epoch.

In the resolution, the Academic Council expressed its satisfaction with the answers of the repentant scholars, including Propp. As O. M. Freudenberg put it, ''Propp, who had been mercilessly harassed because he was German, began to lose his sense of dignity, which he had preserved so long.'' And she recorded how in 1949 Propp fainted in the middle of his lecture and was taken to a hospital (Pasternak 1981, 268, 283).

Neither Propp's admirers nor his critics in Italy knew anything about these events. See Croce's review of *Historical Roots* (1949) and Cirese's introduction to the second Italian edition of the book (de Meijer 1982a). Propp was not deported. He did not even lose his job, but he never recovered from the horror of those spring months. The destruction of culture after the Revolution is an unpopular subject in Soviet historiography, and Propp, whose fame in the West made him a celebrity at home, has been portrayed by his biographers as a man bent on conquering one peak after another. B. N. Putílov, Propp's pupil and associate, wrote ''It is not easy to understand and explain the interests of a great scholar. The program outlined succinctly in the last pages of *Morphology of the Folktale* expressed the interests and possibilities of the young Propp, who viewed his way as long but straight. In real life everything turned out to be more complicated . . . '' (Putilov 1971, 206). Few people will know what complications are meant, the more so that Putilov, following *Russkij fol'klor,* excluded the reviews of the literary hoodlums from the bibliography of Propp's works (see Levin 1967, 38 and Gorelov 1972, 254, both of whom mention only the antiformalist drive); and cf. monstrosities like Zemljanova 1975, 157-59.

Unable to use his morphological insights ("formalism") and works in foreign languages ("cosmopolitan syncophancy"), Propp concentrated on the bylinas and brought out his third major book *Russian Heroic Epic Poetry* (1955), the fruit of ten years' labors. Not a single reference to Western sources tainted its pages, and hardly a mention is made of morphology. But by incredibly bad luck, Propp's timing was always wrong. He wrote a book full of structural revelations (*Morphology*) when the glorious epoch of Russian Formalism had come to an end and its practitioners had been banished or silenced. He published a treatise in which Russian wondertales were assigned a slot in the general evolutionary scheme of world folklore (*Historical Roots*) when the isolationist tendency in Russian history had won a complete victory; finally, he came out with a thick volume informed with a patriotism verging on chauvinism, and at that moment the frost broke. He was again late, and his reviewers (Meletinskij 1956; Uxov 1956) wondered why Propp had so blatantly ignored Western scholarship. Why really? In 1958 Propp brought out the second edition of his book; the spring freshets ran all over the place, but he introduced only a few insignificant changes into his text (for instance, he removed quotations from Stalin and Kalínin and added several noncommittal references to Mazon and Trautmann).

Although Propp worked long, his list of publications grew slowly. *Morphology* was opus 2 (preceded by a two-page abstract bearing the same title), *Historical Roots,* opus 18, and *Russian Heroic Epic Poetry,* opus 26; by 1955 Propp had been an active scholar for nearly thirty years. He still had fifteen years before him, and each of them seems to have been filled with research. Between 1955 and 1970 he wrote fifteen long articles and as many reviews, several notes, and together with M. Ju. Mel'c compiled five annual bibliographies of Russian folklore. He was an indefatigable editor and prepared ten books for publication, a reprint of Afanás'ev's tales among them.

In 1963 Leningrad University published Propp's book *Russian Agrarian Festivals,* a volume of the same size as *Morphology,* and akin to both *Morphology* and *Historical Roots.* Propp set out to investigate the structure and origins of the traditional Russian calendar. The book begins in a way typical of the post-1928 Propp, "although most people in our country have broken with religion, as I. Kryvelev points out, 'the habitual content of the festivals is always more stable than its mythological meaning.' As a result, the festivals have not yet disappeared from our life altogether. 'In many cases, people who have already broken with religion or are quite indifferent to it, to say the least, sit on the fence, as it were, and resort to religious rites and rituals.' The best way to fight such survivals is to explain the original meaning, which is incompatible with our outlook.

The present work serves just this aim'' (p. 4). Krývelev is the author of an insignificant article (1961) in the central ideological journal *Kommunist* [*The Communist*]. But of course, Propp's book is not a cheap piece of antireligious propaganda, but a thorough investigation of the festivals (Chapter 1. Honoring the Dead; Chapter 2. Ritual Meals; Chapter 3. Greeting the Spring; Chapter 4. Greeting Songs and Incantations; Chapter 5. The Plant Cults; Chapter 6. Death and Laughter; Chapter 7. Games and Entertainments). Propp traced the festivals to the economic factor, namely, the peasants' struggle for the increase of the land's fertility (for example, people ate ritual food and believed that the force contained in this food would be transferred to them and their surroundings; in spring young men and girls tied the tops of two birch trees together and passed under this arch with songs, because they believed that the force of the trees would be captured, etc.). True to his pattern of causal hypotheses, Propp rejected all other explanations and disregarded the merry-making itself. *Homo ludens* seems to have been alien to Propp. (This circumstance was also noted in Turbín's unconventional, almost unreadable review [1964]). There are brief synopses of the book in Finnish (Haltsonen 1963), Russian (Nosova 1964a), and German (Nosova 1964b).

Propp's last, posthumous, book is called *Problems of Laughter and the Comic,* and it appeared six years after its author's death: Propp 1976b. (Propp died on August 2, 1970.) The original sent by Propp himself to his prospective publishers contained three chapters: "The Philosophy of the Comic," "Mocking Laughter," and "Other Types of Laughter." The publishers removed the first chapter (Erjomina 1979, 204) and apparently were not happy about the work; they mentioned in the annotation that "the book is very incomplete," yet "they chose to publish it." The sections of the book are as follows. Section 1. Several methodological remarks (pp. 5-15); Section 2. Mocking laughter (pp. 15-123): Types of laughter and mocking laughter as a type, those who laugh and those who do not laugh, the ludicrous in nature, some preliminary observations, man's outward appearance, the comic aspects of similarity, the comic aspects of differences, man disguised as an animal, man as a thing, the deriding of professions, parody, comic exaggeration, thwarted plans, duping, alogisms, falsehoods, the verbal devices of the comic, comic characters, role exchange: "Much Ado About Nothing"; Section 3. Other types of laughter: kind laughter, cruel and cynical laughter, ritual laughter, carnival laughter; conclusion: additions and results, literary mastery (pp. 125-81). One can see at once that Propp is in his element: he has taken a difficult phenomenon and offered a meticulous classification of species and genera. He reviewed several theories of the comic and came to the conclusion that laughter is caused by the discrepancy between what we expect and what we find in real life; it is provoked by relatively small imperfections (otherwise, our reaction is indignation, loathing, etc.), and only if the discovery of the imperfection is sudden. The same principle underlies the comic effect in verbal art. His generalization is not a breakthrough, but his data are varied and interesting.

Also in 1976, a book of Propp's articles came out in Moscow (Propp 1976a), including the answer to Lévi-Strauss, never published in Russian before. A volume *V. Ja. Propp in memoriam* (Meletinskij and Nekljudov 1975), like the 1976 miscellany, opens with an essay by Putilov and contains a list of Propp's publications (Propp's bibliography can also be found in *Russkij fol'klor* 10 (1966): 337-43, and 13 (1972): 258-59; for an abridged English version of Propp's bibliography see Levin 1967, 47-49).

Those who wrote about Propp mainly described his works; yet they mention his kindness, readiness to help, and excellent teaching abilities. Propp always looked for one unifying principle behind diversity, which accounts both for his insights and dogmatism. His first book (*Morphology*) was his greatest achievement, but his subsequent works do not strike the reader as anticlimactic, because at least three of them are the building blocks of one edifice. *Historical Roots* is a natural sequel to *Morphology*, and *Russian Agricultural Festivals* belongs to the same series. *Russian Heroic Epic Poetry* represents a different line of Propp's research, but it too is closely connected with his other works: like its predecessors, it focuses on typology and history, and his theory of archaic epos grew from his studies of the wondertale. Propp's talent was recognized at once, and his earliest effort won the approval of such luminaries as Zelenin, Eixenbaum, and Žirmunskij (Žirmunskij recommended *Morphology* to the Academic Press). Roman Jakobson never forgot the book either and had it translated into English. Jurij Sokolov ventured to praise it in 1941.

Propp must have been a very reserved man. Not a single joke or verbal twist can be found in his entire published heritage; even the book on laughter is couched in the mechanical language that makes the reading of *Morphology* so difficult. His style is dry and repetitive. In his evaluation of other scholars, he never disclosed his own personality. He had great respect for I. I. Tolstoj (1880-1954), but in his introduction to Tolstoj's posthumous miscellany (Propp 1966b) he spoke only about that scholar's academic achievement. In Tolstoj he admired the traits that he had developed in himself: great learning, the gift of seeing similarity where no one else detected it, a lifelong interest in historical typology, and distrust of borrowings in folklore. He never lost his reverence for Goethe and Veselovskij and must have had a strong aversion to deductive reasoning. In his answer to Lévi-Strauss, he proudly called himself an incorruptible empiricist. He was not vindictive; in an obituary of P. D. Uxov (1963c), Propp expressed his admiration for his late colleague (Uxov's prodigious memory, profound knowledge of the bylinas, and a truly remarkable power of observation appealed to Propp very much), but it was only eight years before his death that Uxov had published a critical review of *Russian Heroic Epic Poetry*. Polemics was not Propp's strong point, and his thunderbolts were usually directed against such impersonal enemies as bourgeois scholarship, the Russian Historical school, and the like. But he defended himself when he could. Thus, he clashed with B. A. Rybakóv several times on the historicity of the bylinas, and he responded to Lévi-Strauss's criticism (I think Lévi-Strauss was wrong in calling the rejoinder an offended harangue). His belated international fame could not but come to him as a surprise, but this fame radically changed his status, for after 1958 he was treated by all as the most distinguished student of Russian folklore in the world.

Below I will discuss the conceptions of Propp in the the hope of making him more available to the numerous scholars for whom *Morphology of the Folktale* has opened new prospects.

2. Propp and Structuralism. Propp versus Lévi-Strauss

In the Sixties many Soviet scholars began to study semiotics, and the Tartu school headed by Jurij Lotman was especially visible. Although Propp's ideas occupied a central place in the semiotic revival, to most of his readers in the Soviet Union Propp is primarily a folklorist, and they study his books because they want to learn something about Russian tales, Russian bylinas, Russian festivals, and so on. In the West this aspect of his work interests very few people, and Propp is studied for the sake of the method developed in *Morphology of the Folktale*. Therefore, it is natural to begin an evaluation of Propp with a glance at his structuralism. In my discussion I will concentrate only on those aspects of Propp's theory that make it comparable to the teachings of Trubetzkoy, Jakobson, and Lévi-Strauss. (For a broader treatment of Propp's background and legacy see, apart from the works cited above, Shukman 1976; 1977a; 1977b; and Jason 1977.)

Structuralism has always been a vague term, even when applied to linguistics. From time to time technical terms current within a certain school are put together and published in the form of glossaries. The success of such efforts is dubious. We find that everything ever said by Roman Jakobson between the two world wars, Mathesius, Trubetzkoy, Trnka, Vachek, and some others exemplifies the usage of the Prague Circle, that the numerous statements by Boas, Bloomfield, Bloch, and their disciples make up the creed of descriptive linguistics, and a concordance to Chomsky and Halle's *Sound Pattern of English* will produce a summary of generative phonology. In this way various scholars, each with his or her own meditations and discoveries, are pinned down in separate showcases as representatives of so many species. When several schools are compared, for example, Prague phonology, Danish glossematics, and American descriptive linguistics, the volume of comparison becomes so large that the content is not always worth rescuing. The common denominator of structuralism in linguistics, literature, psychology, anthropology, etc., is still less meaningful. Such "across the board" comparisons are useful only because they disclose the prevailing tendency of human thought during long periods of history. Of necessity, they cannot be very informative. In all discussions of structuralism, linguistics occupies a prominent place. Literary scholars, sociologists, and anthropologists constantly accuse their opponents of underestimating or overestimating the achievements of modern linguistics. Such arguments create the impression that linguistic structuralism is something well defined, which is wrong. Practically all European and American linguistics after World War I has been structuralist. On Russian soil, the process of development was checked by the emigration and suppression of the "formalists," "idealists," etc., who soon lost their battle against state-supported Marxist-Marrian linguistics. In the United States, Chomsky and his followers first called themselves antistructuralists, but they meant "antidescriptivists"; they were with Sapir and Jakobson against Bloomfield and therefore did not leave the womb of structuralism.

The theses common to all twentieth-century Western linguistics are, as I believe, five in number. (1) Language is an autonomous, self-contained system and should be studied as such; philosophy, psychology, aesthetics, and many other branches of knowledge can supply valuable information about language, but language as a system of signs is an object of linguistics, which must study nothing but these signs. (2) It is necessary to distinguish language (*langue*) as a system of elements, and speech (*parole*) as its concrete manifestation. (3) Language is a system of mutually dependent elements: if one element is changed, the entire configuration (structure) is affected. For this reason, each element should be studied in terms of distinctions; it is more important to know the relative than the absolute value of language constituents. (4) Language elements are signs: one side of them refers to something in the world of things (the signified), and the other, to the means of expression, such as phonemes and morphemes (the signifier). (5) Language system and language history are different disciplines, and synchronic description should be carried out without resorting to diachrony.

Today these statements belong to the opening pages of any linguistic manual. We will go over them to establish their role in the development of other areas, especially literature. (1) The role of system is better demonstrable at some levels than at others. Phonemes form a system because their distinctive features are obtained from comparison with other phonemes. The higher the level within the language hierarchy, the less obvious its systemic nature (this is especially true of semantics). But a literary text is of course a system: its parts are organized in such a way that they either call to mind what is absent from the utterance (this is their associative, paradigmatic, or metaphoric value) or refer to other parts in the same text (this is their syntagmatic, or metonymic value). As is the case with language, literature receives countless impulses from psychology, aesthetics, etc., but a literary text as a verbal message is governed by laws of its own, which are the primary object of literary theory. (2) Differentiation between *langue* and *parole* has resulted in the emergence of phonology as a branch of linguistics, with its emphasis on invariant units (phonemes) and realizations (variations, or allophones). The langue/parole dichotomy has proved to be one of the most fundamental achievements of structuralism. In literary studies it has become common practice to distinguish between the invariant (more or less abstract) scheme and its manifestations. Folklore presents an ideal case: "improvised" texts are related to the text known to the community and to active bearers of tradition exactly as speech is related to language (Bogatyrjóv and Jakobson's well known study [1929] is concurrent with Milman Parry's first works). Lévi-Strauss treats myth as an invariant structure and all the concrete texts as its variants. (3) The emphasis on the relative, rather than absolute values of language elements, is the main aspect of every theory dealing with distinctive features. All minimal units are treated as bundles of such features. Although Lévi-Strauss operates with "bundles," they are quite unlike Trubetzkoy's bundles, but one side of the feature approach has been very popular outside phonology. Jakobson offered to reduce all oppositions to binary ones, and, following his example, Lévi-Strauss and many other scholars have subjected their data to binary analysis. (4) The discovery that language consists of signs was very important for the humanities. Semiotics unites students from many fields, and in the final analysis structuralism is an attempt to find the message (signified) and the ways of its expression (signifier). The goal itself is not new, but the idea that the message produces its own unique artistic means and that the plane of content and the plane of expression have comparable structure is original and fruitful. (5) Separation of synchrony from diachrony is equally important for language and literature and follows from the proposition that each system is not only connected with many other systems but is also self-contained, which justifies a structural view (thesis 1). Literary scholars are especially prone to substituting the study of biography, social environment, parallels, and so forth for the study of the text as it stands. This danger is not so conspicuous in linguistics, but both linguistics and literature have suffered from historical explanations where they are not wanted. We know why the words *man, mouse,* and *foot* have anomalous forms in the plural, but a mere reference to Old English does not say anything about the status of these plurals in present-day English. In similar fashion, the origin of a literary style and its modern function are different things. In linguistics de Saussure's structuralism was, at least partly, a reaction against the Neogrammarians, a German school for which theory and history were near synonyms.

Linguistics has taught literature many things. Literary theory has become aware of invariants and realizations and has begun to look upon itself as a branch of semiotics; it has learned to distinguish between text as a self-contained unit and text as a product of outside influences. It may therefore seem that linguistic and literary structuralism have a lot of common ground. This is also the impression created by surveys, introductions, popular lectures, and philosophical overviews. But this impression is deceptive, because now that almost a century has passed since Baudouin de Courtenay and de Saussure made their ideas public, the importance of structuralism lies not so much in its theoretical principles as in the methods of application. It is one thing to accept the bilateral nature of the sign and the decisive role of oppositions in various kinds of material, and quite a different thing to show how these concepts work in each concrete case. And here we find that linguistics and literature often part company.

Structuralism is supposed to have proved itself in linguistics, but this is what nonlinguists think. In fact, the structural *method* has been very successful only in phonetics, which is a privileged level of linguistics for several reasons. It works with a finite set of units, and the number of phonemes in any language is small. The ambiguous nature of the sound needs very little proof. Indeed, living speech contains an immeasurable number of vowels and consonants (it is hardly possible to pronounce exactly "the same" sound twice, and no two people ever produce "the same" sounds; the word "same" is rarely applicable to the process of phonation), but, on the other hand, only a limited number of typical vowels and consonants really matter in the process of communication and the existence of alphabets is based precisely on those types (phonemes). Phonology is a set of procedures by which the linguist reduces the infinity of sounds to a finite set of phonemes. This process of reduction consists of three stages.

The substance with which the phonologist works, whether it is represented by a curve or a spectrogram, does not immediately reveal the presence of phonemes, because from a physical point of view speech is a continuous flow. Curves have points of varying height, and spectrograms show darker and lighter spots, but the correlation between the highs/lows and the formant structure of speech on the one hand and the division of speech into such units as words, morphemes, and phonemes on the other is complex. A spectrogram is meaningful only from a linguistic point of view; the acoustician is unable to read it alone. So the first step in phonological analysis is the segmentation of an indiscrete current into discrete units. All languages consist of syllables, and in some of them syllables are further indivisible blocks. However, in a great number of languages, syllables are not the smallest units of segmentation. For example, the English words *boy* and *boys* are both monosyllables, but association with meaning allows us to isolate -*s*, a unit that does not constitute a syllable. Whether -*s* itself is further decomposable we cannot say yet. In words like *reading* -*d*- is segmentable because it gets into the vice between two boundaries: the form is *read-ing* as a morphological entity and *rea-ding* as a phonetic (disyllabic) complex, so the result is *rea-d-ing*. Division into morphemes precedes phonological analysis, and so does syllable division. Phonology begins with the crudest segmentation of the type described above. The linguist cannot work with phonemes until they have been isolated syntagmatically (in the chain of speech). At the earliest stage of analysis the phoneme is only a minimal unit of segmentation.

The next task is to recognize the same phoneme wherever it occurs. We can isolate the phoneme *s* in *sip-s* (because -*s* is a grammatical formant indicating the plural, if *sips* is a noun, or the third person singular, if it is a verb), but we have no means of identifying this *s* with *s* at the beginning of the word. This is where the machinery of distinctive features comes in. In languages with at least some words having alternating forms and others making up recognizable clusters, phonemes enter into natural groups: cf. *plastic—plasticity* (*k:s*), *house—houses* (*s :z*), *wife—wives* (*f:v*), *feet—foot* (*ee:oo*), *speak—speech* (*k:ch*), *serene—serenity* (*e: ĕ*), and so forth. A distinctive feature is a marker that makes *s* unlike *z, f* unlike *v*, etc. Comparison of *wife* with *wives* will not reveal the physical characteristics of the distinctive feature(s) that keep(s) *f* and *v* apart; we can say only that *f* is different from *v* and that some feature *x* makes the differentiation possible. Since each phoneme is opposed to a number of phonemes, each will end up as a bundle of many features. This is the second step of assembling the phoneme. Initially, the phoneme emerged as the smallest unit of segmentation; now it has been represented as a bundle of distinctive features such as XYZ, AXY, XY, AZ, etc.

The decoding ends with mapping these relational features onto the phonic substance of language. When the physical (articulatory and acoustical) substance of the distinctive features has been ascertained, phonemes become recognizable in any position: *f* in *five* and *f* in *wife*, word initial and word final *s* in *sips*, etc., will be labeled as variants of *the same* phonemes, which signifies a decisive leap from parole to langue, from speech in its concrete manifestations to the system of language. The phoneme, previously a minimal unit of segmentation and a bundle of abstract distinctive features culled from the available oppositions but tied to the place where the oppositions occur, assumes the role of the invariant of a multitude of sounds sharing the same distinctive features.

Language is a code, and phonology is partly responsible for breaking it. Phonology can perform its task only with the help of semantics and grammar (because phonemes can first be isolated as endings, suffixes, and other meaningful units), but it retains a considerable measure of autonomy owing to the last step. Phonology shows how an indiscrete, continuous current of phones becomes a discrete chain of phonemes, and some of the phonological operations have counterparts in grammar, semantics, literature, mythology, and the other areas that claim to be amenable to structural analysis. We will presently examine the convergences between phonology and the science of folklore, but first it is necessary to dwell on one more general problem.

Once the phonemes have been segmented and described in abstract and physical terms, their interrelationships can be studied from many points of view. Some of these interrelationships will have emerged in the process of decoding. For example, *f* and *v* form a pair because they alternate in *wife—wives, shelf—shelves*, etc., and we can risk the hypothesis that the feature responsible for the differentiation between *f* and *v* is the same that sustains the alternation of the final consonants in *house* [s]—*houses* [z], *path* [θ]—*paths*[ð], *sandwich* [č]—*sandwiches* [ž] (the latter mainly in British English). Thus, we get a correlation of four pairs— *f:v, s:z, θ:ð, č:ž.* On the other hand, *p* and *b, t* and *d, k* and *g* never alternate in the same way, so whichever feature distinguishes *p*, *t*, *k* from *b*, *d*, *g* in English, it is not the same as the one discovered in juxtaposing *f*, *s*, *θ* with *v*, *z*, *ð*. Such classes are often very approximate, and additional scrutiny reveals additional properties of the phonemes as a system. Trubetzkoy's classification of phonemes according to various principles is a miracle of ingenuity and a model worthy of imitation. But the primary grouping of phonemes obtained in the process of decoding has an important advantage: it is absolutely natural. The material itself yields the classes, and they are as incontestable as the sections of an orange. Everything else is hidden and must be brought out by the searching linguist. There is nothing wrong in using one's power of observation, but when we no longer follow the division of the orange into sections we can cut our fruit in many equally plausible ways. Phonology traditionally studies vocalic and consonantal systems, which are represented in the form of more or less controversial schemes and diagrams. To many people, a search for designs in their data is the essence of structuralism. Only in phonology are decoding and structuralization two sides of one process. Phonological analysis obtains structures while breaking the sound code; for phonology, structure (that is, the arrangement of phonemes) is a byproduct of decoding. Outside phonology, the role of decoding diminishes, and the structural method inevitably changes. Bearing all this in mind, we can examine the applicability of the three-step process (as it was outlined for phonology) to grammar and literature, including mythology and folklore.

Step 1. Segmentation looms large at all levels of linguistics. Specialists constantly discuss how to delimit the morpheme. Equally if not more difficult is the concept of a separate word. The ultimate goal of phonology is to produce a set of units like *p*, *t*, *k*, *b*, *d*, *g*, *i*, *e*, *o*, *u*, *a*, which have no meaning of their own. All the other units of language are meaningful from the very start. Consequently, no level of language can be decoded exactly like its sound base. The phoneme is an indissoluble unity of function and phonic material. Without recourse to the physical properties of the phoneme's realizations, even Step 2, let alone Step 3, cannot be completed. Phonemes are *sound* invariants. Semioticians often believe that, since language is a code, its material is accidental, and natural sounds are said to be on a par with light signals and colored flags. This is a mistake. Human language is a sound code, and a number of its essential properties are determined by its substance. De Saussure's emphasis on the purely semiotic nature of language has been both beneficial and harmful for scholarship, because twentieth-century linguistics has greatly neglected the study of limitations that the material imposes on the system of relationships. De Saussure was correct in saying that, no matter what the chessmen are made of, the game will be the same if the rules are the same, but language is not a game of chess, and the language code is not indifferent to its vehicle. Once the code has been broken, it is possible to replace the phonemes by pennons, or dots and dashes; the resulting secondary code will not prove anything about natural language, just as the crutch proves nothing about the structure of the leg. Among the structuralists who are not preeminently linguists, Lotman and Barthes realized quite early the role of material in semiotic analysis (Lotman 1968, 29; Barthes 1965, 1, 2, 7). Higher levels of linguistics and literature do not encounter the specifically phonological difficulties, but segmentation is as acute a problem for them as for phonology. We will see that the deepest difference between the two main trends in structural folklore concerns just the principle of segmenting a coherent text.

Step 2 is a search for distinctive features. It has already been pointed out that the idea of bundles of distinctive, usually binary, features is current outside phonology and even outside linguistics. Only a few details need be added here. A distinctive feature is not another word for any feature. In Trubetzkoy's system, distinctive features are yielded by unidimensional oppositions (two phonemes form a unidimensional opposition if they share some unique feature). His procedure has given rise to endless controversies about the nondistinctive and redundant features, neutralization, etc., but the fundamental idea has stayed. Nonphonological structuralism, which is apt to borrow linguistic principles wholesale and disregard their flaws, has often indulged in truisms just in the chapter devoted to oppositions. It may be true or false that the opposition *p:b* is neutralized in *speak, spend,* etc., after *s*, but the statement itself leads to certain conclusions. The statement that the semantic opposition *day:night* is neutralized in *dusk* is modeled on the previous one, but it leads nowhere. Again, Roman Jakobson's classification of all the phonological features as binary may be true or false; in any case, it is supported by phonetic research and a certain general view of phonology. Outside phonology, binarism is popular only because opposites are easy to find ('up' and 'down', 'man' and 'beast', 'cooked' and 'raw', etc.). Some progress in the search for distinctive features has been made in linguistic semantics, but not in literary studies. The phonologist cannot complete the segmentation of the speech chain or recognize phonemes without obtaining bundles of distinctive features. On other levels the very notion of distinctive has remained a blur.

Step 3 is the assembling of variants covered by a certain invariant. Invariants are in the foreground of every structural discipline. In phonology, all the variants of one phoneme have the same distinctive features, and conversely, only those sounds manifest the same phoneme that can be shown to have the same distinctive features. Apparently, the levels of analysis that do without bundles of distinctive features have difficulties in assembling their invariants.

I will now sum up the foregoing remarks. They may have struck the literary scholar as unnecessarily technical, but without the technicalities the entire argument would have been pointless.

1) The principles of linguistic structuralism, as they were put forward by de Saussure, can be applied to all levels of linguistics and many areas outside linguistics. (2) Like every other "paradigm," structuralism started with formulating its symbol of faith. The Prague Circle translated the general principles

into a method that has proved more durable than several other rival methods. The Circle's main achievement was phonology, classically represented by the works of Trubetzkoy and Jakobson. (3) Phonology is a science of breaking the language code at its lowest level. Its procedures revolve around the segmentation of the speech current, isolating minimal units, describing them as bundles of distinctive features, and representing them as sound invariants. (4) Besides breaking the sound code, phonology aims at representing the sound units of language as a system of interdependent elements. Although the second task is merely an extension of the first, it takes on great significance in many studies and often appears as a problem in its own right. Looking for ordered sets, schemes, and so forth, increases in importance at each higher level, as the role of decoding diminishes, because only phonology works with meaningless units whose purpose it is to serve semantics. (5) In grammar, semantics, and literature there are questions also known in phonology, namely, obtaining minimal units of analysis, describing their (distinctive?) features, and discovering invariants that reduce the infinite number of surface realizations to a definite and usually small number of types. (6) Although each area produces its own variety of structuralism, with the operations determined by its unique substance, in discussions of structural method it is reasonable to keep in view the main concepts of phonological method, that is, minimal units, distinctive features, and invariants, and define their status in each particular system.

I will begin with Propp's variety of structuralism. In his article "The Structural and Historical Study of the Wondertale," which is a rejoinder to Lévi-Strauss, Propp wrote:

> In a series of wondertales about the persecuted stepdaughter I noted an interesting fact: in "Morózko" [Frost] . . . the stepmother sends her stepdaughter into the woods to Morozko. He tries to freeze her to death, but she speaks to him so sweetly and so humbly that he spares her, gives her a reward, and lets her go. The old woman's daughter, however, fails the test and perishes. In another tale the stepdaughter encounters not Morozko but a lešij [a wood goblin], in still another, a bear. But surely it is the same tale! Morozko, the lešij, and the bear test the stepdaughter and reward her each in his own way, but the plot does not change. Was it possible that no one should ever have noticed this before? Why did Afanas'ev and others think that they were dealing with different tales? It is obvious that Morozko, the lešij, and the bear performed the same action. To Afanas'ev these were different tales because of different characters in them. To me they were identical because the actions of the characters were the same. The idea seemed interesting, and I began to examine other wondertales from the point of view of the actions performed by the characters. As a result of studying the material (and not through abstract reasoning), I devised a very simple method of analyzing wondertales in accordance with the

characters' actions—regardless of their concrete form. To designate these actions I adopted the term "functions." My observations of the tale of the persecuted stepdaughter allowed me to get hold of the end of the thread and unravel the entire spool. It turned out that the other plots were also based on the recurrence of functions and that all wondertale plots consisted of identical functions and had identical structure. (pp. 69-70, below)

This is Propp's method in a nutshell. The tales that interested Propp are classified under numbers 300 to 749 in Aarne-Thompson's index. The choice of this particular section did not satisfy Propp as a theoretician. He criticized Aarne's division of all folktales into animal tales, tales proper, and anecdotes, as well as Aarne's wondertale categories: a supernatural adversary, a supernatural husband (wife), a supernatural task, a supernatural helper, a magic object, supernatural power or knowledge, and other supernatural motifs, and yet he recognized that Aarne's intuition had not led him astray. At the beginning of Chapter 2, (1975a, 19) he said: "By 'fairy tales' are meant at present those tales classified by Aarne under numbers 300 to 749. This definition is artificial, but the occasion will subsequently arise to give a more precise determination on the basis of resultant conclusions." Now we know what he meant by a more precise determination. Having described the wondertales from Afanas'ev's collection, Propp deduced their morphology and found that all of them have the same type of structure, so he could say that only those tales are wondertales that have this particular type of structure (morphology). He did not define wondertales, he only redefined them, but this redefinition proved useful.

Propp's functions are akin to motifs but differ from them in one vital point. The term *motif* is used loosely. According to Stith Thompson, a motif is a minimal narrative unit ("once there lived a man and a woman who loved each other dearly, but they were not quite happy, because they had no children"), or a familiar figure (a wicked stepmother), or a familiar object (seven-league boots, a cap of invisibility), though the first meaning (a minimal narrative unit) is by far the most important. Veselovskij also identified the motif with a minimal (he said "the simplest") narrative unit; a group of such units makes up the plot (*sjužet;* the English translation [1975a, 12] most unhappily renders *sjužet* as *theme*). Propp was full of admiration for Veselovskij, which did not prevent him from noticing that Veselovskij had sidestepped the definition of "simplest." In the example given above it is possible to detect at least three motifs: "a man and a woman loved each other dearly," "They were not quite happy," and "(because) they had no children"; "a man and a woman loved each other dearly" similarly falls into two parts: "once there lived a man and a woman," and "they loved each other dearly." This difficulty is obvious while we remain on the syntagmatic plane. It is less obvious that the illusory simplicity of the motif is also destroyed by paradigmatic associations. Propp gives a convincing example: "a dragon kidnaps the tsar's daughter.'' A substitution table provided by the entire corpus of Afanas'ev's wondertales shows that "the dragon may be replaced by Koščéj, a whirlwind, a devil, a falcon, or a sorcerer. Abduction can be replaced by vampirism or various other acts by which disappearance is effected in tales. The daughter may be replaced by a sister, a bride, a wife, or a mother. The tsar can be replaced by a tsar's son, a peasant, or a priest" (Propp 1975a, 12-13). So each element of the sentence "a dragon kidnaps the tsar's daughter" turns out to be a motif too. Propp draws the correct conclusion: the final unit of division does not represent a logical whole.

Propp was surprised that his observation had not occurred to others. As a matter of fact, Propp had a Russian predecessor, who outlined the type of analysis carried out by Propp and even used the word *morphology* in the same sense as Propp (Nikiforov 1928; see its English translations: 1973 and 1975), and in Austria, von Hahn developed a somewhat similar approach four decades earlier (see Taylor 1964, 114-16). Dundes (1976, 87-88) quite correctly points out the similarities between Propp and van Gennep. But Propp's method is not trivial. Propp was the first theoretician of folklore who realized that textual analysis should start with setting up strict procedures of segmentation. In this respect he was not only abreast of the time (the epoch of dying Russian Formalism and nascent phonology), but years ahead of his time. Even in phonology, where segmentation is an inescapable difficulty, it was greatly underestimated (for example, by Trubetzkoy, Bloomfield, and Hjelmslev) and still is.

How nontrivial Propp's conclusions are follows from a small but characteristic example. In 1933, W. R. Halliday discussed the theories of monogenesis and polygenesis in folklore and, while supporting the first of them, said the following (pp. 16-17):

> In the case of stories we must satisfy ourselves that where two tales are claimed to be variants of the same story, they are in fact identical in structure and not merely similar in a general sort of way. . . . The various forms of this tale [of the rash vow of the master builder to sacrifice the first person coming to the bridge and the consequent building up of his wife as a foundation sacrifice] are genuinely variants of the same story because they possess not merely a general resemblance of idea but also an identity of structure. They consist, that is to say, of an identical series of incidents arranged in the same general order of interest.

Today such passages are usually called structuralist insights. There is no doubt that the above quotation reads like an excerpt from the early Propp, but Halliday did not go further and did not produce any theory resembling Propp's. Robert Georges (1970, Notes) gives this quotation and seems to imply that it has a structuralist ring, but if not only folklore but also the history of folkloristics is a system, Halliday should not be allotted a place in the development of folktale morphology.

Incidentally, even the term 'morphology' does not necessarily presuppose a structuralist approach (cf. Honti 1939; for a survey of "Classical' morphological quests antedating Propp's book and some later attempts made in obvious ignorance of Propp see Voigt 1977, 567).

The thirty-one units of the wondertale isolated by Propp are well known. Their number can perhaps be modified: Greimas (1966, 194; first published in 1963), by a series of logical operations, reduced the thirty-one functions to twenty, and E. M. Meletinskij and G. L. Permajakóv offered their own interpretations (see a short discussion of them in Revzin 1975, 82), but in this context the principle is more important than the number.

Here are the first eight units discussed in *Morphology of the Folktale:* (1) one of the members of a family absents himself from home (absentation), (2) an interdiction is addressed to the hero (interdiction), (3) the interdiction is violated (violation), (4) the villain makes an attempt at reconnaissance (reconnaissance), (5) the villain receives information about his victim (delivery), (6) the villain attempts to deceive his victim in order to take possession of him or of his belongings (trickery), (7) the victim submits to deception and thereby unwittingly helps his enemy (complicity), (8) the villain causes harm or injury to a member of a family (villainy)—(8a) one member of a family either lacks something or desires to have something (lack). All the rest are of the same type. A segment of the text qualifies for a separate unit if it contains an action, if this action is a recurrent constant in a number of tales and describes the function of one of the dramatis personae, and if this constant is realized in variables. The last condition is logically not necessary; it just happens that the constants *are* manifested in many different ways (if there were no variety of realizations, Propp's discovery would have been made by the very first investigator of the wondertale).

Propp's method of segmentation is associative and functional. It is associative in the sense that it depends on the presence of the common part. If we said that the words *bit, pit, sit, fit,* and so forth fall into *b-it, p-it, s-it, f-it,* this would be a comparable approach to dividing the phonetic chain. Trubetzkoy segmented words in exactly this way. But a common part is segmentable only if it always plays the same role (in other words, a common part is a separate unit if it is known to be a separate unit!). Cf. the letters *m* and *n*: they have a common part, but it does not follow that *m* can be divided after the second downstroke; the same is true of the oval in *d* and *a* (see Zinder 1960, 38). The mere fact that the hero of the wondertale is given a magic horse or a magic pipe in so many tales is not yet sufficient for segmenting this episode as a unit. It becomes a separable unit because it always plays the same role in the narrative: the hero acquires a tool with which he will overcome his opponents and achieve his goal (that is why Propp's method of segmentation is not only associative but also functional). As a result of Propp's analysis, the wondertale comes to be defined not through the plot, but through composition. Propp wrote:

Function, according to my definition of the term (as used in *Morphology*), denotes the action of the character from the point of view of its significance for the progress of the narrative. If the hero jumps to the princess's window on horseback, we do not have the function of jumping on horseback (such a definition would be accurate only if we disregarded the advance of the narrative as a whole) but the function of performing a difficult task as part of courtship. Likewise, if an eagle takes the hero to the country of the princess, we do not have the function of flying on a bird but one of transfer to the place where the object of the search is located. The word "function" is a conventional term that was to be understood in this and no other sense. I deduced the functions from detailed comparative analyses. (pp. 73-74, below)

Just as thousands of episodes appeared to be manifestations of a few basic "functions," so did the numerous personages of wondertales turn out to be manifestations of several easily recognizable types. Propp's statement that the dragon can be replaced by Koščéj, Vixr' [whirlwind], a devil, a falcon, or a sorcerer, while the daughter can be replaced by a sister, a bride, a wife, or a mother presupposes the same level of abstraction as the statement that abduction can be replaced by vampirism or various other acts by which disappearance is effected in tales. Propp discovered the following types of dramatis personae in the wondertale: the villain (marplot), the donor, the helper, the princess (the sought-for person) and her father, the dispatcher, the hero, and the false hero.

The experience of phonology shows that segmentation has a syntagmatic and a paradigmatic side. In the process of segmentation, phonemes form natural classes and reveal their distinctive features. To a certain extent, successful completion of segmentation is the end of the road: by the time the phonemes have been separated from their neighbors we learn enough or nearly enough about them to be able to characterize each phoneme uniquely. Propp did not need any analogue of bundles of distinctive features in his analysis, but Step 3, as it has been characterized above, has an almost exact counterpart in *Morphology*: a minimal unit of *composition* is assembled as an invariant of so many *narrative* elements sharing the same function. Propp's method of analyzing wondertales bears a strong resemblance to the phonological method in its Prague version; the similarity lies not so much in details as in the general orientation: his process of decoding is reminiscent of what we find in phonology.

This conclusion is not meant as a value judgment. Folklore is not phonetics, but characteristically, Propp both excelled and stumbled exactly where the phonologists always do. More than half a century has passed since the appearance of *Morphology*, and at present nothing prevents us from assessing its true role. Curiously enough, Soviet scholars did not notice Propp's most important weaknesses either before or after 1958. For years their attention was directed away from their own areas; instead of discussing folklore, literature, and language, they searched every work for formalism, idealism, bourgeois influences, and the like. When it became clear that the accusations of seemingly profound philosophical errors were only a form of political blackmail, the Soviet humanities were left without any critical apparatus. The development of Soviet structuralism and semiotics in the Sixties and Seventies is a case in point. Anyone working with the concepts of structuralism was hailed as a serious and innovative scholar. Propp suddenly found himself in the center of a tremendously inflated semiotics, whose practitioners were not so much interested in the truth of his discovery as in the possibility of rewriting his *Morphology* in semiotic terms. Propp's conclusions with regard to the structure of the folktale were accepted uncritically and put into a new and alien context. Serebrjanyj 1966 or 1975 (who obviously emulated Greimas) and Revzin 1975 are typical examples of this trend. Cf. also Klein et al. 1977. The experience of Meletinskij is equally characteristic. Alone and as a joint author, he did a great deal to popularize *Morphology*; however, he never examined the difficulties unsolved in that book.

Propp's *Morphology of the Folktale* and Trubetzkoy's *Grundzüge der Phonologie* are works of incomparable magnitude; yet the same verdict can be pronounced about them: both authors undoubtedly discovered true codes, but both presentations are full of holes. Although Trubetzkoy's theoretical construction is shaky, the entire progress of phonology (and to a certain extent, of all twentieth-century linguistics) consisted in rectifying his "mistakes"; without them there would have been very little to build on. The same holds for Propp: his result (the obtaining of wondertale morphology) is significant, but not all his conclusions and methods are correct. We have seen that Propp's definition of the wondertale is circular, for he rejected Aarne's types and then used them for singling out the wondertale. The idea that the sequence of functions in the wondertale is always the same is unwarranted, and Propp dismissed many exceptions too lightly. It is inaccurate to say that a function is defined only by its consequences and its place in the narrative chain; for example, the hero may receive a magic tool at his birth, at the beginning of his quest or just before accomplishing his feat, but the function will be the same. Several actions, called connectives by Propp, find no place in his morphology. In his model he enumerates thirty-one functions and explains that no tale contains all of them, but we are not told how many functions constitute the minimum. Even assuming that the actions are constant and the actors variable, we should not disregard the actors, for the set of roles (the king, the princess, the witch, the evil stepmother, and so forth) is an indispensable element of the wondertale, just like its structure (in other words, the fairy tale cannot be transposed into another substance and remain the fairy tale). Also inaccurate is Propp's claim that basically there is one type of Russian wondertale. Propp had to split the pivotal function No. 8 into two unrelated functions, and his subsequent analysis of "one type" is strained. See the most important critical remarks on Propp (apart from Lévi-Strauss's review) in Peretc 1930, Fischer 1963, 288-90; Taylor 1964, 126; Nathhorst 1969a (together with Drobin's response, 1969, and Nathhorst's rejoinder, 1969b); Røder 1970; Lüthi 1973 a and b; 1974, 115-21; Bremond, 1973,

20-28. (The often cited review by Šor 1928, as well as Drobin 1970, are mere synopses; Reaver 1959 contains no discussion.)

However, Propp's greatest weakness lies elsewhere. Lévi-Strauss was the first to observe that Propp wants to construct the morphology of the tale before learning its semantics. Unfortunately, Lévi-Strauss reduced the entire difficulty to the imaginary opposition between formalism and structuralism, and Propp did not even notice Lévi-Strauss's remark (but see Nathhorst 1969a, 21, 26 and Steiner and Davydov 1977, 156). Propp says that only actions (the stable elements of the tale) matter for his morphological purposes, whereas the dramatis personae (the variables) do not affect the tale's structure, so all primary definitions should be made solely in terms of actions. But to know that the actions are the same, we have to know who performs them! There is certainly no difference between one villain or another carrying off the bride, *as long as we know that the attacker is the villain*. Propp missed this point and fell into the same trap as descriptive linguistics and many phonologists of different schools after him. How can we isolate (that is, segment and identify) phonemes? Do we need to know anything about morphology and semantics when we start a phonological description, and if we do, just how much? To answer this question, we have to offer a unified theory of language decoding. Likewise, to save Propp's idea, we need a much deeper theory of narrative decoding than the one envisaged by Propp. And this is the only great task worthy of mature structuralism and mature semiotics.

We can now turn to the ideas of Lévi-Strauss, Propp's admirer and severest critic.

Lévi-Strauss has been imitated by so many and criticized so often that a new discussion, especially a brief one, may seem a useless enterprise. The main reason for offering an exploration into Lévi-Strauss's ideas in this essay is almost accidental: in his review of Propp's *Morphology* (1960), Lévi-Strauss opposed his own method to Propp's. Since then the two scholars have been compared a number of times, and it is with the view of adding some details to this comparison that I will cast a glance at Lévi-Strauss's structuralism.

Lévi-Strauss's contribution to the study of folklore is his four volumes of *Mythologiques* (1964; 1966a; 1968; 1971; in English: 1969, 1973b, 1978, 1981), which is a meticulous analysis of more than eight hundred American Indian tales; several of his articles collected in two volumes of *Structural Anthropology* (1958; 1973a; in English: 1967; 1976); and a book on savage thought (1962; in English: 1966b). The first problem that confronted Lévi-Strauss was the same that Propp had to solve before starting his work, namely, delimiting the corpus of texts. Propp's solution was not simple: he found Aarne's classification untenable (at least from a theoretical point of view), then used it for his own purposes, showed that the tales numbered 300-749 in Aarne's index indeed form a remarkable unity of composition, and redefined the wondertale in his own terms ("Morphologically a [wonder]tale . . . may be termed any development proceeding from villainy . . . or a lack . . . , through intermediary functions to marriage, . . . or to other functions employed as a denouement": Propp 1975a, 92). By doing so, he vindicated Aarne's division. Propp emphasized several times that Aarne's weaknesses were less important than his intuitively correct approach to his data; for Aarne usually preferred to be reasonable rather than consistent. Propp realized that the existence of wondertales was only a working hypothesis. He proved that wondertales exist as a uniform structural group, but he also proved that to isolate the wondertale one does not need a structural approach. Such simple concepts as magic and transformation identify it quite well. Propp was unable to break through the usual vicious circle of definitions: cf. his procedure—wondertales are tales of magic and transformation. (Nos. 300-749 in Aarne's index); these tales have a certain uniform structure; only those tales are wondertales that have this structure. The circular logic of this procedure is patent, and as a predictable result not only wondertales can have the morphology described by Propp.

The texts constituting Lévi-Strauss's data are in one sense much more complicated than the tales analyzed by Propp. Myths, unlike wondertales, do not form a homogeneous literary genre (if they form it at all) and lack the structural unity that has always been clear to students of the wondertale. Lévi-Strauss believes that myths reflect such deep-rooted oppositions that they can be studied independently of their original language and natural environment. In practice, he often violates his own dictum and learns a good deal from the vocabulary of his texts (including even the etymologies) and the culture of the American Indians whose tales he studies. Since myths in their entirety lack uniform morphology in Propp's sense, they cannot be recognized on purely literary grounds (unlike the wondertale, the sonnet, or the ballad). Lévi-Strauss does not object to Malinowski's idea that myths are charters for some beliefs or institutions, but he never uses this sociological criterion for separating myths from nonmyths. He analyzes myths without defining them in any way, as if the problem did not exist. And apparently it does not exist for him; he says, "Whatever our ignorance of the language and the culture of the people where it originated, a myth is still felt as a myth by any reader anywhere in the world" (1967, 206). Although relations between myth and history and between myth and romance are always at the center of his attention, Lévi-Strauss mentions the difficulty of rubricating oral literature only once in his *Mythologiques*. This is what he says in the "Overture" to *The Raw and the Cooked* (1969, 4):

> It must not be considered surprising if this work, which is avowedly
> devoted to mythology, draws unhesitatingly on material provided by
> folk tales, legends, and pseudo-historical traditions and frequently
> refers to ceremonies and rites. I cannot accept overhasty pro-
> nouncements about what is mythology and what is not; but rather I
> claim the right to make use of any manifestation of the mental or
> social activities of the communities under consideration which seems

likely to allow me, as the analysis proceeds, to complete or explain the myth.

Personally, I find it very surprising (just as Dundes [1964, 43, with a reference to David Bidney], Nathhorst 1969a, 47, and Maybury-Lewis [1970, 155; first published in 1969] did before me), especially because in his critique of Propp's book Lévi-Strauss says many interesting things about the relationships of myth to the wondertale. Lévi-Strauss's unwillingness to "accept overhasty pronouncements about what is mythology and what is not" means that oral tradition is something whole for him. Myths, folktales, legends, etc., reveal with equal clarity the workings of "savage thought" to Lévi-Strauss, and that is all he is interested in.

Perhaps the most striking difference between Propp and Lévi-Strauss is that Propp remained a literary scholar even in his semiethnographic work *Historical Roots of the Wondertale*, whereas Lévi-Strauss as a mythologist is concerned to clarify "not so much what there is *in* myth . . . as the system of axioms and postulates defining the best possible code, capable of conferring a common significance on unconscious formulations which are the works of minds, societies, and civilizations chosen from among those most remote from each other" (1969, 12). Propp and Lévi-Strauss are not complementary, each espousing his own brand of structuralism; Propp tried to discover the structure of the tale, and Lévi-Strauss, the general laws of the structure itself. Lévi-Strauss has no rivals in noticing convergences and parallels among various myths. Nothing escapes his attention; every detail becomes a part in the jigsaw puzzle that he solves brilliantly and imaginatively. He misses only the obvious, namely, the peculiarities of oral transmission, and insists that everything in a tale reflects its *mythological* structure. This is so obviously wrong that it needs no elaborate refutation. Myths (or what Lévi-Strauss calls myths) are structured as certain messages and as oral tales. No one can bring out the essence of myths, wondertales, epics, and so on without studying the interplay of the two structures (cf. Kirk 1970, 75-77).

Propp examined a closed corpus of tales and discovered the invariant structure of their composition. Each tale was a unit in its own right for him, and he even gave some thought to how to delimit one tale from several tales merged together (Chapter 9 of *Morphology*). Lévi-Strauss works with an open set. He treats hundreds of tales as related on the assumption that at one time they had very wide currency, and when one text does not give him enough information he borrows the missing links from other tales, sometimes registered in quite a different and very remote area of America. This method has often been criticized but not always for the right reason. If "authentic links of a historical or a geographical nature have been established . . . or can reasonably be assumed to exist," there is no objection to the use of the tale as Lévi-Strauss wants it. The real flaw of Lévi-Strauss's method is its mechanistic character. The folklorists of the Finnish school also grouped together all similar motifs, even though they played different roles in their respective plots. Propp's attack was directed against just such coordination. The main lesson of his *Morphology* was that the folklorist is not allowed to compare one magic horse with another or one appearance of Baba Jaga with another, but only one function with another. Everything depends on the role of the magic horse in each episode, because actors change freely, and only their roles remain intact. The danger of Lévi-Strauss's flights over the Americas is not so much in the distances as in the choice of his addressees.

One parallel, called exemplary by Lévi-Strauss himself, will suffice as a typical illustration (1969, M_8, M_{55}, and p. 132). In a Kayapo-Kubenkranken myth of the origin of fire, a young man is left stranded on a rock. He is rescued by a friendly jaguar who first notices the man's shadow and then, covering his mouth, looks up, sees the lad, addresses him, and takes him to his own home. In a Bororo myth of the origin of fire, a monkey dupes a jaguar whom he sends on a foolish expedition to catch the sun. The infuriated jaguar comes back and intends to kill the monkey, but the monkey has climbed a tree. The jaguar makes the tree sway, and the monkey has to jump down. He cries to the jaguar, "I am going to let go, open your mouth." The jaguar open his mouth wide, whereupon the monkey drops into it and disappears in the jaguar's belly. Later the monkey cuts open the jaguar from inside and comes out. Lévi-Strauss has noticed a strange detail in the first myth: before looking up, the jaguar covers his mouth. This enigmatic detail is explained with the help of the second myth, in which the jaguar's open mouth proves to be the instrument of his undoing: "the Bororo myth throws light on the Kayapo one: if the Kayapo jaguar had not covered his mouth with his paw, the hero would have fallen into it and would have been swallowed up, exactly in the same way as the Bororo monkey" (1969, 132). Although this is an embarrassing explanation, it is better than some of his others, because Lévi-Strauss can go much further and compare a South American tale with a Japanese one. Such comparisons are not very common, and Lévi-Strauss admits that they run counter to "the sound method of structuralism," but he resorts to them all the same. Several of them (from the first three volumes of *Mythologiques*) are collected by Marc-Lipiansky (1973, 154-57) under the tactful title "Comparaison informelle." With regard to "jaguars and men," see a very critical discussion in Makarius and Makarius 1973, 141-94, and the defense of Lévi-Strauss by Oppitz (1975, 295ff.).

Returning to the linear structure of myth, we observe that segmentation, so important for Propp, does not seriously interest Lévi-Strauss. He may mention in passing, as he does in the introduction to *Mythologiques IV*, that the tales at his disposal are very loose from a literary point of view, but their imperfection is an inconvenience rather than an obstacle to him. Lévi-Strauss breaks every myth into episodes according to the requirements of his analysis. This arbitrary "chopping up" of the text has troubled Edmund Leach, Mary Douglas, and several other critics, but Lévi-Strauss's practice is quite justified, because the invariant structure of myth that *he* seeks does not depend on the syntagmatic division of the tales. Invariants occupy the very center of Lévi-Strauss's quest, which brings us to Step 3.

According to Lévi-Strauss, all myths are structured alike: allegedly, they tell about some basic contradiction and the way this contradiction is overcome (his own term is "mediated"; extending the phonological metaphor to myths, we could perhaps say "neutralized"). This structure allows people to live with the most basic dilemmas of existence. An especially significant manifestation of mythic structure is an opposition between nature and culture, with cooking and fire serving as mediator. Every work by Lévi-Strauss on mythology supplies numerous instances of such neutralized oppositions. Again I will confine myself to one example, taken almost at random from *The Raw and the Cooked* (M_{15}, M_{16}, and M_{18}). The myths are etiological tales about the origin of wild pigs and deal with two species: *caetetu* and *pecari* (caititu and peccary in English), which Lévi-Strauss identifies with collared peccary (*Dicotyles torquatus*) and white-lipped peccary (*Dicotyles labiatus*). I will skip the story itself and quote only the closing remarks, since it is possible to guess the outline of the tale from the conclusion that follows (1969, 86):

> The three myths allow us to understand the semantic position of the two species: they are associated and contrasted as a pair, which is particularly suited to convey mediation between humanness and animality; since one member of the pair represents, as it were, the pure animal which is nothing but animal, whereas the other has become an animal through the loss of its original human nature, to which it was untrue through asocial behavior: the ancestors of the peccaries were human beings who showed themselves to be "inhuman." The caititus and peccaries are therefore semihuman: the former synchronically, since they constitute the animal half of a pair whose other member is human; and the latter diachronically, since they were human beings before they changed into animals.

This aspect of Lévi-Strauss's teachings is known to a wide range of specialists through his early works on the Oedipus plot and the article "La Geste d'Asdiwal" (twice published in English, the last time in Lévi-Strauss 1976, 146-97). Both analyses are relatively short and easy to follow, which is undoubtedly the reason why they have been discussed so often and with such devastating results for Lévi-Strauss: see Adams 1974 and especially Thomas et al. 1976; like Meletinskij (1976b, 98), I think that a parody is an improper vehicle of criticism, but a parody (as Meletinskij himself admits) can be useful: see Codère 1974. Lévi-Strauss's idea that the message of myth is its structure, even though people may not be aware of it, and his flippant and paradoxical statements about myths leading their own existence have caused a torrent of criticism. A great deal of this criticism is due to misunderstanding. Every artifact, be it a pot, a painting, a symphony, or a tale, is produced by the human brain and hands, but as soon as it is alienated from its creator, it starts a career of its own, subject to the laws of its inner organization. This is the main lesson of Russian Formalism (accused of indifference to content!) and all structuralist efforts. One and the same charge that seems never to grow threadbare with use is laid at the door of structuralism, which is said to sacrifice the aesthetic values for the sake of a dead scheme. But structuralism attempts to discover the mechanism of things, the code that allows them to function. Once this is discovered, the question immediately arises about the relevance of the code for aesthetics (cf. Anonymous 1970, 808). In a living body the skeleton is covered with flesh, and its shape reflects the structure of the skeleton, at least up to a point. But who will dare to reproach osteology with indifference for human beauty? Structures are not easy to disclose, and their relations to aesthetics are rarely studied. Lévi-Strauss has every right to say that "it would perhaps be better to . . . proceed as if the thinking process were taking place in the myths, in their reflection upon themselves and their interrelation" (1969, 12), but he is mistaken when he takes the discovery of the structure for the end result of analysis (cf. Lotman 1963, who, I think, at that time would have sided with Lévi-Strauss). Actually, one runs into more far-sighted statements scattered all over *Mythologiques,* but if we stay with Lévi-Strauss's practice rather than chance remarks here and there, the conclusion is clear: according to Lévi-Strauss, the content of myths is only a vehicle for conveying its structure. This is like saying that symphonies exist for the scores to be printed the way they are. Lévi-Strauss's structure is not selective: names, actions, smells, noises, etc., always form the same simple pattern (two extremes and a mediator), for, as we have seen, according to Lévi-Strauss, everything in a myth is mythic, everything is relevant as part of the myth, everything allows the deep-rooted mythic structure to assert itself in the chaos of manifestations. This, and not an unscrupulous, willful treatment of the data by the scholar, is what Lévi-Strauss calls *bricolage.*

There seems to be nothing "savage" in the progress of thought from the awareness of oppositions toward their resolution. Shakespeare's dramas can easily be reduced to this formula, and the mythological school of literary criticism can discover a myth in any novel. In a restrained way, an enthusiast from the Slavic field has applied Lévi-Straussian categories to Tolstoy, Aksákov, Gogol, and Dostoevsky (Barksdale 1974). One of Lévi-Strauss's paradoxes is that he has described savage thought and proved that there is no such thing, because, according to him, thought processes are intrinsically the same everywhere; they are universal, given the opposition man : animal. This is the main point of his revolt against Lévy-Bruhl's tradition.

Propp's and Lévi-Strauss's invariants are quite distinct entities. Lévi-Strauss's concern is with the level of oppositions (which explains why he adopted Jakobson and Halle's matrices) and the relational code. Propp discovered compositional invariants. The two are neither complementary nor disjunctive. Both may be false or true, or only one of them may be true. If every element in a tale reflects the tendency toward mediating a basic contradiction, nothing follows about the invariant formula of its sequential organization, and, conversely, the scheme of the tale, according to Propp, something formidable like

$$\beta^1 \gamma^2 \zeta^1 \eta^3 \delta^2 \theta^3 A^1 \left\{ \frac{C\!\uparrow[D^1E^1 \text{ neg.}]^3\ [D^1E^1 \text{ neg.}]^3\ F \text{ contr.}}{B^4 C\!\uparrow[D^1E^1 \text{ pos.}]^3\ [D^1E^1 \text{ pos.}]^3} \cdot H^1\text{-}I^1K^4\!\downarrow \right.$$

(Propp 1975a, 130) throws no light on its internal grid. Propp's formulas make sense because each invariant serves a higher level, namely, the plot. The "functions" move the plot along and do it in a predictable (formulaic) way. There is a strong resemblance between the tales as analyzed by Propp and language, because for linguistics the concept of level is of prime importance. Phonetics and grammar are not just two consecutive chapters in a textbook: they are levels by virtue of forming a hierarchy. Units of a lower level make up those of a higher one. A linguistic unit has two main properties: it is an invariant of a class of realizations and a building block of a higher unit. In stratifying the language, we run the risk of striking the bottom or reaching the ceiling, neither of which is a level. The bottom is sounds: they are not units, because they are not invariants of anything but are themselves realizations of phonemes. Phonemes, on the other hand, are classical units: the phoneme is an invariant of an infinite class of sounds and a part of the morpheme, a unit of a higher level. The ceiling is not so visible. For instance, Hjelmslev dismissed phonetics as physiology and semantics as "encyclopedia" and did not treat them as linguistic levels. Whether he was right in regard to semantics is immaterial in the present context. Heated discussions about the status of phraseology and stylistics within the science of language revolve around similar questions.

Lévi-Strauss does not work with levels in the technical sense of this term. He distinguishes many codes, such as the acoustical code, the culinary code, and the cosmological code, among others. A code in Lévi-Strauss's system is a way of organizing the concepts that belong to related semantic fields (that is, all references to sound and silence, to cooking and dishes, etc.). His goal is to show that all codes are structured alike and reinforce the message, because each moves toward the mediation of the polar extremes. The idea that all "levels" (codes) of the tale convey the same information has antecedents in the linguistic theory of isomorphism. Both Lévi-Strauss and his popularizers often refer to the notion of isomorphism; Lévi-Strauss has several symbols for isomorphism, and when he uses this word he means symmetry, equivalence, homology. A short linguistic digression will supply Lévi-Strauss's isomorphism with all the background it needs.

In linguistics, the idea of isomorphism was formulated by Hjelmslev and developed by Jerzy Kuryłowicz. According to Hjelmslev, it is necessary to distinguish between the plane of content and the plane of expression, *each of which has its substance and its form.* This extremely powerful postulate is sometimes vulgarized as meaning that isomorphism obliterates distinctions among the linguistic levels and calls for one methodology in the study of phonetics, grammar, and semantics. In fact, the idea of isomorphism suggests only that both content and expression in language are bilateral; it does not presuppose the congruity of the processes occurring on the two planes. Although Roman Jakobson does not seem to have touched on the theoretical foundations of isomorphism in any of his major works, his analyses of lyric poems (for example, Jakobson and Lévi-Strauss 1962, and Jakobson and Jones 1970) are exercises in isomorphism. James Boon (1972, 54-55) cited Lévi-Strauss's words on the untenability of literary structuralism and wondered what had made Lévi-Strauss become Jakobson's coauthor in the article on Baudelaire's sonnet. The answer is self-evident: Baudelaire's sonnet offered great possibilities for an isomorphic demonstration, and one should hardly add that bricolage is only a trade name for isomorphism (Boon says nearly the same on pp. 56-57 but in different terms).

In my comparison of Propp and Lévi-Strauss I have repeatedly emphasized the noncomplementary character of their teachings. The question arises: Are they both structuralists? As pointed out at the beginning of this section, structuralism can be defined in many ways. Scholars who concur with de Saussure's main principles and recognize the semiotic value of language, literature, and culture and draw some practical conclusions from these principles; scholars looking for the inner structure of things, for their underlying design, for invariants and realizations; scholars interested in some one area (for example, phonology) and investigating it with "structuralist" tools, that is, operating with distinctive features, correlations, and neutralization—all of them are structuralists. The important element is not the creed but the value of the results obtained with its help. Nothing in structuralism guarantees that its practitioners will not produce nonsense. Between the adoption of some principle and the practical results lies method. Only those problems are solved correctly that are solved in a correct way. Many philosophers have thought so ("the way to the truth itself must be of the truth"). If the truth is simply guessed, it is nonverifiable. If no strict method is used to lay bare the sought-for design, the conclusions the structuralists arrived at have no advantage over the conclusions of earlier scholarship, and there is no distinction in being a structuralist and no point in distributing labels. Structuralism begins by assuming the existence of the structure in its object and consists in proving this assumption.

Lévi-Strauss's principal flaw is the weakness of his method. I will examine his analysis of the Oedipus myth, because this celebrated analysis has been cited in every major article and book on Lévi-Strauss, and because it is concise and clear and has both a beginning and an end (cf. Leach 1970, 69-71; Glucksman 1974, 59; Paz 1975, 30-33; Ricœur 1976, 83-84; Freilich 1977; Jenkins 1979, 118, and note 26; Shalvey 1979, 47-48; Kurzweil 1980, 18), so I probably understand it correctly. Lévi-Strauss's representation of the myth (1967, 210) is as follows.

Cadmos seeks his sister Europe, ravished by Zeus			
		Cadmos kills the dragon	
	The Spartoi kill one another		
			Labdacos (Laios's father) = *lame* (?)
	Oedipus kills his father		Laios (Oedipus' father) = *left-sided* (?)
		Oedipus kills the Sphinx	
			Oedipus = *swollen-foot* (?)
Oedipus marries his mother, Jocasta			
	Eteocles kills his brother, Polynices		
Antigone buries her brother, Polynices, despite prohibition			

Lévi-Strauss treats the myth as an orchestra score, which he reads from left to right as well as from top to bottom, with rows supplying the sequence of events and columns reflecting similar relations. The common features of the columns are: the overrating of blood relations (1), the underrating of blood relations (2), the killing of monsters (3), and (provided the etymologies are correct) difficulties in walking straight and standing upright (pp. 210-11).

This is how the "structure" is discovered. According to Lévi-Strauss, the first thing to do is to break down each story into the shortest sentences possible and write each sentence on an index card bearing a number corresponding to the development of the story (p. 207). Each gross constituent will contain a relation, but the true constituent units of a myth are not the isolated relations but bundles of such relations. Lévi-Strauss's explanation is far from clear. The first three columns of the "score" consist of eight summarizing sentences. What has happened to all the index cards, of which there must have been several hundred? How were the so-called gross units obtained? Did the text of the myth look originally like Barthes's *S/Z*, a book that Lévi-Strauss considers dazzling? (1979, 495).

Lévi-Strauss invites us to *discover* the common characteristic of each column, but were the "gross units" not isolated in such a way as to make the discovery possible? The analogy between the mytheme as a bundle of relations and the phoneme as a bundle of distinctive features is interesting because in both cases the distinctive feature is a marker of common behavior. In phonetics, common behavior is an obvious fact (for example, only three phonemes alternate in a certain position, and this is their common distinctive feature); in other areas, distinctive features can play a similar role (a very impressive example is Mary Douglas's [1966, 54-57] analysis of "clean" and "unclean"). But in Lévi-Strauss's scheme the features must be guessed before grouping. All five items in Columns 2 and 3 deal with killings, so why are they arranged they way they are? Since the Spartoi are supernatural beings, this episode can be assigned to Column 3; the distinctive feature of Column 3 will remain "the killing of monsters," and in the sequence of events the slaying of the dragon will still precede the Spartoi episode, as it must. "Antigone buries Polynices" can be grouped with "Eteocles kills Polynices" and form a separate column; the distinctive feature of such a column will be something like "disposing of a relative." "Oedipus kills Laios" and "Oedipus marries Jocasta" can also be shown to belong together. Everything depends on how many "instruments" (columns) we want to have in our score. I alluded exactly to this difficulty when I said that once we refuse to follow the sections, we are free to cut the orange in many equally plausible ways. Lévi-Strauss has reduced all myths to the interplay of opposites. His visible success does not prove that myths are really made up of binary oppositions, but it proves that any kind of material can be represented as a network of pluses and minuses.

In his quest for opposites and their mediators Lévi-Strauss is guided by his miraculous, almost superhuman power of observation. He says that a close relation exists between a riddle and incest (the example is again from the Oedipus myth), for the riddle unites two irreconcilable terms, and incest unites two irreconcilable people. Lévi-Strauss may be correct, but his truth is the truth of a poet, not a scholar. His revelations are only his. Leach has mentioned several times (for example, 1967, xvi; 1970, 62) that Lévi-Strauss's method is not entirely new, for Hocart, Lord Raglan, and Propp "made gropings in the same direction." The direction may have been the same, but the results were quite different. Leach himself, when he works according to Lévi-Strauss's doctrine, is inconsistent. His comparison of two versions of the creation story in the Old Testament is Lévi-Straussian in spirit, but in comparing Adam's and Cain's stories he noticed not so much the similarity of "codes" as the fact that different actors play almost the same drama, and this is the main nerve of Propp's analysis.

Propp's results are reproducible by anyone. Roman Jakobson's essay on Pushkin's statue myth (1979, first published in 1937) is close to Propp's *Morphology,* and so is the oral-formulaic concept of theme. If those who belonged to the Parry-Lord school and took their cue from Magoun's articles on Old English poetry had been more interested in general theory, they would have discovered their predecessors at once. Lévi-Strauss is an incomparably more inventive and resourceful scholar than any of his contemporaries, but his work has engendered only a breed of literary Spartoi: they are either his popularizers and vehement admirers or his severe critics. It would be a dull man who would not learn something from Lévi-Strauss, but brilliance and reliability are different things. So many breathtaking hypotheses have passed before our eyes in the last fifty years; we have been told that all words of all languages consist of the same four elements, that culture and especially literature are totally subservient to economy, that the (probably nonexistent) rules of English stress are innate, that all tales of all times are about the phallus and the vagina. . . .

There is an excellent bibliography called *Claude Lévi-Strauss and His Critics* (Lapointe and Lapointe 1977). Its rubrics show the main lines of discussion: Lévi-Strauss and Christianity, Lévi-Strauss and Marxism, Lévi-Strauss and symbolism, Lévi-Strauss and structuralism, etc. In this carnival comparatively few people have taken the trouble of analyzing Lévi-Strauss's procedures in their entirety. Lévi-Strauss was inspired by structural linguistics and especially by Roman Jakobson's sermon (although the influence of phonology and linguistic terms diminishes noticeably from "The Structural Study of Myth," and even *Le Cru et le Cuit,* to *L'Homme Nu*). His followers and his critics seldom doubt that Lévi-Strauss's structuralism is indeed an extension of Prague phonology; see Simonis 1968; Lima 1968, 19-29; Moravia 1969; Scholte 1969, 101 (with two references to earlier sources); Marc-Lipiansky 1973; Caldiron 1975. The reason for this delusion is that the works of Lévi-Strauss have hardly ever been discussed by linguists. In the late Sixties, when the transformational method reached the peak of its popularity, a few scholars noticed that both Lévi-Strauss and Chomsky use transformations and look for underlying structures, and the two names were rather often coupled in theoretical discussions. Since there is nothing in common between Lévi-Strauss and Chomsky, the discussions were unproductive; a dismaying but fairly typical example of wasted labor is Buchler and Selby 1968. Chomsky himself quite justifiably found no points of convergence between Lévi-Strauss's teachings and his own (Chomsky 1968, 64-65), but his comments are very brief.

Roger Poole touched upon Lévi-Strauss's linguistics in several publications, of which his 1970 article is the most detailed. According to him (Poole 1970, 12), the use of the linguistic model in *Les Structures élémentaires de la parenté* was very effective and in the *Le Totémisme aujourd'hui* and *La Pensée sauvage* the author's methods "were refined to take in not only physical configurations of the tribe and its marriage and kinship structures, but also the substructures of myth and totemic observation, as well as economic, linguistic and exchange structures. . . . " Poole's charges are directed only against *Mythologiques:* structuralism needs great amounts of new data but all Lévi-Strauss has done "is to widen and deepen the implicit possibilities of the method. He has never forced a structure on to his materials: always concerned to see what, by use of the *analogy* of linguistic structures, would come clearer if these structures were fitted like a grid over the materials he is concerned with" (p. 13).

Roman Jakobson collaborated with Lévi-Strauss in the analysis of "Les Chats" (see above) and often referred to Lévi-Strauss's explorations of myth but never subjected them even to the briefest analysis. Martinet (Parret 1974, 227) and Steblin-Kamenskij (1976, 13, 23-27; pp. 27, 36-39 of the 1982 English translation) made do with sneers—easily the worst approach to Lévi-Strauss.

I am aware of only one serious work by a professional linguist on the linguistic foundations of Lévi-Strauss's method. In 1970 Georges Mounin (pp. 199-214, written in 1969) assembled most of Lévi-Strauss's references to general linguistics and phonology and came to the inescapable result that Lévi-Strauss shows a poor understanding of both. In Mounin's opinion, Lévi-Strauss is mistaken when he insists that structure and opposition are specific linguistic concepts and his pluses and minuses in the matrices have nothing to do with linguistic relevance; he has mixed up diachrony and syntagmatics (for he equates sequence with history) and has been carried away by the untenable syllogism that since language is a communicative system, every communicative system is a language. Mounin sums up his discussion by saying that for Lévi-Strauss linguistics is only an authority and a metaphor (see the English version of Mounin's chapter on Lévi-Strauss in Rossi: 31-52, printed with a commentary by Marshal Durbin: 53-59).

Most scholars take Lévi-Strauss at his word and even accuse him of unduly stretching the phonological principles. Several quotations that follow (chosen from a large stock) show how even the most erudite anthropologists misrepresent the problems of linguistics. "Linguistics and any analysis modeled on linguistics can only be synchronic sciences. They analyze systems. In so far as they can be diachronic it is in analyzing the before-and-after evolution of systems." "In language the message is consciously communicated and consciously received by native or fluent speakers. It is not found at the level of syntax. . . . Nor do linguists expect to find universals at the level of syntax." "Structuralist theory maintains that what we discriminate are not the sound elements (phonemes) as such, but the distinctive features which underlie the sound elements, such distinctions as vowel/consonant, compact high-energy sound/diffuse low-energy sound. These distinctions are, in effect, second-order data, 'relations between relations.' . . . It is this 'distinctive feature' version of transformational phonology [!] which has been mainly exploited by Lévi-Strauss in his application of structuralist ideas to social anthropology."

In spite of his involvement with linguistics, Lévi-Strauss learned very little from it. Leach has remarked (1970, 8) that Lévi-Strauss's method is as much linguistic as anthropological and that it is the method that is interesting rather than the practical tests to which it has been put. It is hard to accept this verdict. Aside from being puzzled how one can praise a method that gives no results, I believe that Lévi-Strauss's method bears the most superficial resemblance to the methods of linguistics and is too undeveloped to arouse more than a passing curiosity; however, the conclusions he has reached in a roundabout way are sometimes thought-provoking. No wonder that, though Lévi-Strauss admired Propp's *Morphology*, he misunderstood it. Only one point should be made in connection with the dialogue of the two scholars. After Lévi-Strauss's review it has become customary to call Propp's approach syntagmatic and Levi-Strauss's, paradigmatic. Structuralism can never be only syntagmatic, for every unit exists in relation to its neighbors (the syntagmatic aspect) and to other units, which are absent from the concrete situation (the paradigmatic aspect). The same is true of Propp's "functions" (cf. the remarks to this effect in Hendricks 1973b).

3. Propp and Marxist Theory: Synchrony

If Lévi-Strauss fell in love with Marxism at the age of seventeen, Propp, together with all his Soviet contemporaries, was bullied into it after the Revolution. But, as Anna Axmatova once said, children can be born even from a marriage of convenience, and Marxist ideas pervade everything Propp wrote between 1928 and the mid Sixties.

The Soviet brand of Marxism has many overlapping aspects. Readers of Soviet works on literature, general linguistics, and anthropology, let alone history, sociology, and philosophy, are constantly reminded of the line that separates Soviet and bourgeois scholarship. Bourgeois scholarship is then divided into Russian prerevolutionary scholarship, which, admittedly, made a number of grave errors but which is not entirely beyond redemption (the last aspect came to the foreground in the Forties and Fifties), and West European/American scholarship, which must be unmasked, exposed, pitied for its crass ignorance, falsified, and robbed wherever possible. For decades, the phrase "the only correct path" dominated the printed page in the Soviet Union. The opposition between *us* and *them*, between Soviet and bourgeois scholarship, occupies a prominent place in Propp's legacy. This opposition assumes several shapes. First of all, Propp used a pool of quotations that allowed him to feel safe under the most diverse circumstances. At the close of the article "The Nature of Folklore" Propp says: "Marx characterized even Greek mythology as 'nature and social forms that had already acquired an *unconscious* artistic treatment in the people's imagination.' If Marx was not afraid of this word, there is no reason for us to avoid it" (p. 14, below). In another work ("Folklore and Reality") we read: "Lenin said, 'In every folktale there are elements of reality. . . . ' If we examine Lenin's words more closely, we will see that, in his opinion, the folktale does not consist entirely of elements of reality. He said only that they are present" (pp. 17-18). The first work was published in 1946 (a very black year), the second, in 1964 (a rather liberal year by Soviet standards), but the approach is the same: there is a quotation, it contains ultimate wisdom, regardless of whether the author knew the subject, and it is the Soviet scholar's business to use this quotation in the best way possible. References to the four classics of Marxism—Marx, Engels (especially Engels),

Lenin, and Stalin—turn up in every major contribution of Propp; after 1952 only three of them remained. The Soviet temple of Marxism consists of two chambers: the classics and the Russian radical critics: Belínskij, Dobroljúbov, and Černyšévskij; in folklore studies Gorky follows Černyševskij. Quotations from these authors are almost as valuable as those from Marx-Engels-Lenin(-Stalin), as is evidenced by Propp's book *Russian Heroic Epic Poetry.*

The spirit of criticism is well captured in the following statement: "I will not dwell on individual works written by representatives of many prerevolutionary schools. In the study of folk poetry, older Russian academic scholarship did not and could not have fundamental, major achievements, since its premises and methods were false. There could be and in fact there were only correct specific observations that we can use. The most progressive scholars collected masses of invaluable material, but this did not save their theories from total bankruptcy" (p. 155 below). "Did not and could not" was one of the standard formulas.

The main enemies of the Marxist are idealism and metaphysics. Both became ghosts long ago, but they are belligerent ghosts set loose at the slightest provocation. Idealism is especially active. Genetics, structuralism, cybernetics, and several other areas of knowledge were eradicated as idealistic. One could also lapse into the heresy of agnosticism: any statement to the effect that a certain prehistoric feature is beyond reconstruction (for want of evidence) qualified its author as an agnostic (for example, as a "right-wing Neo-Kantian"). In 1939 Propp called Polívka "a very cautious scholar, whose caution verged on agnosticism" (p. 125 below). Another bugbear is metaphysics. The Marxist should study all things in their interconnection, or else some ties will be severed. Idealism is the main enemy, but the snares of metaphysics are nearly as dangerous; the key word is "dissociation" (or "rupture," or "severance", or "disunion"; none renders the ominous *otrýv* 'tearing away' quite well): thought can be dissociated from language, syntax from morphology, folklore from reality—all with catastrophic consequences, and inasmuch as every special study presupposes concentration on some one question, metaphysics ever and anon waylays its unwary victims. The following statement made in 1946 may seem a joke to some, but Propp did not mean to be funny when he said: "My first premise is that among folktales there is a particular category called wondertales that can be isolated and studied independently. Such an approach may cause doubts: have we not violated the principle of the interconnection of all phenomena? In the final analysis, all things are interrelated; yet science always isolates some of them. The point is when and how the line is drawn" (p. 102, below). He was only safeguarding himself against allegations of metaphysics (cf. his quotation from *Anti-Dühring* on p. 125, below).

Metaphysics has a synonym in Soviet literary studies, namely, formalism. Formalism has been charged with dissociating content from form, the worst crime of all. The Russian Formalists were vilified by a unanimous chorus of critics. If Lévi-Strauss had had any first-hand knowledge of the Russian scene, he would never have accused Propp of formalism. Luckily, the translation of *Morphology* and Lévi-Strauss's review fell in the period when such an accusation, especially from a "bourgeois" scholar, did not interest anybody; besides, by 1960 Propp had fully proved his loyalty and was out of danger. Propp explained to Lévi-Strauss that formalism is a meaningless term, because in literature one never knows what is content and what is form. This explanation from Propp addressed to Lévi-Strauss verges on a farce (Janović 1982, 48, also comments on the irony of Lévi-Strauss's reproach).

The alleged superiority of Soviet scholarship could not be maintained without denigrating the opponents, who either worked among the horrors of the prerevolutionary past or had the misfortune of being born outside Russia. The cautious Polívka was accused of agnosticism. The famous classical scholar Wilamowitz "refused to see any connection between Greek literature and folk culture," and "this approach, which denies any folk quality to ancient myth, opens the way to all kinds of reactionary theories" (p. 111, below). The truth, formulated once and for all, was easily covered by the magic formula "everything is created by the people"; the slightest deviation from this loose Romantic formula sounded like a reactionary, bourgeois, and undemocratic theory, or a *so-called* theory (with ironic emphasis on *so-called*), or a theory in quotes. Hans Naumann, with his idea of sunken cultural property, caused more indignation than any other scholar. S. D. Kacnel'son, a leading Soviet linguist, analyzed Naumann's dialectology and characterized his attitude as profascist (a typical accusation between 1933 and 1939), and Propp called Naumann a reactionary in 1946 (p. 123, below; cf. the diatribe against Vsevolod Miller on p. 154). In *Russian Heroic Epic Poetry*, Propp reached the lowest point of his career. In it the Mythological school was proclaimed not only wrong but subversive, because it viewed Prince Vladimir of the Russian bylinas as a human embodiment of the sun, but luckily "the political aspect of this trend was revealed by Dobroljubov and Černyševskij" (p. 153). The campaign against the cosmopolitans, which very nearly cost Propp his life, also found an approving response in that book. This is what he said about the comparativists: "In studying Russian epic poetry, they traced it sometimes to the epic poetry of oriental, Asiatic peoples (Potánin), sometimes to borrowings from Byzantium or from Western Europe (Veselovskij and his school). Comparisons of this type suggested that the Russian people had created nothing and that in its culture it had only followed other people" (p. 154, below). As late as 1958 he still admired the Party decree of 1936, which wiped out the Russian Historical school and thus did irreparable damage to the science of folklore (more of this decree will be said in the next section). Another way of fighting bourgeois scholarship was a conspiracy of silence against the most distinguished colleagues in the West. After the publication of *Historical Roots*, references to European and American works disappeared from Propp's articles and books for many years.

Some people may say that, however sad Propp's personal predicament under the Soviet regime might be, it had nothing to do with Marxism and that the picture drawn above is an evil parody of Marxism. Yet insofar as Marxism claims to be not a faith but a theory, the same yardstick should be applied to it that is applied to all other theories. Marxism has existed for nearly a century and a half, and at present it can no longer be treated as only a sum of undeveloped ideas; the level of application is at least as important as the creed. These are the most general principles common to all Soviet studies in the humanities.

1) Marxism provides a powerful tool of analysis in the social sciences. The insights gained through the application of Marxism make most of previous scholarship look antiquated. Marxist method is superior to other methods. (2) There is a constant struggle going on between materialism and idealism, as well as between dialectics and the many approaches that concentrate on fragments at the expense of the whole and ignore the dynamic properties of the object. Dialectical materialism is the highest peak of both dialectics and materialism; its classical application can be found in the works of Marx, Engels (and Lenin). (3) The struggle between materialism and idealism is not confined to philosophy. It permeates literature, linguistics, sociology, etc. (4) Idealism, which once had its heyday, has long since become the ideology of the reactionary classes. Even if a scholar is a well-meaning and honest person, he (she) can objectively be the mouthpiece of the bourgeoisie (the reactionary class of our time). To recognize the truth, one should consistently analyze the data as well as other scholars' theories from a class point of view.

If this is not true Marxism, then what is? Propp's thinking after 1928 is in full harmony with the principles formulated above.

Another idea that may occur to many is that Marxism is a sort of survival kit for Soviet scholars or perhaps a mask: they had to put it on, but inwardly they always resisted it. This is wishful thinking. To be sure, in the Dragon's school, some are the best pupils, others are satisfied with a C, and still others writhe under the ferrule. But no one graduates from this school without learning a good deal.

The first thing that changes irrevocably is the style. Everybody begins to speak like the master. For many years the favorite words of Soviet humanistic scholarship have been *problem* and *category*. Fairy tales, metaphor, phonemes, or whatever as objects of analysis appeared under the titles of "the problem of fairy tales," "the problem of metaphor," "the problem of the phoneme," etc. Propp's mirthless 1975 book is called *The Problems of Laughter and the Comic*. "Category" was almost automatically appended to *space* and *time*; hundreds of hours sacrificed for learning "the categories of dialectics" were well spent. However, deterioration of style was a relatively superficial phenomenon; the general process of corrosion went much deeper. The truly outstanding scholars resented political demagoguery, but few could remain independent thinkers when confronted with state-supported Marxism. As time went on, a number of things began to look respectable even to the most critical minds. The shortest walk in the necropolis of Soviet philology will prove this point (one can begin at the graves of Eixenbaum, Vinográdov, and Žirmunskij). Of special importance is the Marxist thesis of the basis and superstructure. Propp's views on this subject will emerge from the small array of quotations that follow.

When social differentiation leads to the rise of classes, creative art is differentiated in the same manner. (p. 13, below)

The folktale is an ideological phenomenon, a reflection of the world in men's minds. It is not a reflection of itself. We know what calls forth phenomena of the superstructure, and what causes them: there is no need to go into the theory of basis and superstructure. If the folktale reflects the forms of production that existed at very early stages, one may speak about the paleontological analysis of a folktale motif. (p. 125)

We live under socialism and have developed our own premises for the study of culture. But in contrast to the premises of other epochs, which led the humanities into a blind alley, our epoch has formulated premises showing them the only correct path. I mean a general law for studying all historical phenomena: "The mode of production of material life conditions the social, political, and intellectual life process in general" (Marx). It follows that we must find in history the mode of production that gave rise to the wondertale. (p. 103)

Just as at one time there was 'naive realism,' we now have a trend that can be called 'naive Marxism' and that postulates an *immediate, mechanical* correspondence between the basis and superstruc-ture. . . . The correspondence between the basis and superstructure is understood as a *synchronic* one, whereas it is *historical*, and the synchronization is not always necessary. . . . We should discover the social-economic formation, the stage in the development of this or that formation within whose framework the plot arose because it *had* to arise. Consequently, in order to grasp any literary phenomenon (and the wondertale is a case in point), we should turn to material culture, economy, and the social phenomena connected with them. It follows that in the comparative study of the wondertale we cannot only com-pare one wondertale with another. Elements of the wondertale must be compared with elements of production, with the social life, rites, rituals, and beliefs of the people among which the wondertale is cur-rent, and of the peoples which stand at the same level of economic and cultural development. (1934, 129-30)

Ritual and myth are conditioned by economic interests. (p. 112, below)

It is quite probable that further searches will give a clearer, more precise, and better substantiated picture for each type of laughter and uncover whole layers of material that I have missed. Nevertheless, this work can begin, even if its only value is an attempt to go beyond the limits of formalist comparativism and look at folklore as a type of ideological superstructure. (p. 128)

It is interesting to juxtapose Propp's point of view with that of Bogatyrjov and Jakobson:

Once the unity of the composition of the wondertale was established, I could do no less than ask myself the cause of this unity. It was clear to me from the beginning that the cause would not be found in immanent laws for form and that it should be sought in early history, or prehistory, that is, in the stage of human society studied by ethnology and ethnography. (p. 71, below)

[The limited number of folklore plots] cannot be accounted for by either the common sources, common psyche, or common circumstances of existence. Common plots arise on the basis of the common laws of poetical composition. (Bogatyrjov 1971, 381)

Propp's Marxist views are directly related to his definition of folklore. In prerevolutionary Russian scholarship, folklore was identified with the well-known peasant genres: bylinas, popular tales, and so forth. Hardly anyone thought of defining folklore in strict terms, and hardly anyone needed such a definition. The situation changed after the Revolution, when the concepts of the social sciences were reexamined in light of the basis and superstructure and from a class point of view. Folklore, which along with literature and art went over to the superstructure, was supposed to reflect the changes in the basis. At this juncture the concept of Soviet folklore was born. According to the early predictions, the 1917 economic upheaval would produce Soviet bylinas, Soviet fairy tales, and the like. Lenin seems to have had some hopes of new folklore couched in traditional forms. Responsive to the efforts of the collectors, this new folklore sprouted up: fairy tales and bylinas with a sharp political edge to them, cheerful laments, proverbs and aphorisms perpetuating the values of socialism, oral tales (that is, so-called memorates) about the heroes of the Civil War, and above all a spate of songs— many of them in bylina style—about Lenin, Stalin, and their "fellows-in-arms," about poverty before 1917, and a happy life after 1917. The grateful collectors gathered and classified this luxuriant crop; doctoral dissertations like *The Image of I. V. Stalin in Moldavian Folk Poetry* were defended as late as 1954. The final chapter of Propp's *Russian Heroic Epic Poetry* was written long after the campaign had reached its peak (it started in the Twenties and culminated in the mid and late Thirties). Propp regarded Soviet bylinas and songs as true folklore but concluded that the old forms are no longer productive. Even in 1958, in the second edition of the book, published after a heated discussion of the fortunes of Soviet folklore, he did not admit that the pitiful production known as Soviet folklore has no scholarly or artistic value. See Oinas 1961, 1973, and 1978, all with numerous references, Oinas and Soudakoff 1975, 303-4, Klymasz 1976 and

1978 and Schlauch 1944, 219-22 (the latter on the verge of self-parody). Dorson's (1963, 97-99) main or only source was Oinas 1961 (several names are misspelled).

Another important aspect of the Marxist definition of folklore is revealed by Propp's 1946 article (No. 1 in this book). Marxism requires not only the treatment of artistic activity as belonging to the superstructure but also a class perspective in literary analysis. At first, Soviet scholars worked with the same features of folklore as everyone else and encountered the same theoretical difficulties. It was said that folklore must be traditional, collective, oral, and anonymous (cf. Dundes's attempt to define the American concept of folklore: Dundes 1966). None of these features has anything to do with the stratification of society into classes. Following Gorky, Propp defined folklore as the literary output of the exploited classes. Since he did not allow the ruling classes to have their folklore, he excluded practically all ancient recorded poetry from the sphere of folklore. Propp was strongly opposed to the theory of the aristocratic origin of the Russian bylinas, but he knew better than to believe that the *Iliad* had been produced by foreign slaves or the poorest peasants. In his comments on preclass society, Propp labeled the entire literary activity of that period folklore, and it seemed perfectly normal to everyone that the main criterion for evaluating literature is of a sociological nature, even though the criterion is so patently wrong. Were the lays of Sigurth folklore in the tenth century and literature in the thirteenth only because classes began to appear in Iceland? Would *Gilgamesh* not have been folklore, had there been no slavery in Mesopotamia? The real trouble, however, that could not be dismissed or ignored concerned the Soviet period. Supposedly no class distinctions exist in the USSR, so, according to Propp's principle, opposition between literature and folklore is ruled out: either everything is again folklore as thousands of years ago, or everything is literature. The first solution is hopeless, but the second is also bad. Scholarship found itself at an impasse: Soviet folklore exists, as evidenced by an army of folklorists, and at the same time it does not, because there is no class struggle in the country. Above, I have mentioned this sudden twist of dialectics among the pseudoproblems conjured up by the triumph of the official ideology. Understandably, Propp had little to say about this issue and devoted one paragraph to it.

> Under socialism, folklore loses its specific features as a product of the lower strata, since in a socialist society there are neither upper nor lower strata, just the people. Folklore indeed becomes *national* property. What is not in harmony with the people dies out; what remains is subjected to profound qualitative changes and comes closer to literature. Further research will show what these changes are, but it is clear that folklore under capitalism and under socialism are different things. (p. 5, below)

Although rather vague, Propp's comment was the best one under the circumstances; Propp did not guess what turn "further research" would take, but his solution anticipated a good deal of what was said on this matter in later years. The debate concerning the nature of Soviet folklore, which started in 1948, flared up with unexpected violence in 1954, when for the first time in nearly thirty years one could risk a slightly unorthodox opinion and stay alive. The debate still smolders, but all the arguments have been put forward, countered, and put forward again long ago, and no interesting or original contributions have been made since 1962 (see Oinas 1976). Between 1948 (1954) and 1962 the bylinas and fairy tales about Soviet life and the rest of this production were called the only name they deserved—"fakelore." The features of folklore appeared to be totally inapplicable to the newest samples, none of which were oral (because almost everybody could read and write), traditional, or anonymous. Furthermore, all over the country people preferred literary songs to traditional ones, and, whenever good folklore turned up, it invariably proved old. Only the more or less spontaneous jocular songs (*častúški*) remained productive, but they could not justify the existence of Soviet folklore (see Lopatin 1951: the most detailed survey of such songs in English). The inevitable conclusion was reached that there is no such thing as specifically Soviet folklore, even though people sing, dance, tell stories, and remember some old customs.

The most difficult feature to analyze was 'collective.' It transpired that nobody knew what 'collective' means. Some equated collective with anonymous, others referred to the process of polishing the texts ('polishing' [*šlifóvka*] stood for 'improving,' because Stalin once said that the people polishes its works for centuries, and this dictum ornamented every work in folklore). Some thought that 'collective' presupposes teamwork. Many scholars pointed out that folklore is collective because it is common property and thus shifted the emphasis from the process of composition to the process of transmission. Still others claimed that, since the narrator draws on traditional sources, folklore is collective by definition. This instructive controversy showed that the Soviet science of folklore, which was used to discussing only ideological problems, had lost touch with true scholarship and was unprepared to tackle a really serious question; cf. what was said above about the limpness of Soviet semiotics. The notion of collective is a cornerstone of the science of folklore. It inspired and puzzled the Romantics; both Veselovskij and the Russian Historical school grappled with the paradox of the individual input to the collective forms of art; the Parry-Lord school made an important step in defining authorship and improvisation in folklore. But in the mid Fifties and early Sixties most Soviet folklorists knew only that folklore is the collective production of the exploited classes. In 1946 Propp said that folklore has no individual authors, that it is like language (it is invented by no one and changes independently of people's will when circumstances are appropriate) and that folklore is part of ritual: when the ritual dies, its verbal element acquires independence and comes into its own. He also emphasized that folklore is always traditional, oral, and changeable. B. N. Putílov praised Propp for his determination to return the concept of impersonal to the science of folklore. At the end of his 1946 article Propp did really mention the unconscious element in folklore. As usual, to protect himself from allegations (probably, of Freudian or Jungian sympathies), he referred to Marx and quoted Marx's statement about the unconscious character of Greek mythology, but this ruse saved him neither in the campaign against the "cosmopolitans" (see Kuznecov and Dmitrakov 1948, 237, who qualified all such quotations as a strategem of the entrenched idealist) nor later (see Emel'janov 1964, 44, who pointed out that Marx's formula cannot cover all Greek folklore). But regardless of Marx, how far did Propp's courage go? He himself admitted that he had returned to Busláev's and Veselóvskij's ideas; actually, he returned to Jacob Grimm's *das Volk dichtet*. (I am leaving out of account the hypothesis of all folklore deriving from ritual; it had a strong hold on Marr's school, and in later years Propp modified his views.) There is no doubt that the people creates poetry, but the real question is how the process of creation goes on. Marxism did not help Propp to answer it.

In the debate on Soviet folklore there was no unanimity among the contestants, but those who defended the existence of Soviet folklore said only two things: first, that everything is folklore as long as it is produced by nonprofessional authors (identified with "the people"); second, that denying Soviet folklore is tantamount to denying the creative potential of the Russian people under socialism; neither argument is worthy of refutation. Propp did not take part in the discussion. I think he sided with those who exposed the true nature of postrevolutionary folklore, but for some reason he preferred to keep silent.

Propp undoubtedly believed in everything he said about the basis and superstructure. His entire historical conception is informed with this belief. He also may have come to believe in the concept of bourgeois scholarship and lost interest in this scholarship. Otherwise it would be hard to explain his ignorance of Lévi-Strauss's works as late as 1966. He called himself an incorruptible empiricist and Lévi-Strauss, a philosopher. Lévi-Strauss had every reason to be surprised. It even seems as though the deadening uniformity of taste and thought enforced on the Soviet people began to please him. In the article "Folklore and Reality" (1963) Propp discussed the folktale about a man who sells his mother's corpse and, among other things, said, "If a modern Soviet writer decided to write a story about how a mother is murdered and how the murderer later used the corpse to extort money, no one would publish such a story, and if it were published, it would provoke readers' justified indignation" (p. 19). Apparently, his political and ideological statements came from the heart; he did not mind Big Brother.

4. Propp as a Historian

A. General

Before examining Propp's reconstructions of the wondertale and heroic epic poetry we must form an idea of the climate in which Soviet historical investigations were conducted between the mid Twenties and the mid Fifties. The fundamental principle of such investigations, namely, the dependence of the ideological superstructure on the basis, was discussed in the previous section. Under Marr, the chief figure of postrevolutionary linguistics, language was also treated as part of the superstructure. Later, Stalin allowed language to be neither basis nor superstructure, but literature (including folklore) has never changed its status. According to the officially recognized theory, the economic basis determines the life cycle of the superstructure, which reflects its basis indirectly and which can lag behind the new basis, creating temporary incongruence between the two. Another batch of quotations from Propp will illustrate this theory:

Poetical art is a phenomenon of the superstructure. To explain a phenomenon means to trace it to its causes, and these causes lie in the economic and social life of the people. (p. 9, below)

The similarity of works of folklore is only a particular case of the historical law by which identical forms of production in material culture give rise to identical or similar social institutions, to similar tools, and, in ideology, to the similarity of forms and categories of thought, religion, rituals, languages, and folklore. (p. 7)

In the study of folklore special attention should be directed to the basis, which is primarily the forms of production, and for the folklore of the feudal period the basis is mainly the forms of peasant labor. In the last analysis, the development of forms of thought and art is explained by the development of forms of production. (p. 48)

Historical songs are the products of social development. (p. 35)

After the Revolution the entire development of Russia has been exposed to new scrutiny. The periods in the history of the USSR have been established anew, in conformity with historical materialism. . . . The historical study of epic poetry must consist in revealing the connection between the development of epic poetry and Russian history and in determining the nature of this connection. (p. 158)

We should study epic poetry in conjunction with the epochs, or periods, of its development, rather than with so many separate events. Initial distribution of the data is determined by the sequence of formations in Russian history: primitive-communal society, feudalism, capitalism, and socialism. (p. 163)

Inherited folklore comes into conflict with the old social system that
created it and denies this system. It does not deny the old system
directly but rather the images created by it, transforming them into
their opposites or giving them a reverse, disparaging, negative coloring. (p. 11)

Basis is a difficult concept, and links between a *concrete* mode of production
and a *concrete* song, tale, riddle, and so on, especially at the level of a whole
plot, are seldom demonstrable. It is easier to proclaim Marxist theory of art than
to live up to it. Propp was not the author of manuals of philosophy but a folklorist,
so he had to put Marxism to some practical use. Let it be repeated that Propp
was sincere in his declarations. His most distinguished colleagues, people of his
or greater stature, could have treated with irony Khrushchev's epoch-making contributions to Marxist aesthetics; at one time the boldest of them dared to
acknowledge to themselves that Stalin's pronouncements on poetry and language
were ignorant nonsense or offensive banalities and that Lenin's articles on Tolstoy
and Hertzen are classic examples of aesthetic deafness, but reverence for Marx
and Engels was most firmly driven into them. It would be ridiculous to believe
that hypocrisy was or is the main driving force of Soviet scholarly life. Propp,
who did not as much as mention Marxism in *Morphology*, became a Marxist in
the Thirties. Like many, he began with perfunctory references and ended up among
the aggressive orthodox. Besides, in comparison with Ždanov and Kalínin, Marx
and Engels seemed thoroughly acceptable. Nearly everything written by Propp
after *Morphology* is devoted to the history of folklore, and for this reason it is
his historical teachings that show his deepest obligation to Marxism. As pointed
out, links between folklore and economy are seldom apparent. Propp was well
aware of this and replaced the notion of the economic basis by Černyševskij's
loose notion of reality. Compare his three programmatic statements:

1. Folklore, like any other art, derives from reality. Even the most
fantastic images are based on reality. Materialistic scholarship must
find the historical basis of folklore. . . . 2. Independently of the intentions of its creators and performers, folklore reflects real life. The
forms and content of this reflection differ according to the period and
the genre. They are subject to the poetics of folklore. 3. A folk artist
sets himself the goal of representing reality. Such a purpose
characterizes the historical song and workers' folklore. (p. 38, below)

Propp's reality comprises economy, ritual, and so-called primitive thought.

One can easily assume that folklore reflects social or some other relationships directly. This would be a wrong assumption. Folklore,
especially in its early stages, is not a description of life. Reality is not
reflected directly but through the prism of thought, and this thought is
so unlike ours that it can be difficult to compare a folklore

phenomenon with anything at all. In this system of thought, connections of cause and effect do not yet exist; other connections prevail, but we often do not know which. There are no generalizations, no abstractions, no concepts. Space and time are perceived differently from the way we perceive them. The categories of singular and plural and the qualities of subject and object (identification of oneself with animals) play a role completely different from the one they play for us. What we never consider real is considered real and vice versa. Primitive man sees the world of things not as we do, and his views change from one stage to another. Therefore, we can look in vain for an existential reality behind a folklore reality. (p. 10)

Propp seems to have been satisfied when he could show that folklore reflects at least something in the surrounding world, that is, when he could refer to any factor but "immanent laws of form"; no wonder that a gang of critics in 1947-48 accused him of idealism.

The Marxist principle that the development of the superstructure should be explained by the changes of the basis is inwardly hostile to the study of form as a separate entity. Long ago Engels wrote that it would be ludicrous to try to interpret the German Consonant Shift in economic terms. It might seem ludicrous to him, but it did not amuse others: one need only look at Lotman's battery of pathetic arguments meant to prove that structuralism is not incompatible with Marxism (Lotman 1968, 3-17). The almost pathological fear of "formalism" that has racked Soviet scholarship for over fifty years (and everybody from Šklovskij to Šostakovič has appeared guilty) was aroused not so much by the formal excesses of this or that trend as by the attempts to allow form to be governed by its own laws. It would be unthinkable for a Soviet scholar to remain in good standing and claim that painting or poetry grows under impulses from within, for example, in order to reach a measure of inward stability. Propp always gravitated toward extraliterary explanations of literary history (but not of a given literary text!), so in this respect his way through the wilderness of 1930-1955 was smooth.

Marxism did more than alert Propp to the dependence of the superstructure on its basis; it taught him that every phenomenon should be studied in a historical perspective (cf. the requirement to study every phenomenon in all its interconnections). Several statements to this effect appear in Propp's works.

All the humanities can now be only historical. We examine every phenomenon in its development. (p. 9, below; with a subsequent thrust at positivist scholarship)

One of the basic requirements of contemporary scholarship is that all phenomena of human culture be studied in their historical development. . . . Attempts at the historical study of folk poetry were also

made even before the Revolution. We must know about these attempts
in order to avoid mistakes of bourgeois scholarship. (p. 153)

The historical principle is far less innocuous than it may seem at first glance.
Not all phenomena should always be studied in their historical development.
Present-day human society, a language arrested at a certain moment, the wondertale as a genre, and thousands of other phenomena are interesting for their own
sake, quite independently of accretions of the past in them. But for decades Soviet
linguistics and literature dreaded to "disassociate" synchrony from diachrony,
and this almost superstitious dread blocked the way to the mildest forms of structuralism. Of course, *Morphology* is a triumph of the synchronic approach to
folklore, and Propp knew it better than anybody else. In 1968 he again ventured
the following statement:

All genres of Russian folklore can be studied from the standpoint of a
broad conception of history. . . . But historical study *follows* the study
of forms. To discover the history of the wondertale, we need first to
investigate its morphology. Likewise, without knowing the typology of
charms, the poetics of riddles, the structure of ritual songs, and the
forms of lyric songs, we will never reveal the oldest stages in the
emergence and growth of these genres. (p. 50, below)

There is no arguing this point, but Propp did not dare make it for forty years.
Propp's historical views discussed so far can be summed up in the following
theses: (1) All the humanities are now historical; (2) All the phenomena of social
life belong to the superstructure, and their past can be understood only in light
of what happens to the basis; (3) The basis, at least in regard to folklore, is
synonymous with reality, which subsumes economy, ritual, and primitive thought.
To this must be added another statement, the most important of them all for Propp's
practical work: (4) History is a succession of stages. I will follow Lawrence
Thomas's (1957) example and refer to this principle as stadialism (the Russian
word is *stadiál'nost'*).

The most influential Russian literary scholar who espoused stadialism was Aleksandr Veselovskij, the teacher of all twentieth-century Russian literary scholars
and by 1948 "the last undethroned idol of bourgeois scholarship." His name
sometimes turns up in European and American studies, in which he is usually
called a forerunner of Russian Formalism, but such a vague reference is not sufficient for the appraisal of Veselovskij's role. Veselovskij was a school and an
epoch in himself. His erudition was boundless, and his greatest ambition was
to represent the development of literature as a historically determined process.
For the dawn of civilization, he reconstructed the stage of mythological thought
and one syncretic art, with poetry, singing, and dance undifferentiated. He paid
special attention to group and amoeban singing, which he treated as an expression of collective emotionality. Individual lyric songs signified to Veselovskij not

only a higher stage in the growth of poetry than choral singing but also a higher stage of man's consciousness, for in the lyric song, man emerges as an individual opposed to the group. For this reason, Veselovskij viewed epic poetry as a more ancient stage than lyric poetry. Drama, according to his scheme, arose from the choral dance and ritual action. Veselovskij equated the stages of literary development with the stages of man's development. This equation is taken for granted by M. I. Steblin-Kamenskij, Veselovskij's last truly original disciple (see Steblin-Kamenskij 1971 [1973]; 1976 [1982]). Veselovskij relied on Tylor and Andrew Lang in his ideas of primitive thought and, predictably, was close to Lévy-Bruhl.

The all too familiar literary scheme Classicism-Romanticism-Realism (the latter represented by critical realism and socialist realism) is also stadial because it considers the succession of styles in literature and art to be an ascending scale, with socialist realism at its peak (just as history existed to produce socialism, so literature has evolved in the direction of socialist realism).

A similar teleological assumption forms the foundation of the linguistic teachings of Marr. Marr took some of Veselovskij's ideas (for example, he believed that sound language derives from the collective choral song), which he crossed with the theories of Lévy-Bruhl and Noirée and grafted on Marxism. His highly eclectic doctrine is remembered in the West (by those few who have ever read Marr) for its dubious, ridiculous, and anecdotal statements. Such are indeed beyond number; for example, language is part of the superstructure; pronouns appear only after man has become aware of the right of property; articulate language could not have arisen before man learned to produce tools; the protoword of language is *hand*; social terms go back to tribal names; since sound language (which followed the kinetic form of communication) has always been a class phenomenon, class differentiation must have existed at the end of the early Neolithic period; both semantics and morphology are determined by economy (thus, the positive, comparative, and superlative degrees of adjectives are a relic of the lower, middle, and upper classes, respectively); all words of all languages go back to the same four elements: *sal, ber, yon, roš*, and they can still be detected everywhere (this was called paleontological analysis), and so on. Marr's works, even his 1928 concise course for the uninitiated, are difficult to read. Their fluid, evasive syntax transmits fickle, changeable thought; ideas chase one another; and the whole sometimes strikes the reader as cleverly disguised glossolalia.

Yet this eloquent shaman exercised a lasting influence on the Soviet humanities. In the army of careerists and toadies that surrounded him were several gifted people (cf. Lotman 1976). A few outstanding anthropologists were dazzled by his brilliance. Students caught his enthusiasm, but even the most talented were ruined by him, because he made them investigate all sorts of nonsense (such as ablaut in light of tribal migrations and economic conditions), infected them with his own arrogance and his contempt of "bourgeois scholarship," and barred them from the achievements of European and American linguistics and from the possibility of making Marxist linguistics respectable (see Vološinov 1973). When the cudgel of the 1950 linguistic "discussion" crushed Marrism, his pupils recanted at once, and the short era of Stalin's linguistics set in. The apostasy of Marr's students, disciples, and friends tells us something about the climate of the Fifties, but it should not be taken seriously. To be sure, no one cared for the so-called philosophical aspects of linguistics, and when Stalin proclaimed that language is neither basis nor superstructure (nor an intermediate phenomenon, for such, according to Stalin, are not recognized by Marxism), the new status of language did not affect anybody's interests. But Marr's school had been taught to believe in stadialism, which is indeed part and parcel of Marxism. Although the whole of Marr's teachings was repudiated and dismissed as folly, Stalin did not touch on this particular problem; so the position of stadialism remained unclear and still is. Since then Stalin has been dethroned and soon rehabilitated, together with his victims and the victims of his victims. Everybody has won, and all must have prizes.

The stadial views of Marr are close to Tylor's (with the same emphasis on survivals) and of course to Engels's, as they emerge from his book *The Origin of the Family, Private Property and the State*. The three types of languages, namely, amorphous (Chinese), agglutinative (the Turkic family), and inflectional (Latin), were traced by Marr to the changing economic base and treated as three consecutive stages of development. Marr's successor (Marr died in 1934) was I. I. Meščanínov, a somewhat more solid scholar. True to the spirit of Marr's doctrine, Meščaninov regarded the entire history of language as a unidirectional process and also believed that similar forms of thought produce similar forms of expression in language. According to him, the unity of language development finds its best proof in stadial periodization.

If we dismiss as totally ungrounded the idea that syntax reflects economy, we will be left with the truism that Chinese, Turkish, and Latin represent different grammatical models. No one has ever doubted that, just as no one will argue that Keats, Dante Gabriel Rossetti, and T. S. Eliot represent different styles. *The main question is whether these types and styles form a historical hierarchy.* A stadial analysis of language and literature can be passed off as typology with almost no effort, because the postulated *stages* are also coexistent *types*. This is exactly what has been done with Marr's and especially Meščaninov's heritage in the Sixties and Seventies when Western scholars responded to Jakobson's appeal and began to study the universals of language and Soviet scholars followed suit. The old data collected by Marr's pupils were salvaged and appeared quite respectable (as they sometimes were), but the guiding principle that had inspired Marr and Meščaninov was hidden; by an easy trick, diachrony became synchrony. Today even Vjačeslav Ivánov has a kind word for Marr (Ivanov 1976, 28).

Stadialism has had a precarious existence in the last fifty years. In early Soviet scholarship, stadialism and comparativism, though both endorsed by Engels, were torn apart because Marr was a convinced stadialist but a sworn enemy of comparative linguistics. In 1948 there must have been some confusion among the leaders of ideology, for Dement'ev (1948, 85) in his speech against the "cosmopolitans" made several scathing remarks about "the survivals of comparativism and objectivist methodology in the science of literature" as represented by the "the so-called theory of stadialism" and crushed V. M. Žirmunskij (who was both a comparative linguist and Veselovskij's disciple in historical literature), I. M. Tronskij (one of the foremost classical scholars in the Soviet Union, also a student of language and literature), and G. A. Gukóvskij (a distinguished scholar and the author of an original theory of stadialism as applied to Russian literature; he did not recant publicly, was deported, and perished; Žirmunskij and Tronskij, though also Jewish, survived). However, the subsequent purge did not affect stadialism, and, as mentioned above, even the routing of Marr's school two years later passed it over, perhaps because stadialism is the main point at which comparativism meets Marxism. Veselovskij's theories were certainly not an offshoot of Marxism: Veselovskij, Engels (who learned his anthropology from Morgan), and Lévy-Bruhl worked independently and arrived at partly comparable results. (Cf. the epilogue to the American edition of Steblin-Kamenskij's *Myth*, where more is said of these matters).

In the West, stadialism died together with Tylor and his followers and found convinced grave diggers in Franz Boas and Boas's pupils. Melville Jacobs (1966, 414) speaks of stadialism with great disdain: "Scattered historicist or comparativist researches, even now, feature various European anthropologists who are little known or whose orientation is Marxist. The unsophisticated worldwide grab-bag procedure known as 'the comparative method,' with its smaller manifestations in studies limited to single regions, is virtually dead in anthropology. But not quite so in folklore." Edmund Leach introduces Steblin-Kamenskij's *Myth* in the same condescending way (and nearly says that the author is little known and his orientation Marxist).

Older scholarship has bequeathed us two questions: Do similar historical conditions (broadly taken) produce similar literary forms? (for example, does a certain type of social relationships and of world outlook tend to engender heroic poetry?) and conversely: Do certain literary forms arise only at a certain "stage" of human development (for example, can heroic poetry arise only when it usually does and does it presuppose myth as its indispensable foundation?). These questions, which cannot be answered by any other method except comparative and to which most literary scholars usually return a reluctant yes, are the very essence of stadialism and have nothing to do either with Lévi-Strauss's brave postulate that the logical structure of thought is the same at all times or with the Marxist idea about economy underlying the "superstructure."

But to return to Marr.

Marr exercised a strong influence on early Soviet folkloristics. In his youth,

Marr studied Georgian and Armenian medieval literatures, but he never addressed himself to the theoretical aspects of folklore (even his old and new admirers have been unable to find anything but a few insignificant remarks: see Azadóvskij 1935; Gel'gardt 1976; there is some discussion of Marr in Astaxova 1966, 82-83). However, he viewed philology as an indissoluble whole, that is, he did not doubt that in folklore as in linguistics the main approach is paleontology, its analytical tool, stadialism, and its material, semantics (cf. Azadovskij 1935, 13). These principles came to the foreground when Marr was appointed Chairman of the Sector of the Semantics of Myth and Folklore, which set out to extend the new linguistic principles to folklore. Again, some of his associates were excellent scholars, others, self-seeking nonentities. The best-known product of Marrian folklore is a book entitled *Tristan and Isol'da*, which is a dismal failure (Marr 1932). In historical linguistics Marr disregarded phonetic laws and took into account only semantics; hence the fantastic etymologies. In comparative literature, he also was mainly interested in semantics and taught that no plot should be analyzed outside its historical context, because every plot is called forth by its environment (so the laws of form were again left out of account). The chief principles of the collective miscellany *Tristan and Isol'da* are as follows. Every plot is a phenomenon of the ideological superstructure; themes and motifs change constantly, but their semantics makes them indestructible; the only "source" of the plot is the plot itself, that is, its previous stage, and parallels should be examined from this point of view: the scholar's task is to establish the semantic equivalencies of the parallels in the ideological systems of the stages to which they belong. B. V. Kazánskij, the author of one of the best contributions to the book (see Kazanskij 1932), adds several more concrete theses to the general scheme: Isolda's free love is a relic of the matriarchate, as it existed among the Picts, and the triangle Tristan-Isolda-Mark is also traceable to the early state of Pictish society (a typical borrowing from the castigated "bourgeois Anthropological school"); the stages of Isolda are such: a mistress of nature—the healing fairy and hunting nymph—the stronger of the two lovers; Isolda can be the ancient symbol of water (*hand* and *water* formed, according to Marr, a diffuse semantic bundle) and Tristan, of the sun (Marr was very close to Max Müller, and Marr's followers constantly defended their teacher from this embarrassing similarity); but possibly the basis of the plot is not a triad but the diad goddess/mother/mistress : god/son/lover, itself traceable to the seasonal group marriage and initiation. The authors of the other articles discovered variations on the Tristan—Isolda theme and defined the stage of these variations in each national folklore. The book was supposed to prove Marr's etymology: Isolda ‖ Ishtar (the heroine of the Semitic myth of Tammuz and Ishtar) and was criticized for excessive zeal immediately after its appearance.

Propp referred to Marr rarely, but he was far from immune to Marr's influence and never threw a stone at him after 1950. Again, I will let Propp speak for himself:

We arrange our data according to the stages in the development of peoples (a 'stage' is the level of culture, defined by the features of material, social, and spiritual achievement) and obtain a 'historical poetics' in the real sense of this word, the historical poetics whose basis was laid by Veselovskij [This was said before the campaign against the cosmopolitans (p. 12, below).]

Each motif must be listed and examined in terms of socio-economic stages and of the changes in the motif that correspond to them, rather than in terms of territorial distribution and formal differences ('variants'). Many folktales have preserved such unambiguous traces of tribal organization, hunting, and early forms of agriculture as the basic form of production, together with traces of the social institutions that went with them, early forms of thought, family relations and marriage, etc., that a careful comparison of the folktale and the past leaves no doubts about the historical roots of most folklore motifs. (p. 126)

[So-called wondertales of primitives] are products of earlier stages of economic development, products that have not yet lost the connection with their economic base. (p. 109)

According to Marr, the idea of a protolanguage is a bourgeois racial fiction. In history he saw nothing but hybrid formations and looked on every language as a cross between two tribal dialects. One of Marr's works was devoted to the means of locomotion, and we find an echo of it in Propp's 1946 article:

The old and the new can exist not only in a state of unresolved contradictions; they may also enter into hybrid formations. Folklore and religious ideas are full of such hybrid formations. The dragon, or serpent, is the combination of the worm, the bird, and other animals. Marr showed that when the horse had been domesticated, the religious role of the bird was transferred to it. The horse acquired wings. Flying ships, winged chariots, etc., become understandable. Research into the religious role of fire will show why the horse is combined with fire and becomes a fiery horse and how the idea of a fiery chariot arises. Such hybrids are possible not only in visual images, they are deeply hidden in the most diverse ideas and relations. Entire new plots can arise by transference of the new to the old. The plot with the hero killing his father and marrying his mother, that is, the plot of *Oedipus*, arose as a result of the transfer of a hostile attitude toward the daughter's future husband—the son-in-law and heir—to the son-heir, and the transfer of the role of the king's daughter as the transmitter of the throne by marriage to the king's widow. This formation is not accidental or isolated: it is in the nature of folklore. (pp. 11-12, below; cf. p. 143, end of section 8)

When Propp qualified his study of the princess who could not laugh as "an attempt to go beyond the limits of formalist comparativism and look at folklore as a type of ideological superstructure" (p. 128), not only did he pronounce a usual Marxist incantation, he also bowed to Marr, because it was Marr who branded comparative studies as formalist. Propp was also willing to apply Marr's paleontological analysis to folklore. He called this method ("demonstrated for linguistics by Marr") "risky and difficult, but necessary and inevitable, where early stages are not represented by first-hand data" (p. 12; paleontological analysis in linguistics meant only etymologizing with the four elements). He added that "if the folktale reflects the forms of production that existed at very early stages, one may speak about the paleontological analysis of a folktale motif" (p. 125). Propp's mention of the myth's semantics (p. 112) and his untraditional use of the term 'totemic' (= mythic) are also shibboleths. Propp kept repeating that language and folklore are similar in many respects. When this old idea occurred in Propp's works it had only Marrian connotations. His structuralism was largely unconscious; he was not interested in structural linguistics, must have resented Bogatyrjov and Jakobson's ideas and later missed Lévi-Strauss's works. He followed Marr, who taught that the same semantics underlies language, folklore, and ritual. Incidentally, this thesis allowed many students of culture to call themselves Marr's pupils (cf. Lotman 1976), and, since the thesis was general and the linguistic core rotten, it was easy to deny the teacher the moment the cock crowed.

B. The Wondertale

The ideas developed in *Historical Roots of the Wondertale* go back to the time when Propp wrote his *Morphology* (Berkov 1966, 112; Putilov 1971, 203), and a series of later articles, all oriented toward ethnography (Propp 1934, 1939a; 1939b; 1941, 1944), belong together with *Historical Roots*. But before turning to these works, we should pay special attention to the article "Transformations of the Wondertale," which was meant as a special chapter of *Morphology*.

Any scholar interested in reconstruction has to decide how to distinguish archaic forms from innovations. In linguistics, Rasmus Rask, one of the founders of the comparative method, gave this question much thought. For example, he believed that the more complex the grammar of a language, the more ancient it is. In folklore, the Grimms operated with the concept "perfect" and viewed the life of tales as a process of deterioration, so the more perfect the tale seemed to them the more ancient it turned out to be. The first detailed research into this problem is less than a century old and is the product of the Finnish school of folklore. The guidelines were formulated by Julius Krohn, Antti Aarne, Walter Anderson, and several other Scandinavian scholars and were codified by Kaarle Krohn. Propp's principles of reconstruction will make more sense if they are compared with those of the Finnish school. My source for the Finnish school is Krohn 1971 (originally published in 1926).

1. A variation that occurs in only one or a very few geographically related

examples can in general be viewed as a chance form that was accepted with approbation, or survived only in a restricted area. *Between two alternatives represented by a significant number of transcriptions, statistical quantity is not a decisive factor.* A rather small number of widely scattered variants may adopt some one characteristic independently of each other or alter it in a similar manner (pp. 99-100, my emphasis). 2. With regard to the direction of geographic diffusion of a tradition, greater reliability must be attributed to the version that lies nearer the point of origin. However, at some place far removed from the site of origin a version older than those closer to home may sometimes appear, perhaps distinguished only by a single feature (p. 100). 3. An older manuscript has in general claim to greater attention than a later transcription from the same area, but it often happens that in a later transcription by the descendants of the original informant some item forgotten by him may come to light (p. 101). 4. The occurrence of a version in a colony that is separated from the motherland can, if later transplantation or borrowing from neighboring areas is out of the question, suggest the existence of the version before the date of colonization (p. 102). 5. In Märchen research the "wave theory" must replace the genealogical theory used in investigating manuscript texts (p. 153). 6. A variant whose characteristics have in general been well preserved should be given greater attention in certain cases than one that has been corrupted in many details (p. 103). 7. More precise descriptive features are usually older than the less descriptive ones (p. 118). 8. If two areas are not in direct contact but preserve the same tradition whereas the area between them lacks it, the interposed area probably had this tradition but lost it. The smaller the interposed area, the more certain the assumption that the tradition in question previously migrated through the region and that it was once diffused throughout it (p. 68). 9. In the choice between various versions, the one is older from which the others can be shown to have evolved directly or indirectly. A later variation can also be recognized if it is traceable to another feature in the same tradition or even in some other one (pp. 104-105). 10. If there are two versions employing the same motif and it is indispensable only for one, it probably belongs originally to this version and is a borrowing in the other. At its inception every motif had its place in one particular song or tale only (p. 105). 11. A truly new creation or creative alteration does not occur in stages but rather in one stroke (p. 96).

At least one principle of those enumerated above came directly from linguistics: Johan Schmidt offered to replace Schleicher's theory of the *Stammbaum* (a reconstructed genealogical tree of the Indo-European languages) by the *Wellentheorie* (a wave theory, according to which the change is like a stone thrown into the water: the stone forms the epicenter of the change, and rings spread outward from it; the farther away from the stone, the weaker the ring). Schmidt's book was a major event in historical dialectology, and Walter Anderson's idea (point 5 above), along with many other ideas of the Finnish school, derives from this book.

Areal linguistics (or Neolinguistics), as it is known from the works of Bartoli, Bonfante, Bottiglioni, and later Coseriu and Porzig, also owes much to Schmidt's *Wellentheorie*. If one disregards a number of small points of the type "sound change cannot go back and forth" (that is, *a* cannot change to *o* and back to *a*; a very dubious law), the principles of the Neolinguistic school overlap those of the Finnish school to a considerable degree: cf. (1) The more archaic forms tend to be preserved in isolated regions, in peripheral regions, in larger areas, and in areas of later colonization. (2) If a language is represented by two states, one of which has (nearly) disappeared and the other is in active use, the first state is older.

The pupils of Bartoli and Julius Krohn started with the same book (Schmidt) and came to similar conclusions. For example, Axel Olrik claimed that the legend of Loki had reached the North from the Caucasus, transmitted by the Goths. Kaarle Krohn rejected Olrik's reconstruction point blank, on the grounds that if we had the same legend in such remote areas as Scandinavia and the Black Sea steppes, it would have been known in the interjacent area as well. In a similar fashion, Joseph Emonds (1972, 112-13) reexamined the First Consonant Shift. This change, well known from Germanic, has a counterpart in Armenian. Emonds argued that since the shift has been attested in two unconnected areas and nowhere between them, the norm preserved in Germanic and Armenian is archaic; consequently, it is the rest of the Indo-European world and not Germanic and Armenian that underwent the shift! Emonds missed the extremely important discussion of Armenian consonantism on the pages of *Voprosy jazykoznanija* (1959-62) and used insufficient and antiquated material, so his conclusion can be disregarded, but it is good as an illustration of a certain principle. Krohn was also wrong, but for different reasons. Von Sydow showed that folklore does not spread like language, for its existence and dissemination depend on active bearers of tradition, rather than on large masses of population (von Sydow 1965, 229-42; first published in Swedish in 1922).

Several other analogous principles have been put forward; for instance, according to Kacnel'son, nonproductive types are usually more ancient (which almost follows from the definition of *productive*), great uniformity is probably the result of later levelings, while areas with many coexisting types point to the original (more archaic) state; optional variants are often late signs of the system's decay, so the obligatory variants are more reliable material for reconstruction (see Liberman 1968, 125-27).

By 1928 both the Finnish and the Italian theories had wide currency in their own parts of the world (but nowhere else, thus proving the law of the peripheral regions). As pointed out several times, Propp's *Morphology* was a well-planned attack on Aarne's types and motifs. However, it did not try to explode the Finnish theory of transmission. There is no evidence that Propp was aware of the Italian Neolinguists, but Paolo Toschi (1949, 41) was correct in saying that, since (in *Historical Roots*) Propp rejected Krohn's ideas of diffusion, he thereby set himself in opposition to Bartoli (Toschi mentioned only the law known as the norm of the larger area).

The main difference between Propp and Krohn is that, with one exception (see point 6, below), Propp was not interested in the areal aspect of folklore and focused on the plot. Here are his principles (1928). (1) If the same form occurs both in a religious monument and in a wondertale, the religious form is primary and the wondertale form is secondary. Especially any dead religious phenomenon is older than its artistic reflection in a modern wondertale. (2) If the same element has two variants, one of which derives from religious forms and the other from daily life, the religious formation is primary and the one drawn from daily life secondary. (Propp added here, "In applying these principles, we must observe caution. It would be an error to trace all basic forms to religion and all derived ones to reality.") (3) A fantastic treatment of a wondertale component is older than its rational treatment. This viewpoint is based on the link between the wondertale and religion, but it may prove invalid with respect to other types of tale, which may be older than the wondertale. (4) A heroic treatment of a wondertale is older than a humorous treatment; this is just a variant of the preceding case. (5) A form used logically is older than a form used nonsensically. (6) An international form is older than a national one. (On the attitude of Russian folklorists toward the Finnish school see Jason 1970—a succinct but informative article. See also Wosien 1969, 58-59.)

The principles formulated by the Finnish school, the Neolinguists, and Propp (or by anyone dealing with reconstruction) are only working hypotheses supported by observation and common sense. Everybody knows it; hence the abundance of such words as *usually, probably,* and *obviously.* These principles are not laws and can be reversed or revoked at any moment. In 1963 Propp wrote an article "Folklore and Reality," in which he said:

> The nonobligatory character of external motivations is inherent in all types of folklore, both prose and poetry. Logic is possible, but not mandatory. The artistic logic of the narrative does not coincide with the logic of causal thought. It is the action that is primary, not the reason for it. In comparing variants of the same plot, we discover that the motives for identical actions can be very different. . . . Logical motivations are introduced later in history, and there can be no doubt that a well-motivated narrative arose or was developed after a poorly motivated or unmotivated one. The version of the tale about the ill-fated corpse in which the motive for the murder is jealousy and the attempt to dispose of the corpse is made from fear that the murder will be discovered is a later version than the one about the fool who killed

his mother by accident. Characteristically, it was the motivated version that found its way into written literature. This version meets the aesthetic requirements and forms of thought of literate urban people. (pp. 26-27, below)

While writing this very persuasive passage, did Propp remember that "a form used logically is older than a form used nonsensically"?

In *Historical Roots* Propp again formulated the premises of his historical analysis. The ideas that interested him in 1926-1928 were different from those of 1934-1946. In the book Propp offered the following ten propositions (see No. 8 in the present volume).

(1) Wondertales form a specific group within folktales. They can be isolated and studied independently. (2) All wondertale motifs should be studied with reference to one another. (3) All wondertale motifs should be studied in their relations to the whole. (4) We must find in history the mode of production that gave rise to the wondertale. (5) The wondertale must be compared with the historical reality of the past, and its roots should be sought there. (6) The roots of the wondertale must be sought in the social institutions of the past. The wondertale preserves traces of vanished forms of social life. (7) The wondertale should be compared with ritual and custom. (8) The wondertale should be compared with the myths of ancient civilizations as well as with those of primitive, preclass societies. (9) In a study of the genesis of the wondertale, forms of primitive thought should be taken into consideration. (10) An investigation can begin even if the data have not been exhausted.

The first three theses sum up the ideas of *Morphology*. Numbers 4-6 answer the question about the most general roots of the wondertale and reflect the viewpoint of historical materialism. Numbers 7-9 specify what it is in reality that brought forth the wondertale; they are the key to Propp's stadialism. Today it is hard to believe that as late as 1946 someone could defend theses 4-9 in such a rigid form. We can see that the statements formulated in "Transformations of the Wondertale" are not repeated in the book, because in *Historical Roots* Propp did not investigate which forms of the wondertale are archaic and which are late. As regards ties between the wondertale and religion, this whole question is lost, but Propp's early suggestions are dissolved in the statements about the relations between the wondertale and primitive thought, myth, ritual, and social life in general.

Propp, following Tynjanov and other Formalists, differentiated the genesis of the wondertale and its history, and in the 1946 book he studied the genesis, the origin, rather than the subsequent development or transmission of the tale. He assumed that the wondertale had always reflected "reality" and had been brought to life by some ritual (a debatable conclusion that hardly needed elaborate Marxist support). It is worth investigating to what extent Propp remained a structuralist in his historical studies. Lévi-Strauss said that Propp had been torn between his formalist vision and a need for historical explanations. This remark only shows how thoroughly Propp was misunderstood by his critic. A view of language as a system is applicable both to synchrony and diachrony, but historical phonology (to take the clearest example) is a theory of sound change, not of the origin of language.

We usually do not know why sounds, art forms, tastes, beliefs, etc., change. In most cases it is difficult or impossible to state whether a particular change started under pressure from within or from outside. The morphology of English underwent radical transformations after the Norman conquest, but it probably would have changed in the same direction even if left alone. On the other hand, insular cultures are usually conservative (in keeping with Neolinguistic doctrine). Many sciences, from linguistics to geology, ask similar questions about change and answer them in a rather similar way. A functional point of view and concern about shifts that affect the entire system give birth to historical structuralism. When at some point the system becomes unstable and begins to move in a definite direction (whatever the initial causes of the change), certain laws of instability set in, and research into these laws is the structuralist's domain. This domain is limited, because it covers the process only after the process starts. *Historical Roots* is all about origins, so the structural apparatus could not have been used in it. But Propp (as he pointed out in his rejoinder to Lévi-Strauss) retained a systemic view of his data, and this was his main strength. He compared the wondertale with the rites of initiation and funeral rites and concluded that *the whole of the wondertale* mirrored *the whole of the rites. Historical Roots* is a detailed demonstration of this thesis. According to Propp, initiates were told what would happen to them during the rite, and later, after the desacralization of the tales, their texts came to be known as the wondertale.

Propp was not the first to maintain a holistic view of folklore origins: psychoanalysis does the same (with regard to Propp cf. Skeels 1967, 250). Nor was he the first to trace the wondertale to initiation and funeral. In Soviet scholarship S. Ja. Lur'é and B. V. Kazánskij investigated initiation, though on a very limited scale. Before them, Gidéon Huet and E. N. Trubetzkoy derived the other world of folklore from the kingdom of death, and Saintyves wrote a book on Perrault's tales (1923), in which he classified all of Perrault's plots into three groups: *les contes d'origine saisonnière, les contes d'origine initiatique,* and *les contes inventés par les sermonnaires.* The second group (the tales of initiatory origin) comprises "Le Petit Poucet," "La Barbe-Bleue," "Riquet à la Houppe," and "Le Maistre Chat ou le Chat botté." Cocchiara noticed the proximity between Propp and Saintyves at once: see Propp 1949, 16 and Cocchiara 1981, 509, and so did Propp's persecutors in 1947. Kaarle Krohn (1971, 169) did not accept Saintyves's reconstruction, because, apart from the obscurity of the rite, Saintyves operated with what Krohn called "individual variants and their frequently fortuitous characteristics." Propp (1946a, 42) said the same about Saintyves and added that his predecessor's ethnographic material is meager. Propp's own material is very extensive, but he, too, used "individual variants and their frequently fortuitous characteristics." He was obliged to reconstruct the initiation rite from many odds and ends picked up from all over the world (a weakness made much of in the anticosmopolitan purge). In later days, Propp has been much admired for his erudition, but the reverse side of his erudition was the extremely diffuse geographical space of his research.

Nor was this the only difficulty. Propp began with the idea that the initiation rites were similar everywhere, because their function is always the same: the boy undergoes ritual death and is reborn a man, a member of his community, and a potential bridegroom. The uniformity of the rites explains, according to Propp, why all wondertales are made to one cut. Implicitly, this theory presupposes the polygenesis of the wondertale. Propp must have been out of sympathy with the theory of monogenesis in folklore, as his repudiation of the Finnish school shows, but he never came to grips with this theory in open polemics, so his views on the subject of polygenesis versus monogenesis are unclear. Apparently, if a certain tale originated in India and reached Russia in the seventeenth century, initiation as we find it in Africa is not a very reliable source for reconstructing the Russian plot. Propp's belief in polygenesis could have been reinforced by Marr, who did not admit linguistic borrowings of any importance and as pointed out above, fought against the concept of protolanguage (when he was young, Marr detected a non-Indo-European substratum in Armenian, and in his mature years he asserted that the farther we delve into the past, the more different the related languages turn out to be, and their modern similarities are the result of later convergences). The idea of the prototale was unacceptable to Propp, and since he believed that both the ritual and the tale derived from the economic basis, the theory of polygenesis must have seemed satisfactory to him.

Still another difficulty that confronted Propp was a consequence of his strength. He worked with a 31-unit tale and attempted to trace it to a structured rite. Whether initiation is as uniform as Propp believed to be is a special question, but the wondertale, in spite of its constantly repeating scenario, cannot be squeezed into one single type (Žirmunskij 1947, 100, with a vague reference to earlier criticism; Taylor 1964, 126; Tudoróvskaja 1972, 149-50, Guépin 1973, 132). When the rigid pattern Propp established failed to cover his data, he, exactly like Lévi-Strauss, resorted to the idea of transformations. These transformations, outlined in Propp's 1928 article, are numerous: reduction, expansion, contamination, inversion, intensification, attenuation, substitution (not fewer than six types), modification, and assimilation (six types). Nearly all of them are obvious, because they can be accounted for by the laws and circumstances of oral transmission. Krohn (1971, Chapter 15) offered a similar list. According to Krohn, transformations occurring in oral prose are caused by substituting a synonym or replacing an obscure word; by adjusting a piece of foreign folklore to the new local conditions (with regard to flora, fauna, custom, belief, and so on); by the law of parity (words that belong to one and the same category tend to combine in parallel constructions); by the laws of similarity and contrast (sisters are substituted for brothers, wolves for bears; the villain is forgiven instead of being punished); by the law of spatial, temporal, and causal contiguity; by various assimilations.

Propp was less successful when he applied the idea of transformation to the remotest past. The main type of transformation in his quest for the wondertale's prehistory was inversion, and here the similarity between Propp and Lévi-Strauss is striking: both twist their material in practically the same way. Even Propp's most sympathetic critics (Žirmunskij, Toschi) did not accept his inversions. For instance, Propp derived the motif of dragon fighting from ritual swallowing and regurgitation, so he explained the fight with a fish that swallows the hero as the first stage of dragon fighting: previously the swallowed one was the hero, now the slayer of the swallower is the hero (inversion); when swallowing disappears altogether, we obtain dragon fighting in its modern form (1946a, 218). A baby put into a barrel and thrown into the sea is said to be another inverted form of swallowing and regurgitation (1946a, 224). Such examples abound in this book. They are especially common when Propp is carried away by his functional analysis and ignores the material. Then fishes and barrels, dragons and birds, all of which are interchangeable as variants in the narrative texture of the tale, are said to be historically interchangeable entities as well. A structural approach to language and folklore often does show how similar functions result in the rise of similar manifestations. But material (and we again return to the most fundamental question of structuralism) is not dead matter. Material serves the function as best it can, but its inertia is very strong, and its change in a certain predicted direction is only a possibility. If Lévi-Strauss had read the Italian translation of *Historical Roots* (he seems only to have looked through the book) and if Propp had read Lévi-Strauss's "Structure et dialectique" (1958; Chapter 12 of *Structural Anthropology 1*), with such statements as "a structural analysis of the myth content . . . furnishes rules of transformation which enable us to shift from one variant to another by means of operations similar to those of algebra," and "the semantic values are the same; they are merely permuted in relation to the symbols which express them," the two scholars could perhaps have learned something from each other.

Propp worked with an inflexible mold (initiation as it is reflected in the tale), and this simplistic solution was bound to spring a leak in more cases than one. In addition, as Mircea Eliade (1963, 196) noted in his discussion of Saintyves and Propp, "the whole problem is to determine whether the tale describes a system of rites belonging to a particular stage of culture, or if its initiatory scenario is 'imaginary,' in the sense that it is not bound up with a historico-cultural context but instead expresses an ahistorical, archetypal behavior pattern of the psyche" (first published in 1956). See also Meletinskij 1976a, 263-64 (the same objection).

The main chronological idea of Propp's reconstruction is that the wondertale is a later phenomenon than myth because the wondertale is a desacralized myth. It is very probable that wondertales are later than myths (I discuss the whole problem in Liberman, forthcoming), but there is no way of proving that, in spite of the common scenario that unites the initiation rite, the postulated initiation myth, and the wondertale, the tale was actually *derived* from myth. Tales of dragon fighting and of the fight between children and an ogre living in the wood are current and popular among the peoples that still offer sacrifices to snakes and observe the initiation rites.

No one seems to have noticed that Propp disregarded a basic literary aspect of the wondertale. Initiation focuses on the hero's death and rebirth, whereas the wondertale shifts the emphasis to the moral aspect of the adventure. If the wondertale is "about" anything, it is about the inevitable triumph of good over evil. The initiation drama, at least from what we are told in *Historical Roots*, knows nothing of this ethical problem. Neither does the early European ritual drama, insofar as it retains its pre-Christian features. If the wondertale was at one time a sacral text and attended a ritual, how did it acquire its most salient literary traits? Especially given Propp's preference for polygenesis, the uniform choice by all peoples of the initiation myth as the basis of the wondertale *with the same aesthetic consequences* is almost a miracle.

Historical Roots must have seemed antiquated to many as far back as 1946, and still it is worth reading today because a number of Propp's observations are insightful, correct, and not yet appreciated. But, in spite of Propp's hopes, even having read this excellent book we know as little about the origin of the wondertale and its relations to myth as ever.

C. Epos

Russian Heroic Epic Poetry is the only survey of such magnitude in any language; it is even bigger than Trautmann 1935 and is interesting both as a compendium and as a monument to its time. The book opens with an introduction (No. 10 of the present volume), which is followed by six parts: (1) Epic poetry at the time of the disintegration of primitive-communal society; (2) Russian epic poetry under developing feudalism; (3) The Russians' fight against the Mongol invasion; (4) Epic poetry during the formation of the Russian centralized state; (5) Epic poetry under capitalism, (6) Epic poetry today.

It is clear from the table of contents that Propp paid more than lip service to the theory of economic formations, because he recognized the division of human history into primitive-communal society, (slavery), feudalism, capitalism, and socialism as a relevant factor of literary history. In this Propp was not original. By the early Fifties no other scheme existed in Soviet works; Propp distinguished himself only by an unusually rigorous application of this scheme. Few scholars of his talent went so far. In *Russian Heroic Epic Poetry*, just as in *Historical Roots of the Wondertale*, Propp formulated his premises (1955, 57-58). These premises are reproduced below.

Since the peoples living at the primitive-communal stage have (or had) very rich epic poetry and the change of the economic formations is a universal law of history, the Russians must also have developed such poetry at the same stage, that is, long before the emergence of Kievan Rus'. The scholars who thought (or think) otherwise are wrong. Epic poetry arises when the primitive-communal order is nearing its end; it is directed against the tribe (kin). Its hero fights for a wife, because the principal concern of epic poetry is the setting up of the monogamous family—the new, progressive unit of society. Epic poetry is also directed against myth, the main ideological reflection of the primitive-communal stage. The concept of mythological epos is untenable. The basis of mythology is the religion of the so-called masters of nature. Early man is at the mercy of these masters. The stronger the element of fight against the masters, the closer such a tale is to epos. Myth and epos are ideological opposites. Epic poetry inherits from myth the idea of two worlds: one inhabited by human beings, the other in which the masters live. Later this idea is overcome, and the masters, reinterpreted as monsters, turn into the hero's enemies. Unlike the mythic hero and the wondertale hero, the epic hero possesses no magic tools or talismans; he performs his feats himself. The epic hero is selfless and disinterested; not only does he obtain a wife, but he also becomes a benefactor of his people. As long as the ruler (prince, khan, etc.) heads the union of related tribes, he is the hero of epic poetry, but when he begins to represent the exploiting class, he acquires the features of a negative figure (cf. Vladimir, who is the beloved prince and also a despot, coward, and traitor). When a ruler appears in class society, his literary counterpart attracts heroes who serve him. Cyclization is not the result of form's inner development, it is a purely ideological phenomenon. "Insofar as epic poetry necessarily reflects the economic and social structure of a people, the epic songs of the peoples at the same stage of social development will be similar and permit comparison" (p. 31). Even the earliest epic songs are highly artistic. A typical device of early epos is hyperbole. Epos can be in prose, in verse, and mixed; poetry without any prose insertions is probably the latest medium. The epic songs of some peoples consist of many links: new adventures are added to the initial story, and the song swells. Russian epic songs concentrate on one plot that is allowed to develop fully; this more perfect form is probably late. Russian tradition knows many epic heroes; this also is a later stage that was preceded by one-hero epos.

Propp's premises are supported by the facts collected from multinational epic tradition on the territory of the Soviet Union. As already mentioned, in the entire first edition of the book there is not a single reference to a foreign scholar, not even to Heusler or Menendez Pidal, who investigated very similar questions.

In the introduction Propp highlights four principal features of epic poetry: its content is heroic, its hero fights for his people's ideals, it is always sung, it has its own poetics. The third point is postulated rather than proved, and the fourth remains undeveloped.

Russian Heroic Epic Poetry is full of political statements but is almost divorced from literary analysis. For example, Propp examines Prince (King) Vladimir from a class point of view, lavishing abuse on him. Although it is true that Vladimir's relations with the heroes serving him are often strained (more so in later versions) and that the image of the Prince in the bylinas is not flattering, it is equally true that the epic Vladimir is not the Grand Duke of Russian history (as Propp himself knew very well) but a conventional literary figure, and his kin are many other outwardly illustrious but inwardly weak rulers. Arthur and Mark (inactive cuckolds), Anfortas (the suffering, impotent Graal King of *Parzival*), the hesitating Gunther in the first part of the *Nibelungenlied*, the pathetic Etzel in the second part of the same poem, and Charlemagne (a dignified supernumerary alongside of Roland)—all resemble Vladimir. Beowulf performs his chief deeds before he becomes king. Once on the throne, he is aware that the roles of a great warrior and a great ruler are incompatible and accepts the final challenge reluctantly; he is old and not afraid to die, but he knows that he is more useful to his subjects alive than dead. Vladimir is neither good nor bad; he is indeterminate. At the beginning of most bylinas he is represented feasting. During his first meeting with the hero he is ''neutral'' and unpredictable. He only sets the action going by sending the hero on an errand. He is never allowed to eclipse the hero; on the contrary, his frailty is emphasized to make the hero's service really worthwhile. If Vladimir, Hrothgar, and Mark could obtain their brides and kill monsters themselves, what would Il'ja, Beowulf, and Tristan do? Vladimir is even weaker and less heroic than his wife or daughter (another international device constantly used to humiliate the epic ruler).

The evolution of the heroic and royal ideals in epic poetry is a complex process, and a class point of view is too rude a tool for its analysis. Skaftymov (1924, 113-15; in English: Oinas and Soudakoff 1975, 137-54) proved that for the bylina the main element is the hero's feat. Vladimir is in the background of the tale; his function is to provide a situation in which the hero will be able to shine to advantage. He is endowed with the qualities necessary for the development of the heroic plot. The function of the background and the foreground, of right and left in an Old Russian icon can be described in comparable terms (see Uspenskij 1976a and b: both in English). Medieval art and literature usually have the same organizing principle (cf. the interlace structure of Old English and Old Norse poetry and the northern pictorial design). By and large, the same is true of modern poetry, painting, and music (the baroque, the rococo, Romanticism, Impressionism, etc.). Ancient Russian poetry and art were no exception to this law.

Propp reconstructed many centuries of pre-Kievan epic poetry. As he himself said, his only argument was the doctrine of historical materialism. In his opinion, the pivotal moment of Russian epic poetry was the formation of the state. If we can judge by Celtic and Germanic literatures, the formation of the state (a vague concept under the best of circumstances) does not affect literary development at all.

From time to time Propp shed the class point of view and began to analyze the text before him, and then he was like the Propp who wrote *Morphology of the Folktale*. This is what he says about the bylina of Mixájlo Pótyk (1958b, 119):

A bylina cannot end in marriage. . . . Marriage is a usual finale of wondertales, not of bylinas. The bylina plot needs a continuation, and only the first part of the lay concludes with marriage. The ancient epic required that after the hero's marriage a misfortune should befall his wife. Usually she is abducted. This always happens in the hero's absence. Therefore, when Potyk, after having married, again leaves Kiev, again absents himself from home, we know that this is a way of preparing the misfortune that will befall his wife during his absence. Hence the great variety of motivations used to explain his departure; the goal of his journey is practically immaterial.

But such passages are rare. In nearly all cases Propp uses the notorious ideological message to explain everything in the bylina, preferably the message as it was formulated by Belínskij. Time and again we come across passages like the following:

What will happen? Will Il'ja refuse to help?'' [He has been incarcerated by Vladimir, and Kiev is besieged by Tatars.] It is quite obvious that Il'ja cannot let Tatars devastate his native land. Will Il'ja and Vladimir be reconciled? It is equally obvious that such a solution is out of the question, because there cannot be any reconciliation between the people and the ruling power alien and hostile to them. What happens testifies to the depth of the people's thought. (1958b, 322)

If my considerations are correct, it follows that the bylinas present Vol'ga as a typical feudal and serf-owner *(krepostnik)*, who sets off to squeeze tribute from his subjects. In addition, he is a warrior. Now we understand why the half-forgotten Vol'ga had to be revived: he will be opposed to Mikúla. Class differentiation leaves its stamp on the warrior's image. . . . Vol'ga's army defends not their land's but the Prince's interests: it will help him exercise his feudal rights. (1958b, 378)

And a final flourish about Vladimir:

We have already seen the people's various attitudes toward Vladimir in epic poetry: on the one hand, Vladimir attracts the heroes as the center of Russian state unity, on the other hand, the people begin to understand the class character of power. With the development of epic poetry, the negative attitude toward Vladimir becomes more and more apparent. In the later bylina he is described not only as a statesman: the people depict his depravity, show him as a vicious despot, an abject human being who despises all morals. It means that in the people's eyes Vladimir is totally discredited. Social injustice is represented as a vice, as a moral evil. This is a typical peasant point of view. (1958b, 388)

One feels almost surprised that the peasants' leader Emelján Pugačév proclaimed himself tsar and that, given such a degree of class consciousness, Russia did not have its 1917 October Revolution at least in the seventeenth century.

Propp as a theoretician of folklore fought two schools: the Finnish school and the Russian Historical school. The method of *Morphology* is a reaction against Aarne's principles of classification, and the ideas of *Russian Heroic Epic Poetry* are opposed to those of the Russian Historical school. Propp attacks this school in the opening section of *Historical Roots* and in his article "Historicity of Folklore" (pp. 52 ff., 60 ff.). He usually added the expression *so-called* before the name of this school. In fact, the Russian Historical school represented a most fruitful trend. Its outstanding representatives (such as L. N. Majkov, V. F. Miller, M. N. Speránskij) attempted to establish connections between heroic poetry and the historical environment that brought it to life. They avoided the sweeping generalizations that became popular in Soviet historiography and that underlay Propp's conception, but they were certainly not the simpletons the statement on p. 100 implies. Unlike Marr, they preferred to work with the text in its recorded form and, by comparing it with other texts, to draw all the possible conclusions about its history. They did not aspire to reconstruct the spiritual life of the Slavs of the late Neolithic or even of the primitive-communal epoch. And since they were both cautious and well informed, their periodization of the Russian bylinas and many of their conclusions have not become antiquated in fifty or even a hundred years (Majkov's book was published in 1863). The school had its limitations, but much of what is solid in the science of Russian heroic epic poetry is based on the findings of Vsevolod Miller and his followers.

To better understand the ideas of the Historical school, it will be useful to discuss the differences between the bylina and the so-called historical song. The bylinas are more or less fantastic lays of varying length, from several hundred to several thousand lines, about the older heroes *(bogatyrí)*. Their action is usually set in and near Kiev, but Novgorod also had a rich epic tradition. The bylinas tell of olden days and have a recognizable system of stylistic devices. They are felt to constitute a genre, though they run the gamut from semimythological tales to ballads. Besides the bylinas, Russian folklore includes songs describing comparatively recent events, for instance, sieges of towns and feats of popular commanders; from an artistic point of view the songs are very heterogeneous and do not belong to one genre. They are sometimes long, but most are not; their length is not their significant feature.

The origin of the bylinas is unknown. The *Lay of the Host of Igor*, allegedly composed in the twelfth century, is quite unlike the bylinas; in its treatment of language and plot it can be compared to such bookish productions as the *Cantar de mio Cid* and the *Chanson de Roland*. The narrator of the *Lay* starts by dissociating himself from the style of the legendary singer Boján, with his ornate style. Russia may have had both "classical" (mythological-heroic) and "skaldic" tradition. If so, the *Lay* is antiskaldic; there even seems to be an uncomplimentary reference to the use of kennings in the opening lines of the poem (cf. Šarypkin 1973 and the bibliography cited there).

The earliest recorded historical song goes back to the fourteenth century. Whether any songs of this type were known at an earlier period is a matter of speculation; the few attempts to reconstruct pre-fourteenth-century songs have not been very successful. Although in their entirety the historical songs cannot pretend to be a genre, they seem to be opposed to the bylinas by the criterion of historicity: the bylinas treat history in a vague way, whereas the songs were presumably brought to life by concrete events. These events are often misrepresented, and familiar turns of the plot are used indiscriminately in different situations, but, when all is said and done, there is a clear line between Dobrýnja Nikítič killing a dragon and Ivan the Terrible attempting to kill his son, even if the epic Dobrynja and the historical Dobrynja share some features. However generalized the image of Ivan IV or Peter I may be, they are not literary descendants of Vladimir, and Hrothgar, Mark, and Anfortas are no longer their kin. Propp insisted that, since the historical song is dependent on actual fact and has a poetics of its own distinct from the poetics of the bylina, the bylina's independence of fact is proved. But this is an obvious non sequitur. The bylinas, too, may have drawn their inspiration from concrete facts but reflected (or refracted) them in their own way. This was the point of view of several representatives of the Historical school. Veselovskij regarded the historical song as a preparatory stage in the development of the bylina. According to him, the bylina is a song whose ties with the event have come to be forgotten. This reconstruction does not account for the aesthetic differences between the bylinas and the historical songs *as we know them*, but the more realistic theory, which traces the historical song to the later epoch, shatters against a very similar obstacle: it cannot explain what caused the appearance of the song with its peculiar style. The artistic aspect is the only one that matters here, for, even if we admit that the rise of historical self-awareness needed new ways of expression, we will not say anything about the emergence of a new poetics. (Heusler's theory of Germanic heroic poetry is a good basis for comparison in a situation of this type.)

From the point of view of Slavic literary tradition it would be difficult to decide whether the lays of the *Elder Edda*, the "Hildebrandslied," and the Finnsburg fragment are historical songs or bylinas. The Historical school treated all heroic poetry as based on fact, compared it with the chronicles, and attempted to discover the events that underlie each text, usually at the level of separate episodes. The excesses of this method and the many untenable conclusions reached by the Historical school have diminished its credibility but could not invalidate the quest itself. Bookish heroic poetry, such as *Beowulf,* the *Cantar de mio Cid,* the *Chanson de Roland*, the *Nibelungenlied*, and the *Lay of the Host of Igor*, is a mixture of accurate information, legend, *loci communes*, and what we now call fantasy. The historical truth (again, in our sense of the word) glimmers through countless international motifs and fiction not yet realized as such. The bylinas are not bookish, but their treatment of history was or at least could have been similar to what we find in heroic poetry. B. N. Putílov, Propp's alter ego, admitted (1966, 123-24) that there are four types of facts in the bylinas as compared with the chronicles: (1) some realities (dates, names, etc.) made their way into the chronicles from the bylinas; (2) some coincidences are fortuitous; (3) some coincidences are dubious and should better be left alone; (4) some coincidences are indeed based on historical facts, and so in this instance the bylina and the chronicle describe the same event. Putilov explained away the fourth category by saying that familiar names come to be tied to stereotyped situations in retrospect, so the apparent historicity of the bylinas is late; for example, all the invading kings are alike to Russian poetry, and at one time they are called Kálin or Kudrevánko, at another Skúrla, Mamáj or Bátyj (that is, Batu). This is Propp's theory all over: Putilov is unwilling to give credit to actual fact in the bylina; he refers to history in general, rather than to concrete events; and he operates with the mold that remains stable and changes only its content from one epoch to another (Propp reasoned similarly in his reconstruction of the wondertale). But if Putilov is correct, how did the mold come about? Surely, at one time there must have been a concrete stimulus for the creation of at least some of the lays (e.g., those that deal with the Mongol invasion). Skaftýmov struggled with a similar difficulty: he claimed that the bylina, at its inception, was interesting to the audience as a narrative about some event, but later developed according to its own laws, which are the laws of poetics. This hypothesis is not irreconcilable with Veselovskij's (that is, first the song, then the bylina), and again it leaves unexplained the change of focus from historicity to pure aesthetics. Putilov's analysis is less subtle than Skaftymov's, because he does not specify how the bylina plot originates and develops. He remains within the circle drawn by Propp and is mainly concerned about refuting Rybakóv, whose dogmatic reading of the bylinas is easy prey for criticism but whose conclusions have little to do with the value of the Historical school (cf. p. 28 below).

Inasmuch as some names, dates, and routes, mentioned in the bylinas are accurate, everything in Russian heroic poetry should be studied with a chronicle in hand. Extreme caution and a sense of measure are necessary in such a study, because, as Putilov says, there are all kinds of convergences between history and epic poetry.

The usual question that scholars ask about Russian bylinas and their origin is: Do bylinas have a foundation in fact? But what we should ask is: How are historical facts reflected in the bylina? We need not be particularly interested in whether Dobrynjna's fight against the dragon tells the story of the introduction of Christianity to Kievan Rus'. Quite apart from the consideration that allegory is alien to both myth and heroic poetry, there is no great hope of discovering the historical core of purely fabulous events. Verifiable hypotheses are hardly possible on such material. Other scenes in the bylinas are more amenable to historical analysis. Old poetry knows many approaches to fact. When Beowulf killed Grendel, the court poet "described" the event by extolling a hero of old; by implication, Beowulf was like that hero. Beowulf himself learned about Grendel's inroads from songs, but we do not know what kind of songs they were. The Old English Chronicle glorifies the victory at Brunanburh and laments the defeat at Maldon, but both poems contain more formulas than information. When heroic poetry wanted to describe a contemporary event, it usually offered an ancient parallel. Cf. the famous episode told by Saxo Grammaticus: before the murder of St. Knud in 1131, a Saxon minstrel tried to warn him by singing about Kriemhild's treachery; the king did not take the hint and was killed. But in the same period and much earlier, Iceland knew a flourishing skaldic tradition, and the skalds could describe contemporary events very well, in spite of the extreme complexity of their style. If the bylinas are comparable to Eddic poetry, they were probably past-oriented from the very beginning and could never be too accurate. Characteristically, to glorify the Russians' fight against the Mongols (Tatars), the singers of bylinas had to set the action in old Kiev.

To bring this discussion to a close I would like to give a quotation from Putilov's main work (1960, 160). As pointed out above, Putilov follows Propp in everything and is a mouthpiece for Propp's ideas.

The scholars who assumed that every historical song is an artistic reworking of some real facts (or a reworking of legends based on these facts) made unsuccessful attempts to explain "Kostrjúk" by resorting to all kinds of questionable arguments. This assumption inevitably resulted in the idea that history is "distorted" in the song, that the singers had forgotten the facts, messed them up, etc. However, nothing is forgotten in "Kostrjuk" and nothing is messed up; everything is exceptionally consistent and logical. "Kostrjuk" is not a distortion of history and not a lampoon; it is a definite conception of history, which found a peculiar artistic expression. The warp and woof of this conception is not historical realities; realities are totally determined by this conception, totally dissolved in the traditionally epic movement of the plot. The historical realities of the song are important not in and of themselves but as an object of artistic interpretation and description, and only to the extent they can be used in the melting pot of the chief artistic design. "Kostrjuk" was never meant to be a song of "the tsar's marriage" or of "the valiant wrestler Mamstrjuk Temrjukovič." "Kostrjuk" was not meant to be a song of any concrete fact. The relation between fact and fiction in

"Kostrjuk" is of the same nature as in bylinas. In epic poetry we also run across personages and motifs that seemingly correspond to those in the chronicle, but there is no inner artistic link between them. It is true that some facts from the chronicles can be connected with the facts from epic poetry and that the connection is not always fortuitous, but these facts could not have been the base or the object of artistic description; on the contrary, they were drawn into the system of epic poetry, became part of this system and were reworked and reinter- preted according to its laws. This is what happened with "Kostrjuk," so "Kostrjuk"—at least in one respect—is closer to the bylinas than to the historical songs.

The Historical school undoubtedly fell into many traps (as was known to its practitioners and made very clear by Skaftymov), but the alternative offered by Propp and Putilov is even less convincing than the hypotheses of Vsevolod Miller and his followers. Did medieval Russian narrators indeed have "a conception of history" powerful enough to merit such a name? What shaped this concep- tion? Putilov's singer must have reasoned like this, "I have heard that when Tsar Iván Vasíljevič married a Circassian princess the bride's brother Kostrjuk (or Mamstrjuk) Temrjukovič came to Moscow and was defeated in a wrestling match by a Russian, who stripped him of all his clothes, to the delight of the spectators, but I will sing the song my own way, paying no attention to what I have heard, because I do not believe in the tale; and anyway I am interested in generalities rather than in concrete facts." What grounds are there for reconstructing such a conception? And what heroic songs do we know that were not even meant to depict any concrete facts? Perhaps only the most fantastic Euro- pean romances, but not *Beowulf, Roland, Cid,* the *Nibelungenlied*, or Homer's poems. Unlike Milman Parry, Propp and Putilov never attempted to reconstruct the process of epic composition; hence the vagueness of their notions and the unrealistic character of their conclusions.

There are three rival theories of the origin of epic poetry in modern Soviet scholarship. According to Propp, heroic poetry is opposed to myth and grows from prestate poetry, in which the hero's enemies are monsters. According to Meletinskij, heroic epic poetry is a continuation, rather than the negation, of myth- ological epic poetry (he distinguishes between archaic and classical epos). Ac- cording to Žirmunskij, heroic poetry derives from the bogatyr tale; his main material is Slavic and Turkic, and his views are not unlike Heusler's.

The methods (and weaknesses) of the Historical school are also alive today (Rybakóv, Pliséckij, partly D. S. Lixačév), but the school itself has only recently recovered from the blow that was dealt it in the Thirties. (See Azbelev 1982, 5-42, for the latest survey of the field; Propp's ideas are subjected to severe criticism in the book). In 1936 the official Kremlin poet Dem'ján Bédnyj pro- duced a farce on a bylina theme (a politically oriented revision of an old com- edy). For reasons that are not quite clear, this farce was condemned in a special decree of the Central Committee as unpatriotic and disparaging of Russia's heroic past, and Bednyj fell into contempt. For still more obscure reasons, someone connected Dem'jan Bednyj's play with the Historical school, which was accused of reactionary tendencies (because it favored the idea of the aristocratic origin of heroic poetry), and with Hans Naumann's teachings. (The best account of these events in English is Oinas 1971b.) A "discussion" ensued, and the school stopped existing. The critics of the school (at that time all active folklorists) claimed that V. Miller and his pupils had reduced each bylina to some concrete fact and thus distorted the principle of historicity in folklore. Propp took the "discussion" very seriously and opposed all attempts to revive the Historical school in any of its forms. He wrote, "Followers of the old Historical school do not understand the nature of epic poetry as a specific genre. . . . A bylina is not a novel by Tolstoy. A bylina has a historical foundation and reflects it, but the active representation of current historical reality and current events is neither its objective nor a part of its aesthetics and poetics" (p. 56, below). How did Propp know that "the active representation of current historical reality and current events is neither [the bylina's] objective nor a part of its aesthetics and poetics"? Is it not precisely the thesis that needed proof? Propp formulated the principle (from which he deviated in a few cases) that epic poetry does not reflect any *concrete* features of historical reality but only the people's *major* ideals and aspirations characteristic of whole epochs (cf. Emel'janov 1976; 1979; and Aníkin's spirited but unconvincing polemics: Anikin 1979).

The first edition of *Russian Heroic Epic Poetry* (1955) was received rather coolly. (Kovács 1956 is only a sympathetic survey; Emel'janov 1955 is unavailable abroad, and I am not aware of any analytical reviews of the 1958 edition but see Astaxova 1966, 67-69, 82-83, 85, 120-21.) Meletinskij (1956) praised Propp for his excellent style and general attitude but disagreed with his treatment of myth versus epos. He especially contested Propp's idea of a passive mythical hero dependent on the "masters" and opposed archaic, mythological epos to classical, heroic epos. Propp specifically denied the existence of mythological epos. Meletinskij also refuted Propp's strange idea (an abortive paraphrase of Morgan-Engels) that heroic poetry was concerned with the creation of the monogamous family, his dogmatic treatment of Vladimir as the enemy of the Russian heroes and the Russian people, and his improbable sociological explanations. Uxov (1956) expressed his dismay at Propp's lack of interest in "bourgeois scholarship," his disrespectful tone of criticism, and his political demagoguery. Followers of the Historical school also struck back (see Pliseckij 1960 and Rybakov 1963, 42-43 and passim).

Propp, armed with the tenets of historical materialism and treading "the only correct path," intended to revolutionize the study of the bylinas. This he did not achieve, but his book remains a useful source of information on the subject of Russian heroic poetry.

Conclusion

Soviet literary scholarship, despite all the translations and surveys, is a sealed book to the West. Even if some works become well known in Europe and America, they are rarely understood in their true context. Propp is a case in point. His *Morphology* made him very famous, but the ties that connected him with his predecessors and contemporaries remained hidden. The real, demythologized Propp was quite unlike the semilegendary father of structuralism in folklore, as he is represented by his admirers on both sides of the Atlantic.

Propp's legacy is varied; it contains articles and books on almost every genre of folklore. It was mentioned at the beginning of this essay that Propp has a following in the West only as the author of *Morphology*. The other works from his pen occasionally appearing outside the Soviet Union are most often treated as extensions of *Morphology* and appraised as contributions to structuralism and semiotics. This approach is inadmissible. It is true that Propp, inspired by the ideas of Russian Formalism, investigated ''how the wondertale was made,'' and his first attempt, even though not flawless, turned out to be a major event in folklore studies. The book pursued a narrow goal, namely, to describe wondertales from Afanas'ev's collection, and, as we know now, Propp viewed *Morphology* as an introduction to the history of the wondertale. In this, he was part and parcel of Russian structuralism. One of the main lessons of the Prague Circle is that diachronic studies should follow a meticulous synchronic analysis of the data. The methodological value of this lesson is great, and the science of folklore has not yet learned it. The numerous attacks on the origin of the wondertale, be it the ridiculed solar hypothesis, the antiquated theory of survivals, or the popular Freudian-Jungian approach, share common cause in their indifference to the structure of the tale, to its literary features, and to its aesthetic message. Propp himself made only one step in the direction he envisaged. His partial failure to reconstruct the beginnings of the wondertale testifies less to the weakness of structuralism than to Propp's insufficiently rigorous application of the structural principle. It is not clear what Propp would have achieved, had he been more consistent, but his ideas cannot be brought to their logical conclusion until the whole of his legacy becomes available to an international audience.

All his life Propp looked for invariants in folklore. His *Morphology, Historical Roots,* and *Russian Agrarian Festivals* are milestones on this road. His experience shows that to discover an invariant does not always mean to discover the truth. Few scholars' works provide a better basis for discussing the ultimate goals of folklore than Propp's, but again it is necessary to review all three books and all his articles, not just the most conspicuous ones.

It is important to begin treating Propp's concrete investigations as seriously as his theoretical views. Propp shares the fate of the other founders of structuralism in that people mine him for his general ideas and disregard his everyday work. De Saussure's *Course* has been torn to quotations, but his brilliant *Mémoire* attracts only the Indo-Europeanists, who care more for the author's results than for his method. A reference to Trubetzkoy's *Grundzüge* is a standard embellishment in works on semiotics, but these references seldom go beyond the first eighty pages, though Trubetzkoy's genius is displayed in the later chapters much more strongly than in the introduction to the book. Independent of whether one is ready to accept Propp's theory of the wondertale, his *Historical Roots* and his articles are a treasure house of information, and his reasoning remains a mighty stimulus to his supporters and opponents alike.

Propp's Marxism poses another question. No one can appreciate Marxism without studying its Soviet face. Many scholars will probably try to evaluate Propp's experience in this area. Some will be strengthened in their conviction that the principles of dialectical materialism and a class point of view are profitable in literary analysis, some will agree with the principle but criticize Propp's application of it, and some will dismiss the whole attempt. *Russian Epic Heroic Poetry* is an invaluable book for all those who investigate the impact of Marxism on comparative and historical literature, including folklore.

Propp wrote an important chapter in the science of folklore, and it is essential that it be accessible to the large community of scholars outside his own country.

Note

In 1981 the Leningrad University Press announced V. Ja. Propp's new book *The Russian Folktale* [*Russkaja skazka*]. According to the catalog, it is a work of about 400 pages never published before. "It presents in a systematic way a holistic conception of the origin and development of the Russian folktale in its principal varieties." The book was due in July-September 1982. By April 1984, this book announced once more in the 1983 catalog has not appeared. No detailed description of the volume exists, but this work is definitely distinct from *Morphology of the Folktale* and *Historical Roots of the Wondertale*.

I. The Nature of Folklore

Chapter One.
The Nature of Folklore

The Social Nature of Folklore

Problems of folklore are acquiring more and more importance nowadays. None of the humanities, be it ethnography, history, linguistics, or the history of literature, can do without folklore. Little by little we are becoming aware that the solution to many diverse phenomena of spiritual culture is hidden in folklore. Nevertheless, folklore has not yet defined its objectives, its material, or its own specific character as an area of knowledge. We have some works pertaining to general theory, but life proceeds at such a rapid pace that the propositions put forward in these works no longer conform to the extremely complex picture that emerges from current research. To define the subject and essence of our discipline, to determine its place among related disciplines, and to define the specific character of its material has become a vital matter. Correctness of methods and, consequently, of conclusion depends on the correct understanding of the essence and objective of research. The way problems of general theory are formulated has a cognitive and philosophical meaning and affects their concrete solution.

Western Europe has no lack of theoretical works either, but these works satisfy us even less than early Soviet works. Folklore is an ideological discipline. Its methods and aims are determined by and reflect the outlook of the age. When an outlook disappears, the principles of scholarship it has created also disappear. We cannot be guided by the scholarly views of Romanticism, the Enlightenment, or any other trend. We need to create a discipline with the outlook of our own age and country.

What is meant by "folklore" in the most recent Western European scholarship? To answer this question it suffices to open any monograph with an appropriate title. If we take the book of the well-known German folklorist John

Meier *Deutsche Volkskunde* (1921), we will see the following sections: the village, buildings, farmsteads; plants; superstitions; language; legends; folktales; folk songs; bibliography. This picture is typical of all Western European scholarship, primarily German and French, to a lesser extent of English and American. Journals discuss the same subjects but with greater specializations, for example, the smallest details of buildings: platbands, shutters, the ridges of roofs, the structure of stoves, utensils, household goods, vessels, cradles, distaffs, clothing, headgear, and so on and so forth. Along with this are studied rituals, weddings, holidays, and also folktales, legends, songs, proverbs, etc. There is nothing fortuitous in this choice of subjects. It reflects a definite understanding by scholarship of its objectives. The premises and principles on which this scholarship is built amount to the following: (1) the culture of only one stratum of the population is studied, namely, that of the peasantry; (2) the subject of scholarship is both material and spiritual culture; (3) the subject of scholarship is the peasantry of only one nation, and in most cases it is the researcher's nation.

We can accept none of these premises. We separate the material and spiritual spheres and make them the subject of different, although related, close, interconnected, and interdependent areas of scholarship. The view that the material and spiritual culture of the peasantry can be studied by one branch of scholarship is that of a gentleman folklorist. Nothing like this is done for the culture of the ruling classes. The history of technology and architecture, on the one hand, and the history of literature and music, on the other, are different areas of scholarship, because here one is dealing with the upper strata of society. But when one is dealing with the peasantry, the structure of old stoves and the rhythm of lyric songs can allegedly be studied together. We know very well that the closest connection exists between material and spiritual culture, but we separate the material and the spiritual, just as it is done for the culture of the upper classes. By folklore we mean only *spiritual* production, and only verbal, poetical products. Since poetry is almost always connected with music, musical folklore forms an autonomous discipline within folklore.

This understanding of folklore has long since characterized Russian scholarship. What we call folklore is called *traditions populaires, tradizioni populari, Volksdichtung,* and the like in the West, and there it is not the subject of a separate area of knowledge. We, on the other hand, do not consider folklore as it is defined in the West to be a special area of knowledge but at best recognize it as the popular-scientific study of one's native country.

In the West it is the poetical works of the *peasants* and always of the *contemporary* peasants that are studied, though only insofar as their contemporary culture has preserved elements of the past. The subject is "living antiquity," and it persisted rather long in Russia as well. Such a point of view is unacceptable to us because we study all phenomena in the *process* of their development. Folklore had existed before the emergence of the peasantry. From a historical perspective, the entire creative output of peoples is folklore. For peoples who have reached the stage of class society, folklore is the output of all strata of the population except the ruling one; the latter's verbal art belongs to literature. Folklore is, first and foremost, the art of the oppressed classes, both peasants and workers, but also of the intermediate strata that gravitate toward the lower social classes. One can speak with some reservations of lower middle class folklore, but never of the folklore of the aristocracy.

In the West folklore means the peasant culture of *one* people, most commonly of the researcher's own people. The principle of selection is quantitative and national. The culture of one people serves as the object of one branch of knowledge, namely, folklore, *Volkskunde*. The culture of all other peoples, including primitive peoples, is the object of another discipline that has many names: anthropology, ethnography, ethnology, *Völkerkunde*. There is no precise terminology here.

Although we fully acknowledge the possibility of a scientific study of national cultures, the principle outlined above is completely unacceptable, and it can easily be reduced to the absurd. Indeed, if a French scholar studies French songs, this is folklore, but if the same scholar studies Albanian songs, this is ethnography. We must dissociate ourselves from such a conception and put forward our own point of view: the science of folklore embraces the art of all peoples, no matter who studies them. Folklore is an international phenomenon.

We can now summarize our premises and say that by folklore we understand the art of the lower social strata of all peoples, irrespective of the stage of their development. For peoples before the formation of classes it is their entire art taken together.

The question naturally arises: what is folklore in a classless society, under socialism? It would seem that folklore, which is a class phenomenon, should disappear. However, literature is also a class phenomenon, but it does not disappear. Under socialism, folklore loses its specific features as a product of the lower strata, since in a socialist society there are neither upper nor lower strata, just the people. Folklore indeed becomes *national* property. What is not in harmony with the people dies out; what remains is subjected to profound qualitative changes and comes closer to literature. Further research will show what these changes are, but it is clear that folklore under capitalism and under socialism are different things.

Folklore and Literature

All this defines only one aspect of the matter, namely, the social nature of folklore, and is insufficient for singling out folklore as a form of verbal art and the science of folklore as a branch of knowledge.

Folklore is the product of a special form of verbal art. Literature is also a verbal art, and for this reason the closest connection exists between folklore and literature, between the science of folklore and literary criticism. Literature and folklore overlap partially in their poetic genres. There are genres specific to literature (for example, the novel) and to folklore (for example, the charm), but both folklore and literature can be classified by genres, and this is a fact of poetics. Hence there is a certain similarity in some of their tasks and methods.

One of the literary tasks of folklore is to single out and study the category of genre and each particular genre. Especially important and difficult is to study the inner structure of verbal products, their composition and makeup. The laws pertaining to the structure of the folktale, epic poetry, riddles, songs, charms, etc., are little known. In epic genres consider, for example, the opening of the poem, the plot, and the conclusion. It has been shown that works of folklore and literature have different morphologies and that folklore has specific structures. This difference cannot be *explained,* but it can be *discovered* by means of literary analysis. Stylistic and poetical devices belong here too. Again we will see that folklore has devices specific to it (parallelisms, repetition, etc.) and that the usual devices of poetical language (similes, metaphors, epithets) have a different content in folklore and literature. This too can be determined by literary analysis.

In brief, folklore possesses a most distinctive *poetics*, peculiar to it and different from the poetics of literary works. Study of this poetics will reveal the incomparable artistic beauty of folklore.

Thus, not only is there a close tie between folklore and literature, but folklore is a literary phenomenon. Like literature, it is a verbal art.

In its descriptive elements the study of folklore is the study of literature. The connection between these disciplines is so close that folklore and literature are often equated; methods of literature are extended to folklore, and here the matter is allowed to rest. However, as just pointed out, literary analysis can only *discover* the phenomenon and the law of folklore poetics, but it is unable to *explain* them. To avoid the error of equating folklore with literature, we must ascertain not only *how literature and folklore are alike,* related, and to a certain extent identical in nature, but also *how they differ.* Indeed, folklore possesses a number of features so sharply differentiating it from literature that methods of literary research are insufficient for solving all its problems.

One of the most important differences is that literary works invariably have an author. Folklore works, on the contrary, never have an author, and this is one of their specific features. The situation is quite clear: either we acknowledge the presence of *folk art* as a phenomenon in the social and cultural history of peoples or we do not acknowledge it and claim that it is a poetical or scientific fiction and that only individuals and groups can create poetry.

We believe that folk art is not a fiction, that it really exists and that the study of it is the basic objective of scientific folklore. In this respect we make common cause with such older scholars as F. I. Busláev[1] and Orést Míller[2]. What older scholarship felt instinctively and expressed naively, awkwardly, and not so much scientifically as emotionally must now be purged of romantic errors and elevated to the height of modern scholarship, with its consistent methods and exact techniques.

Brought up in the traditions of literature, we are often unable to conceive that a poetical work can have arisen not as a literary work arises when created by an individual. It always seems to us that someone must have been the first to compose it. Yet it is possible for poetical works to arise in completely different ways, and the study of those ways is one of the most fundamental and complex problems of folklore. I cannot go into this problem here and will only mention that in its origin folklore should be likened not to literature but to language, which is invented by no one and which has neither an author nor authors. It arises everywhere and changes in a regular way, independently of people's will, once there are appropriate conditions for it in the historical development of peoples. Universal similarity does not present a problem. It is rather its absence that we would have found inexplicable. Similarity indicates a regular process; the similarity of works of folklore is a particular case of the historical law by which identical forms of production in material culture give rise to identical or similar social institutions, to similar tools, and, in ideology, to the similarity of forms and categories of thought, religion, rituals, languages, and folklore. All of these live, influence one another, change, grow, and die.

With regard to the problem of conceiving *empirically* the origin of folklore, it will suffice to note that in its beginnings folklore can be an integral part of ritual. With the degeneration or decline of a ritual, folklore becomes detached from it and continues to live an independent life. This is only an illustration of a general trend. Proof can be supplied by concrete research, but that folklore originated in ritual was already clear, in the last years of his life, to A. N. Veselóvskij.[3]

The distinction discussed here is so important that it compels us to single out folklore as a special type of verbal art and the science of folklore as a special discipline. A literary historian interested in the origin of a work looks for its author. The folklorist, with the aid of broad comparative material, discovers the conditions that brought forth a plot. But the difference between folklore and literature is not confined to this distinction; they are differentiated not only by their origin but also by their forms of existence.

It has long been known that literature is transmitted through writing and folklore by word of mouth. Until now this distinction has been considered to be purely technical. However, it captures the innermost difference between the functioning of literature and folklore. A literary work, once it has arisen, no longer changes. It exists only when two agents are present: the author (the creator of the work) and the reader. The mediating link between them is a book, manuscript, or performance. A literary work is immutable, but the reader always changes. Aristotle was read by the ancient Greeks, the Arabs, and the Humanists, and we read him too, but all read and understand him differently. True readers always read creatively. A work of literature can bring them joy, inspire them, or fill them with indignation. They may wish to interfere in the heroes' fortunes, reward or punish them, change their tragic fate to a happy one, put a triumphant villain to death. But the readers, no matter how deeply they are aroused by a work of literature, are unable and are not allowed to introduce any changes to suit their own personal tastes or the views of their age.

Folklore also presupposes two agents, but different agents, namely, the performer and the listener, opposing each other directly, or rather without a mediating link.

As a rule, the performers' works are not created by them personally but were heard earlier, so performers can in no way be compared with poets reciting their own works. Nor are they reciters of the works of others, mere declaimers reproducing someone else's work. They are figures specific to folklore, and all of them, from the primitive chorus to the folktale narrator Krjúkova[4], deserve our closest attention. Performers do not repeat their texts word for word but introduce changes into them. Even if these changes are insignificant (but they can be very great), even if the changes that take place in folklore texts are sometimes as slow as geological processes, what is important is the fact of *changeability of folklore compared with the stability of literature.*

If the reader of a work of literature is a powerless censor and critic devoid of authority, anyone listening to folklore is a potential future performer, who, in turn, consciously or unconsciously, will introduce changes into the work. These changes are not made accidentally but in accordance with certain laws. Everything that is out-of-date and incongruous with new attitudes, tastes, and ideology will be discarded. These new tastes will affect not only what will be discarded but also what will be reworked and supplemented. Not a small (though not the decisive) role is played by the narrator's personality, taste, views on life, talents, and creative abilities. A work of folklore exists in constant flux, and it cannot be studied in depth if it is recorded only once. It should be recorded as many times as possible. We call each recording a variant, and these variants are something completely different from a version of a work of literature made by one and the same person.

Folklore circulates, changing all the time, and this circulation and changeability are among its specific characteristics. Literary works can also be drawn into the orbit of this circulation. For example, Mark Twain's *Prince and the Pauper* is told as a folktale; Lermontov's 'Sail,'[5] Del'vig's "Nightingale,"[6] etc., are sung.

What do we have in this instance: folklore or literature? The answer is fairly simple. If, for example, a story from a chapbook, a saint's life, or the like, is recited from memory with no changes from the original, or if "The Black Shawl"[7] or an excerpt from *The Peddlers*[8] are sung exactly as Pushkin and Nekrásov wrote them, this case differs little from a performance on the stage or anywhere else. But as soon as such songs begin to change, to be sung differently, as soon as they begin to form variants, they become folklore, and the process of their change is the folklorist's domain. To be sure, there is a difference between folklore of the first sort, which often originated in prehistoric times and has variants all over the world, and poets' verses, freely used and transmitted by word of mouth. In the first case, we have pure folklore, that is, folklore both by origin and by transmission; in the second case, folklore of literary origin, that is, folklore by transmission but literature by origin. This distinction must always be kept in mind. A song that we consider pure folklore can turn out to be literary, can have an author. The universally known and seemingly pure folk songs "Dubínuška"[9] and "Íz-za óstrova na stréžen' "[10] were composed by obscure poets, one by Tréfolev, the other by Sadóvnikov. Such examples are numerous, and ties between literature and folklore, as well as the literary sources of folklore are among the most interesting subjects both in the history of literature and in folklore.

This case again brings us to authorship in folklore. We have taken only two extreme cases. The first is folklore that was created by no one individual and arose in prehistoric times within the framework of some ritual or in some other way and that has survived through oral transmission to the present. The second case is obviously an individual's recent work circulating as folklore. In the development of both literature and folklore, between these two extremes occur all sorts of intermediate forms, each of which is a special problem. Modern folklorists are well aware that such problems cannot be solved descriptively, synchronically, but should be studied in their development. The genetic study of folklore is just one part of *historical* study, for folklore is not only a literary but also a historical phenomenon and the science of folklore not only a literary but also a historical discipline.

Folklore and Ethnography

All the humanities can now be only historical. We examine every phenomenon in its development, beginning with its emergence, trace its development, its peak, and, possibly, its degeneration, decline, and disappearance. This does not mean, however, that we hold an evolutionist point of view. Evolutionist scholarship, having established and traced the fact of development, goes no further. Genuinely historical scholarship requires not only the establishment of the fact of development but also its *explanation*. Poetical art is a phenomenon of the superstructure. To explain a phenomenon means to trace it to its causes, and these causes lie in the economic and social life of the people.

The earliest forms of material culture and social organization are the object of ethnography. Therefore, historical folklore, which attempts to discover the origin of its phenomena, rests upon ethnography. There cannot be a materialist study of folklore independent of ethnography.

We do not know precisely just what and how much originates in primitive society. In any event, the folktale, epic poetry, ritual poetry, charms, riddles as *genres*, etc., cannot be explained without enlisting ethnographic data. Likewise, many motifs (for example, those of the magic helper, marriage to an animal, and the faraway kingdom)[11] find their explanation in the ideas and religious-magic practice of the past. Ethnographic data are equally important in the genetic study and in the study of the initial development of folklore; for not only the origin of genres, plots, and motifs, but also their subsequent functioning depends on the forms of material and social life.

Realization of this principle is interesting and fruitful when it is applied in depth, when the smallest details of both folklore and ethnography are taken into account. It is not enough to say that the motif of noble animals is of totemic origin, that the *Edda*[12] was created at the stage of disintegration of tribal society, etc. All this must be demonstrated in an unambiguous way on extensive comparative material. For example, to study the hero's marriage (and courtship is one of the most widespread motifs in myth, in the folktale, and in epic poetry), we must study the forms of marriage that existed at various stages in the development of human society. Furthermore, we need very detailed knowledge of wedding ceremonies and customs. We must know precisely at which stages and among which peoples the bridegroom undergoes a trial and what the character of this trial was. Only then will we properly understand the corresponding phenomenon in folklore.

One can easily assume that folklore reflects social or some other relationships directly. This would be a wrong assumption. Folklore, especially in its early stages, is not a description of life. Reality is not reflected directly but through the prism of thought, and this thought is so unlike ours that it can be difficult to compare a folklore phenomenon with anything at all. In this system of thought, connections of cause and effect do not yet exist; other connections prevail, but we often do not know which. There are no generalizations, no abstractions, no concepts. Space and time are perceived differently from the way we perceive them. The categories of singular and plural and the qualities of subject and object (identification of oneself with animals) play a role completely different from the one they play for us. What we never consider real is considered real and vice versa. Primitive man sees the world of things not as we do, and his views change from one stage to another. Therefore, we look in vain for an existential reality behind a folklore reality.

In folklore, characters behave in one way or another not because things actually happened so, but because this is how they were perceived according to the laws of primitive thought. Consequently, this thought and the whole system of primitive outlook should be subjected to special study. Otherwise, we will understand neither the composition, the plots, nor the individual motifs and run the risk of falling into a kind of naive realism or of treating folklore phenomena as something grotesque, exotic, as the free play of unbridled fantasy.

It can be taken for granted that one of the manifestations of this thought is religious concepts, which have the closest connection with folklore. Not only religious *concepts* and thought images are important but the very religious-magic *practice*, that is, the whole complex of ritual and other acts by which primitive man believed he could influence nature and defend himself from it. Folklore itself is a part of the system of religious-ceremonial practice.

It follows that the textual study of folklore, the study of texts taken independently of the economic, social, and ideological life of peoples is a fallacious method. In the West, collections of texts alone are usually published; the scholarly apparatus of such collections consists of indexes of motifs, plots, and sometimes plot variants, but there is no information on the people among whom the texts were collected, on the forms in which they exist and function, or on the specific conditions of performance and recording.

All these considerations show how close the connection between folklore and ethnography is. Ethnography is especially important when we study the genesis of folklore phenomena. There ethnography constitutes the base for the research, and without this base folklore hangs in the air.

Folklore as a Historical Discipline

It is obvious that the study of folklore cannot be limited to the investigation of origins and that not everything in folklore goes back to a primitive state or is explained by it. New formations occur in the entire course of peoples' historical development. Folklore is a historical phenomenon and the science of folklore, a historical discipline. Ethnographic research is its first step.

Historical study should show what happens to old folklore under new historical conditions and trace the appearance of new formations. We cannot ascertain all the processes that occur in folklore with the transition to new forms of social structure, or even with the development within the existing system, but we know that these processes occur everywhere with surprising uniformity. One of them is that inherited folklore comes into conflict with the old social system that created it and denies this system. It does not deny the old system directly but rather the images created by it, transforming them into their opposites or giving them a reverse, disparaging, negative coloring. The once sacred is transformed into the hostile, the great into the harmful, evil, or monstrous. But sometimes the old is preserved without any noticeable changes and gets along peacefully with new forms and relations. Folklore enters into contradiction with itself, and such contradictions are always present. Folklore formations arise not as a direct reflection of life (this is a comparatively rare case), but out of the clash of two ages or of two systems and their ideologies.

The old and the new can exist not only in a state of unresolved contradictions; they may also enter into hybrid formations. Folklore and religious ideas are full of such hybrid formations. The dragon, or serpent, is the combination of the worm, the bird, and other animals. Marr showed that when the horse had been domesticated, the religious role of the bird was transferred to it. The horse acquired wings. Flying ships, winged chariots, etc., become understandable. Research into the religious role of fire will show why the horse is combined with fire and becomes a fiery horse and how the idea of a fiery chariot arises. Such hybrids are possible not only in visual images, they are deeply hidden in the most diverse ideas and relations. Entire new plots can arise by transference of the new to the old. The plot with the hero killing his father and marrying his mother, that is, the plot of *Oedipus*,[13] arose as a result of the transfer of a hostile attitude toward the daughter's future husband—the son-in-law and heir—to the son-heir, and the transfer of the role of the king's daughter as the transmitter of the throne by marriage to the king's widow. This formation is not accidental or isolated: it is in the nature of folklore.

Finally, the old can be reinterpreted, the types of reinterpretation being numerous. The old is changed in accordance with the new life, new ideas, new forms of consciousness. Transformation into an opposite is only one type of reinterpretation. Changes can be carried so far as to make things unrecognizable, and discovery of the original forms is possible only given a great deal of comparative data on various peoples and at various stages of their development.

This method is called *the study by stages*. We arrange our data according to the stages in the development of peoples (a 'stage' is the level of a culture, defined by the features of material, social, and spiritual achievement) and obtain a 'historical poetics' in the real sense of this word, the historical poetics whose basis was laid by Veselóvskij.

The path indicated here is a historical path, leading upward from the old to the new. Modern ethnography and history are of insufficient help in this respect. We do not have a clear periodization of the stages of development. Lewis H. Morgan's scheme, corroborated by Engels, has not as yet been worked out on extensive material, developed, or completed.

Together with the study upward, study in the opposite direction, downward, is customary in folklore, that is, reconstruction of the early "mythological" bases by means of analysis of late data. This paleontological study, demonstrated for language by Marr, is in essence correct and quite applicable to folklore. This method, which is more risky and difficult, is necessary and indispensable where early stages are not represented by first-hand data. It can turn out that for some peoples folklore will prove a valuable historical source by which the ethnographer can reconstruct both the social system and the ideas.

The method outlined here is an achievement of Soviet scholarship. In the West the predominant principle is still that of simple chronology, rather than of stages. There, Classical material will always be considered more ancient than the material recorded today. Yet Classical material can reflect a relatively late stage of an agricultural state, whereas a modern text can reflect much earlier totemic relationships.

Each stage must have its own social system, ideology, and art. Folklore, like other phenomena of spiritual culture, does not register changes immediately and preserves for a long time old forms under new conditions. Since any people passes through several stages in its development, and all of them find their reflection in folklore and leave traces in it, folklore always combines a number of stages, and this is one of its distinctive features. Scholarship should *stratify* this complex conglomerate and thereby recognize and explain it.

The process of reworking the old into the new is the basic creative process in folklore, observable right up to the present. To say this is not to belittle the creative aspect of folklore. The concept of creative art does not mean the production of something absolutely new. Folklore is creative by its very nature, but creation is not an arbitrary process; it is governed by *laws*, which scholarship must explain.

We know what happens with peoples whose folklore has been recorded in our lifetime, peoples living at the most diverse stages of development and under the most diverse conditions. But some stages are no longer represented by an extant people; they have irretrievably receded into the past and we cannot have any direct evidence about their folklore. Such is an early slave-owning agricultural state of various types and various natural conditions, for example, the ancient Oriental states of Egypt, Greece, and Rome. The folklorist studying any data historically, be they genre, plot, motif, or something else, feels lost there; for in those times no one recorded folklore. This is an especially painful loss, since the slave-owning stage first witnesses the formation of classes. At this stage agriculture and agricultural cults develop and a new consciousness is formed. Apparently, folklore must have undergone deep changes, but we have no immediate knowledge of them.

Where no direct sources exist, indirect sources, to a certain degree and tentatively, permit filling the gap. When social differentiation leads to the rise of classes, creative art is differentiated in the same manner. With the development of writing among the ruling classes, literature (*belles lettres*) springs up, that is, the fixation of word by means of recording. We know that this early literature is entirely or almost entirely folklore. Since the beginning of literature is recorded folklore, the scholar's situation is not hopeless. The study of such ancient works of literature as the Egyptian *Book of the Dead*,[14] the myth of Gilgamesh,[15] the myths of ancient Greece, Classical tragedy and comedy, etc., is indispensable for the folklorist. All this is not folklore, pure and simple; it is reflected and refracted folklore, but if we succeed in making a correction for the ideology of priests, for the consciousness of a new state and class, for the specific quality of new literary forms developed by this consciousness, we will be able to see the folklore basis behind this motley picture.

Here the aims of the folklorist and the literary scholar coincide. What happens to folklore and literature at this stage of development is extremely significant for an understanding of all history of spiritual culture. Folklore is the womb of literature; literature is born of folklore. Folklore is the prehistory of literature. All the literature of peoples at this stage can and must be studied on the basis of folklore. The process of transmission basically proceeds upward; it can be observed in feudalism of all types, it is equally apparent in the folklore and literature of Mongol peoples, it is becoming clear for the European Middle Ages as well. Although in other forms, we can see the use of folklore sources in literature at the end of the eighteenth and during the nineteenth centuries; it is present in our time as well.

The process described above is normal and historically determined. Therefore, attempts to assert the opposite, to represent folklore as "a sunken cultural property"[16] (that is, descended from the upper social classes) are unscientific. Such assertions usually arise because people sing songs created by the dominant social classes. Indeed they do. But to elevate this particular phenomenon to a general principle is a very serious error, characteristic of outlooks foreign and hostile to us.

Literature, which is born of folklore, soon abandons the mother that reared it. Literature is the product of another form of consciousness. This does not mean that literature is realized through individuals isolated from their environment; it means, rather, that the individuals *represent* this environment and their people but do it in their own individual, unique, personal way. In the lower social strata, creative art continues to exist on the old basis, sometimes in interaction with the art of the ruling class. It is transmitted from mouth to mouth, and we have already discussed its distinctive features. We should add only that the art of the lower strata (for us—until the Revolution, and in the West—to the present day) is determined by other forms of consciousness than the art of the upper classes. Older scholarship called this art "unconscious" or "impersonal," and although these terms may be not very precise and do not exhaust the matter, they do reflect an idea correct in itself. Marx characterized even Greek mythology as "nature and social forms that had already acquired an *unconscious* artistic treatment in the people's imagination" (my emphasis). If Marx was not afraid of this word, there is no reason for us to avoid it. Our task is to *develop* and to *refine* what is hidden behind it all, but we cannot disregard the specific character of folklore as an expression of forms of consciousness yet little known.

Like any genuine art, folklore possesses not only artistic perfection but also a profound message. The discovery of this message is one of the objectives of the science of folklore. Older scholarship, as represented by Busláev and his followers, was again correct when it saw in folklore the reflection of a people's moral principles, although, perhaps, it did not see these principles and ideals where we see them now. The ideological and emotional content of Russian folklore can in brief be reduced not to a concept of good but to a category of strength of spirit. This is the same strength of spirit that leads our people to victory.[17] The study of Russian folklore shows that it is indeed saturated with *historical self-awareness*. This is evident in heroic poetry and in historical songs, later in the songs of the Civil and Great Patriotic Wars.[18] A people with such an intensity of historical consciousness and with such an understanding of its historical tasks can never be defeated.

Chapter Two.
Folklore and Reality

According to a widespread opinion, there are no fundamental differences between the ways reality is represented in folklore and in *belles lettres*. Reality is thought to be portrayed with an equal degree of accuracy in both. For example, M. M. Pliséckij, in his book on the historicity of Russian bylinas, refused to agree with those who believe that the bylinas represent the aspirations of a particular period, rather than its events. Why, he asked, are historical events depicted in the songs about the siege of Kazan[1] and about Stepán Rázin,[2] why can the *Lay of the Host of Igor*[3] faithfully depict the campaign of the Cumans against the Russians, why could Leo Tolstoy in *War and Peace* and Alexej Tolstoy in *Peter the First* portray historical persons and events and the bylina cannot do this? "Why are the bylinas not permitted to do this?" the author exclaimed (Pliseckij 1962, 105-6, 109-10). He saw no fundamental difference between the ways bylinas, historical songs, the *Lay of the Host of Igor*, and historical novels of the nineteenth and twentieth centuries represent reality.

This somewhat primitive approach, which ignores the artistic devices of folklore and literary genres, the social milieu that creates art, and the centuries of the people's development, though palpably unhistorical, is rather characteristic of one contemporary trend. Even the wondertale is sometimes supposed to depict life with the same fidelity as the bylina and to reflect class struggle as it existed in the nineteenth century (see Tudorovskaja 1955; Nagiškin 1957, Anikin 1959). This is what E. A. Tudorovskaja (1955, 314) wrote about the wondertale: "The ancient class enmity between the serf-owning oppressors and the downtrodden masses is faithfully shown." When it comes to examples, we read the following, "Bába Jagá, the mistress of the forest and animals, is represented as a real exploiter, oppressing her animal servants . . ." (pp. 316-17). In Tudorovskaja's opinion, class struggle in the wondertale acquires the "form of fiction." "This

16

somewhat limits the realism of the wondertale" (p. 315). The wondertale emerges as a realistic genre, but allegedly it has one defect: it contains an element of fiction, which diminishes and limits its realism. A logical consequence of this opinion would be the assertion that if there were no fiction in the wondertale it would be better.

Such curious opinions would not be worth mentioning if Tudorovskaja's viewpoint were unique. But it is not. V. P. Anikin, for example, wrote: "Immediate social and historical experience is the source of faithful representation of reality in folklore." Anikin discerned class struggle in animal tales, which he declared to be allegories. "Social allegory is a most important feature of animal tales, and without it the people would not need the folktale" (Anikin 1959, 70). We are told that the people does not need the folktale; it needs only the social allegory. The author tried to prove that the wolf is an "oppressor of the people." The bear is also said to belong with the wolf. In the wondertale, Koščéj[4] and the hero's other opponents are considered social oppressors of the people. Anikin's book contains many correct observations, but when the book was written such conceptions passed as mandatory and progressive.

I will not enter into further polemics but will try to answer the question of how reality is represented in folklore and how folklore differs from realistic literature by studying the data themselves rather than by abstract speculation. I will try to show that the poetics of folklore has its own specific laws, different from those of professional art. The question ought to be approached historically; however, before doing this we have to understand the situation as it is today. I will examine monuments of folklore in recordings of the eighteenth through the twentieth centuries and leave origins and development for the future.

There are laws common to all or many genres of folklore, and there are laws peculiar to individual genres. In my survey of the problem by genres, I will make no attempt to characterize them exhaustively but confine myself to the relation of folklore to reality.

I will start with the folktale, for its relation to reality is rather obvious. The folktale will also permit us to discover certain general laws of narrative genres. Lenin said: "In every folktale there are elements of reality. . . ." (1962, 19). The most cursory glance at the folktale will bear out the truth of this statement. In wondertales such elements are fewer; in other types of folktales they are more common. The fox, wolf, bear, hare, rooster, goat, and others are the very animals the peasant deals with; peasants and their wives, old men and women, stepmothers and stepdaughters, soldiers, gypsies, farmhands, priests, and landowners also entered the folktale from life. The folktale reflects prehistoric reality, medieval customs and morals, and the social relations of feudalism and capitalism. Soviet and foreign scholars carefully study these elements of reality, and considerable literature exists on them (see, for example, Propp 1946a; Kahlo 1954; Röhrich 1956).

However, if we examine Lenin's words more closely, we will see that, in his opinion, the folktale does not consist entirely of elements of reality. He said only that they are present. As soon as we turn to the question of what these realistic peasants, soldiers, and other personages do in the folktale, that is, as soon as we turn to plots, we plunge into the world of the impossible and the invented. Consider the Aarne-Andreev index of folktale plots, section *Novellas*. Who has ever seen fools deceiving everyone and never bested? Do there exist clever thieves who steal eggs from under a duck or the sheet from under a landowner and his wife? Are shrewish wives tamed in life as in the folktale, are there fools who look down the barrel of a rifle to see how the bullet comes flying out? In the Russian folktale there is *not a single* credible plot.

I will not go into details but will take a typical folktale as an example. This is the tale of an ill-fated corpse (Andreev 1929, Nos. 1536, 1537, 1685-I, 1730-I). The story goes roughly as follows. A fool accidentally kills his mother: she gets caught in a trap or falls into a pit that the fool has dug in front of their house. Sometimes he kills her on purpose; she hides in a trunk to learn what the fool discusses with his family; he knows this and pours boiling water on the trunk. He seats his mother's corpse on a sleigh, puts a spinning bench or distaff, comb, and spindle into her hands and sets out. A landowner's troika rushes toward him. He does not swing off the road and the sleigh is overturned. The fool cries that his mother, the tsar's embroiderer, has been killed. He is given a hundred rubles smart money, travels farther, and now seats the corpse in a priest's cellar; in his mother's hand he places a jug of sour cream and a spoon. The priest's wife thinks that the corpse is a thief and hits it on the head with a stick. The fool once again gets a hundred rubles. After this he puts his mother in a boat and sets her afloat in a river. The boat drifts into fishermen's nets. The fishermen beat the corpse with their oars, it falls into the water and "drowns." The fool cries that his mother has drowned and gets a hundred rubles from the fishermen. He returns home with the money and tells his brothers that he has sold his mother at the market in the city. His brothers kill their wives and take them to be sold. The police put them into prison and the brothers' wealth goes to the fool. With this property and the money he begins to live like a king.

There is another version of this folktale that can be considered another folktale. Here the action proceeds somewhat differently. A peasant's wife is entertaining her lover. Her husband is spying on them. When the wife goes into the cellar for butter, her husband kills the lover and shoves a pancake into his mouth so that people will think that he has choked to death. Then begin all the swindles with the corpse, which can partially coincide with the previous version or have a different form. In this case the husband has to get rid of the corpse in order to avert suspicion. The peasant leans the corpse against a house where a wedding feast is in progress and begins to curse. The guests run out, thinking that it was the peasant leaning against the wall who was cursing, and beat him on the head.

When they see him dead, they are frightened, and to get rid of the corpse, they seat it on a horse, tie it fast, and let the horse go. The horse runs into the forest and damages a hunter's traps. The hunter beats the corpse and thinks that he has killed it. He puts the corpse in a boat and the action ends as in the previous version: the ill-fated corpse is struck by a fisherman, falls into the water, and disappears.

If a modern Soviet writer decided to write a story about how a mother is murdered and how the murderer later used the corpse to extort money, no one would publish such a story, and if it were published, it would provoke readers' justified indignation. Yet the folktale provokes no indignation, even though peasants treat the dead with special reverence. This tale is popular among many European peoples (AT 1536, A, B, C; 1537).[5] It has penetrated even to the Indians of North America. How has such an outrageous plot gained popularity? This has been possible only because the tale is an amusing farce. Neither the teller nor the listener treats it as reality. It is the scholar who can and should treat it as reality and determine what called this plot to life, but this procedure is part of scientific, not artistic perception. What we have before us is not a case of reduced or limited folktale realism, not an allegory or fable, but a *folktale*.

I have dwelt on this example in such detail because it is significant and typical. The folktale is deliberate and poetic fiction. It never passes itself off as reality. What makes the folktale attractive if the representation of reality is not its purpose? First of all, its unusual narrative. The lack of correspondence with reality, fiction as such, offers special delight. In many humorous tales, reality is intentionally turned inside out, and this is why people find them so fascinating. True, the unusual occurs in *belles lettres* as well. It is stronger in Romantic prose (the novels of Sir Walter Scott, Hugo) and weaker in realistic prose (Chekhov). In literature, the unusual is depicted as something possible and arouses emotions of horror, rapture, and amazement; we are ready to believe in the events described. In folk prose, the unusual acquires dimensions impossible in life. True, in folktales about ordinary people the laws of nature are seldom violated. Nothing is quite improbable here. But the events are so unusual that they could never have occurred in reality and that is what makes them interesting. In folklore the narrative is not based on normal characters or normal actions in a normal situation; just the opposite: folktales choose things strikingly unusual. The folktale cannot even be compared with realistic literature. It is not worth the narrator's time to tell about the ordinary and humdrum, about what surrounds man every day. Anyone can recount what actually happened the previous day, today, a little while ago, or long ago, but the people attaches no artistic significance to such stories. They do not perform aesthetic functions, although from an objective point of view, they can possess certain artistic qualities (stories from someone's life, eyewitnesses' recollections of the Revolution, war, remarkable people, etc.).

One of the characteristics of the folktale is that events that did not occur and could never have occurred are recounted with certain intonations and gestures, as though they did actually take place, although neither the teller nor the listener believes the tale. This discrepancy determines the *humor* of the tale. The tale of the ill-fated corpse is significant in this respect. The story concerns the most evil deeds, but the way they are told makes listeners laugh with pleasure. Tales about a fool, clever thieves, a duped priest, unfaithful or shrewish wives, and many others, in a word, all tales of everyday life, are of the same type. Wonder-tales, animal tales, and so forth, are permeated by a light, good-natured humor, which stems from the feeling that all this is only a folktale, not reality.

Yet, in spite of its distortion of reality, the folktale, and especially the tale of everyday life, is an ancestor of written realistic literature. In Renaissance Europe, when the hold of the church over men's minds began to loosen and secular narrative literature in prose appeared, it drew its plots from folklore. In Russia this process began in the seventeenth century; in Western Europe, much earlier. The plot of the ill-fated corpse was used by the Italian short-story writer Masuccio (ca. 1420-1500).[6] Comparison of his version with folklore is instructive for the study of both the poetics of folklore and early realistic narrative art. His novella may be called *The Innocent Murderer*. In Salamanca at the time when King Fernando of Aragon ruled in Castile there lived a learned young theologian, a Minorite monk named Diego. This beginning signifies a completely different style of narration. The place of action is mentioned in the novella, but not in the folktale; still more important is that the events are transferred to an ordinary environment. They are told not only as credible but as having happened in a definite location, at a definite time, and to definite people. The humorous fiction of reality is absent here. This is also clear from the subsequent narrative. We hear a romance filled with details of everyday life. The learned monk Diego falls in love with the wife of a wealthy nobleman and besieges her with letters. She fears publicity and tells everything to her husband, who is malicious and hot-tempered. He lures the monk into his home and has him suffocated in the darkness and the corpse carried to the monastery lavatory and seated there. I will not retell the plot or analyze it. The differences between it and the folktale are manifest. Here we have everyday life, the motivated connection of events, etc. As in the folktale, the corpse passes from one supposed murderer to another. Again we have a corpse stood up against the wall of a house and a corpse seated on a horse, etc. The last supposed murderer is caught, tortured, and condemned to execution. Then one after another the supposed murderers appear in court and testify against themselves and last of all the real murderer appears. The king, on hearing this incident, finds it amusing and pardons the murderer.

The story has been transformed into a "true" one. The distinctive feature of the novellas that have moved from folklore into literature is that they are about unusual, uncommon but actual occurrences. People liked to hear something incredible and fabulous. But this is no longer folklore. The penchant for unusual, uncommon stories lasted a long time. Typical people in a typical setting[7] do not form the subject of early literature at its juncture with folklore.

Another characteristic of the folktale is the exceptional dynamics of the action. Let us note at once that this feature is typical of all narrative folklore. I will broaden the area of my observations somewhat and touch on other narrative genres, both prose and verse.

The narrator or singer and the listener are interested only in the action and nothing more. They have no interest in the surroundings of the action. The environment in which a peasant lives and works is not reproduced in narrative art. For the peasant his house, his barnyard with its stable and cattle shed, his field, his garden, his meadow, as well as the people around him, including his family, do not exist as the object of art. True, small features, details that reflect the real life of the peasant are interspersed here and there, but the narrator does not attempt to represent this reality. Nor is he interested in the characters' outward appearance. The art of the portrait is absent from epic and narrative genres. It matters little to the narrator what the soldier or old woman functioning in the story looks like. A princess is supposed to be a beauty, but the narrator refuses to give her portrait; she is so beautiful that "one cannot describe her beauty in a tale, nor write about it with a pen."[8] The looks of a personage are usually not mentioned at all, and if they are, some details pertaining to the hero as a type, rather than an individual, are given. The figure of Il'já Múromec,[9] when he rides on a horse, his gray beard flying in the wind, is full of dignity, but this is not a psychological portrait. In the bylinas about Vasílij Busláevič[10] mention is made of Potánjuška, the stoop-shouldered hunchback: Vasilij Buslaevič strikes him on the head so as to test his strength, but we do not see his face. Bába Jagá is sometimes portrayed rather expressively in the wondertale, but this does not mean that the wondertale possesses the art of individual portraiture. The hero's equipment and clothing (Djuk's[11] fine attire, the boyar's[12] fur coat, Mikúla's[13] morocco leather boots, etc.) depict his figure, but this is not a portrait. We do not know what Vasilij Buslaevič, Dunáj,[14] Dobrýnja,[15] Aljóša,[16] and other folktale personages look like. This applies not only to the folktale and epic poetry but to the historical song. Not Ivan the Terrible, Pugačëv,[17] Kutúzov, Napoleon nor any other historical figure is ever described. The same is true of the ballad. What Vasílij and Sóf'juška,[18] Prince Dmitrij,[19] and Domna[20] looked like makes no difference to the narrator.

The same applies to landscape. Forest, river, sea, steppes, city walls, etc., are mentioned when the hero jumps over or crosses them, but the narrator is indifferent to the beauty of the landscape. The situation changes only in lyric poetry.

This indifference to the circumstances under which the action is performed and to the outward appearance of the characters distinguishes folklore from the realistic art of written literature. The peasant houses, the various faces and types of servants and masters described by Tolstoy in *A Landowner's Morning* would be quite impossible in folklore. In folklore the story is told only for the sake of the events.

The result of the exceptional dynamic quality of action is that only those persons who contribute to the development of the plot figure in the narrative. Folklore does not deal with personages who are introduced for the sake of a milieu or society. In *Eugene Onegin* we see the Larins' guests, who differ in their appearance and typify the milieu and period depicted by Pushkin but who have not done and will not do anything in the story. In folklore everyone is assigned a role in the narrative and there are no extra characters. All will act, and only in terms of their actions do they interest the listener. For this reason folklore tends to have only one protagonist. One character is central, and around him and his actions are grouped other people, his opponents, helpers, or those whom he saves. Russian folklore never deals with more than one hero, and the "overcrowding" that is sometimes observed in novels is alien to folklore, indeed impossible in it.

Action is always performed physically, in space. Psychological novels based on the complexity of human interrelations, with dialogues, explanations, and so on, do not occur in folklore. Compared with space in realistic novels and novellas, space in folklore has certain peculiarities that can probably be accounted for by early forms of human thought. Folklore focuses only on empirical space, that is, on the space that surrounds the hero at the moment of action. Anything that occurs outside this space does not become the subject of narration. Therefore, in folklore two theaters of action do not exist in different places simultaneously. This is the so-called *law of chronological incompatibility*, well known in relation to Homer's epic poems and little noticed by Russian folklorists (Zelínskij 1896). The term means the incompatibility of several actions occurring simultaneously at different points. Complex composition, as in *War and Peace*, with actions performed simultaneously at the front and in the rear, in St. Petersburg and in Moscow, in Kutuzov's camp and in Napoleon's camp, is out of the question in folklore.

When the narrative has only one hero, the situation is clear. Action is performed in accordance with the movement of the hero, and what lies outside this movement lies outside the narrative.

In the wondertale and in epic poetry the action often begins with the hero's leaving home. His journey is the axis of the tale. This is a very old form of composition. The narrative ends either with the hero's return home or with his arrival in another city or another land. Plots that are constructed differently are, as a rule, younger. Ballads are not subject to this scheme, which is one of the indications of the ballad's later origin.

This type of composition is especially characteristic of epic poetry. Aljóša Popóvič leaves home and comes to Kiev; there, at a feast at Vladímir's [21] court, he sees the monster Tugárin[22] and kills him. Il'ja Muromec leaves home, liberates Černígov[23] on his way, kills Solovéj the Robber,[24] and arrives in Kiev. In such instances space and time are uninterrupted, as this is not required by the narrative. In epic poetry there are indeed plots with two, sometimes three, characters. However, they never appear in different theaters of action simultaneously. The narrative is about only one hero, whereas what happens to the other(s) remains unknown. A case in point is the bylinas about Dobrýnja's departure and Aljoša's attempt to marry his wife. Dobrynja leaves home for all sorts of reasons. When he is lost sight of, Aljoša takes over. He compels Dobrynja's wife to marry him, and this is recounted at length and in detail. When the wedding day comes, Dobrynja reappears *ex machina* and thwarts the wedding. Where he was at the time and what he was doing remains unclear. Although a law of epic poetry does not permit two heroes to act in different places simultaneously, this law was sometimes broken by nineteenth-century performers. Trofím Grigór'evič Rjabínin[25] contaminated this bylina with another, the one about Dobrynja and Vasílij Kazimírovič.[26] The way he did it is instructive. The foundation of the plot is the bylina about Dobrynja and Vasilij Kazimírovič. Dobrynja takes his leave, orders his wife to wait for him, and departs. The singer follows Dobrynja's exploits; his house has been left behind, and what happens there is unknown. Together with Vasilij Kazimírovič, Dobrynja sets out for the Soróčincy[27] area and defeats King Butján Butjánovič.[28] On returning home, Dobrynja suddenly learns from a prophetic dove that his wife is planning to marry Aljoša. We are not told anything about the courtship. A short account of what had taken place is put into the mouth of a messenger; the narrator himself cannot tell what happened to Dobrynja's wife while Dobrynja was away.

The bylina about Kozárin[29] is also revealing. The Tatars abduct Kozarin's sister, and he rescues her. It would seem that the plot is very simple, but for epic poetry there are certain insuperable difficulties here. The singer can begin in two ways. In some cases he begins with the abduction of the girl. She disappears from sight, and the narrator does not follow her; he follows her brother Kozarin, who finds her among the Tatars in a tent and rescues her. In other cases the narrative follows the girl from the very beginning. She is in one of the Tatars' tents, and the Tatars argue over whose she is to be. Kozarin appears unexpectedly and rescues her. The singer cannot recount what was happening to Kozarin and to his sister at the same time, that is, what was happening to the sister while her brother was looking for her, or what was happening to the brother while his sister was in the tent.

A somewhat different manifestation of this law also exists. While one hero is active, the other is inactive: sometimes he is merely sleeping. We have this in the bylina about Kálin and Il'ja Muromec. The Tatars advance on Kiev. Il'ja cannot repel them alone. While he prepares to rescue the city, the other bogatyrs are inactive; they are somewhere in the field, in tents, far from Kiev. Il'ja prepares for battle, and the other heroes, Dobrynja, Aljoša, and Samson, do nothing or are even asleep. When Il'ja summons them (sometimes waking them from sleep with a shot from his bow), they all fall upon the Tatars at the same time. Such observations are important to those historians who see a direct representation of reality in epic poetry. The reflection of reality is subject to the laws of epic poetry and unless scholars take them into consideration they will never solve the question of the historicity of epic poetry.

The law of chronological incompatibility reveals itself in the wondertale even more clearly than in epic poetry. The composition of the wondertale is more complex than that of epic poetry. In the former, besides the protagonist there are helpers, donors, the hero's opponents, and persons whom he saves or rescues. The law of chronological incompatibility can be violated in wondertales recorded in the nineteenth century, but, on the whole, it is valid for the genre. A stepdaughter has been driven from home. In this instance the narrator speaks only about her as the one in motion and not about her parents, who remain at home in immobility. The feelings of her father, for whom the expulsion of the girl is a tragedy, are of little concern to the narrator, or rather the description of the father's suffering cannot become the subject of the narrative because of the poetics of the wondertale.

In the wondertale the dragon appears from without, as if from another space; but this space is given as an unknown, unclear, dark space lying not only beyond the hero's horizon but also beyond our world. The dragon, Koščej, Vixr',[30] etc., appear out of nowhere, always unexpectedly, and abduct the princess. In this case the wondertale follows not the abducted princess, who is in a state of immobility, but the hero who sets out to find her, that is, not the passive personage but the active one. Where several personages are present, only one of them is always active. Thus, when three brothers set out in turn on a quest, the first two suffer defeat. The oldest is imprisoned in a witch's cellar, turned to stone, etc. As soon as the first hero loses his power to move, the second "comes alive," and then the third. The same thing happens when the hero is doubled. Two Ivans, a soldier's sons, marry princesses. One suffers a misfortune, that is, he is plunged into immobility (enchanted by his wife or the like), and the other, who will rescue him, appears on the scene.

When one of two characters gets into trouble, the other must learn about it. This explains the importance of messengers bringing news from the hero: in epic genres they are doves, prophetic horses, wise wives who know what is going on outside the hero's field of vision, etc.; the heroes, on parting, may give each other an object that in time of trouble changes shape, bleeds, or turns black.

Space in epic folklore is a special subject. It is closely connected with composition, and even the few examples cited above show that narrative folk art is based on principles completely different from those of modern narrative prose.

Unity of space is inseparable from unity of time. Like space, time in folklore cannot admit interruptions. Pauses do not exist. If the hero's action is stopped, another personage swiftly takes it up. Once begun, the action will rapidly develop to its conclusion. There is no general concept of time in folklore. Just as there is only empirical space, there is only empirical time measured not by dates, days, or years but by the personages' actions. It exists as a real factor only relative to these actions. In folklore action is performed mainly in space, but time as a form of thought does not seem to exist. In his struggle with nature, prehistoric man—a primitive hunter, fisher, and later a farmer—had to migrate to sustain life; therefore, space was mastered and assimilated empirically, while awareness of time is the result of a certain abstraction. For all intents and purposes, measurement of time begins to play a role in culture only with the full-scale development of agriculture. In its awareness of time, folklore reflects the pre-agricultural stage, and its designations of time are therefore always fantastic. Dobrynja departs and asks his wife to wait for him for three, nine, twelve, or thirty years, and she does so but never grows older.[31]

Counting is closely connected with space and time. Counting by threes is a question in Indo-European folklore that we will not consider now. Probably at some stage the number three was the limit in counting. Counting by fives and tens (on the fingers) is a later accomplishment. *Three* must have meant "much" or "many," and *much/many* must have meant "greatly," "very," that is, intensity was denoted by a large number. For this reason the difficulty of an undertaking and victory, the heightened interest in the narrative, and the delight caused by it are expressed by repetitions limited to the number three. In the folklore of some peoples, counting by fours and fives plays the role that counting by threes plays for us. The question requires further study, but one thing is clear: in folklore counting is just as arbitrary as space and time.

Such are some features of narrative folklore.[32] They are determined by early, in part very archaic forms of thought that also determine some of its other characteristics. Basically, this is not cause-and-effect thought. In folklore, reasons, or to use the language of poetics, motivations, are not required for actions.

A good example is cumulative tales ("Kolobók,"[33] "The Cock that Choked to Death," etc.). Units of the tale follow one another, but it is not necessary that this succession be motivated. The units can follow one another according to the principle of agglutination. Thus, in the tale "The Fly's Hut" various animals invite themselves into the fly's hut one after another, usually in order of increasing size: a louse, a flea, a mosquito, a mouse, a lizard, a hare, a fox, and a bear. The appearance of these animals is determined by artistic logic, not by cause-and-effect thinking. Although the agglutinative principle is expressed most clearly in cumulative folktales,[34] we also observe it in other types of folktale. For instance, the fox can play the most diverse pranks, one after another, without any particular connection. In the tale about a husband who leaves home because of a stupid wife and seeks to find out whether there are people even more foolish than she, the hero meets a group of simpletons who do the most improbable things.

Such tales consist of units that adhere to one another. They can be broken off and concluded anywhere or continued at the storyteller's discretion.

The absence of logical motivations is somewhat different in wondertales. Quite often the development of the action depends on chance. In the wondertale the hero is powerless; he sets out without knowing the way but then unexpectedly meets an old man or Baba Jaga, who shows him where to go and helps him. This meeting has no external motivation, but it determines the subsequent narrative. The artistic logic of the tale is that the hero must get hold of a magic means, and it alone accounts for the meeting with someone who will give him this means or help him find it. Another example: in the tale of the frog-princess, the king suddenly begins to assign his daughters-in-law difficult tasks. Why he does this is never said. Formally, his actions are not motivated. But the folktale canon requires that false heroes be put to shame and the real hero exalted. Assigning difficult tasks leads to the happy conclusion.

There is no external logic in tales of everyday life either, or in any case, such logic is not a requirement of folk aesthetics. In the tale of the ill-fated corpse, the actions of the simpleton who killed his mother and played pranks with her corpse are not externally motivated; he never plays his pranks for the purpose of deceiving people and getting money from them: he just takes advantage of an opportunity and swindles people, and this causes the listeners' delight. Fortuity of events, which determines the course of action and its favorable outcome, would be a defect in terms of realism, but it is not a defect in terms of the folk narrative. The scholar can always ascertain what circumstances brought forth these principles of composition. They are not at all products of "free" fantasy; they result from the development of the poetics of folklore. When the hero of the folktale is a "fool," this means not only that he is foolish, but also that he (and consequently the narrative) is not bound by the listener's norms of conduct and behavior.

The nonobligatory character of external motivations is inherent in all types of folklore, both prose and poetry. Logic is possible, but not mandatory. The artistic logic of the narrative does not coincide with the logic of causal thought. It is the action that is primary, not the reason for it. In comparing variants of the same plot, we discover that the motives for identical actions can be very different. In the bylina about Dobrynja and the dragon, Dobrynja leaves home to go for a swim, to have a look at the sea, to look at people and to show himself, or whatever. But these are only pretexts. The artistic reason for his departure is that he must meet the dragon. Logical motivations are introduced later in history, and there can be no doubt that a well-motivated narrative arose or was developed after a poorly motivated or unmotivated one. The version of the tale about the ill-fated corpse in which the motive for the murder is jealousy and the attempt to dispose of the corpse is made from fear that the murder will be discovered is a later version than the one about the fool who killed his mother by accident. Characteristically, it was the motivated version that found its way into written literature. It meets the aesthetic requirements and forms of thought of literate urban people, whereas the actions of the fool lack a clearly defined reason and purpose; this fact prevented the earlier version from entering literature.

In the ballad, which is a later genre, actions are sometimes internally motivated not by the requirements of the canonic outcome, but by the nature of the characters. Thus Sof'juška's mother-in-law poisons her and Vasilij; in another ballad, a cruel mother-in-law kills her grandson and then falsely accuses her daughter-in-law. The dead boy's father kills his wife. Prince Román[35] kills his wife because he wants to marry another woman. Singers never mention the motives for these actions. The listener must guess them.

In some ballads, however, the action is based on pure chance. Such is the ballad "The Robber Brothers and Their Sister." The brothers give their sister in marriage and become robbers. Three years later they fall upon travelers on a road, kill a man and a child, and dishonor a woman who turns out to be their sister.[36] There are a number of such ballads about an unfortunate fate.

Characters in narrative folklore and literature are completely different. In literature they are unique individuals; they typify a period or social milieu, generalize the features of many people and reflect a great number of prototypes, but remain individuals. They have their own names and possess their own personalities. In the wondertale, the hero does not normally have a name. There are several types of wondertale and, correspondingly, several types of hero, but they are not individual characters. The name *Ivan* is the name of a type, not of a person. The type may represent a social position: a tsar, tsarevich, prince, merchant, soldier, priest, gentleman landowner, peasant's son, or farmhand. In literature, each personage belongs to a definite plot and cannot be transferred from one work to another. In folklore, Ivan Tsarevič is the same personage in different plots. So is Ivan the peasant's son. So is the tsarevna, whether she be called Eléna, Anastasija, Vasilísa, or Már'ja the Beautiful. The same principle applies to tales of everyday life. The folktale priest is always the same person. Different tales and different plots about priests reflect only different aspects of one type. A glance at the gallery of priests depicted by Chekhov and Leskóv will make the point clear. The folktale is not unique in this respect. Il'ja Muromec is an epic type, the same in all plots about him. But epic poetry has progressed further than the folktale: epic heroes have certain traits that are expressed in their actions. One observes, for example, the wise composure of Il'ja, his generosity, implacability toward his enemies, etc. Dobrynja and Aljoša also are names associated with character types. Yet the number of epic types is limited; each of them is represented by a cycle rather than one plot, and within this cycle the image of the hero does not vary.

In the historical song psychological individualization is also limited. We perceive Ivan the Terrible, Ermák,[37] Skópin-Šújskij,[38] Razin,[39] Peter,[40] etc., as different people. In some cases the historical song can even achieve a certain mastery in depicting characters (cf. Ivan the Terrible, Anastasija Romanovna, and Nikíta Romanovič in the song about Ivan's anger at his son).[41] However, this is not the purpose of the song, and, on the whole, its characters are poorly described. They can even be interchangeable. The reason for this is not only the limited individualization, but also the law according to which action is of prime importance. This law is observed even when the historical truth has to be violated for its sake. Songs about Ermak can circulate with Razin's name; songs about Razin, with Pugačëv's name; the Swedish king is easily replaced by the Turkish sultan and even Napoleon; songs about Arakčéev[42] circulate with Dolgorúkov's[43] name (or vice versa), etc. Here too we deal with types, not with individuals.

In narrative folklore all characters are either good or bad. In wondertales this is quite apparent, but the same is true elsewhere. "Average types" (which constitute the majority in life) do not occur in folklore.

The image of a good hero may not always conform to society's moral code. The idealized hero of wondertales is the tsarevich. In epic poetry all basic heroes are good and embody national ideals. Nevertheless, their behavior is sometimes at variance with contemporary ethics. Aljoša Popovič performs several deeds incompatible with the morality of his time, but he remains a genuine hero. In the tales of everyday life this situation is still more obvious. The hero is the one who wins, irrespective of the means, especially if he defeats a stronger opponent. Perhaps this is why most of such tales turn on making a fool of someone. The same holds true for animal tales and partly for wondertales. Intellect and cunning are the strength of a weak person: with these qualities, the hero overcomes a stronger enemy. In the folktale we will not find realistic descriptions of the struggle of the oppressed peasantry against the landowners. The folktale deals with only one type of social struggle and social satire: the gentleman landowner and priest are always duped and deceived by a clever hired man (the latter overpowers the devils themselves). Another such hero is the clever thief who robs a landowner, a boyar, sometimes the tsar's treasury. Even the tsarevich, the idealized hero of the wondertale, may achieve his goals by deception. In the wondertale, the hero usually steals the objects of his quest: the firebird, a horse, a princess, the apples of youth, etc. Prometheus steals fire for people, and this plot occurs at very early stages of social development. Magic objects like a flying carpet, self-propelled boots, and a self-spreading tablecloth are frequently obtained by deception. Cunning and deception are the tools of the weak against the strong, and this conforms to the moral requirements of the listener.

Animal tales are almost entirely about tricks that clever animals, especially the fox, play on other animals. The victory of the weak over the strong must have very ancient roots. Among hunting peoples, women and children told stories of the fox's tricks when the men were hunting. Success of the weak and their victory over the strong in the story were intended to promote success in reality. At this stage animal tales were not yet folktales: they became folktales when faith in their effectiveness had been lost.

The folktale sheds light on certain features of epic poetry, for the latter partially reflects archaic forms of thought. Hence, the conventional representation of space and time, the absence of motivations, the division of all characters into "good" and "bad," and the predominance of types over individual characters in it. But there are profound differences between the folktale and epic poetry. The relation to reality in epic poetry is different from that in the folktale. The bylina is sung, and this is not an external characteristic of performance, but a feature that determines the very essence of the genre. Storytellers do not believe in the reality of their tales. With epic poetry the situation is different. Singers give diverse and contradictory answers when asked whether they believe in what they sing about. Confusion is caused by an incorrect question. Unlike the storytellers, the singers cannot admit that the heroic, great, or merely dramatic events they describe are a lie, but though they perceive a deep artistic truth in their works, they do not know how to express their intuition. They realize that such events are impossible in contemporary life and attribute the action of the bylinas to antiquity. The folk name for bylinas, *stáriny* "tales of olden times," is revealing: everything in the song is the truth, and consequently it did take place, but it took place long ago and will not happen again.

Like other epic genres, the bylina gives a transcript of reality according to epic laws and does so much more broadly than the folktale. Celebration of past events and actual people is not an aim of the bylina: the poetics of the bylina is not yet mature enough for such a task. This aim will be met later by the historical song. But independently of performers' intentions and of their aesthetic desires, historical reality breaks through in epic poetry. In the bylina about Sadkó,[44] the plot of which is a pure wondertale, we observe sailors' mythological ideas of the master of the sea, recollections of sacrifices to the Sea King, cooperative forms of fishing and the organization of trade, and the very trade routes of ancient Novgorod; this bylina tells of the beginnings or early forms of the social struggle between the poor, represented by the peasant Sadko, and the rich merchant class. Similar observations apply to many other bylinas. What a rich field for historians!

We can study the armament of heroes, battles, social relations, property relations, and the entire field of everyday life and material culture. But some scholars persist in understanding historicity only as the representation of historical events and persons, that is, the very things that are absent from epic poetry. When historical names turn up in epic poetry, those who bear the names are subject to the poetics of the bylina and become epic characters. The historical Mamáj[45] and Batu[46] acquire the generalized features of enemies of the Russian land, and in this they are not differentiated from King Kalin, Kudrevánko, and other enemies whom Il'ja Muromec drives from his native country with a wave of his hand.

A different relation to reality characterizes the ballad. If in epic poetry events are thought of as having occurred in the remote past, in the ballad they are attributed to a potential reality, although perhaps not the reality that surrounds the performer. These works are no longer stariny, though people call some of them that. The ballad preserves many laws of epic poetry, but it differs from the epic in its subject matter. The ballad does not deal with heroic feats performed by bogatyrs[47] for the glory of the fatherland but with human passions, especially love. The exceptional nature of events inherent in all folklore enters into the ballad too but acquires its own character. Unusually strong passions lead to unusual, terrible deeds. Passion overcomes all obstacles, even generally accepted morals, and goes as far as murder. In the ballad, crime is never atoned for, which was impossible in earlier genres. The boy's mother poisons two lovers (Vasilij and Sof'ja) but suffers no punishment. The lovers are buried near a church, trees grow from their graves, and their tops intertwine. This signifies the complete justification of the young lovers and condemnation of their murderer. The criminal is condemned by the performer and the listener, but retribution does not follow. The performer no longer concentrates alone on the plot and begins to display an interest in internal aspects of life. This is a great step forward. In balladry, the new type of plot results in new poetic devices.

Yet certain old features of the poetics of folklore are kept intact in the ballad, the inability or unwillingness to motivate events among them. Motives are sometimes obscure and can be understood and interpreted in various ways. What provokes Domna's mockery of Dmitrij (an event precipitating the finale) is not mentioned. It remains unclear why Vasilij's mother poisons the young lovers Sof'ja and Vasilij, etc. We will not enumerate plots. The pattern is already clear: in the ballad the events are motivated psychologically. The characters are impelled by love, hate, and jealousy. This is a new feature, but the framework is old. The love affair is never defined in words, for the requisite artistic means are still lacking. As before, the singers are concerned only with events and do not attempt to determine their causes.

The type of characters is also new in ballads. Bogatyrs are gone; all personages are ordinary people from various walks of life; they are no longer heroes and villains. Criminals are not epic villains; reality is not idealized or exaggerated. The darker sides of life now find their reflection in art. The ballad is tragic, which is almost never the case with epic poetry.[48] The few bylinas in which a woman rather than an enemy is killed or in which suicide is mentioned (Dunáj,[49] Danílo Lovčánin,[50] Suxmán[51]) are an intermediate link between the bylina and the ballad. Sometimes the ballad borrows from these plots. The ballad tends to represent real people and their conflicts. It is much closer to realism than are epic poetry and the folktale, which in no way determines the degree of its artistic perfection. Each folklore genre has its own degree of perfection, just as it has its own bounds and limitations. The ballad depicts the struggle against family despotism of the Russian Middle Ages. The listener believes in the events narrated in it and is deeply moved. In most cases, the ballad is performed by and for women. The ballad certainly gains in realism, but it is not as monumental as epic poetry and its artistic theme is less significant.

In general, the development of narrative genres among the people has ceased or is gradually ceasing.

The decline of narrative genres results from their own specific features and from the ever-growing discrepancy between the type of art and the new requirements of life. When remnants of archaic thought began to disappear and came at cross purposes with life's demands, the artistic possibilities associated with these forms of thought were exhausted. Productive development of the wondertale was completed long ago. Even the Middle Ages could no longer provide new plots for wondertales, and storytellers fell back on certain everyday plots for purposes of satire. The development of epic poetry must have been completed by the seventeenth century.

Yet some genres continued to develop: lyric poetry, for example, which treated reality in a new way and was not hampered by the ancient forms of thought that fettered narrative genres.

There cannot be a lyric attitude toward such deliberate poetic fiction as the folktale. A lyric attitude is possible toward the bylina, which is supposed to contain the truth of the remote past. An active, sincere, and varied attitude toward reality occurs only when the subject of art is contemporary life. Unlike basically collective epic art, lyric art is individual, and it acknowledges the feelings of each person. The collective character of the most ancient folklore is another instance of the collective forms of ancient man's life and work. The primitive communal system entailed not only common possession of property but also the closest cooperation of people in everything they did. An individual did not matter. Folklore reflected these forms of life and consciousness for a very long time. And in agricultural Russia this situation was particularly tenacious.

One of the genres in which aesthetic principles other than those discussed above are quite apparent is laments for the dead. Laments occupy an intermediate position between epic, lyric, and ritual poetry. The power of the emotions they express makes laments part of lyric poetry; in function they belong to ritual poetry; with regard to the narrative elements they contain they are close to epics. Laments are a more recent genre than the folktale. It is immaterial at what stage of social development they arose. Laments must have been very widespread in ancient Rus', for they are reflected in old Russian literature beginning with the eleventh century. Much in these laments derived from Byzantine rhetoric, much from church oratory, but still more from folk laments, and this can be easily proved by comparing certain monuments of old Russian literature with nineteenth century recordings of peasants' laments.

Important differences occur: the fragments of laments interspersed in saints' lives and chronicles are always devoted to saints, princes, or members of their families. The lament is often represented as national: for example, the laments about Dmitrij Donskój[52] and Aleksandr Nevskij. Here certain standard devices were developed: similes, metaphors, addresses, mournful exclamations, which do not, however, give a clear understanding of the life and personality of the deceased.

Folk laments are quite different. Here we also observe a canon, that is, a number of devices repeated from one lament to another. Repetition of these devices can even seem somewhat monotonous. Sometimes less talented mourners merely combine such repetitive elements, which sound like variants. Among traditional motifs is the poetic ("rhetorical") question to carpenters: for whom are they making the cramped mansion with no windows or doors? the question to the deceased: for what journey has he fitted himself out? etc. Each part of the funeral ceremony has its traditional motifs. They occur in numerous laments and do not define the genre. The genre is defined by those parts of the laments that are improvised, that is, composed for a particular case. For the first time we observe a phenomenon not in the least typical of folklore: just as no man is like another, though all men share the same features, so no lament is similar to another, despite the presence of traditional motifs. A lament is composed on the death of someone close. No two laments are identical, nor can they be, and laments do not have variants. Each lament contains unique motifs, for example, a kind of biography. A woman in mourning abandons herself to recollections of her life and the life of the dead person. A widow recollects her entire past: her happy childhood in her father's house, her proud and independent character, her unhappy marriage. She depicts her future with children and no provider. The relations of laments to reality is different from that of epic genres. There is no way of reconstructing the life of the Russian village from folktales, but from laments we can reconstruct it with details not mentioned in other sources. This is why Nekrásov studied them so attentively. A widow describes her future life. Family relations in the Russian village prior to the Reform,[53] the "big family," its terrifying patriarchal customs and gradual decline, the tragic fate of the lone widow who can neither return to the big family nor support herself and her children and who is doomed to become a beggar—all this stands out in relief in the laments. We see a cold, unheated hut; children frozen to the bone who have no choice but to live by begging; a deserted field with no one to work it. Laments mirror the actual life of the village; they represent reality directly. The lament called "The Drunkard" (on the death of a husband who died from drinking) paints in vivid detail the blood-curdling picture of the gradual ruin of the farm and the disintegration of the family. If necessary, the lament gives exact descriptions of nature. The lament about a man who drowned in Lake Onéga describes the storm and all the circumstances surrounding the deaths of the father and his young son. Laments also express the rebellious feelings of the peasants. One of the best laments of the renowned mourner Irína Fedósova[54] is about a village *stárosta* ("elder"). The elder was arrested by the local arbitrator[55] because the peasants did not appear for an assembly, which was viewed as an act of mutiny. Fedosova gives a dynamic portrait of the arbitrator, who pounds on the table, waves his fists, and spouts curses, oaths, and threats. Yet the singer never transcends her peasant psychology. She does not incite the peasants to rebel but prays that God will punish the arbitrator for the tears and grief he caused by his extortions and cruelty.

Here we do not find the laws that characterize epic genres and that halted their development. Rather, we see an art based on a subjective evaluation of reality. Nevertheless, laments are a short-lived genre. They are lyrical in their emotional tension, but from a functional point of view they belong to ritual poetry. When the soil that nourished ritual poetry has been exhausted, this genre, despite its high achievements, begins to disappear. The last excellent examples of this fading poetry were collected by Bazánov and Rázumova (1962).

Quite a different case is the lyric song per se, which still exists and will apparently always exist. We do not know when the Russian lyric song originated, but we do know that the most primitive peoples had both ritual folklore (incantations) and improvised songs about themselves, their life, about what they saw, and what happened to them. As V. V. Senkévič-Gudkóva observed, the Kola Lapps improvise songs about their surroundings, and the simplest of them consist of only one word: the name of one's child, the word *sun* repeated many times with interjections, or the name of a deer (Senkevič-Gudkova 1960; see also Mikušev 1960). The words may be accompanied by epithets ("my fine deer, clever deer"), one line may be chanted endlessly ("Dunja, Dunja, Dunja loves me" or "the boat sails, sails", etc.). There are longer songs of love and of everyday happenings, and songs similar to those that Russians perform at celebrations. This is not a national peculiarity of the Lapps. All lyric poetry developed from such beginnings, and Veselovskij was wrong in asserting that it originates in ritual poetry. Ritual poetry, whose purpose was to accompany rituals and dances and promote by magic all kinds of luck, existed from time immemorial quite independently of lyric poetry. F. A. Rubcóv (1962) also showed that the musical and intonational systems of ritual and slow lyric songs are based on dissimilar principles.

Samples of improvised exclamations do not yet constitute songs. This is lyric poetry in an embryonic state, and it is still naturalistic. The lyric song proper arises when artistic images appear in it and when its momentary significance for one person and for one time gives way to a general significance and to the desire to repeat the song.

We cannot trace the development of the Russian lyric; we can speak only about its phase represented in recordings beginning with the eighteenth century. The developed Russian peasant lyric and the epic genres are based on entirely different principles and a different attitude toward reality; their artistic devices are also different. The subject of the lyric is a real man, his life, and his emotions. If it is true that realism increases in folklore, the origins of this realism are in the lyric, not the epic.

The basis of the narrative is the plot, and the poetic treatment of the plot determines all the features of a folklore genre. The basis of the plot is action. But in the lyric song, there is no plot, no action with a beginning, development, and end; therefore, the lyric song is not bound by the laws of composition. Although the song tells of events from the singer's life, these are represented by one situation, which is always rooted in the present, so the singers directly or indirectly relate the songs to themselves.

We can compile an index of plots for the folktale, epic poetry, and the ballad, but only an index of plot situations for the lyric song. However, we do not yet have such a list,[56] and if we did, we would understand the extent to which the lyric song is connected with the life of the peasant village. To be sure, the peasant's economic life is absent from the lyric song. The peasant considers his life as a producer unworthy of representation in art. He treats his economic concerns as work; his attitude toward them is practical, technical, not lyrical, so songs do not come in here. Social struggle is somewhat more widely represented: there are songs about the crimes of gentlemen landowners and their wives, about the sufferings of their victims and about the curses against those who cause the sufferings. But they are very few for the same reasons that there are no lyric songs about peasants' work. We will not find the depiction of peasant riots and uprisings: not because there were none—on the contrary, they were numerous— but because according to the poetics of folklore, only certain aspects of reality are reflected in folk poetry. If we wanted to follow the growth of peasant revolutionary feelings in lyric songs, we would get an incorrect and one-sided picture. However, the situation gradually changed. Real life outside the sphere of love and personal relations in general penetrated more and more into popular lyric poetry. The later the song, the closer it is to real life and social struggle. Recruits' songs, including laments, robbers' songs, soldiers' songs, prison songs, songs of the penal colony and exile are different from love songs; and this is not only a difference in genre but a historical difference that reveals the evolution of folk poetry and the direction of the evolution.

Although peasants' work is not the subject of their lyric songs, two aspects of life that are almost absent from epic poetry begin to appear in lyric poetry: landscape and portrait. This is of course a lyric landscape, with azure flowers, silken grass, birch trees, and willows, but it is a genuine Russian landscape just the same. Lyric portraits are also conventional, but they are present, whereas in epic narrative art they are absent altogether.

The song, too, has its conventions and limits, but inasmuch as they are not determined by the nature of the genre, they are at times overcome. The changeability, breadth, and freedom assure the song its longevity. One of the features of the lyric is its imagery; popular lyric poetry begins to employ allegories, which acquire the form of similes, parallelisms, and metaphors and make it impossible to speak about life as directly as in early, primitive lyric poetry. Popular lyric poetry is based on the poeticization of life, and what does not lend itself to such poeticization cannot become its subject.

It follows that the relation to reality and the means of representing reality in folklore change and develop as the people develop historically.

One of the comparatively late folklore genres is the historical song. We saw that the historical song is governed by general epic laws; we still have to show the advance made by this genre. The historical song would be impossible without the previous development of epic poetry, in particular, the bylina. The form of some of the early songs, for example, sixteenth-century songs about Ivan the Terrible, clearly derives from the bylina. But the historical song overcomes the conventions that fettered the bylina and checked its growth. Its other source is the lyric song, which gave the historical song its emotional tenseness, musical character, and variety of forms. Many historical songs can be classified as lyrics. This applies primarily to certain songs about Ermák and later about Rázin. But the historical song overcomes the subjectivity of the lyric song and is not limited to the inner, spiritual world of man. One of the basic new features of historical songs is their scope. Historical songs are about the people's past and present political life. Events are not only depicted but also evaluated. Class struggle, so weakly reflected in the lyric song, finds its expression in the songs of the peasant uprisings. Russia's many wars and the war for national independence are the subject matter of military historical songs. This is why historical songs have such diverse forms. Unlike other types of folk poetry, historical songs do not possess a common poetic system. The song about Ščelkán is a buffoon's song, the song about Ivan the Terrible's anger at his son is close to bylinas in form, the song about the poisoning of Skópin[57] can be classified as a ballad, the song about Ermák is a lyric, whereas the lament of the streléts,[58] or soldier, about Ivan the Terrible or Peter is close to funeral laments. Ksenija Godunóva's[59] lament can be classified as a lament from everyday life. The variety of forms is so great that the genre of historical song cannot be defined by these forms alone. Indeed, what do Ksenija Godunova's lament and the happy song about Plátov[60] in Napoleon's camp have in common? B. N. Putílov (1956) suggested classifying historical songs according to their poetic system, and this is correct, since there are several such systems. Historical songs share similarity of content, which relates directly to Russian history.

Historical songs are the products of social development. Folklore ceased to be the peasants' exclusive property. The oldest historical songs about Ščelkán Dudént'evič was composed by the urban population of Tver'.[61] In style it belongs to the art of buffoons. The song about the siege of Kazan by Ivan the Terrible comes from gunners, and the song about Ivan's anger at his son from the lower strata of Moscow. Songs about Ermak, Razin, and later Pugačëv had their origin in a Cossack milieu. Beginning with the eighteenth century, soldiers produced military folklore. These social strata were not the peasantry, although in their psychology they were close to it.

Historical songs started in a very special way. Basically they were created by participants in or witnesses to the events. Hence, a new attitude toward what is represented as something seen and heard, and this attitude is inconceivable in epic poetry, the folktale, and the ballad. Even when the content of a song is fictitious, it is invented in the milieu in which the event could have taken place. Thus, details of the song about the siege of Kazan are not attested in historical sources; they were invented in a gunners' milieu. This is one of the basic features that permits distinguishing the historical song from other genres. From this point of view the song about Avdót'ja Rjazánočka,[62] which is usually classified as a historical song, does not belong here. The event is fantastic; it did not have actual participants or witnesses, nor were they possible. This song should be classified as a ballad. Such a relation to reality means that a new type of oral folklore has arisen, a type fundamentally different from all previous ones.

Earlier we discussed the collective character of peasant folklore and its dependence on certain conditions. Such conditions were absent at the rise of historical songs. Historical songs were produced by people some of whom were talented and poetically gifted; what they created others took up. This is not yet individual creation in the strict sense of the word (although some songs may have been composed by individuals); it is an intermediate stage between two extremes: collective creation of traditional folklore by the peasants and individual creation by professional writers.

Understanding which events are selected by historical songs is especially important, for the selection seems strange. Songs may recount minor, insignificant events, while the great events of Russian history may be ignored. Why, for example, are there no songs about the battle of Borodinó?[63] Borodino, unlike Smolénsk, Možájsk, Berezíná, and Paris, is not even mentioned. The reason for this is not to be sought in a deep philosophy, folk wisdom, or historical consciousness. Historical songs were composed by participants in the events themselves. The battle of Borodino was such that there were no people or groups that could have composed a song at that time. The same holds for the battle of Poltáva,[64] which left very few traces in folklore, in spite of its great importance. The absence of a song never means that the people did not understand the event. It means only that conditions for the creation of a song did not exist.

Unlike traditional peasant epic and lyric folklore, the historical song aims at depicting and evaluating the reality witnessed by the singer. In epic folklore time and space are conventional. In the historical song they are defined historically and geographically or topographically, although deviations are possible.

> In the month of September
> On the twenty-fifth
> In the year seventy-one
> In the city of Jaik[65]
> Swift news came to us—
> We would not remain in that place.

Thus begins a soldiers' song about Pugačëv.

In the historical song wars are not waged as in the bylinas: Il'ja can no longer take a wiry Tatar by the feet and swing him in the air. Epic poetry does not deal with regular commanders, does not describe Russan armies, while the historical song names popular commanders, understands the role of military organization, and describes the movements and bloody clashes of armies.

The heroes of songs are historical people who have names and possess individuality. In some cases their psychological characterization is deep and complex; consider the image of Ivan the Terrible in the song about his anger at his son. The romantically colored Razin, the bold Platov, the calm Kutuzov, and many others make up a whole gallery of characters and types. The wondertale and epic poetry are governed by certain laws of composition. The historical song does not obey them: its composition is as free and diverse as life itself.

There is no need to define all the poetic devices of the historical song. We have seen that it overcomes traditions and creates a new art. Yet it retains the interest in unusual happenings characteristic of all folklore. Many historical songs are actually anecdotes, with the main emphasis on the narrative rather than on character delineation, so personages are not always linked with events. Despite the progress made by the historical song, its action can sometimes be transferred from one person to another. The defense of Pskov against Stephen Báthory[66] is attributed in different variants to Semjón Konstantínovič Karámyšev, Mixaíl Vasíl'evič Skópin-Šújskij, Nikíta Románovič Vol'xónskij, and Borís Petróvič Šeremétev, although none of them has anything to do with this event (for some details see Putilov 1962, 328-29). One and the same plot can likewise be connected with different places and times. The story in which a city is taken by sapping the walls and putting powder barrels under them must originally have belonged to the siege of Kazan, but we also find it in songs about the siege of Azóv,[67] Oréšek,[68] and Riga.[69]

If we believe that the aim of the song is to describe actual events, then all such elements look like nonsense. But the song aims at transmitting the significance of the event, not just at recounting it. The people does not care whether it is Karl of Sweden,[70] Napoleon, or the Turkish sultan that threatens to conquer Russia, and whether it is Kutuzov, Lopuxín, or someone else who answers the letter. The people only wants to make it clear that Russia will not fall to any foreign aggressor.

D. S. Lixačëv (1958, 120) noted that "old Russian literature did not have a recognizably fictitious hero." The literary heroes of ancient Rus' are historical persons or saints in whose existence people believed. Literary heroes in the strict sense of the word appear only beginning with the seventeenth century, mainly under the influence of folklore. The development of folklore itself proceeded in the opposite direction: from the fictitious heroes of epic poetry, the wondertale, and the ballad to real people and events. The means of folklore were limited, but with them the people created the most perfect and profound works of art, which inspired a new literature and which have been a source of inspiration ever since.

We have not examined all genres, but in light of what has been said we can examine and understand other types of folklore: various legends and tales, častúški,[71] and workers' poetry. In workers' folklore the artistic tendencies of the historical song were developed still further. At this stage, folklore came close to literature, a process that requires special study.

The relation of folklore to reality may be of three types:

1. Folklore, like any other art, derives from reality. Even the most fantastic images are based on reality. Materialistic scholarship must find the historical basis of folklore. This applies to absolutely all folklore.

2. Independently of the intentions of its creators and performers, folklore reflects real life. The forms and content of this reflection differ according to the period and the genre. They are subject to the poetics of folklore.

3. A folk artist sets himself the goal of representing reality. Such a purpose characterizes the historical song and workers' folklore.

Most mistakes in the study of folklore result from the failure to distinguish these three aspects.

In his dissertation *The Aesthetic Relations of Art and Reality,* Černyševskij (1958, 94) wrote: "In all folksongs there are mechanical devices; we can see the familiar mainsprings without which songs never develop their themes . . . " Černyševskij understood that to clarify the problem of the aesthetic relation of folklore to reality, one must know the laws of folk poetics. The science of folklore should discover and describe these laws.

Chapter Three.
The Principles of
Classifying Folklore Genres

In any field of knowledge, classification is the basis for and prerequisite of in-depth study. However, classification is the result of long and detailed research. To define the object of study means to assign it correctly to a definite class, genus, and variety. In folklore this work has not yet been done. Considerable attention has been paid to only one genre, namely, legends. In the International Society for Folk-Narrative Research a *Sagen-Kommission* was formed, which met at a special conference in Budapest October 14-16, 1963, and a number of important and interesting papers were given there [see Ortutay 1964]. Besides the attempts at cataloging already in print, several additional projects were suggested, most of them based on extensive data. In my article I use data from that conference.

Before we begin to classify individual genres, we must agree on the general principles of classifying folklore. Classifications can be of applied or of strictly scholarly, cognitive significance. The former are arrived at in an empirical way, gropingly, and they can prove useful despite some logical and other errors, but indeed only until principles of scientific classification have been worked out. Classifications are necessary for libraries, archives, compilers of bibliographies, collectors and publishers of folklore, and the like. Everyone who publishes collections of texts or prepares notes from a field trip first systematizes them. Too strict requirements should not be imposed on such classifications: if they meet the immediate purposes of organizing the material at hand, they can be considered satisfactory. Even if a bibliography lacks a scientific system but is so structured that one can find everything in it without much effort, the aim of systematization will have been partly realized. Examples of such imperfect empirical classifications, useful as technical tools, are well known.

Everything changes when we turn to problems of scientific classification, such as are entailed in the process of compiling indexes and cataloging folklore in archives, with their millions of items in need of precise systematization.

In Soviet scholarship, the basic unit for any study of folklore, including classification, is genre. On the one hand, it is subordinate to more general categories; on the other, it can be broken down into smaller categories. Genre is a purely arbitrary concept, and we need agreement on its meaning. Etymologically the word *genre* goes back to Latin *genus* and corresponds to German *Gattung*, but in fact it refers to a narrower concept, namely "kind," "sort," and corresponds to German *Art*. In Russian literary scholarship *genre* designates not a *general* but a *specific* concept. As long ago as 1841, Belínskij wrote about *the division of poetry into genera and species* and began his intended critical history of Russian literature with it (see Belinskij 1954, 7-67). The continuation of this chapter would have been another long chapter in which Belinskij for the first time defined and characterized several genres of Russian folk poetry. For him, as later for Veselóvskij, the problem of genres was central in creating a history of literature as a law-governed process. It is common knowledge that the *genera* of poetry are epic poetry (more precisely, narrative poetry and prose), drama, and lyric poetry. Genera consist of species, and we call these species genres.

Not everything is clear in such a definition, however. First, the concepts "genus" and "species" belong to the area of classification. An exact definition of what is meant by genre is impossible outside a classification of genres; each genre must be defined both in and of itself and in its relationship to other genres from which it must be distinguished. *Defining* genres and *classifying* them constitute two aspects of one problem.

How can genre be defined, if we bear in mind the nature of folklore as a type of verbal art? In literary criticism, genre is defined by the entire poetic system. The same principle is valid in folklore. In the broad sense of the word, a genre is a group of monuments united by a common poetic system. Since folklore consists of works of verbal art, we should begin by studying the properties and laws of this art, its poetics. Poetics refers to devices used for expressing artistic goals and reflecting the emotional and intellectual world; it is form in connection with a specific content (the plot and the message that goes with it). Zoologists were able to create a scientific classification only when they had studied the skeletons of animals, the structure of their bodies, their means of locomotion, their relation to their environment, the peculiarities of their feeding, reproduction, etc. Mutatis mutandis, the same complicated situation characterizes our science.

Poetics understood as the laws of people's creative process has been somewhat neglected in both the Russian and foreign science of folklore. This is one of the reasons why we lack a scientific classification of folklore genres. To be sure, concern about the necessity of studying oral art forms was voiced at the Budapest congress. Oldřich Sirovátka mentioned this problem in his presentation "The Morphology and Cataloguing of Legends" [1962], and so did some others, but no practical conclusions were reached.

The character of a genre is determined by the kind of reality it reflects, the means by which reality is expressed, the relation to reality, and its assessment. Unity of form results in unity of content, if by content we understand not only the plot but also the intellectual and emotional world reflected in the work. It follows that unity of form is sustained by everything called content and that the two cannot be separated. In his article on Kol'cóv, Belinskij said, "When form is the expression of content, it is so closely connected with content that to separate it from content means to destroy that very content; and conversely, to separate content from form means to destroy form" (1955, 535). Even today Belinskij's words have not lost their significance either in the theory of literature or in the practice of literature as art.

The form of a work of art cannot be changed without detriment to its entire poetical system. When we say that a work belongs to a particular genre we do not mean only one of its formal properties; genre affiliation determines the whole artistic fabric down to its finest threads, especially in the minute, subtle details that can evoke admiration of mastery, give great aesthetic enjoyment, and thereby infuse the work with life and arouse the reader. Nevertheless, the boundaries of genre are not always stable and are sometimes overstepped. The structure of each genre is different. We should study composition, for plot is closely connected with it. Different plots can have the same composition, as in the wonder-tale. Plot must often serve as the basis for classification. Plot is realized by characters, and there will be instances in which classification can be made in terms of characters. Everything that belongs to style is also part of poetics. We can distinguish prose and verse genres. Genres differ greatly according to the type of prose; various genres of song have dissimilar rhythm and structure, and this fact can serve as a criterion for differentiating them.

Consistent application of these principles will yield a more or less precise inventory of folklore genres for every people and will introduce important corrections into many popular ideas. For instance, the folktale is generally considered a genre, even though folktales subsume works differing in their poetical nature. From a structural point of view wondertales are quite unlike cumulative tales and tales about *pošexóncy*.[1] Consequently, folktale is a broader concept than genre. The same can be said about some other types of folklore.

The first task of classification is to determine the inventory of folklore genres of each people. The inventory of folklore genres valid for one people cannot be mechanically transferred to the folklore of another people. It is the principles of classification not the material that is international. Defining genre and determining the number and nomenclature of genres should start with research into the poetics of folklore.

In literary criticism, the definition of genre ends here. In folklore the situation is not quite the same. Although the poetical system is one of the basic criteria for defining folklore genres, we must bear in mind a number of other features absent from literature. In folklore there are genres characterized by their application to everyday life, and this must be the second criterion of classification. There are songs sung only at weddings, at funerals, or on certain holidays. Use in particular situations is a basic feature of some genres.

The third criterion that can prove essential in defining genre is the type of performance. For example, Russian singing-and-dancing in a ring (*xorovód*), is accompanied by certain body movements by each individual performer and by all together; stanzaic structure and other peculiarities of this singing cannot be fully understood if the movement is disregarded. The same, but in greater measure, applies to game songs. Finally, no type of drama can be studied only as text; we need to know what the actors do.

One more peculiarity of folklore distinguishes it from literature. All Russian verse folklore is sung. To study it independently of its music means to understand only half of it, for the metrics of the verse is inseparable from its rhythm and melody. In this area, great progress has been made of late and further cooperation of folklorists and musicologists cannot but bear fruit. Russian songs other than round-dance, game, and folk-dance songs are not stanzaic. The text does not indicate the presence of stanzas, but the recurring melody does. A song sometimes has a hidden stanzaic structure, which can be important for determining its genre and origin. In some cases the decisive factor for determining the genre is musical performance. Thus, only those works belong to classical heroic poetry that are sung. The story of the encounter of Il'já Múromec with Solovéj the Robber is either sung (and then it is epic poetry) or told (and then it is folk prose: a folktale or a bookish narrative).

In sum, a genre is determined by its poetics, application, type of performance, and relation to music. As a rule, no single feature is sufficient to describe a genre, which is determined by all of them together. Not all are needed in every case, but for verse folklore they are obligatory. Neither literary, ethnographic, nor musicological folklore alone can solve all the problems that confront our science.

When a genre has been studied, it must be characterized as precisely as possible and in accordance with the data. At the Budapest conference several definitions of *Sage* were put forward. But some participants were of the opinion that definition of a genre is of subsidiary importance (for example, Ina-Maria Greverus [1964]), and this is definitely a wrong opinion. Kurt Ranke and some others treated the concept of *Sage* too broadly and somewhat formally, including in it myths and legends. In defining a particular genre, the historical period must also be taken into consideration; here this was not done.

The folklore genres of every people should be inventoried and defined. Then we will know how the folktale and various types of legend differ from one another. We will discover which types of lyric and epic songs each people has. Going over one isolated genre after another cannot yield firm conclusions, since works of different genres are often interconnected; it cannot bring out the wealth and originality of the folk poetry of each people or the features peculiar to a particular people.

When this first, basic problem has been solved, we will have to determine the broader and more general categories from which a genre is derived and also to break down each genre into the smaller categories of which it consists, that is, to include it in the system of classification as a whole. There is a great fear of small categories in the science of folklore. Attempts to subsume the existing material under more general categories or, conversely, to break it down are seldom made, and the need for subordination of the first, second, etc., degree is not even recognized. In A. I. Sobolévskij's large, seven-volume collection of Russian folk songs, for example, the material is divided as follows: narrative songs (volume 1), family songs (volumes 2 and 3), love songs (volumes 4 and 5), songs of recruits, soldiers' songs, songs about captives, robbers' songs, prisoners' songs, barge haulers' and servants' songs (volume 6), humorous, satiric, and game songs (volume 7). From a logical point of view such a division is strikingly inconsistent, but in many empiric classifications, either the material is not subdivided at all or the classification consists of two, three, or at most four categories. For comparison one has only to pick up an elementary text on zoology and see how thorough and careful the system of classification is according to phyla, classes, orders, families, genera, species, varieties, etc.

A classification can be of cognitive value only when there are as many categories in it as in the material itself. A good example is the meticulous classification *Czech Tales of Superstitions* (2nd variant, 1963), which gives a clear idea of such tales among the Czechs. All the texts are divided first into two basic classes, then into twelve coordinate groups, and finally into sixty-nine distinct types. We need just such precise multilevel divisions. Although the terminology for designating the rubrics is still lacking, it can be worked out. A number of terms exist like genus, area, genre, species, variety, type, plot, motif, variant, etc., but a different terminology is also possible.

Any classification is based upon some one feature. At the Budapest conference, the opinion was expressed that since folklore is alogical, logic is inapplicable to it. This opinion should be rejected point blank. Dagmar Klímová-Rychnová correctly said, "The system of headings must be subordinate to a unified logical conception." In folklore classifications, just as in all others, even the slightest logical errors are inadmissible, since they can lead to a distorted idea of the data.

The following considerations are of importance.

1. The selected feature must reflect relevant aspects of the phenomenon. What is relevant and what is not is determined by the goals of the investigation, but some objective criteria exist. An example of a correct classification is the scheme proposed by N. P. Andréev for various legends, which he grouped according to characters (there are tales about dead men, devils, witches, wood goblins, water sprites, brownies, and the like; see the supplement to his *Index*, 1929). Essen-

tially the same classification was proposed by Simonsuuri (1961) for a certain part of his index of types and motifs in Finnish mythic legends. On the other hand, arrangement of proverbs in alphabetical order cannot be of scholarly value, since the feature of alphabetization is irrelevant. In a similar fashion, it would be wrong to arrange works according to their size. Riddles, proverbs, and the like are often classified as small genres (*Kleindichtung*), but such a definition based on a purely external feature is of no use.

2. The selected feature must remain the same throughout the classification; it cannot vary. Application of this principle to folklore runs into serious difficulties, since folklore itself is in a constant process of change. The wedding ceremony is not observed now, and songs that accompanied this ceremony are sung as lyric songs. The same happens with round-dance and calendar songs. However, we can determine the genre of a song in its original form and refer to those genera that cover the song now. Numerous variants, the shift from one plot to another, etc., require a great deal of study. Another example: with the disappearance of epic poetry some plots are transformed into folktales. In this case we have two different genres employing one plot. We are dealing with the general problem of stable and variable (or changeable) elements in folklore. I once attempted to prove that the stable elements in the wondertale are the actions of the characters, whereas the performers of these actions are variable, and that, therefore, a scientific classification of wondertales and plots can be based only on the characters' actions (Propp 1928a). It is not clear whether we have a general or a specific law of epic folklore here. Czech classifiers of local legends also had to grapple with this problem. Originally their classification was based on local features, but it turned out that the same plots can be tied to various localities, and the entire classification had to be redone in terms of plots (Pourová 1963). Classification by stable features, as logic requires, is possible in folklore after we have learned what is stable for each genre and what is not. For example, classification by characters is possible only when we have determined that a particular character is indeed connected with definite actions and plots. There is a legend of how some underwater creatures summoned to their aid a midwife from a village. The plot is customarily classified under the heading "water sprites," but it is also known under the rubric "dwarfs living underground"; consequently, it cannot be classified according to characters but only according to plot.

3. The basic feature must be formulated clearly, so as to preclude the possibility of different interpretations. This requirement is very often violated. In Czechoslovakia an attempt was made to classify songs by main motifs; according to this idea, the *Leitwörter* should be found and arranged in alphabetical order (Sirovátka 1962). Such a classification is based on a subjective selection of primary and secondary elements. As a result, many cases will lend themselves to nonunique solutions. It is rather common to classify folklore data by themes or groups of themes (*Themenkreise*). But what is a theme? Let us take the ballad about Sof'ja and

Vasilij,[2] in which Vasilij's mother poisons the lovers because they do not attend church; later, trees with intertwining tops grow on their graves. What is basic here: the theme of a touching love that continues beyond the grave, the theme of a fanatic murder, or the right to love in spite of the teachings and outlook of the church? The concept of theme is applicable for a monograph on one plot, but it is inapplicable for scholarly classification.

To sum up, the features used as the basis for classification must be relevant, stable, and unambiguous. When the basic features have been found, classification proper can start. Three cases are possible here: classification is made according to the presence/absence of one particular feature, according to varieties of one feature, or according to mutually exclusive features. *Within the limits of one category (class, genus, species), only one method is admissible.* Definition according to the presence/absence of one feature is normal when broad categories are set up. For instance, works of folklore can be divided into those accompanied by musical performance (singing) and those without such accompaniment. Sung poetry is often divided into ritual and nonritual, which is correct both formally and in essence. Songs in a Rumanian anthology are arranged according to the following principle: types connected with definite occasions (Christmas carols, wedding songs, funeral songs) and types whose performance is not connected with such occasions (songs in the strict sense of the word) (Rădulescu 1961). Nonritual songs can be divided into those performed with certain rhythmic body movements (round-dance, game, folk-dance songs) and those performed without them, by voice alone (while standing, sitting, moving, or working). In prose folklore the same principle permits separating works in which people do not believe from those in which they do. It may seem that the basis for the latter classification is the subjective attitude of the speaker, but this is not so. In the first case we have artistic fiction (all formations of the wondertale type) and in the second, an artistic transcript of reality or what is believed to be reality (all types of legends). The two types are differentiated by their poetics and aesthetics.

Classification according to varieties of some feature is especially common. G. A. Megas (1964) reminded us of Linos Polites's classification, who categorized his data according to the subject of the narrative. Some legends concern natural phenomena (the sky, stars and planets, meteors, the earth, animals, plants); the rest are ethnological legends, which are grouped in another category. From a logical point of view such a classification is correct, but it will be actually correct if the subjects of the narrative are permanently associated with corresponding plots; classification within a group should be carried out according to varieties of one feature and not several features at once. If a child says that he has white, red, yellow, and wooden blocks, the inconsistency is immediately obvious. Such an error is not always evident at first glance, but it makes a classification untenable and is the scourge of almost all proposed classifications. I will limit myself to a few examples. In the Aarne-Thompson *Index* the wondertale ''The Bladder, the Straw, and the Bast Shoe'' (AT 295) is assigned to animal tales. N. P. Andréev, who reworked this index for Russian tales, assigned "The War of the Mushrooms," "The Frost, the Sun, and the Wind," and some others to animal tales as well. Following in Sobolevskij's footsteps, scholars usually set up categories of love, family, and humorous songs, despite the fact that half of all humorous songs are love songs. Equally untenable is the division into love, family, and round-dance songs, for round-dance songs are predominantly songs about love. The error lies in the circumstance that the features are from various groups and are not mutually exclusive. Aarne divided wondertales into the following categories: the magic adversary; the magic spouse, brother, and the like; the magic task; the magic helper; the magic object. All seems fine, for the categories are united by the concept of magic. However, the first two categories are defined by character, the third by motif, the fourth by object. This error in logic cannot but entail factual errors. A magic task is always performed by a magic helper. What will we do with the wondertale about Sívka-Búrka,[3] in which the magic task of jumping up to the princess's window on horseback is performed by the magic helper, the horse? The Aarne-Thompson index is used internationally and has been translated into many languages, but the time has come to say that it is useful only as a technical tool for want of a better one.

Even the careful classification of legends developed by a special commission of the International Society of Folk-Narrative Research and circulated by Kurt Ranke is not free from similar errors [Ortutay 1964, 131]. In it historical legends subsume local legends and legends relating to early history. Two principles are confused in this system: local and temporal. How will we classify the legend about the founding of Kiev by three brothers: as local (Kiev) or as historical? Mythic legends contain the headings *devil* and *demon of sickness*. But what will we do with plots in which the devil possesses a woman and thereby causes her illness? In one of the papers at the Budapest congress some northern legends about magi were classified thus: professional magi, nonprofessional magi, and women. The logical inconsistency here is apparent at once. If we go over publications of folklore texts and examine how data are set out there, we can give hundreds of such examples. However, some of them are only the result of awkward wording. Thus, in Simonsuuri's index, in which the material is correctly arranged from both a logical and a factual point of view by types of character, we suddenly find the heading *interdictions*. But the author means people who violate the folk code of ethics and belief, rather than types of interdiction. The confusion can be easily rectified by changing the heading.

Classification by mutually exclusive features is applied in setting up folklore genres (riddles, proverbs, charms, etc.). This method is clear enough, but errors are possible even here. It is especially difficult to distinguish epic genres, which sometimes merge into one another. Classifiers should check themselves and be fully aware of the feature they have chosen, of how they are making the classification, and to what degree their method is applicable to their data.

I have by no means attempted to exhaust the question; many difficulties lie ahead. I only wished to call attention to two aspects of classification that are usually neglected, namely, the necessity of studying the poetics and laws of folklore and of observing the rules of logic. In the classifications of the natural sciences there are and can be no errors of logic. We must also aim at similar results, although our data are qualitatively different.

Chapter Four.
On the Historicity
of Folklore

At present one hardly needs to offer special proof that every art, including folklore, is derived from reality and reflects it. Difficulties arise when we attempt to interpret the historical process and to decide how history has been reflected.

Two trends are clearly observable in modern folklore. One develops the ideas of pre-Soviet scholarship and conceives history as a chain of foreign and domestic events. Events can always be dated exactly. They are caused by the actions of people who really existed, that is, concrete people with concrete names. The historical basis of folklore is understood as the reflection of such real events and persons. A scholar is expected to show which events and which persons are depicted in individual monuments and to date them accordingly.

The other trend proceeds from a broader conception of history. This trend differentiates genres. The historical basis of genres is diverse. For some of them it is possible to treat folklore as a representation of history and persons. For others such a narrow understanding of history is insufficient. The driving force of history is the people itself; individual persons are a derivative of history, not its impetus. From this point of view, everything that happens to a people belongs to history in one way or another. In the study of folklore special attention should be directed to the basis, which is primarily the forms of production, and for the folklore of the feudal period the basis is mainly the forms of peasant labor. In the last analysis, the development of forms of thought and art is explained by the development of forms of production. The field of history encompasses forms of society down to the smallest details in the relations between boyar and peasant, landowner and serf, priest and farmhand. There are no names or events here, but this is history. The history of forms of marriage and family relations that determine wedding poetry and the greater part of lyric poetry also belongs here. In a broad conception of history, the historical basis includes the whole of a people's life throughout its existence.

The relations of folklore to reality can be of three kinds:

1. Folklore is engendered by reality but does not contain any direct traces of the concrete reality or epoch that has engendered it. A case in point is the wonder-tale images that seem fabulous to us. Fiery dragons, winged horses, or enchanted princesses have never existed. These are fictitious images. However, monuments containing such images should also be studied and elucidated. Historical research will discover when, in what epoch, at what stage of human society, thought forms, and artistic creativity such works and ideas are bound to arise.

2. The second type of relation of folklore to reality presupposes a fictitious plot that contains obvious traces of peoples' lives. Reality finds reflection even though such reflection was not the performer's aesthetic aim. For instance, in the wondertale about a stepmother and a stepdaughter, the stepmother sends the girl to some monster, which is sure to kill her, but Bába Jagá, or a bear, or Morózko [Frost] tests her and rewards her. This narration is the performer's objective. But in passing, the tale describes the peasant's hut, the unhappy family life of a remarried widower who has children by his first wife, pictures of Russian nature, etc.

3. In the third case the performer intends to describe reality. Such are soldiers' songs about the draft, the hardships of service, raids, battles, and death in battle. Which folklore genres belong here and how reality is related to folklore according to genre will be shown below.

For a correct understanding of the historical basis of folklore one should bear in mind that folklore does not exist as a unified whole, that it breaks down into genres. The prerevolutionary science of folklore did not even use the word "genre," but nowadays the study of genres is gradually attracting the attention it deserves. Genre is the primary unity with which our study must begin. One of the basic features of genre is its poetics: each genre has a poetical system of its own. Genre has other features, but this one is the most important. Each genre possesses specific features. A difference in poetical devices is not of merely formal significance; it reflects a difference in the relation to reality and determines the various ways in which reality is represented. Each genre has its own very strict boundaries beyond which it does not and cannot go lest it become a different genre, which also occurs in folklore. A bylina, for example, can develop into a wondertale. Until the specific features of a genre have been determined or at least outlined, we cannot study the individual monuments constituting it.

Each genre is characterized by a specific relation to reality and by a method for its artistic representation. Various genres are formed at various periods, have various fortunes, pursue various aims, and reflect various aspects of the political, social, and everyday history of a people. The wondertale does not reflect reality like the funeral lamentation, nor does the soldiers' song reflect it like the bylina. We do not know enough about genres, but we can no longer do without a specific concept of genre. Consequently, we must first examine each genre separately and only then draw conclusions about the historicity of folklore as a whole.

All genres of Russian folklore can be studied from the standpoint of a broad conception of history. Each of them, in one way or another, refracts the reality of various periods: from very ancient times to the present day. But historical study *follows* the study of forms. To discover the history of the wondertale, we need first to investigate its morphology. Likewise, without knowing the typology of charms, the poetics of riddles, the structure of ritual songs, and the forms of lyric songs, we will never reveal the oldest stages in the emergence and growth of these genres. Russian peasant life of the nineteenth century can be deduced from wondertales, songs, laments, proverbs, dramas, and comedies. None of them deals with historical events or names, but we can examine them historically, although not all ages are represented in them equally well. These are some of the genres that can be studied from the point of view of the broad conception of history.

There are other genres, in which the representation of historical reality is the chief goal. They can be analyzed from the standpoint of a narrower conception of history and historicity. First come legends. In Russian folklore, legends have been investigated very little. They have attracted almost no interest, and the number of recordings is really small. On the contrary, in Western Europe the *Sage* occupies the center of attention; it forms the subject of international congresses. By their nature *Sagen* are very diverse and can be mythological and historical.

Historical legends are probably very ancient. Naturally, we do not have recordings from pre-Kievan Rus' and the Russian Middle Ages. But we can form an opinion by analogy with other peoples. G. U. Èrgis (1960) published an excellent edition of the historical legends and stories of the Yakuts. He characterized them as follows, "Legends and historical tales contain narratives about real events connected with real individuals and reflect the people's economic and cultural achievements" (p. 13). The presence of such a genre among the Yakuts is especially interesting, because the Yakuts have a splendid, highly developed, and very poetic epic poetry. Characteristically, the people never confuse the genres of epic poetry and legends; nor do scholars. Ergis wrote, "Historical legends and stories, as distinct from oral fictional genres proper, can be called the Yakuts' historical folklore based on real events" (p. 15). The main thematic cycles of these legends concern the migration of the Yakuts from the South to the Lena, their fights with hostile tribes and peoples, their settlement of the Viljuj and Kobjaja[1] river basins, and the incorporation of Yakutia into the Russian state. There are special legends about lineage, on the basis of which ramified genealogical tables can be drawn up. All this is somewhat reminiscent of Icelandic family sagas.

Did the Eastern Slavs have historical legends? We may suppose that they did. Fragments have been preserved in chronicles and other sources and have been examined by B. A. Rybakóv (1963). The folklorist is accustomed to oral recordings. Consider the well-known recordings of legends about Stepán Razin, Peter I, Pugačëv, the Decembrists,[2] several tsars, etc.

In an insightful and interesting article, V. I. Čičerov (1959, 263, 264) said: "Historical legends treat events and persons of the past as if they were real. . . . By preserving the memory of past events and narrating about the heroic behavior of some person, the historical legend lives in the people's memory as oral, unwritten history." I think that these observations are correct, although many legends have a fantastic character. From an artistic point of view legends are usually poor. As Èrgis observed, this is not an aesthetic genre. The narrator seeks neither consciously nor unconsciously to embellish the story, but wants only to transmit what he considers reality.

In this respect legends are very different from historical songs. We have a huge literature on historical songs; in the Soviet period alone there have been heated debates about their nature and genre. However, some of their features are indisputable. They do not deal with fictitious characters but with historical and usually outstanding persons who really existed, e.g., Ivan the Terrible, Ermak,[3] Peter I, Razin, Pugačëv, Suvorov, Kutuzov, Napoleon, etc. As a rule, some attested event underlies the plot (the capture of Kazan, the birth of Peter I, Napoleon's invasion, the Sebastopol campaign, etc.), but the characters and the actions do not have to correspond completely to recorded history. Although the people can give rein to their historical fantasy and their artistic imagination, the general character of historical songs remains unimpaired: their historicity lies in the people's expression of its historical self-awareness and in its attitude toward past events, persons, and circumstances rather than in the songs' correct depiction of historical persons or relation of events considered real. Historical significance is an ideological phenomenon.

Thus, the Cossack chief (*atamán*) Platov[4] never visited Napoleon's headquarters in disguise and never spoke with Napoleon incognito. Yet, the song about this event can be called a historical song. In this merry *skomoróšina*,[5] the people expressed its mocking attitude toward Napoleon and its admiration for one of the most daring partisan leaders. Herein lies the historicity of this song.

Historical songs were composed by those who witnessed or participated in events. The song about the capture of Kazan[6] arose among the gunners of that time. Songs about Ermak were composed by the Cossacks; songs about Kutuzov, in the Russian army of that time; songs about the Decembrists, by the eyewitnesses to the events of 1825.

It is easy to date historical songs, but not their genre, and there is no unanimity among Soviet scholars about this question. The peak in the development of the historical song undoubtedly falls in the sixteenth century, that is, in the reign of Ivan the Terrible. Only one unquestionable fourteenth-century skomoróšina has come down to us, namely, the song about the murder of Ščelkán Dudént'evič (the historical Ševkal, Deden's son).[7] There are good reasons for the sudden flowering of this genre in the sixteenth century. The greatest historical aspiration of the people expressed in epic poetry, namely, the creation of a powerful, centralized state and complete liberation from the Mongol yoke, had been realized. A great cultural change set in. The whole character of warfare changed radically. The invention of firearms and the rapid improvement of Russian artillery pushed to the background the epic bogatyrs with their swords, spears, and cudgels, as well as the bogatyrs who won an easy victory by swinging a wiry Tatar and cutting swaths through the enemy's army. Instead of lone bogatyrs, an army with regular commanders now appeared and instead of bylina-style victories, hard-won battles, so that "the land was bathed in blood." This is the background for the appearance of the historical song as a genre. Realistic historical songs come to take the place of the monumental bylina.

The purpose of my remarks was to show that as far as historical songs are concerned, the methods of the old Historical school, which sought in folklore chiefly the representation of events and persons, were correct. This does not exclude studying historical songs from a broader historical point of view. Most historical songs are about war. They give a many-sided picture of the soldiers' way of life, sometimes down to the smallest details of clothing, food, and so forth.

The same is true of workers' poetry. In a certain respect, workers' songs are the heir to historical songs. They depict with even greater force everyday reality and the conditions under which the Russian proletariat lived and worked. Foreign events are not their domain; those are reflected in historical songs proper. Such events are noticed only when they provoke the wrath of the whole people, as in soldiers' and sailors' songs about the Russo-Japanese War. But they recreate rather than reflect unintentionally everything in the life of workers, as we can already see in the mining songs of the eighteenth century, with their description of daily life in the workers' barracks, from reveille at five o'clock in the morning to running the gauntlet and sending the injured to the hospital. The exposition is dry and factual. Still a song can rise to great pathos, as in the description of the events of January 9[8] and in the curses against Nicholas II. Such events as strikes, demonstrations, clashes with the police, arrests, and exiles are depicted realistically.

I have for the time being deliberately avoided the question of the historicity of bylinas. This question has caused heated, sometimes passionate arguments, and I would like to dwell on it at greater length.

The publication of L. N. Májkov's dissertation *On the Bylinas of the Vladimir Cycle* in 1863 marked the appearance of a new trend in folklore, later known as the Historical school. Majkov examined all the historical accretions in the Russian bylina. He realized that the content of bylinas is fictitious, but the *circumstances* are historical. The book consists of three chapters, the second of which, "Examination of Bylinas as Monuments of the People's Life," is the central one. Here he studied the historical realities of Russian bylinas: the prince's (knjaz's) court and his retinue, buildings, feasts, armor, weapons, utensils, food and drink, etc. He also paid some attention to agrarian relations and the like. Examination of the realities led Majkov to the conclusion that the content of the bylinas of the Vladimir cycle had developed during the tenth, eleventh, and twelfth centuries and had been fixed not later than the time of the Mongol Yoke, that is, in the thirteenth and fourteenth centuries. Generalizing Majkov's point of view somewhat, we can say that in his opinion Russian epic poetry as a genre emerged in the period of Kievan Rus' and in the following centuries up to the Mongol invasion.

This point of view predominated for a long time and still enjoys some support. However, the overwhelming majority of Soviet scholars believe that epic poetry arises long before the formation of the state. The Revolution opened our eyes to the untold epic treasures of peoples of the USSR who had lived under tribal conditions up to 1917. It is these peoples with the most archaic forms of life that have epic poetry; they belong to the Paleo-Siberian group: Nivxi, Čukči,[9] and others. The most archaic of all epic poetry attested so far, that of the Néncy,[10] has now been published (Kuprijánov 1965). We know better the epic poetry of the Karelians. The Yakuts have created splendid epic poetry, extraordinary in scope and artistry. The epic poetry of the Altaic peoples is no less perfect; the monuments of the Šórcy[11] are known especially well. The Tajiks, Uzbeks, Turkmens, Kazakhs, Kirghiz, and the peoples of the Caucasus possess rich epic poetry. It follows that epic poetry as a special type of folklore arises before the formation of the state. In this respect, the Eastern Slavs could not have been an exception. That they had epic poetry is part of the nature of things. The epic poetry of the Eastern Slavs sprang up before the emergence of the Kievan state. The forms and stage of development of an epic poetry correspond to the stage of a people's social and historical development. All these observations and propositions underlie my book on Russian epic poetry (Propp 1958b, 29-59).

The view that Russian epic poetry arose within so-called Kievan Rus' has proved tenacious. Thus, Rybakov (1963, 44) wrote, "Bylinas as a genre must have arisen at the same time as the Russian feudal state." This is far from evident. He also said, "In his struggle against the bourgeois Historical school, Propp severed Russian bylinas from historical reality altogether and declared that a significant part of Russian epic poetry had arisen in tribal society" (p. 42). This criticism denies tribal society the status of historical reality. The opinion of Majkov and his contemporary followers that the bylina was born in so-called Kievan Rus' is untenable and indeed finds little support among Soviet folklorists. If it is true that epic poetry originates before the state, the primary objective of historical research must be to compare the epics of various peoples at various stages in their development and to determine which plots originated before the rise of the state and which after it.

The number of prestate plots in Russian epic poetry is very great, much greater than it may seem at first glance. Plots in which the hero meets a monster (a dragon, Tugarin,[12] Idolišče,[13] and others) or sets out to court a bride and sometimes fights a monster (Pótyk,[14] Iván Godínovič[15]), plots in which he finds himself in the other world (Sadko[16] in the sea kingdom), plots in which there are amazons with whom the hero stays or whom he marries, the fight of a father with his son, and certain others could not have arisen or been invented under the conditions of an organized state. It is historically impossible for the plot of dragon-fighting to have originated in Kievan Rus'. All these plots are earlier, and they can be documented in the epic poetry of the peoples of the USSR.

When a people begins to form a state, its epic poetry changes considerably. Old epic poetry undergoes reworking, and a new epic poetry arises that reflects the state and its interests (cf. bylinas about the struggle with the Tatars). The ideology of tribal society comes into conflict with the interests of the young state. The clash of two ideologies in old plots should be accorded detailed treatment, and this sort of treatment also can be called historical. The dragon that used to abduct women now also captures Russians. It is no longer a maiden but Kiev that the hero frees from the dragon's raids. Such is the plot of the Russian bylina about Dobrynja[17] the dragon-fighter in light of comparative data, and this is just one example. Apparently, we cannot date such bylinas. They do not go back to one day or hour or year; they are the result of a long historical process. Majkov erred in tracing the origin of epic poetry to the tenth through twelfth centuries, but he was correct in discovering the historical realities. When historical reality changes, epic poetry absorbs the new reality. The process of absorption continues later as well. Epic poetry is like those layers of earth containing deposits of various geological epochs.

Majkov's initiative was not taken up by subsequent Russian scholarship. In the works of Vsevolod Miller and his followers the problem of the historicity of epic poetry lost its edge. Although Miller and others continued to study the way of life as described in Russian bylinas (and these works and pages will never become antiquated), the basic and most important, if not the only problems of their research became the historical prototypes of bylina heroes, the exact events presented in bylinas, and dating bylinas. Since the bylinas themselves contain no direct, clear traces of past events, they were declared to be a distorted representation of what happened in history by uneducated, ignorant peasants, and the main objective of research was reduced to eliminating these distortions. A long succession of works on the prototypes of Russian heroic poetry appeared. Solovéj Budimírovič[18] turned out to be not Solovej Budimirovič but the Norwegian king Harald; Djuk[19] was traced to the Hungarian king Stephen IV; Potyk, to the Bulgarian saint Michael from the city of Potoka; Dobrynja's fight with the dragon turned out to be not a dragon fight but the baptism of Novgorod, etc.

No unanimity existed among scholars, and they constantly disputed one another. Especially debatable is the prototype of Vol'ga, the hero of a well-known bylina. P. A. Bessónov thought that Vol'ga is Oleg, a son of Svjatosláv (born in 960). B. A. Rybakov repeated this theory. Orest Miller (1869, 188 ff.) believed that

Vol'ga was both an Indo-European hunting deity and the historical Prophetic Oleg. A. N. Veselovskij (1890, 23-26) compared Vol'ga with the Germanic hero Ort-nit. I. N. Ždanov (1895, 404-24) distinguished the plot of Vol'ga and Mikula and the plot of an Indian raid. The first Vol'ga allegedly goes back to the apocryphal Novgorod tale of Simon Volxv, while the second is none other than Robert the Devil of the German legends. S. K. Šambinágo (1905) discerned in Vol'ga the features of Ol'ga and the Prophetic Oleg as they were known from the chronicles. N. I. Koróbka (1908) traced Vol'ga to Ol'ga. After the Revolution A. N. Robinson (1951, 149) analyzed Vol'ga as a blend of Oleg and Vsesláv, Duke of Polock. D. S. Lixačëv (1953, 200-1) thinks that the bylina hero has absorbed Oleg, Vseslav, and someone else (undefined).[20] Why was there such disagreement? Perhaps the scholars lacked erudition? On the contrary, they were among the most prominent scholars in the field. The reason lies in their erroneous methodology. In his book *The Poetics and Genesis of Bylinas* A. P. Skaftýmov (1924) showed convincingly how strained their conclusions were. The principles of the Historical school were subjected to severe criticism. But this criticism only temporarily halted attempts at similar historical interpretations. At present the Historical school of Vsevolod Miller is being resurrected. Attempts are made to avoid some of its mistakes, for instance, the assertion that epic poetry arose in an aristocratic milieu, and neglect of the artistic features of epic poetry, but basically everything has remained as it was. Rybakov (1963, 43) claimed that one must approach the bylinas "verifying anew and broadening the historical comparisons made a hundred years ago." These words mean that we must remain true to the views held a hundred years ago and only enlarge the material quantitatively, verify it anew, and then everything will fall into place. This is quite untenable. What is needed is not a quantitative increase in the data but a qualitative reexamination of the methodological premises. What was progressive a hundred years ago in bourgeois scholarship cannot be considered progressive in contemporary Soviet scholarship. The methodology of the Historical school proceeds from one basic premise, which is that in bylinas people wanted to represent current political history and actually represented it. Thus, M. M. Pliseckij (1962, 141) wrote, "Epic lays arose for the purpose of fixing historical events." If this premise is correct, then the trend that looks for the representation of political events and historical figures in bylinas is legitimate. If this premise is incorrect, the methodological basis of this trend collapses.

The premise is indeed false. Moreover, it is antihistorical. It attributes to people of Old Russia aesthetic intentions and a form for realizing them that could not have existed before the fourteenth and fifteenth centuries. Russian man of the early Middle Ages could not represent actual reality in his verbal art. This intention became prevalent in folklore much later, namely, in the sixteenth century, when the historical song came into its own. There are two types of folklore genres: in one, reality is reflected independently of the narrator's intentions, and in the other, the reflection of reality is the artist's basic purpose. The bylina does not belong to those genres whose conscious aim was to represent actual history. The historicity of bylinas lies in another plane. Compare the fine arts of Old Russia. Russian icon painting, like any art, originated in reality and indirectly reflected it. It is the art of the Russian Middle Ages; it depicted various types of people: the young and the old, men and women, the bearded adult and the beardless youth, the stern and the angelic, etc. But the art of realistic portraiture and genre painting is alien to icon painting. The icon painter did not represent events and did not paint people's portraits. In his own way he elevated people and transformed them: he created the images of saints. This general truth does not rule out the fact that in some cases real people were depicted: Jaroslav Vsévolodovič (1199—the Church of Our Savior on the Nerédica[21]), Boris and Gleb.[22] Even in these rare cases, the representation is conventional and subordinate to the style of this art. He who ascribes to icon painting the intention of representing actual reality does not understand the differences between an icon by Rubljov[23] and a picture by Répin[24] and attributes to Old Russia the aesthetic intentions of the nineteenth century.

The case of verbal art is essentially the same. In an icon, human beings are transformed into saints, and in epic poetry common people are transformed into grand heroes who accomplish the greatest exploits, which only they are able to accomplish. Therefore, one cannot recount these feats, one can only sing about them.

Followers of the old Historical school do not understand the nature of epic poetry as a specific genre; hence their mistakes. Pliseckij's statement is typical; according to him, if concrete events are represented in the *Lay of the Host of Igor*, in songs about the siege of Kazan and about Stepan Razin, and in good historical novels (he even cites Leo Tolstoy's *War and Peace* and Alexey Tolstoy's *Peter the First*), then "why are bylinas not allowed to do this?" It is very simple why: because they are genres of different epochs, with different social intentions and different aesthetic systems. A bylina is not a novel by Tolstoy. A bylina has a historical foundation and reflects it, but the active representation of current historical reality and current events is neither its objective nor a part of its aesthetics and poetics. The question of the representation of historical reality is legitimate for legends and historical songs but not for bylinas. Adherents of the Historical school deliberately deny the distinction between these genres. The bylina, the historical song, and the legend are the same thing to them. Pliseckij tried to erase all distinction between the bylina and historical song, which is recognized by several Soviet scholars. He disagreed that the historical song, as opposed to the bylina, is made up by participants in and witnesses to events. "There is no doubt," he wrote, "that the bylinas, like other heroic and historical works, were composed either by direct participants in events or by those who were very close to them" (Pliseckij 1962, 109). But how is one to conceive of the participants in such events as the transfer of Svjatogór's power to Il'já Múromec?²⁵ There are only two people in the scene, so which of them created the bylina? What witnesses could watch and celebrate in song the dance of the Sea King on the bottom of the sea, while Sadko accompanied him on the gusli? On this question I wish to express my solidarity with V. I. Čičerov. Two of his works are an early article entitled "On the Stages in the Development of Russian Historical Epic Poetry" (Čičerov 1947) and a later one, which I have already mentioned, "On the Historicity and Genres of Russian Bylinas and Historical Songs." In these works he expressed different, even opposite, opinions. In the first, the very term "historical epic poetry" shows that, following Vsevolod Miller and others, he believed that concrete events are the basis of both bylinas and historical songs. To him the bylina was just a very ancient form of the historical song; he did not detect any significant difference between them and treated "historical epic poetry" as bylinas and historical songs taken together. Later Čičerov studied the historical song in depth. He realized what a profound difference there is between the bylina and the historical song. I will not repeat Čičerov's arguments but rather refer all those seriously interested in the problem to his works. Čičerov briefly formulated his view thus: "Historical songs are not composed like bylinas." Indeed, they arise at different periods, their principles of reflecting and representing reality are different, and their poetics and aesthetics are different. Pliseckij (1962, 103) insisted on the opposite: making a distinction between the bylina and the historical song is absolutely without foundation. A superb collection of historical songs, the first volume of which was published by Pushkin House, provided a firm material basis for the study of the historical song as a genre,²⁶ and B. N. Putilov's doctoral dissertation on the folklore of the historical song of the thirteenth through the sixteenth centuries provides a theoretical basis for the correct understanding of this problem (Putilov and Dobrovol'skij 1960; Putilov 1960).

A few words about the methods of the historical study of folklore are now in order. I believe that in folklore one can use only the inductive method, that is, one proceeds from data to conclusions. This method is firmly established in the exact sciences and linguistics but not in folklore. Here deduction has always predominated, that is, research has proceeded from a general theory or hypotheses to facts that were examined in accordance with a set of postulates. Some scholars tried to show that absolutely all epic folklore is traceable to the solar cult, others tried to prove the Oriental, Byzantine, or Romano-Germanic origin of folklore, still others asserted that the heroes of epic poetry were historical figures, and yet others that folklore was entirely realistic, etc. And although each of these hypotheses contains a grain of truth, a correct methodological foundation should be different. With a preconceived hypothesis, we do not prove anything but only select data to fit the postulates. Many works in folklore are of this type.

Very often scholars use only the facts that confirm their initial hypothesis and ignore the others. Sometimes they do not even know all the facts and draw wrong conclusions from incomplete data. In any textbook, in popular works, and in scholarly works one can read that the Sadko of the Russian bylina is a historical personage, because, according to the chronicle, in 1167 a certain Sotkó Sytínyč founded the Church of Sts. Boris and Gleb.[27] The bylina Sadko also sometimes has a church built, though indeed not that of Sts. Boris and Gleb, but this discrepancy is usually dismissed. S. N. Ázbelev (1962, 44-51) collected every mention of Sotko Sytínyč's enterprise (including several unpublished ones). He found twenty-two texts. Azbelev studied all the facts about Sadko's name and all the variants of the bylina and came to the irrefutable conclusion that the bylina hero and Sotko Sytinyč have nothing in common. Another example: it is widely believed that the bylinas arose from eulogies, the encomiastic songs (slávy 'glories') addressed to the victorious princes. The expression pojút slávy 'they sing glory' occurs in the Lay of the Host of Igor. This belief is widespread, though with regard to their content the bylinas have nothing in common with the eulogies. B. N. Putilov (1960, 43-48) collected all the references to "glories" in Old Russian literature, examined them, compared them with the songs, and came to the conclusion that the "glories" and bylinas are not related. The scope of the collected material is important because in the compendia of Russian heroic poetry each bylina is accorded two or three pages; the data in such sections are scanty and the conclusions ungrounded. We are in great need of exhaustive monographs on individual plots, a rare genre in our scholarship. Mályšev 1956 is an exception. If we had more of such excellent works, we would make great progress in the study of the bylinas.

But sometimes the Russian material alone is insufficient. A genuinely historical method should be comparative in the broad sense of the word. International congresses of Slavists have taught us a great deal. For example, the plot of the bylina about Ivan Godinovič is usually treated as originally Russian; attempts have even been made to determine the time and place of its origin. Yet this plot is typical of prestate epic poetry. One can speak only of the Russian form of this plot. The plot of the bylina about Dunaj[28] and his quest for a bride for Vladimir has been compared with the story in Russian chronicles about the marriage of Prince Vladimir to Rognéda.[29] There seem to be two objects for comparison. However, B. M. Sokolóv (1923) compared this plot with the cycle of tales about Koltoma, with the cycle of Germanic legends of the marriage of Gunther to Brünhilde in all its versions (the Nibelungenlied, the Elder Edda, Völsunga Saga, Tidriks Saga), with Russian chronicle materials, and with all the variants of the bylina. It appears that there are no longer two objects for comparison but many more. The international character of this plot, despite all its national traits, becomes evident. Representatives of the modern Historical school ignore Sokolov's work and do not consider it necessary to dispute it.

The most important thing in a bylina is its plot taken as a whole. The plot must be studied in all its details and versions. This is the main task of investigation.

In a bylina the plot is not reducible to an entertaining adventure. It always expresses a certain idea, which one must understand and determine. Since ideas are born not of themselves but at a certain time and in a certain place, the historical study of a bylina consists in determining when the idea embodied in a particular form could arise. In most cases bylinas display accretions of several periods, so their ideas can clash. The presence of collisions is one of the most interesting though most complex facts of bylinas. The objective of historical research is to determine the historical meaning and significance of a bylina's idea and to discover when such a complex entity could spring up.

In many works, historicity is deduced not from the entire plot and its historical significance but from individual details. For example, the historicity of the bylina about Sadko is argued on the basis of one element, namely, his building of a church. The hero of the bylina is identified with a person in the chronicle, and this is said to constitute its historicity. The plot as a whole, the conflict between Sadko and Novgorod, his descent under water, the figure of the Sea King, etc., are not studied by representatives of the so-called Historical school; patent fiction does not interest them. However, even if it did turn out that the historical Sotko Sytinič was the prototype of Sadko, the historical significance of this bylina would not be explained.

Historical realities can be of great assistance in explaining the fate of a plot. The bylina is rich in realities, and the number increases as epic poetry develops. Among such realities are proper and place names, which must be studied in accordance with contemporary onomastics and toponymics and not by means of the conjectural association of like-sounding words.

An example of how richly the most diverse realities are represented in epic poetry is the comparatively late bylina about Mikúla Seljanínovič.[30] The bylina raises many questions. How do we interpret the act of allotting cities to Prince Vol'ga? What rights and obligations accompanied such allotments and which of them are reflected in the bylina? When were such allotments possible? Can one find these cities on the map? What does the name Vol'ga mean, and how did it find its way into the bylina? Who are Vol'ga's retainers? What is the legal and social position of the peasant in relation to the prince in the bylina? On whose land does Mikula plow? How is his plow constructed? How is he dressed? What agrarian relations are depicted in the bylina? In the bylina Mikula goes to get salt; what is his route? Is natural economy reflected here? In the bylina there are obscure traces of the salt trade being subject to a duty: what monetary system is reflected? The analysis of such details will not bring out the plot's message. The significance of the meeting and conflict between the plowman Mikula and Prince Vol'ga will emerge only from the study of the work's artistic fabric. But the analysis of historical realities helps us to set up the historical meaning of the bylina. There is much for the historian to do here, and the folklorist awaits his assistance. But scholars who represent the method of narrow historical study seize on only two problems of the entire complex: which cities are represented in the bylina and who is the historical prototype of Vol'ga? The idea that Vol'ga may have no prototype at all and that the names of the cities are arbitrary and are of no significance for historical study is not admitted. Mikula, as a patently fictitious personage, has not been studied from this point of view. When he was studied at all, the fact that he wore fine clothes was used in declaring him a representative of the kulaks and of kulak ideology[31] (B. M. Sokolov). This is what the study of details in isolation from the whole can lead to.

Any study of folklore is based on diverse and manifold comparisons. However, we have worked out neither the technique nor the methodology of comparison; so many works, both old and new, abound in false analogies and erroneous conclusions.

I would like to dwell on B. A. Rybakov's treatment of the bylina about Ivan Godinovič (Rybakov 1963, 44-47). His theory is plausible at first sight, but it will not bear close scrutiny. Rybakov dates the bylina to the ninth-tenth centuries. His main argument is as follows: a drinking horn banded with silver was found in Černígov. On the band there is a scene, which, according to Rybakov, reproduces the culmination of the bylina. Archaeologists date the horn to the ninth-tenth centuries, and Rybakov proposes the same dating for the bylina. His syllogism is wrong. We have only the *terminus ante quem*: by the ninth-tenth centuries the plot had already existed, but it could have existed for decades or even centuries before. I believe that this is a prestate plot, later drawn into the Kiev cycle, and reworked in the period preceding the Mongol invasion (Propp 1955, 121-26; 1958b, 126-34).

Let us see what is said in the bylina and what is represented on the horn. The bylina gives the following picture: there is an oak, and Ivan Godinovič is tied to this oak. Close by stands a tent, in which Koščéj Trípetovič and Nastás'ja (Marja) are having a rest. Nastas'ja has been taken away from Ivan Godinovič with her own assistance. On the oak two doves are billing, i.e., they are doing on the the tree what Koščej and Nastas'ja are doing in the tent. This picture annoys Koščej; he takes a bow and shoots at them. But lo and behold! The arrow meant for the doves turns against Koščej and strikes him in the heart, killing him. The denouement is well known: Ivan Godinovič visits a cruel punishment on Nastas'ja and returns to Kiev.

Now what about the horn? There is no oak tree, no tent, no billing doves, and no Ivan Godinovič. Only a huge bird, taller than a man, stands on the ground. Rybakov says that it resembles an eagle, but it is not an eagle; allegedly, it corresponds to the doves. Why so? One singer (Nikífor Próxorov) mentions a prophetic raven instead of the doves. Among the forty-nine variants of the bylina this case occurs only once, but Rybakov relies on it completely and calls the others unimportant and unoriginal.

What else can we see on the horn? There are two human figures, which are represented running and which Rybakov takes for Koščej and Nastas'ja. But where is Ivan Godinovič, the hero of the bylina? Rybakov finds an easy answer: since Ivan Godinovič is absent, he is not the protagonist of the bylina. Who then is the protagonist? The prophetic bird mentioned by one singer is. Rybakov writes, "The absence of Ivan Godinovič proves that the chief personage in the fight against Koščej is not so much Nastas'ja's bridegroom as the bird, which prophesied the death of Koščej, the carrier of evil, and which killed him. This was the view both of the old painter and the bylina." But in the bylina (in one variant) we read:

> A bird, a black raven came,
> The raven alighted on the oaktree
> And said with human words:
> Not Tsar Koščej, Tripet's son,
> But Ivan Godinovič
> Will have Marja Dmitrievična.

(Rybnikov 1910, No. 122, lines 105-110)

Three lines of prophecy are devoted to the bird. The raven does not win any victories. Rybakov believes that the raven, not the doves, represents the oldest form. Can it be so? The raven's prophecy turns out to be false (Ivan Godinovič does not marry Nastas'ja; he kills her); obviously, we are dealing with an individual and unsuccessful treatment of the original motif (the doves).

Let us see what else is represented on the horn. In the air, behind the man, are three arrows, one of which is broken. According to Rybakov, these arrows clinch his argument. He writes, "Now there can be no more doubts about the identity of the bylina and the scene on the horn. The ninth century engraver knew the bylina, in which Koščej is hit not by the first but by the third arrow, as always in folklore tradition: in bylinas and wondertales episodes happen three times." The trouble is that in the bylina Koščej is invariably hit by the first arrow, and this episode does not and cannot treble. Koščej's hand is directed by fate, Providence, justice, and Providence cannot make mistakes.

The doves are messengers of Heaven; some women singers even say that they are angels. They avert Koščej's arrow and direct it against him. So this argument has no foundation in the texts either: the bylina knows nothing of the trebling of the arrows. Some other discrepancies between the bylina and its analysis by Rybakov are also worthy of note.

The bylinas are not tied to the Kiev cycle. But Rybakov is unhappy about the fact, because Vladímir Svjatoslávovič's activity (and Rybakov is certain that the epic Vladimir is the historical Vladimir Svjatoslavovič) falls in the tenth to the beginning of the eleventh centuries, whereas the bylina is dated to the ninth-tenth centuries. What is to be done? Rybakov declares that in this bylina Vladimir is a chance figure. He dissociates the bylina from the Vladimir cycle and calls its ties with the cycle "enforced" and "ornamental." But again the texts tell a different story. In the forty-nine recordings there are hardly three in which Ivan Godinovič sets off on his wooing expedition not from Kiev and without Vladimir's blessing. The bylina is an integral part of the Vladimir cycle.

Let us return to the horn. Rybakov describes the beginning of Ivan Godinovič's expedition so, "In the bylina the hero goes to Černígov through dark woods full of beasts and allows his army to hunt." In fact, there is *not a single* case of a journey through the woods. Either the landscape is not described at all (this is normal) or they go "through the field" (*čistym polem*). Why did Rybakov need wild animals? "On the horn," writes he, "we can see beasts, birds, monsters, and two small dogs." None of this is mentioned in the bylina. Sometimes, on their way back, the heroes discover the tracks of animals in the steppe or on the snow, but no animals, let alone dogs and monsters, occur in the bylina. Ivan Godinovič tells his army to follow the tracks, but this is a transparent device: the hero must meet his adversary alone, and therefore the army (if it is mentioned) is sent hunting. When Ivan Godinovič is accompanied only by a boy, the boy is sent to Kiev with the message that the bride has been obtained.

If the horn indeed represents a folklore plot, there is one that corresponds to it better than the bylina; I mean the wondertale about the hero's unfaithful sister who has a lover resembling Koščej and who tries to undo her brother (Aarne-Andreev, no. 315). She fails in her plans, because her brother has helpers—all kinds of animals called Ivan's hunt. Among them are two dogs, which could explain dogs on the horn. The hero must punish (kill) his sister, but he is unwilling to do so himself. He lets the ordeal settle the matter: though he shoots an arrow into the air (this episode is sometimes trebled), the arrow hits the woman and kills her. All this could also explain why the woman is running away from the man: she is hiding from the arrows that fly in the air behind his back. The bird would be explained too. It is not a raven or eagle, but a hyperbolized hunting falcon or gyrfalcon, the hero's mythic helper. It will not let the woman escape and appears before her like a formidable obstacle. The horn is a hunting trophy, so it can well represent a scene in which the hero is a hunter and in which the "hunt" saves him from a woman's wiles.

I do not imply that the horn represents a wondertale rather than a bylina plot; I only wish to show that more plausible explanations than Rybakov's can be advanced. In all probability, what we see on the horn (a hunting trophy) is an epic hunt with many animals, real and fabulous, dogs, and a falcon. The man has broken and used up his arrows (hence the arrows flying all over the place) and is running to the woman, who has a huge quiver at her belt. Both are running, and this is a common occurrence during the hunt. Incidentally, it is far from clear that the second figure is a woman. Perhaps it is a boy, a servant, an armor bearer with another bow and a big, heavy quiver.

Rybakov reproaches Soviet folklorists with the lack of historicity. Where does he himself see the historicity of this bylina? According to the precepts of the Historical school, the first sign of historicity is exact dating. But if the horn does not represent the plot of the bylina about Ivan Godinovič, the dating, the ninth-tenth centuries, flimsy as it is, collapses altogether. The methods of the Historical school require the analysis of names. Rybakov does not interpret Ivan Godinovič's name, but pays attention to Koščej's name. Strictly speaking, Koščej is not a name: it is the designation of a wondertale personage.[32] In the *Lay of the Host of Igor* the Pečeneg Končák[33] is called "a heathen Koščej." Rybakov concludes that the Koščej of this bylina also refers to the Pečenegs, and, since the horn was found in Černigov, the bylina reflects "an epic tale about the victory of Černigov over the nomadic Pečenegs." Ergo, Koščej is a Pečeneg and a nomad. Nothing is said about who represents the people of Černigov in the bylina, but, since the hero responsible for the victory is admittedly the raven, the raven alone appears to represent Černigov, and Koščej must represent the defeated Pečenegs.

Rybakov goes even further. Until 1917 in the Černigov coat of arms there was an eagle with wings outspread. Rybakov identifies this eagle with the bird on the horn and the prophetic raven in the bylina. This is the last argument for the theory that the bylina's historical foundation is the fight of Černigov against the Pečenegs.

I have examined in minute detail the analysis of one bylina by a distinguished modern follower of the prerevolutionary Historical school. This was just a sample. I could have gone over similar argumentation in the works of other adepts of this school. By now the school can offer nothing, and a return to it is impossible, in spite of some achievements in the works of its representatives.

In a short article one certainly cannot elucidate all the problems of the historicity of folklore. I have touched only on those which are now the most pressing and whose solution is necessary for the further development of the Soviet science of folklore.

II. The Wondertale

Chapter Five.
The Structural
and Historical Study
of the Wondertale

Morphology of the Folktale was published in Russian in 1928 and elicited two kinds of reaction. Some folklorists, ethnographers, and literary scholars received it favorably, while others accused its author of formalism, and this accusation has often been repeated even in our day. The book, like so many others, would probably have been forgotten or remembered occasionally only by specialists, but a few years after the war it emerged again. It was frequently mentioned at congresses and in articles, and it was translated into English (Propp 1958a; 1968a). The cause of this renewed interest should be sought in the revolutionary discoveries made in the exact sciences through the use of much more advanced and reliable methods of research and computation. Attempts to apply similar methods extended to the humanities as well. Structural and mathematical linguistics sprang up, and other disciplines followed, poetics among them. Then it appeared that the concept of art as a system of signs, the procedure of formalization and modeling, and the possibility of using computation had been anticipated in *Morphology*, although at the time it was written the concepts and the terminology with which poetics operates today did not exist. Once again this work was evaluated in two different ways. Some considered it useful and necessary in the search for new methods, whereas others, just as before, found it formalistic and devoid of any epistemological value.

Among the opponents of the book is Professor Claude Lévi-Strauss. He is a structuralist, and the structuralists themselves have often been accused of formalism; Lévi-Strauss has used *Morphology*, which he takes for a basically formalistic book, to show the difference between structuralism and formalism (Lévi-Strauss 1960). Let the reader decide whether or not Lévi-Strauss is right; but when one is attacked, one tries to defend oneself. If the arguments of the adversary seem faulty, one can put forward counterarguments, and such a polemic may be of general interest. Therefore I gladly accepted the invitation of the Einaudi Publishers to write a rejoinder. Lévi-Strauss has thrown down the gauntlet, and I am ready to pick it up. Readers of *Morphology* will thus witness our duel and will be able to determine the winner, should there be one.

Lévi-Strauss has a very important advantage over me: he is a philosopher, whereas I am an empiricist, indeed an incorruptible empiricist, who first scrutinizes the facts and studies them carefully, checking his premises and looking back at every step in his reasoning. However, the empirical sciences are also all different. In some instances the empiricist can and even must limit himself to a mere description, especially if the object under study is an isolated fact. Such descriptions, provided they are correct, are in no way devoid of value. But if we are describing a series of facts and their relationships, our description will bring out what is essential in the phenomenon, and, apart from being of interest to the specialist, will invite philosophical meditations. In my book such meditations were present too, but they were hidden in the epigraphs to some chapters. Lévi-Strauss knows my work only in an English translation; the translator, however, has taken an unpardonable liberty. He missed my point and did not understand the function of the epigraphs. At first glance, they do not seem to belong to the text, so he decided that they were useless embellishments and barbarously suppressed them. Yet the epigraphs were from Goethe's works collected under the title of *Morphology* and from his journals; their purpose was to express certain things not stated in the text of the book.[1]

The highest goal of every science is to discover laws. Where the naive empiricist sees only disjointed facts, the empiricist-philosopher recognizes a law. I noticed a law in a small and narrow area—one type of folktale, but it occurred to me even then that the discovery of this law could also be of some general importance. The word *morphology* was not borrowed from manuals of botany whose chief purpose is classification, or from grammatical treatises; it came from the writings of Goethe, who used this unifying term in the title of his works on botany and osteology. Behind Goethe's term, we can see the prospect of discovering general laws that permeate all nature. It is not by chance that Goethe went on from botany to comparative osteology. I can heartily recommend these works to the structuralists. And if the young Goethe, like his own Faust seated in a dusty laboratory among skeletons, bones, and herbaria, saw nothing in them except the mortal dust, the aging Goethe, a master of precise comparisons in the field of natural sciences, saw in individual phenomena the common and general principle that permeates all nature. But two Goethes, the poet and the scholar, do not exist; the Goethe of *Faust*, who longed for knowledge, and Goethe, the naturalist, who attained it, are one and the same person. By starting some chapters with epigraphs, I paid homage to him. The epigraphs also emphasized that the realms of nature and human creativity are not separated. Something unites them;

laws common to both can be studied by related methods. This idea, still vague at that time, now underlies the search for exact methods in the humanities. This is one of the reasons that the structuralists have supported me. On the other hand, some structuralists failed to understand that my goal was not to arrive at the broad generalizations alluded to in the epigraphs but to investigate a specific area of folklore. The puzzled Lévi-Strauss twice asked a question about what had made me apply my method to the wondertale. He himself stated these reasons, of which, he believes, there are several. He asserts that I am not an ethnologist and therefore could not avail myself of mythological material and that I have no idea of the relationships between the wondertale and myth. It turns out that I studied the wondertale because of my scholarly limitations; otherwise, I would probably have tested my method on myths, not on wondertales.

I will not dwell on the logic of these arguments ("since the author does not know myths, he studies wondertales"). This logic seems poor to me, and I think that no scholar can be forbidden to do one thing and urged to do another. According to Lévi-Strauss, a scholar first finds the method and then begins to think where to apply it; in my case it has been applied, regrettably, to wondertales, an area of little interest to the philosopher. But things never happen so in science; nor did they happen this way in my case. Before the Revolution, Russian universities cared very little about the literary training of philologists. Folk poetry in particular was completely neglected. To fill that gap, I devoted myself after graduation to the study of Afanas'ev's famous collection. In a series of wondertales about the persecuted stepdaughter I noted an interesting fact: in "Morozko" [Frost] (No. 95 in Soviet editions) the stepmother sends her stepdaughter into the woods to Morozko. He tries to freeze her to death, but she speaks to him so sweetly and so humbly that he spares her, gives her a reward, and lets her go. The old woman's daughter, however, fails the test and perishes. In another tale the stepdaughter encounters not Morozko but a *lešij* [a wood goblin], in still another, a bear. But surely it is the same tale! Morozko, the *lešij*, and the bear test the stepdaughter and reward her each in his own way, but the plot does not change. Was it possible that no one should ever have noticed this before? Why did Afanas'ev and others think that they were dealing with different tales? It is obvious that Morozko, the *lešij*, and the bear performed the same action. To Afanas'ev these were different tales because of different characters in them. To me they were identical because the actions of the characters were the same. The idea seemed interesting, and I began to examine other wondertales from the point of view of the actions performed by the characters. As a result of studying the material (and not through abstract reasoning), I devised a very simple method of analyzing wondertales in accordance with the characters' actions—regardless of their concrete form. To designate these actions I adopted the term "functions." My observations of the tale of the persecuted stepdaughter allowed me to get hold of the end of the thread and unravel the entire spool. It turned out that the other plots were also based on the recurrence of functions and that all wondertale plots consisted of identical functions and had identical structure.

If the translator has done the reader a bad turn by leaving out the epigraphs from Goethe, the original Russian publisher also violated the author's will, for he changed the title of the book. I called it *Morphology of the Wondertale*. To make the book more attractive, the editor replaced the word *wondertale* and in this way led everybody (including Lévi-Strauss) to believe that the book would concern itself with the general laws of the folktale. A work with this title could be included in a series of studies like *Morphology of the Charm, Morphology of the Fable, Morphology of Comedy*, and so forth. But my intention was not to study all the various and complex types of the folktale; I examined only one strikingly distinctive type, viz., the folk wondertale. The book is devoted to a specific area of folklore. The analysis of narrative genres according to the functions of the characters can perhaps be applied to other tales and even to any narrative. If so, in each case the results will be different. For instance, cumulative tales and wondertales are based on totally dissimilar principles. English folklorists call cumulative tales formula tales, and the types of formulas can be isolated and defined, but the schemes of the cumulative tale and the wondertale will not coincide. Thus, though several kinds of narrative occur, they can be analyzed by the same methods. Lévi-Strauss cited the statement in which I admit that my conclusions are not applicable to the tales of Novalis and Goethe and to the *Kunstmärchen* in general and turned it against me: allegedly, if my statement is true, my conclusions are wrong. But they are not wrong; they merely lack the universal character that my esteemed critic wished to attribute to them. The method is broad, but the conclusions are valid for the type of narrative that yielded them in the first place.

I will not respond to all of Lévi-Strauss's charges and will dwell only on some of the most important ones. If these prove to be unfounded, the other, less important ones, derived from them, will fall by themselves.

His main charge is that my work is of a formalistic stamp and for that reason alone cannot be of any epistemological value. Lévi-Strauss has not provided a precise definition of what he means by formalism; he just limits himself to some characteristics that he points out as he goes along. One of them is that the formalists study their data without reference to history. Lévi-Strauss attributed such a formalistic, ahistorical method to me too, but then, in a seeming attempt to mitigate his harsh judgment somewhat, informed the readers that I had renounced formalism and morphological analysis after I wrote my *Morphology* and devoted myself to the historical and comparative study of the relationships between oral literature (as he calls folklore) and myths, rites, and institutions. He did not, however, specify which study he meant. In my book *Russian Agrarian Festivals* (1963a) I used the same method as in *Morphology*. I discovered that all the principal agrarian festivals consist of identical elements organized differently. This work could not at that time have been known to Lévi-Strauss, so he is evidently referring to my *Historical Roots of the Wondertale*, which appeared in 1946. If he had taken a look at that volume, he would have realized that it begins with an exposition of the theses developed in *Morphology*. There the wondertale is defined not through the plot, but through composition. In fact, once the unity of the composition of the wondertale was established, I could do no less than ask myself the cause of this unity. It was clear to me from the beginning that the cause would not be found in immanent laws of form and that it should be sought in early history, or prehistory, that is, in the stage of human society studied by ethnology and ethnography. Lévi-Strauss is perfectly right when he says that morphology is sterile if it is not bound directly or indirectly to data from ethnology. For this very reason I did not abandon morphological analysis but set myself the task of searching for the historical foundations and historical roots of the system revealed by a comparative study of wondertale plots. *Morphology* and *Historical Roots* represent, so to speak, two parts, or two volumes, of a single work—the second proceeds directly from the first, the first is the premise of the second. Lévi-Strauss cited my statement that morphological research should be connected with historical inquiry and once again turned my words against me. Insofar as this research is absent from *Morphology*, he is right, but he has underestimated the fact that these words were the expression of a specific principle. In addition, they represented a promise to do this historical research in the future, a bill that I honestly paid, even if many years later. So when he says that I am torn between the "formalist vision" and the "obsession with historical explanations," he is simply wrong. Using the most rigorously consistent means possible, I went from the scientific description of the phenomena and facts to an explanation of their historical roots. Lévi-Strauss knows nothing of all this and even claims to have detected some sort of repentance in me that presumably made me abandon my formalist illusions for historical investigations. But I do not feel any remorse and do not have the least twinge of conscience. Lévi-Strauss maintains that a historical explanation of wondertales is impossible "because we know very little about the prehistorical civilizations in which they sprang up" and regrets the lack of texts for comparison. But the problem is not confined to texts (which, incidentally, exist in quite sufficient quantity); what really matters is that plots are engendered by the life of the people and the forms of thought at the early stages of social development and that the appearance of these plots is historically determined. It is true that we still know little about ethnology, but scholars have gathered enough data to make such inquiries reliable.

Clearly, questions of principle are more important than the ways in which *Morphology* was conceived. It is inadmissible to separate formal inquiry from the historical approach and juxtapose them. On the contrary, formal analysis, that is, a careful systematic description of the material, is the first condition, prerequisite, and the first step of historical research. Individual plots have been studied in great detail: cf. the works of the Finnish school. But their authors see no connection among the plots; they do not even suspect that such a connection exists or is possible. This is the characteristic orientation of the formalists, for whom the whole is a mechanical conglomeration of disjointed parts. Consequently, the wondertale is represented by them as so many individual plots. The structuralist, on the other hand, detects a system where the formalist inevitably fails to see one. The method elaborated in *Morphology* makes it possible to rise above the plots and study the genre of the wondertale as a whole, rather than pass from plot to plot, as is done by the Finnish school, which has been justly accused of formalism, all its merits notwithstanding. The comparative study of plots opens up wide historical perspectives. What needs historical explanation is not individual plots but the compositional system to which they belong. This approach will bring out the historical connections among them and pave the way for the study of individual plots.

The relation between formal and historical analysis covers only one aspect of the question. Another aspect is the relation between content and form and the methods of studying them. The term *formalistic* usually implies the study of form divorced from content. Lévi-Strauss even speaks of the two as being juxtaposed. His conclusions do not differ from those of contemporary Soviet literary scholars. Thus, according to Jurij Lotman (1968, 11), one of the most active literary structuralists, the principal flaw of the so-called formal method was the view of literature as a sum total of devices, a mechanical conglomeration. To this can also be added that for the formalists form is governed by its own independent laws and its development is free from the pressure of social history. Literary development is treated as an immanent process subject to the laws of form.

If this is what is meant by formalism, *Morphology of the Folktale* cannot possibly be defined as formalistic, even though Lévi-Strauss is far from being my only accuser. Not every study of form is formalistic, and not every scholar who examines form in oral and visual art is a formalist.

I have already cited Lévi-Strauss's statement that my observations regarding the structure of the wondertale are an illusion, *une vision formaliste*. This is not a casual opinion; the author is deeply convinced that I am a victim of illusions. Out of many tales I allegedly constructed one that never existed, and this one is "an abstraction so vague and general that it tells us nothing about the causes of the existence of so many tales." That my abstraction, as Lévi-Strauss calls my scheme, does not reveal the causes of diversity is true; only historical research can do that. But it is not true that the scheme is vague and represents sheer illusion. Lévi-Strauss's words suggest that he failed to understand my empirical, concrete, and detailed investigation. How could that have happened? Lévi-Strauss complained that my work was in general difficult to understand. It happens quite often that people who have many ideas of their own have difficulty following those of other people. They do not see what is clear to any unprejudiced person. My approach is at variance with Lévi-Strauss's, and that is one of the reasons for the misunderstanding. Another is related to me. I wrote the book when I was young; I believed that it was enough to put forward an observation or an idea for everyone to grasp and share it immediately. My style was terse; I expressed myself in theorem form and did not care for detailed proofs, because I thought that even in that form they would be clear at first view. I was wrong about that.

Let us begin with the terms. I must admit that Goethe's term *Morphology*, which was once so dear to me and to which I attributed a meaning not only scientific but in part philosophical and even poetic, was not a good choice after all. I should have spoken not of morphology but of a much more narrow and accurate concept, that of composition, and should have entitled the book *Composition of the Folk Wondertale*. But even "composition" ought to be defined, because it can mean many things. So what do I mean?

As stated above, my analysis originated in the observation that in the wondertale different characters perform identical actions, or, what is the same thing, that identical actions can be performed in very different ways. I have cited as evidence the tales of the persecuted stepdaughter, but this observation is valid not only for the variants of this plot but for every wondertale plot. So, for example, if the hero leaves home in quest of something, and the object of his desires is far away, he can reach it by magic horse, eagle, flying carpet, flying ship, astride the devil, etc. I will not enumerate all the possibilities. It will be easily seen that in each case we are dealing with the transfer of the hero to the place where the object of his search is located, but that the forms in which the transfer is realized are different. We have both constants and variables. Let us take another example. The princess does not wish to marry, or her father does not want her to marry a suitor he or she dislikes. The suitor is required to perform impossible tasks: to jump to her window on horseback, bathe in a cauldron of boiling water, solve the princess's riddle, procure a golden hair from the sea king, etc. To the uninitiated listener all these variants seem completely different, and in a way he is right. But to the sophisticated scholar this diversity conceals a logically determinable unity. In the first series of examples we are dealing with the transfer to the place of the search, whereas in the second we have the motif of difficult tasks. The content of the tasks varies, but the presence of a task is something stable. I called such stable elements the functions of the characters. The goal of my investigation was to establish which functions appear in the wondertale, to determine whether they are limited in number and what sequence they follow. In my book I discussed the results of this analysis. The functions turned out to be few, their forms many, the sequence always the same. A picture of surprising regularity has been obtained.

It seemed to me that all this was simple enough and easy to understand. I still think so. I did not, however, take into account that the word "function" has many different meanings in the languages of the world. It is used in mathematics, mechanics, medicine, and philosophy. Those who do not know all these meanings understand me easily. Function, according to my definition of the term (as used in *Morphology*), denotes the action of the character from the point of view of its significance for the progress of the narrative. If the hero jumps to the princess's window on horseback, we do not have the function of jumping on horseback (such a definition would be accurate only if we disregarded the advance of the narrative as a whole) but the function of performing a difficult task as part of courtship. Likewise, if an eagle takes the hero to the country of the princess, we do not have the function of flying on a bird but one of transfer to the place where the object of the search is located. The word "function" is a conventional term that was to be understood in this and no other sense.

I deduced the functions from detailed comparative analyses. Therefore, I cannot agree with Lévi-Strauss when he says that the functions were established in an altogether arbitrary and subjective way. On the contrary, they were established through the comparison, juxtaposition, and identification of hundreds and thousands of cases. But Lévi-Strauss gives the term "function" a meaning completely different from the one adopted in *Morphology*. To show that the functions were arbitrary, he refers to the example of different people guarding a fruit tree: one would consider fertility most important, another, deep roots, whereas a savage would attribute to it the function of joining heaven and earth (the tree can reach up to heaven). From the point of view of logic, fertility can indeed be defined as one of the functions of a fruit tree, but fertility is not an action, much less an action of a character in a narrative. I devote myself only to narratives and their specific laws. Lévi-Strauss gives my terms a generalized, abstract meaning that they do not have and then rejects that meaning.

We can now turn to composition. By composition I mean the sequence of functions as given in the tale itself. The resultant scheme is not an archetype or the reconstruction of a single imaginary tale (as my critic thinks) but something altogether different: it is the compositional scheme underlying all wondertales. Lévi-Strauss is right about one thing: this compositional scheme has no real existence. However, it is realized in the narrative in many different forms: it is the basis of the plot and is, so to speak, its skeleton. To make my idea clearer and avoid further misunderstandings, I will give one example of what is meant by the plot and by composition. Let us imagine that a dragon has carried off the king's daughter. The king appeals for help, and a peasant's son decides to search for her. He sets out and on the way meets an old woman who asks him to look after a herd of wild horses. He does so, and she gives him one of the horses, which carries him to the island where the dragon guards the abducted princess. The hero kills the dragon and returns, and the king rewards him by bestowing upon him the hand of his daughter. This is the plot of the tale, whereas the composition can be outlined as follows: a misfortune occurs; the hero is asked to help; he sets off; on the way he meets someone who puts him to the test and rewards him with a magic tool; with its help he finds the sought-for object; the hero returns and is rewarded. The same composition can lie at the bottom of many plots and, conversely, many plots are based on the same composition. Composition is a constant factor; the plot, a variable one. But for a danger of further terminological misunderstandings, I could have referred to the plot and composition together as the structure of the wondertale. Composition has no real existence, just as all general concepts have no existence in the world of things: they are found only in man's mind. But with the use of these general concepts we explore the world, discover its laws, and learn to control it.

In studying the wondertale we note that some functions (actions of the characters) are binary. For example, a difficult task implies its solution, pursuit ends with rescue, the battle leads to victory, the initial misfortune or disaster is liquidated at the conclusion, and so forth. According to Lévi-Strauss, binary functions are complementary and should be reduced to one. That may be true on a logical plane. In a certain way, battle and victory do form one whole. But for the study of composition such mechanical associations are unsuitable and misleading. The binary functions are performed by different people; e.g., the difficult task is imposed by one character and resolved by another. The second half of a binary function can be positive or negative. In the wondertale we encounter a true hero and a false one: the first accomplishes the task and is rewarded, the second fails and is punished. Again, binary functions are separated by intermediate ones. Thus, the abduction of the princess (the initial misfortune) is found at the beginning of the tale, while her return takes place only at the end. Therefore, in the study of composition, that is, of the sequence of functions, reduction of the binary elements to a single one will not reveal the laws that govern the development of the plot. A logical arrangement of functions is detrimental to our search.

For the same reason I cannot accept another recommendation. I tried hard to discover the order in which narrators arranged their functions. It turned out that the order is always the same, a very important discovery to the folklorist. The narrative action develops in time, and therefore the functions are ordered in sequence. Lévi-Strauss does not approve of this method of analyzing and ordering the functions. He uses the letters of the alphabet A B C D for designating the sequence. Instead of a natural order, he proposes a logical system. He would like to arrange the functions vertically and horizontally. This sort of arrangement is one of the requirements of the structuralists' technique, and it is present in *Morphology*, only in another form. Probably my critic did not pay enough attention to the end of the book, to the appendix entitled "Materials for the Tabulation of the Tale." The rubrics given there represent the horizontal. The table is a detailed compositional scheme of what is designated in the text by letters. Under these rubrics one can put the actual material of the tale, and this would constitute the vertical. There is no need to replace this completely concrete scheme derived from the comparison of texts with another, which is the result of pure abstraction. The difference between my way of reasoning and that of my critic is that I draw my abstractions from the data, whereas Lévi-Strauss draws abstractions from my abstractions. He asserts that there is no way back from my abstract schemes to the material, but if he had taken any collection of wondertales and compared them with my scheme, he would have found that the scheme does indeed correspond to the material and that the structure of the wondertale is a fact. Moreover, with the scheme as a starting point one can compose an infinite number of tales, all constructed according to the same law as the folktales. If we leave out certain incompatible varieties, we can calculate mathematically the number of possible combinations. If one wishes to call my scheme a model, this model reproduces all the constructive elements (constants) of the wondertale and passes over the nonconstructive elements (variables). My model corresponds to what was modeled and is based on a study of data, whereas the model Lévi-Strauss proposes does not correspond to reality and is based on logical operations not imposed by the data. An abstraction drawn from data serves to explain them; an abstraction drawn from abstractions is an end in itself; it is divorced from data, may find itself at odds with the facts of the real world, and hence is incapable of explaining it. Lévi-Strauss carries out his logical operations in total disregard of the material (he is not in the least interested in the wondertale, nor does he attempt to learn more about it) and removes the functions from their temporal sequence. The folklorist is unable to endorse such a procedure, because the function (act, behavior, action), as it is defined in my book, is played out in time and cannot be removed from it. Incidentally, the concepts of time, space, and number in the wondertale are completely different from those to which we are accustomed and which we tend to consider absolute. This is a special problem, and I have alluded to it only because the forced removal of the functions from the temporal sequence destroys the artistic fabric of the narrative, which, like a fine and elegant web, falls apart at the slightest touch. This is another reason for setting the functions in time, as the narrative itself demands, and not in an atemporal series *(structure a-temporelle)*, as Lévi-Strauss would have it.

The folklorist and the literary scholar are mainly interested in the plot. In Russian the term *plot (sjužét)* has a well-defined meaning; it refers to all actions and incidents developed in the course of the narrative. The English translator has rendered *sjužet* quite accurately by the word *plot*, and, as we know, the German periodical devoted to narrative art is entitled *Fabula*. But the plot is of no interest to Lévi-Strauss, and he translated this word into French as *thème*. Evidently he preferred *thème* because the plot is a temporal category, whereas *thème* is not. No student of literature will ever accept this substitution. The terms *plot* and *theme* can be understood in very many ways but they can never be used interchangeably. This lack of interest in the plot and narrative is also seen in other instances of imprecise translation. Thus, when the hero encounters an old woman (or another character) who puts him to the test and gives him an object or a magic device, this character, in exact accord with his function, was defined in my work as *darítel'* (giver). The magic objects that the hero receives have been called magic gifts (Germ. *Zaubergaben*) by folklorists. This is a specific term. The English translator has rendered the word *daritel'* as *donor,* which fits the wondertale perfectly and perhaps is even better than *daritel'*, because the gift is not always voluntary. Lévi-Strauss translated it as *bienfaiteur*, which once again lends the term such a general and abstract sense that it becomes meaningless.

After all these digressions necessary for a better understanding of what follows we can get down to form and content. As has been mentioned earlier, it is customary to call the study of form divorced from content formalistic. I must admit that I do not understand what all this means and understand neither the statement nor its practical application. Perhaps I would understand it if I knew where, in a work of art, to look for form and where for content. One can indulge in endless discussions of form and content as philosophical categories, but the arguments will be fruitless as long as they concern form and content in general, without reference to the data.

In folklore aesthetics, the plot makes up the content of a work. For the people the content of the tale "Firebird" is the story of how this bird flew into the king's garden and stole the golden apple and how the prince went in search of it and returned not only with the firebird but with a horse and a beautiful bride. What happened in the tale constitutes the entire interest. Let us assume for the moment the point of view of the people (incidentally, a very clever point of view). If the plot is the content, then composition is not. Thus, we reach the conclusion that composition belongs to form. If that is true, different kinds of content can be put into a single form. But I said earlier that composition and the plot are inseparable: the plot cannot exist without composition, nor composition without the plot. On our own data, we have arrived at the well-known truth that form and content are inseparable. Lévi-Strauss himself says: "Form and content have the same nature and are subject to the same analysis." This is without doubt so, but if form and content are inseparable and even identical in nature, he who analyzes the one necessarily analyzes the other. Where then is the sin of formalism and what is my crime when I analyze the plot (content) and composition (form) in their indissoluble union?

Yet this idea of content and form is not so common after all, and it is not clear whether it can be applied to other kinds of verbal art. Form usually means genre; therefore, the same plot can take the form of a novel, a tragedy, a film script, etc. Lévi-Strauss's idea is brilliantly confirmed by attempts to rewrite a narrative work for the stage or adapt it for the screen. A novel by Zola as a book and on the screen are two different works that usually have very little in common. Again, content in most cases refers not to the plot but to the message, to the author's idea, world outlook, and views. Innumerable attempts have been made to study and appraise the writer's outlook but in most cases they have been hopelessly amateurish. Leo Tolstoy used to deride such attempts. When asked what he intended to say in his novel *Anna Karenina*, he answered, "If I wished to say in words all that I intended to express in the novel, I would have to write from the very beginning the same novel that I had already written. And if critics understand and can express in a newspaper article what I want to say, I must congratulate them" (Tolstoy 1953, 268-69). If in literature the work of art is the form in which an idea is expressed, it is all the more so in folklore. Here we have such strict laws of form (in composition) that ignoring them results in great mistakes. According to his own political, social, historical, and religious conceptions, the scholar will attribute to the tale and folklore his own view of the world and discover mystical, atheistic, revolutionary, or conservative attitudes in them. This in no way means that ideas of folklore cannot be studied, but it does mean that idea ("content") can be analyzed scientifically and objectively only after the formal laws have been clarified. I quite agree with Lévi-Strauss when he demands research into history and literary criticism. However, he demands them as a substitute for what he calls formal study, and I am convinced that preliminary form analysis is the prerequisite for both historical and critical inquiry. If *Morphology* is, in a certain sense, the first volume of a broad investigation and *Historical Roots*, the second, the third could have been literary criticism. Only when the wondertale has been studied formally and its historical roots have been determined is it possible to analyze objectively and scientifically the growth of folk philosophy and folk morality as they are found in the tale. This analysis will reveal a stratified organization, a structure similar to that of geological sediments in which ancient layers are combined with the more recent and even modern ones. We will examine all variable elements, all the colors of this structure, for the tale's artistry is not restricted to its composition. To study and understand all this, we must first know the foundation underlying the amazing variety of the wondertale.

I cannot respond to all of Lévi-Strauss's observations; however, I would like to dwell on a specific but interesting question, that of the relationships between the wondertale and myth. For the present discussion this is not a very important problem, because my research is devoted to the wondertale rather than to myth, but Lévi-Strauss is an expert in mythology, and here again he does not agree with me.

In my book, I said very little—and that concisely and without proof—about the relationships between the wondertale and myth. I made the mistake of expressing my ideas apodictically, but unproven concepts are not always wrong. I believe that myth as a historical category is older than the wondertale; Lévi-Strauss maintains the opposite. This is no place for going into the problem, but it deserves at least a brief mention.

What constitutes the difference between the wondertale and myth for the

folklorist and in what respects are they alike? One of the properties of the wondertale is that it is based on poetic fiction and is a distortion of reality. In most
languages the word *tale* is a synonym for *lie* or *falsehood*. "The tale is over;
I can't lie any more"—thus do Russian narrators conclude their stories. Myth,
on the other hand, is a sacral narrative; not only is it believed to be true, it also
expresses the faith of the people. Consequently, the difference between them is
not formal. Myths can take the narrative form that should be studied, even though
this has not been done in my book. According to Lévi-Strauss, "myth and the
wondertale exploit a common substance," which is perfectly true if by substance
is meant the advance in the narrative or the plot. There are myths based on the
same morphological and compositional system as the wondertale. Such are, for
example, classical myths of the Argonauts, Perseus and Andromeda, Theseus,
and many others. At times they correspond, down to minute details, to the compositional system studied in *Morphology of the Folktale*. In some cases, myth
and the wondertale have the same form. But the correspondence is by no means
universal: a great number of myths from antiquity (actually, most of them) have
nothing in common with the wondertale system. This is even more true of the
myths of primitives. The cosmogonical myths, myths of the creation and origin
of the world, animals, men and things are totally different from the wondertale
and cannot be transformed into it; they are based on a morphological system of
their own. Many such systems exist, and mythology has been studied very little
from this point of view. Where the wondertale and myth are based on the same
system, myth is always older than the wondertale, as follows, for instance, from
the history of the plot of Sophocles' *Oedipus* (Propp 1944). In Hellas it was a
myth. In the Middle Ages the plot acquired a sacral Christian character, and its
protagonist became the great sinner Judas or a saint such as Gregory, Andrew
of Crete, or Alban, who were redeemed from great sin by their great virtue. But
when the hero loses his name and the story loses its sacral character, myth and
legend are transformed into a wondertale. Lévi-Strauss is of another opinion.
He does not agree that myth is older than the wondertale and says that they can
coexist and do coexist to this day. "In present times, myths and folktales exist
side by side. One genre cannot then be held to be a survival of the other" (Lévi-
Strauss 1976, 130). [2] The example of *Oedipus* shows, however, that in the course
of historical development plots can shift from one form (myth) to another (legend)
and from that to a third (wondertale). Any folklorist knows that plots very often
migrate from genre to genre (the plots of the wondertale end up in epic poetry,
etc.). But Lévi-Strauss is not referring to actual plots. He uses the words *myths*
and *wondertale* as vague cover terms, that is, myth "in general" and the wondertale "in general"; he considers the genre as such, without distinguishing types
and plots. Therefore he speaks of their coexistence up to the present day. In this
instance he is not thinking like a historian. Of importance are not the centuries
but historical periods and social structures (formations). Study of the most ar-

chaic and primitive peoples shows that *all* their folklore (as well as visual art) is of sacral, or magical, character. What is passed off in popular publications and, at times, even in scholarly editions as wondertales of primitives very often has nothing to do with the wondertale. It is well known that animal tales were once told not as tales but as magic stories whose purport was to contribute to a successful hunt. Such material is abundant. The wondertale originated later than myth, and for a certain time they can indeed coexist, but only if the plots of myths and wondertales belong to different systems of composition and represent different plots. Classical antiquity recognized both wondertales and myths, but their plots differed. The myth of the Argonauts and the wondertale of the Argonauts cannot coexist among the same people. There could be no wondertales about Theseus where his myth was alive and where he was the object of a cult. Finally, in present-day advanced social formations, the existence of myths is no longer possible. The role of sacred tradition that they played at one time has been taken over by sacral legends and religious narrative. In the socialist countries even these last remnants of myths and sacral legends are disappearing. So the problem of the relative antiquity of myth and the wondertale and the possibility or impossibility of their coexistence cannot be solved in a general way. The solution depends on the stage of historical development. It is necessary to know and understand different morphological systems and to know how to distinguish them in order to be able to determine affinities and differences between the wondertale and myth and to judge their relative antiquity and the possibility or impossibility of their coexistence. The question is more complex than Lévi-Strauss seems to think.

We can now draw some conclusions. The philosopher will consider correct those statements that correspond to a particular brand of philosophy. The scholar will consider correct those that follow from the study of the data. Lévi-Strauss says that my conclusions do not correspond, as he puts it, to the nature of things; yet he does not mention a single instance in which my conclusions concerning the wondertale were found to be wrong, though only such concrete objections are the most dangerous to the scholar and also the most desirable, useful, and valuable.

Another important problem is method. According to Lévi-Strauss, my method is wrong because actions can be transferred from one person to another and the same actions can be performed by different characters not only in the wondertale. This observation is quite correct, but it argues for, rather than against, my method. Thus, if in cosmogonical myths the crow, the mink, and the anthropomorphic creature or divinity can assume the role of the demiurge, this means that myths can and must be studied by the same methods as the wondertale. The conclusions will differ, and many morphological systems will emerge, but the methods can remain the same.

It is very possible that the method of analyzing narratives according to the functions of characters will prove useful both for the narrative forms of literature and folklore. However, the methods proposed in my book before the appearance of structuralism, as well as the methods of the structuralists who aim at the objective study of literature, have their limitations. They are possible and profitable where recurrence is the norm, as in language and folklore. But when art becomes the product of a unique genius, the use of exact methods will yield positive results only if the study of recurring elements goes hand in hand with the study of the unique, which to us is simply a miracle. It matters little how we will classify *The Divine Comedy* or Shakespeare's tragedies: Dante and Shakespeare stand alone, and exact methods will not explain their genius. At the beginning of this article I emphasized the affinity between the laws of the exact sciences and the humanities. I would like to conclude it by stressing the fundamental specific difference between them.

Chapter Six.
Transformations
of the Wondertale

1. The study of the wondertale may be compared to the study of organic formations in nature. Both the naturalist and the folklorist deal with species and genera of essentially the same phenomena. The Darwinian problem of "the origin of species" arises in folklore as well. The similarity of phenomena in nature and folklore resists any direct, objective, and absolutely convincing explanation. It is a problem in its own right. Both fields allow two points of view: either the internal similarity of two externally unrelated phenomena cannot be traced to a common genetic root (theory of spontaneous generation) or else this morphological similarity results from a genetic tie (theory of origin by metamorphoses or transformations traceable to certain causes).

To resolve this problem, we need a clear understanding of what is meant by similarity in wondertales. Similarity has so far been defined in terms of a plot and its variants. Such a method is acceptable only to those who believe in the spontaneous generation of species. Supporters of this method do not compare plots; they feel such comparison to be impossible or, at the very least, erroneous.[1] We do not deny the value of studying individual plots or comparing them solely from the standpoint of their similarity but propose another method, another basis for comparison. Wondertales can be compared from the standpoint of their composition and structure; their similarity then appears in a new light.[2]

We can see that the characters of the wondertale perform essentially the same actions as the tale progresses, no matter how much they differ in shape, age, sex, occupation, nomenclature, and other static attributes. This determines the relationship between the constant and the variable factors. The functions of the characters are constant; everything else is variable. For example:

1. The king sends Ivan after the princess; Ivan departs.
2. The king sends Ivan after some wonder; Ivan departs.

82

3. The sister sends her brother for some medicine; he departs.
4. The stepmother sends her stepdaughter for fire; she departs.
5. The smith sends his laborer for a cow; he departs.

The dispatch and the departure on a quest are constants. The dispatching and departing characters, the motivation behind the dispatch, and so forth, are variables. Further along, stages of the quest, obstacles, etc., can again be basically the same but differ in their realization in images. The functions of the characters can be isolated. Wondertales exhibit thirty-one functions, not all of which are found in any one tale; however, the absence of certain functions does not interfere with the order of appearance of the others. Together they constitute one system, one composition. This system has proved to be very stable and widespread. The folklorist can demonstrate that, for instance, the ancient Egyptian tale of two brothers,[3] the tales of the firebird,[4] of Morózko [Frost],[5] of the fisherman and the fish,[6] and a number of myths follow the same general pattern. Analysis of the details bears out this conclusion. Thirty-one functions do not exhaust the system. Such a motif as "Baba Jaga gives Ivan a horse" contains four elements, only one of which represents a function, while the other three are of a static nature.

All in all, the wondertale displays about one hundred and fifty elements, or components. Each of these elements can be labeled according to its role for the progress of the plot. Thus, in the above example, Baba Jaga is a donor; the word "gives" signals the moment of transfer: Ivan is the recipient, and the horse is the gift. If we write down the labels for all one hundred and fifty elements in the order dictated by the tales themselves, such a table will cover all wondertales, and conversely, any tale that fits such a table is a wondertale, whereas any tale that does not belongs in another category. Every rubric is a component of the wondertale, and reading the table vertically yields a series of basic and a series of derived forms.

It is these rubrics that should be compared. Such a procedure would correspond in zoology to a comparison of vertebrae with vertebrae, teeth with teeth, etc. But between organic formations and the wondertale there is a significant difference that makes our task easier. In the first instance, a change in a part or feature brings about a change in another feature, whereas each element of the wondertale can change independently of the others. This phenomenon has been noted by many scholars, although there have so far been no attempts to evaluate it methodologically or otherwise.[7] Thus, Kaarle Krohn, though he agrees with Karl Spiess on the instability of separate elements, considers it necessary to study the wondertale in terms of entire *structures* rather than components, but he does not supply any convincing arguments to support his views (which are those of the Finnish school). I believe that the elements of the wondertale can be studied independently of the plot they constitute. The vertical rubrics reveal norms and types of transformations. What holds true for an isolated element also holds true for entire structures, because the components are joined to one another in a mechanical manner.

2. The present work does not claim to exhaust the problem. I will indicate only certain guideposts that may subsequently form the foundation of a broader theoretical study. But even in a brief outline, before we go on to the transformations themselves, we must establish the criteria by which to distinguish basic and derived forms. The criteria can be expressed in two ways: in terms of general principles and in terms of special rules.

First, the general principles. In order to establish them, the wondertale has to be examined in connection with the *environment* that gave rise to it. Life and religion (in the broad sense of the word) are of special importance here. The causes of transformations often lie outside the wondertale, and we will not understand the evolution of the tale unless we consider some comparative data from its environment.

The basic forms are those connected with the *origins* of the wondertale. Obviously, the tale is born out of life; however, the wondertale is a weak transcript of reality. Everything that derives from reality is secondary. To determine the origins of the wondertale, we must draw upon the broad cultural material of the past.

The forms that, for one reason or another, are defined as basic are linked with religious concepts of the remote past. We can formulate the following premise: if the same form occurs both in a religious monument and in a wondertale, the religious form is primary and the wondertale form, secondary. This is particularly true of archaic religions. Any dead religious phenomenon is older than its artistic reflection in a modern wondertale. This statement cannot be proved here. Indeed, such a dependence in general cannot be *proved*; it can only be *shown* on a mass of material. This is our first general principle; it will be elaborated below. The second principle can be stated thus: if the same element has two variants, one of which derives from religious forms and the other from daily life, the religious formation is primary and the one drawn from life secondary.

In applying these principles, we must observe caution. It would be an error to try to trace all basic forms to religion and all derived ones to reality. To avoid such errors, we need to go into the methods of comparing the wondertale and religion and the wondertale and life.

There are several types of relationships between the wondertale and religion. The first is a direct genetic dependence, which in some cases is patently obvious and in others requires special historical research. Thus, if a dragon (serpent) is encountered in both the wondertale and religion, it entered the tale from religion, not the other way around.

However, the presence of such a tie is not obligatory even if the similarity is very great. Its presence is probable only when we deal with direct *cult* and *ritual* material. Such ritual material must be distinguished from *epic* material of a religious nature. In the first case we can speak of a direct kinship along descending lines, analogous to the kinship line of fathers and children; in the second case we have only parallel kinship or, to continue the analogy, the kinship of brothers. Thus, the story of Samson and Delilah cannot be considered the prototype of the wondertale resembling the Old Testament story, but the tale and the Biblical text may well go back to a common source.

To be sure, the primacy of cult material should be postulated with a certain degree of caution. Nonetheless, in some instances this primacy is beyond doubt. What really matters may concern the document itself, rather than the concepts that are reflected in it and that underlie the wondertale, but we are often able to judge concepts only by documents. For example, the *Rig-Veda*, as yet relatively unexplored by folklorists, is among such sources of the wondertale. If it is true that the wondertale exhibits approximately one hundred and fifty components, then the *Rig-Veda* contains no fewer than sixty. Their use is lyrical rather than epic, but these are hymns sung by high priests, not by commoners. In the hands of the people (shepherds and peasants) these lyrics took on features of the epic. If the hymn praises Indra as the dragon slayer (the coincidence with the wondertale is sometimes complete), the people were able in one form or another to *narrate* how Indra killed the dragon.

Let us look at an example. We readily recognize Baba Jaga and her hut in the following hymn:

To the Lady of the Forest (Aranyāni)

RV 10. 146

1. Lady of the Forest, Lady of the Forest, you who are like one who has become lost!
Why do you not ask about the village? Is it not that fear has found you?
2. When the Ciccika-bird coos to the (bird) whose call is like a bull roaring,
The Lady of the Forest shows herself to be great, as one marching to the sound of cymbals.
3. And as cattle graze or as a house comes into view,
So, at evening, the Lady of the Forest truly creaks like a (heavy) wagon.
4. Someone who calls to the cattle or someone who splits wood,
Remaining in the forest (or: with the Lady of the Forest) at evening—he thinks thus: "Someone is crying out!"
5. Truly, the Lady of the Forest does not kill, nor does any other one attack.
One consumes sweet fruit as one lays down (i.e., dispenses with) one's desires.
6. She who is sweet-smelling with the odor of unguents, rich in food without having tilled the field,
Mother of the wild animals, Lady of the Forest—her I have praised![8]

We have a number of wondertale elements here: a hut in the woods, a reproach linked with inquiry (in the wondertale it occurs in an inverted form), a hospitable night's rest (Baba Jaga provides food, drink, and shelter), a suggestion of the mistress of the wood's potential hostility, and an indication that she is the mother of the wild beasts (in the wondertale she calls them together); the chicken legs of her hut, as well as any indication of her external appearance, etc., are missing. One coincidence is especially remarkable: he who spends the night in the hut seems to hear that someone is chopping wood. In Afanas'ev's no. 99 the father, after leaving his daughter in the hut, straps a boot last to the window. The last flops, and the girl says: "That is my father chopping wood."[9]

All these coincidences are not accidental, for they are not the only ones. A great many exact parallels occur between the wondertale and the *Rig-Veda*. The parallel mentioned here cannot, of course, be viewed as proof that our Baba Jaga goes back to the *Rig-Veda,* but it shows that on the whole the line proceeds from religion to the wondertale and that comparative studies are in order in this area.

However, everything said here is true only if religion and the wondertale lie at a great chronological distance from each other, if, for example, the religion under consideration has already died out and its origin is lost in the prehistoric past. It is a different matter when we compare a living religion and a living wondertale of one and the same people. Here we can observe the reverse dependence that is impossible between a dead religion and a modern wondertale. Christian elements in the wondertale (the apostles as helpers, the devil as villain, and the like) are *younger* than the wondertale, not older. In fact, we really ought not to call this relationship the reverse of the preceding one. The wondertale derives from ancient religions, but modern religions do not derive from the wondertale. Modern religion does not create the wondertale; it merely *modifies* its material. Yet isolated instances of a truly reversed dependence probably do occur, that is, instances in which the elements of religion are derived from the wondertale. A very interesting example is the Western Church's canonization of the miracle of St. George the Dragon Slayer. This miracle was canonized much later than was St. George himself, and the latter canonization took place despite the stubborn resistance of the Church (Aufhauser 1911). Since the battle with the serpent is a part of many pagan religions, it is traceable to them. In the thirteenth century, however, these religions were dead and only epic tradition in the lower strata could play the role of transmitter. The popularity of St. George and of dragon fighting caused the saint's image to merge with that of the dragon fighter; the Church was forced to acknowledge the merger and canonize it.

Finally, alongside of direct genetic dependence of the wondertale on religion, alongside of their parallelism and reversed dependence, we find cases when the two are totally unconnected, despite outward similarity. Identical concepts can arise independently of one another. Thus, the magic horse is comparable to the sacred horses of the Teutons and the fiery horse Agni in the *Rig-Veda*. The former have nothing in common with Sívka-Búrka,[10] whereas the latter coincides with him in all respects. The analogy may be applied only if it is more or less complete. Heteronomous phenomena, however similar, must be excluded from such comparisons.

Thus, the study of *basic* forms makes it necessary to compare the wondertale with various religions. Conversely, the study of *derived* forms in the wondertale shows how it is linked with reality. A number of transformations can be explained as the intrusions of reality into the wondertale. This poses the problem of the methods used in studying the relationship between the wondertale and life.

In contrast to other types of tale (anecdotes, novellas, fables, and so on), the wondertale is comparatively poor in elements borrowed from real life. The role of daily existence in creating the wondertale has often been overrated. We can understand the relationship between the wondertale and life only if we remember that *artistic realism and the presence of elements from real life* are two different concepts and that they do not always overlap. Scholars often make the mistake of searching for facts from real life to support a realistic narrative.

Nikolaj Lerner, for example, takes the following lines from Pushkin's "Bová":

> This is indeed a golden Council,
> No idle chatter here, but deep thought.
> A long while all the noble lords pondered.
> Arzamor, old and experienced,
> All but opened his mouth (to give counsel
> Was the old greybeard's desire),
> His throat he loudly cleared, but thought better
> And in silence his tongue did bite, *etc.*
> (All the council members keep silent and begin to drowse.)

and comments, citing L. N. Majkov:

> In depicting the council of bearded courtiers the poem might have been
> a satire on the government of old Muscovite Russia. . . . The satire
> might have been directed not only against Old Russia but against
> Pushkin's Russia as well. The entire assembly of snoring "thinkers"
> could easily have been observed by the young genius in the society of
> his own day. (Lerner 1907, 204)

However, this is strictly a *wondertale* motif. In Afanas'év (for example, in no. 140) we find: "He asked once—the boyars were silent; a second time—they did not respond; a third time—not so much as half a word." We have the traditional scene in which the supplicant entreats aid, the entreaty usually occurring three times. It is first directed to the handmaids, then to the boyars (clerks, ministers), and third to the hero of the story. Each party in this triad can likewise be trebled. We are not dealing with real life but with the amplification and specification (added names, etc.) of a folklore element. We would make the same mistake if we were to consider Homer's image of Penelope and the conduct of her suitors as corresponding to the facts of life in ancient Greece and to Greek connubial customs. Penelope's suitors are *false suitors*, a well-known device in epic poetry throughout the world. We should first isolate whatever belongs to folklore and only afterward go into the correspondence between specifically Homeric moments and life in ancient Greece.

The problem of the relationship between the wondertale and life is not a simple one. It is inadmissible to draw conclusions about life directly from the wondertale. But, as we will see below, the role of real life in the *transformation* of the wondertale is enormous. Life cannot destroy the overall structure of the wondertale, but it produces a wealth of younger facts that often replace the old ones in a number of ways.

3. The following are the principal and more exact criteria for distinguishing the basic form of a wondertale element from a derived form.

a. A fantastic treatment of a wondertale component is older than its rational treatment. This case is very simple and does not require discussion. If in one tale Ivan receives a magic gift from Baba Jaga and in another, from an old woman passing by, the former is older than the latter. This viewpoint is based on the link between the wondertale and religion, but it may prove invalid with respect to other types of tale (fables, etc.), which, on the whole, may be older than the wondertale. The realism of such tales dates from time immemorial and cannot be traced to religious concepts.

b. Heroic treatment is older than humorous treatment. This is just a variant of the preceding case. Obviously, entering into mortal combat with a dragon is older than beating it in a card game.

c. A form used logically is older than a form used nonsensically (see examples in Karnaúxova 1927).

d. An international form is older than a national one. If the dragon is encountered virtually the world over but is replaced in some tales of the North by a bear and in the South by a lion, the basic form is the dragon, whereas the lion and bear are derived forms.

Here we ought to say a few words concerning the methods of studying the wondertale on an international scale. The facts are so many that a single investigator cannot possibly study all one hundred and fifty elements in the tales of the entire world. He must first work through the tales of one people, distinguishing between their basic and derived forms, then repeat the same procedure for a second people, and then proceed to a comparative study.

The thesis concerning international forms can be narrowed and stated thus: a broadly national form is older than a regional or provincial form. Once we start along this path, we are bound to accept the following statement: a widespread form predates an isolated form. However, it is theoretically possible that a truly ancient form has survived only in a few instances and that all the other varieties are younger. Therefore this quantitative principle (the use of statistics) should

be applied with extreme caution; *qualitative* considerations are of equal importance. Here is a case in point: in the wondertale "Vasilísa the Beautiful" (no.
104 in Afanas'ev) Baba Jaga is accompanied by three mounted riders who sym-
bolize morning, day, and night. The question arises: is this not a fundamental
feature peculiar to Baba Jaga and lost in the other wondertales? Yet special considerations (which I will pass over) show that this hypothesis is untenable.

4. By way of an example I will go through all the possible changes of a single
element—Baba Jaga's hut. Morphologically, the hut represents the abode of the
donor (that is, the personage who gives the hero the magic tool). Consequently,
we will examine not only the hut but all kinds of the donor's abodes. The basic
Russian form of the abode, as I think, is the rotating forest hut on chicken legs.
Since *one* element does not yield all the changes possible in the wondertale, I
will consider other examples as well.

a. *Reduction.* Instead of the full form, we can find the following types of
change:

1. the hut on chicken legs in the forest;
2. the hut on chicken legs;
3. the hut in the forest;
4. the hut;
5. the (pine)forest (Afanas'ev, no. 95);
6. no mention of the abode.

Here the basic form is truncated. The chicken legs, the rotation, and the
forest are omitted, and finally the hut itself can be dispensed with. Reduction is an incomplete basic form. It should be accounted for by the narrator's forgetting the tale, which in turn has more complex causes. Reduction reflects the lack of agreement between the wondertale and its present
environment, its insignificance in a given milieu, in a given epoch, or to
the narrator.

b. *Expansion.* This is the opposite of the preceding. The basic form is extended and broadened by the addition of extra detail. Here is an expanded
form: the hut on chicken legs in the forest rests on pancakes and is shin-
gled with pies. More often than not, expansion is accompanied by reduction. Certain features are left out, others are added. Expansion can be divided
into categories according to origin (as is done below for substitutions). Some
expanded forms derive from daily life, others represent an amplified detail
from the wondertale canon, as in the preceding example. The donor is a
blend of hostile and hospitable qualities. Ivan is usually fed in the donor's
abode. The forms of this entertainment are varied. ("She gave him food
and drink." Ivan addresses the hut with the words: "I will climb in and
have a bit to eat." In the hut the hero sees a table laid, he samples all the
food or eats his fill; he goes outside and slaughters some of the donor's
cattle and chickens, etc.) The donor's hospitality is reflected in his very

abode. In the German tale "Hansel and Gretel" this form is used somewhat differently, in conformity with the childlike nature of the story.

c. *Contamination.* Since the wondertale is in a state of decline today, contamination is relatively frequent. Sometimes contaminated forms spread and take root. The idea that Baba Jaga's hut turns continuously on its axis is an example of contamination. In the course of the action, the hut has a specific purpose: it is a "sentry-box," an outpost, and the hero is tested to see whether or not he is worthy of receiving the magic tool. The hut greets Ivan with its closed side, and consequently it is sometimes called a hut without windows or doors. Its open side, that is, the side with the door, faces away from Ivan. It would appear that he can very easily go around to the other side of the hut and enter through the door. But he is unable to and *never does* so in the wondertale. Instead, he utters the incantation: "Stand with your back to the forest and your front to me," or "Stand as your mother stood you," and so on. The result is usually: "The hut turned." This "turned" has become "keeps turning around," and the expression, "When it has to, it turns this way and that" has become "It turns all the time," which even if vivid is meaningless.

d. *Inversion.* Often the basic form is reversed. Female characters are replaced by male, and vice versa. This procedure can involve the hut as well. Instead of a closed and inaccessible hut, we sometimes see a hut with a wide-open door.

e-f. *Intensification and Attenuation.* These types of transformation apply only to the actions of the characters. Identical actions occur with various degrees of intensity. Here is one example of intensification: the hero is exiled instead of merely being sent on a quest. Dispatch is one of the constant elements of the wondertale; this element occurs in such a variety of forms that all degrees of intensity are demonstrable. The dispatch can be initiated in various ways. The hero is often asked to go and fetch some unusual thing. Sometimes the hero is given a task. ("Do me the service.") Often it is an order accompanied by threats, should he fail, and promises, should he succeed. Dispatch can also be a veiled form of exile: an evil sister sends her brother for the milk of a fierce animal to get rid of him; the master sends his laborer to bring back a cow allegedly lost in the forest; a stepmother sends her stepdaughter to Baba Jaga for fire. Finally, we have exile in the direct sense of the word. These are the basic stages of dispatch, each of which allows a number of variations and transitional forms; they are especially important in the study of tales dealing with exiled characters. The order accompanied by threats and promises can be regarded as the basic form of dispatch. If the element of promise is left out, such a reduction can also be considered an intensification—a dispatch and a threat. Omission of the threat will soften and weaken this form. Further attenuation consists in completely omitting the dispatch. As he prepares to leave, the son asks his parents for their blessing.

The six types of transformations discussed so far can be interpreted as very familiar *changes* in the basic form. There are, however, two other large groups of transformations: substitutions and assimilations. Both can be analyzed according to their origin.

g. *Substitution of One Wondertale Element For Another.* Looking again at the donor's dwelling, we find the following forms: (1) a palace and (2) a mountain alongside a fiery river. These are not cases of reduction, expansion, etc. They are not *changes* but *substitutions.* These forms, however, are not drawn from outside, but from the tale's own reserves. A *transposition, a rearrangement* of forms and material has taken place. The palace (often of gold) is normally inhabited by a princess. Subsequently this dwelling becomes the property of the donor. Such transpositions in the wondertale play an important role. Each element has its own peculiar form. However, this form is not always exclusively bound to the given element. (For example, the princess, usually a character *to be found,* can play the role of the donor, helper, etc.) One wondertale image supersedes another. Baba Jaga's daughter can appear as the princess; in this case Baba Jaga does not live in her hut but in a palace, that is, in the abode normally associated with a princess. Palaces of copper, silver, and gold belong here too. The maidens living in such palaces are donors and princesses at the same time. The palaces could have come about as the result of trebling the golden palace or spontaneously without any connection with the idea of the Ages of Gold, Silver, and Iron, etc.

Likewise, the mountain alongside the fiery river is nothing else but the dragon's abode that now belongs to the donor.

These transpositions play an enormous role in creating transformations. Most transformations are substitutions or transpositions generated from within the wondertale.

h. *Externally Motivated Substitutions.* If we have the forms: (1) an inn and (2) a two-storied house, it is apparent that the fantastic hut has been replaced by forms of dwelling normal in real life. Most of such substitutions can be explained very easily, but there are substitutions that require a special ethnographic exegesis. Elements borrowed from everyday life are always immediately obvious, and, more often than not, scholars center their attention on them.

i. *Confessional Substitutions.* Current religion is also capable of suppressing old forms and replacing them with new ones. Such are instances in which the devil functions as a winged carrier, or an angel is the donor of the magic tool, or an act of penance replaces the performance of a difficult task. Certain legends are basically wondertales in which all elements have undergone this type of substitution. Every people has its own confessional substitutions. Christianity, Islam, and Buddhism leave their stamp on the wondertale of the corresponding peoples.

j. *Substitution Caused by Superstition.* Obviously, superstition and local beliefs can likewise suppress the original material of a wondertale. However, we come across this type of substitution much more rarely than one might expect at first glance (hence the errors of the Mythological school). Pushkin was mistaken in saying that in the wondertale:

> Wonders abound, the lešij [a wood goblin] wanders,
> A mermaid sits in the boughs.

If we encounter a lešij in the wondertale, he is almost always a substitute for Baba Jaga. Mermaids are met with but a single time in the entire Afanas'ev collection, and only in an introduction *(prískazka)* of dubious authenticity. In the collections by Ončukóv, Zelénin, the Sokolóvs, and others, there is not a single mention of mermaids.[11] The lešij finds his way into the wondertale because, as a creature of the forest, he resembles Baba Jaga. The wondertale accepts only those elements that can be readily accommodated in its construction.

k. *Archaic Substitution.* We have already mentioned that the basic forms of the wondertale go back to extinct religious concepts. Knowing this, we can sometimes separate the basic forms from the derived ones. In certain rare instances, however, the basic form (more or less normal in the wondertale) has been replaced by a form no less ancient, which can likewise be traced to a religious source but whose occurrence is unique. For example, instead of the battle with the dragon, in the wondertale "The Witch and the Sun's Sister" (no. 93 in Afanas'ev) we have the following: the dragon's mate suggests to the prince, "Let Prince Ivan come with me to the scales and we'll see who outweighs whom." The scales toss Ivan to the sun's houses. Here we have traces of the weighing of souls. Where this form—well known in ancient Egypt—came from and how it happened to be preserved in the wondertale are questions that need special historical study.

It is not always easy to distinguish between an archaic substitution and a substitution imposed by superstition. Both may have their roots in deep antiquity. But if some item in the wondertale is also found in a living faith, the substitution can be considered a relatively new one (e.g., the lešij). A pagan religion may have had two offshoots: one in the wondertale and the other in a faith or custom. In the course of centuries, they may have crossed each other's way and the one may have superseded the other. Conversely, if a wondertale element is not attested in a living faith (e.g., the scales), the substitution has its origin in deep antiquity and can be considered archaic.

l. *Literary Substitutions.* Literary material is as rarely accepted by the wondertale as current superstition. The wondertale possesses such resistance that other genres shatter against it; they refuse to merge. If a clash takes place, the wondertale wins. As regards other literary genres, the wondertale is the most likely to absorb elements from legend and the bylina. On rare occasions the romance provides a substitution, mainly the chivalric romance, which itself derives from the wondertale. The process occurs in stages: wondertale → romance → wondertale. Therefore, works like *Eruslán Lázarevič*[12] are pure wondertales in terms of construction, despite the bookish nature of individual elements. All this concerns only the wondertale. The *Schwank*,[13] the novella, and other forms of popular prose are more flexible and less impervious.

m. *Modification.* There are substitutions whose origin is not readily ascertainable. More often than not, these are imaginative substitutions owing to the narrator's own preferences; such forms are not typical from an ethnographic or historical point of view. These substitutions play a greater role in animal tales and other types than in wondertales. (The bear is replaced by the wolf, one bird by another, etc.) Of course, they can occur in the wondertale too. Thus, as the winged carrier, we find an eagle, a falcon, a raven, geese, and so forth. As the sought-for wonder, we find a stag with antlers of gold, a horse with a mane of gold, a duck with feathers of gold, a pig with bristles of gold, etc. Derived, secondary forms are usually the ones most likely to undergo modification. This can be shown by the comparison of a number of forms in which the sought-for wonder is simply a transformation of a princess with golden locks. If comparison of the basic and derived forms exhibits a certain descending line, comparison of two derived forms reveals a certain parallelism. Certain elements in the wondertale exhibit a particular variety of forms. One example is the "difficult task." If the task does not have a basic form, it makes little difference to the wondertale's unity of construction what task is assigned. This phenomenon is even more apparent when we compare elements that have never belonged to the basic type of the wondertale. Motivation is one such element. Transformations sometimes create the need to *motivate* a certain act; as a result, we see a wide variety of motivations for one and the same act. Thus, the hero's exile (exile is a secondary formation) is motivated in a number of ways. On the other hand, the abduction of the maiden by the dragon (a primary form) is hardly ever motivated externally, for it is motivated from within.

Certain features of the hut are also subject to modification. Instead of a hut on chicken legs, we sometimes come across huts on goat horns and on ram legs.

n. *Substitutions of Unknown Origin.* We have been discussing substitutions from the point of view of their origin, but since origin does not always appear as a simple modification, we require a category for substitutions of unknown origin. For example, the sister of the sun from the wondertale "Little Sister" (Afanas'ev no. 93) plays the donor's role and may also be considered a rudimentary form of the princess. She lives in the sun's houses. We cannot know whether this reflects a sun cult, the creative imagination of the narrator, or some suggestion by the collector asking the storyteller whether he knows any wondertales dealing with a particular subject or whether thus and so can be found; in such a case, the narrator sometimes fabricates something to please the collector.

This brings us to the end of substitutions. We could, of course, have set up several more varieties that would cover a few isolated cases, but there is no need for that now. The substitutions discussed above are relevant to the entire breadth of wondertale material; their application to isolated cases can be easily demonstrated and supplemented by employing the transformational types.

Let us turn to another class of changes, that of assimilations. By assimilation I understand an incomplete suppression of one form by another, the two forms merging into one. Since assimilations follow the same classification scheme as the substitutions, they will be enumerated in brief.

o. *Assimilation of One Wondertale Element to Another.* An example occurs in the forms: (1) *a hut under a golden roof* and (2) *a hut by a fiery river.*

In wondertales we often meet with a *palace* under a golden roof. A hut plus a palace under a golden roof yields a hut under a golden roof. The same is true of the hut by the fiery river.

The wondertale "Fjódor Vódovič and Iván Vódovič" (Ončukov 1909, no. 4) provides a very interesting example. Two such heterogeneous elements as the miraculous birth of the hero and the pursuit of the hero by the dragon's wives (sisters) have been drawn together by assimilation. The wives of the dragon, in pursuing the hero, usually turn into a well, a cloud, a bed, etc., and stand in Ivan's path. If he samples some fruit or takes a drink of water, he will be torn to pieces.

The motif of the miraculous birth has been used in the following manner: the princess strolls about her father's courtyard quite alone, sees a well with a small cup, and by it a bed (the apple tree has been forgotten). She drinks a cupful and lies down on the bed to rest. From this she conceives and gives birth to two sons.

p. *Externally Motivated Assimilations* take the following forms: (1) *a hut on the edge of the village* and (2) *a cave in the woods.* Here we find that the fantastic hut has become a real hut and a real cave, but the isolation of the dwelling has been preserved; in the second instance the cave is in the forest. The wondertale plus reality produces an assimilation that is purely external.

q. *Confessional Assimilation.* This process can be exemplified by the replacement of the dragon by the devil; however, the devil, like the dragon, dwells in a *lake*. The concept of evil beings of the deep does not necessarily have anything in common with the so-called lower mythology of the peasants; it often goes back to a certain type of transformation.

r. *Assimilation by Superstition.* This is a relatively rare phenomenon. A lešij living in a hut on chicken legs is an example.

s-t. *Literary and Archaic Assimilations.* These are even rarer. Assimilations to the bylina and legend are of some importance to the Russian wondertale. Here, however, we are more likely to find suppression rather than the assimilation of one form to another, with the components of the wondertale preserved as such. Archaic assimilations require a detailed study of each occurrence. They are known to exist, but identifying them is possible only after a great deal of very special research.

Our survey of transformations can end at this point. Perhaps not all wondertale forms will be accommodated by my classificatory scheme, but many will. One can also think of other types of transformations, e.g., *specification* and *generalization.* In the first case, general phenomena become concrete (instead of the remote kingdom, we find the city Xvalýnsk); in the latter case, the opposite occurs (a particular, though remote, kingdom becomes simply a "different, other" kingdom, etc.). Almost all types of specification can also be regarded as substitutions, and generalizations as reductions. This is also true of rationalization (a winged horse becomes an earthbound one), the wondertale becoming an anecdote, etc. If we apply these types of transformation correctly and consistently, we will feel more secure in the study of the wondertale as a historical entity.

What is true of the individual elements of the wondertale is equally true of the wondertale as a whole. If an extra element is added, we have amplification; in the reverse case, we have reduction, etc. Applying these methods to entire tales is important for the comparative study of wondertale plots.

One important problem remains. If we write out all the occurrences (or at least a great many of them) of one element, not all the forms of that element can be traced to a single basis. Let us suppose that we accept Baba Jaga as the basic form of the donor. Such forms are a witch, Grannie-Behind-the-Door, Grandma-Widow, an old woman, an old man, a shepherd, a lešij, an angel, the devil, three maids, the king's daughter, etc. All can be satisfactorily explained as substitutions for and other transformations of Baba Jaga. But then we run into a "fingernail-sized peasant with an elbow-length beard." Such a form of the donor does not derive from Baba Jaga. If it occurs in a religion, we have a form coordinated with Baba Jaga; if not, a substitution of unknown origin. Each element can have several basic forms, although the number of such parallel, coordinated forms is usually insignificant.

5. This outline would be incomplete if I did not show a model for applying my observations. I will use relatively tractable material to discuss a series of transformations. Let us take the forms:

the dragon abducts the king's daughter
the dragon tortures the king's daughter
the dragon demands the king's daughter

From the point of view of the morphology of the wondertale, we are dealing with an element called *the initial misfortune*. Such a misfortune usually serves as the start of the plot. In accordance with the principles proposed in this paper, we should compare abduction not only with abduction, etc., but also with all the various types of initial misfortune as one of the components of the wondertale.

Caution demands that all three forms be regarded as coordinated forms, but the first seems to be basic. In Egypt we find death conceived of as the abduction of the soul by a dragon. But this concept has been forgotten, whereas the idea that illness is a demon settled within the body lives on. Finally, the dragon's demand for the princess as tribute reflects an archaism borrowed from real life. It is accompanied by the appearance of an army that besieges the city and threatens war. However, one cannot be certain. Be that as it may, all three forms are very old, and each allows a number of transformations.

Let us take the first form:

the dragon abducts the king's daughter

The dragon is viewed as the embodiment of evil. Confessional influence turns the dragon into a devil:

devils abduct the king's daughter

The same influence affects the object of the abduction:

the devil abducts the priest's daughter

The dragon figure has become foreign to the village. It has been replaced by a dangerous animal that is better known (externally motivated substitution), the animal acquiring fantastic attributes (modification):

a bear with fur of iron carries off the king's children

The villain merges with Baba Jaga. One part of the wondertale influences another (substitution of one wondertale for another). Baba Jaga is a female and, correspondingly, the person abducted is a male (inversion):

a witch abducts the son of an old couple

In one of the forms constantly complicating the wondertale the hero's brothers steal the prize. The intent to do harm has been transferred to the hero's kin. A canonical form of complicating the action is this:

Ivan's brothers abduct his bride

The wicked brothers are replaced by other villainous relatives from the wondertale stock in trade (substitution of one wondertale element for another):

the king (Ivan's father-in-law) abducts Ivan's wife

The princess herself can take over the same function, and the wondertale can assume more amusing forms. Here the figure of the villain has been reduced:

the princess flies away from her husband

In all these cases a human being has been abducted, but the light of day can be abducted too (an archaic substitution?):

the dragon abducts the light of the kingdom

The dragon is replaced by other monstrous animals (modification); the object of abduction is brought closer to the imagined life of the court:

the mink steals animals from the king's menagerie

Talismans play a significant role in the wondertale. They are often the only means by which Ivan can attain his goal; hence they are often stolen. If the action happens to become complicated in the middle of the wondertale, such theft is even obligatory as far as the wondertale canon is concerned. This middle moment can be transferred to the beginning (substitution of one wondertale element for another). The thief is often a cheat, a landowner, and so on (externally motivated substitution):

a shrewd lad steals Ivan's talisman,
a landowner steals the peasant's talisman

The tale of the firebird represents a transitional stage to other forms; here the stolen apples of gold are not talismans (cf. the apples of youth). The theft of the talisman is only possible as a complication of the wondertale's midpoint, after the talisman has been acquired. The talisman can be made off with at the beginning only if its possession has been motivated, however briefly. It is for this reason that the stolen items that appear at the beginning of the tale are not often talismans. The firebird has made its way from the middle section of the tale to the beginning. The bird is one of the basic means of transporting Ivan to the remote kingdom. Golden feathers and similar features are usually attributed to the animal life of the wondertale:

the firebird steals the king's apples

In every case the abduction is preserved. The disappearance of a bride, a daughter, a wife, etc., is an act of some mythic creature. However, mythic thought is alien to modern peasant life, therefore foreign, imported mythology is replaced by sorcery. Disappearance is ascribed to magic spells cast by evil sorcerers and sorceresses. The nature of the villainous deed changes, but its result is still the same: a disappearance entailing a quest (substitution caused by superstition):

a sorcerer abducts the king's daughter,
a servant bewitches Ivan's bride and forces her to fly away

Again we see the activity transferred to wicked relatives:

sisters force the girl's bridegroom to fly away

Turning to the transformations of our second base:

a dragon tortures the king's daughter

Transformations are similar:

the devil tortures the king's daughter, etc.

Here the torture assumes the nature of detention and vampirism, which can be fully explained ethnographically. Instead of the dragon and the devil we see again another of the wondertale's evil beings:

Baba Jaga tortures the bogatýrs' (warriors') hostess

A third variation of the basic form poses the threat of forced marriage:

the dragon demands the king's daugther

This opens up a number of transformations:

a water sprite demands the king's son, etc.

This form, morphologically speaking, leads to a declaration of war without any of the king's offspring being demanded (reduction). A transfer of similar forms to relatives produces:

the sister, who is a witch, seeks to eat the king's son (her brother)

This case (Afanas'év no. 93) is of special interest. Here the prince's sister is called a dragoness. This classic example of one wondertale element substituting for another points up the need for caution in studying kinship ties in the wondertale. The marriage of brother and sister and other forms are not necessarily survivals of an old custom; rather, they can be the result of certain transformations, as the above case clearly shows.

I anticipate the argument against all of the preceding that anything can be fitted into a sentence with two objects. This is far from true. How would the beginning of the wondertale "The Frost, the Sun, and the Wind" and many others fit into such a form? Second, the observed phenomena represent the same constructional element with respect to the overall composition. The subsequent elements of the plot are also similar in content, even if different in form; compare a plea for help and a departure from home, a meeting with a donor, etc. Not every wondertale containing a theft motif produces this construction. If this construction does not follow, similar patterns cannot be compared, for they are heteronomous or we have to admit that a wondertale element has entered an essentially different construction. Thus we return to the necessity of making juxtapositions on the basis of identical components and not of external similarity.

Chapter Seven.
Historical Roots
of the Wondertale:
Premises

The Basic Question

Before the Revolution folklore was produced in Russia by the oppressed classes—illiterate peasants, soldiers, artisans, semiliterate apprentices, etc. In our time folklore is indeed produced by *the people*. Before the Revolution the science of folklore looked to other areas of knowledge for its concepts. It ascribed to folklore some abstract philosophy, was blind to its revolutionary dynamic, subsumed folklore under literature, and viewed folklore only as part of literary criticism. Now the science of folklore is becoming independent. Methods of prerevolutionary folklore were powerless to deal with its complicated subject; theory supplanted theory, yet none of them holds water. At present the method of Marxism-Leninism—the method of Marx, Engels, Lenin and Stalin—makes it possible to abandon abstract theorizing for concrete investigation.

What does a concrete investigation of the tale mean? Where do we begin? A mere comparison of tales will leave us within the framework of comparativism, *but we wish to find the historical base that brought the wondertale to life.*

At first it seems that nothing is new in this goal. Folklore has certainly been studied historically before. The Russian science of folklore has known an entire historical school headed by Vsevolod Miller. Thus, M. N. Speranskij (1917, 222) said in his course in Russian oral literature, "We attempt to guess the historical fact on which the bylina is based and with that in mind to prove the identity of the bylina plot with some historical events." I intend neither to *guess* historical facts nor prove their *identity* with folklore. I will try to ascertain to which past phenomena (rather than events) the Russian wondertale corresponds and in what measure the past really determines and brings forth the tale. My aim is to discover the sources of the tale in historical reality. However, to study *the genesis* of a phenomenon is not the same as to study its *history*. The study of history cannot be carried out all at once. It needs the efforts of several generations and should be accomplished by our young science of Marxist folklore. The study of the genesis is the first step in this direction.

The Significance of the Premises

Every investigator sets out from some premises. As early as 1873, A. N. Veselovskij insisted on taking a theoretical stand and on a critical assessment of one's method (see Veselovskij 1938, 83-128). On the example of Gubernatis's *Zoological Mythology* (1872), Veselovskij showed how the lack of such an assessment could lead to false conclusions despite the author's erudition and power of synthesis.

Properly speaking, a critical history of folktale studies is in order here, but I will do without it, for such a history has been set forth more than once and is well known. But if we ask why we still lack solid and universally accepted results in this field, we will see that the cause of it lies in the authors' false premises.

The Mythological school believed that the external similarity between two phenomena, i.e., the presence of analogy, testifies to their historical connection. Thus, if a hero grows "not day by day but hour by hour," this rapid growth was supposed to reflect the rapid growth of the rising sun (Frobenius 1898, 242). Yet the sun diminishes, rather than increases, to the eye of the observer; in addition, analogy and historical connection are different things.

According to the Finnish school, the more frequent forms belong to the original state of the plot. Aside from the fact that theory of plot archetypes itself needs proof, we will see more than once that truly archaic forms are rare and that they have often been superseded by widely current new ones (for more details see Nikiforov 1926).

Such examples are numerous, and the fallacy of the initial premise is usually quite obvious. The question arises: Why did the authors themselves fail to see the mistakes that are so clear to us? We will not blame them for their mistakes; they were made by the most outstanding scholars. The crux of the matter is that these scholars could not think differently! Their ideas were determined by the epoch in which they lived and by the class to which they belonged. The question of premises was not even raised in most cases, and the voice of the brilliant Veselovskij, who constantly revised his own premises and started anew many times, remained a voice crying in the wilderness.

Definition of the Wondertale

My aim is to find and investigate the historical roots of the wondertale. Later I will explain what I mean by historical roots, but first it is necessary to discuss the term *wondertale*. The folktale is so rich and varied a phenomenon that one cannot study the whole of it everywhere. Since the data must be limited, I will limit them to wondertales, that is, I postulate the existence of tales that can be brought under this category. Such in fact is my premise. I will designate those tales as wondertales whose structure I have studied in *Morphology of the Folktale* (Propp 1928; 2nd ed. 1969; English translation 1958; 2nd ed. 1968a). In my book, the genre of the wondertale is defined in precise terms. A wondertale begins with some harm or villainy done to someone (for example, abduction or banishment) or with a desire to have something (a king sends his son in quest of the firebird), and develops through the hero's departure from home and encounters with the donor, who provides him with a magic agent that helps the hero find the object of the search. Further along, the tale includes combat with an adversary (the most important form is slaying a dragon), a return, and a pursuit. Often this structure is more complicated, for example, when the hero is on his way home and his brothers throw him into a pit. Later he escapes, is subjected to a trial by difficult tasks, and becomes king and marries, either in his own kingdom or in that of his father-in-law. This is the compositional core of many plots in brief outline. Tales reflecting this scheme will be called wondertales here, and only they will serve as the object of my investigation.

Thus, my first premise is that among folktales there is a particular category called wondertales which can be isolated and studied independently. Such an approach may cause doubts: have we not violated the principle of the interconnection of all phenomena? In the final analysis, all things are interrelated; yet science always isolates some of them. The point is when and how the line is drawn.

Although wondertales are one part of folklore, they are not a part inseparable from the whole; they are not like an arm in relation to the body or a leaf in relation to the tree. While remaining a part, they nonetheless form a whole and are here taken *as a whole*.

Research into the structure of wondertales shows how closely related they are; as a matter of fact, their plots cannot be delimited. This circumstance leads to two more important premises: first, all wondertale plots should be studied with reference to one another; second, all wondertale motifs should be studied in their relation to the whole. My approach to the problem is quite new. Hitherto this sort of work has been conducted as follows: the investigator would select some one motif or some one plot, collect all the accessible written versions, and then draw conclusions by putting the data side by side and comparing them. Jiří Polívka (1924) studied the formula "Russkim duxom paxnet" [it smells Russian], Ludwig Radermacher (1906) the motif of people swallowed and spat out by a whale, and Walter Baumgartner (1915) the motif of people sold to the devil ("give me that which you don't know in your own home"). These authors reach no conclusions and refuse to draw any.

Individual plots have been studied in the same way. For example, Lutz Mackensen (1923) studied the tale of the Singing Bone, and Sven Liljeblad (1927) the tale of the Grateful Dead Man. Such works have seriously advanced our knowledge of the dissemination and life of individual plots, but they have not solved the question of origins. Therefore, at this stage, we should not study tales according to their plots: the wondertale is a whole, and all its plots are interconnected and mutually determined. For this reason, if for no other, it is wrong to study motifs in isolation. If Polívka had not only collected all the variants of the formula but had also posed the questions: Who pronounces this formula? Under what conditions does it occur? Who is greeted with such an exclamation?—that is, if he had studied it *in its connection with the whole*, he might well have come to a correct conclusion. A motif can be studied only within the plot system; plots can be studied only in their mutual interconnection.

The Wondertale as a Phenomenon of the Superstructure

Earlier I indicated that many premises are the product of the epoch in which the author lives. We live under socialism and have developed our own premises for the study of culture. But in contrast to the premises of other epochs, which led the humanities into a blind alley, our epoch has formulated premises showing them the only correct path. I mean a general law for studying all historical phenomena: "The mode of production of material life conditions the social, political, and intellectual life process in general" (Marx 1962, 363). It follows that we must find in history the mode of production that gave rise to the wondertale.

The most cursory glance at the wondertale will show that capitalism did not bring it forth. This does not mean that the capitalist mode of production is not reflected in the wondertale. The cruel factory owner, the greedy priest, the officer flogging soldiers, the deserter, the landowner oppressing farmhands, and the poverty-stricken, drunken, ruined peasantry—all figure in it, but the genuine wondertale, with its winged horses, firespitting dragons, fabulous kings, princesses, etc., is obviously not determined by capitalism; it is much older. The wondertale is also older than feudalism, as will become evident further along. It does not correspond to the mode of production in which it is current. The cause of this lack of correspondence was also explained by Marx: "With the change of the economic foundation, the entire immense superstructure is more or less rapidly transformed" (Marx 1962, 363). The words "more or less rapidly" are very important. A change in ideology does not always occur immediately after a change in the economic base. There is a "lack of correspondence" that is extremely interesting and valuable for scholarship. The wondertale arose on the basis of precapitalist modes of production and social life, and we must discover exactly on which ones.

Lack of correspondence of a similar type allowed Engels to shed light on the origin of the family. Citing Lewis H. Morgan, and referring to Marx, Engels (1962, 192) wrote:

> "The family," says Morgan, "represents an active principle. It is never stationary, but advances from a lower to a higher form as society advances from a lower to a higher condition. . . . Systems of consanguinity, on the contrary, are passive, recording the progress made by the family at long intervals apart, and only changing when the family has radically changed." "And," adds Marx, "the same is true of the political, juridical, religious, and philosophical systems generally."

The same is true of the wondertale. Originally, it was not tied to the mode of production of the early nineteenth century, the time when it was first recorded. This fact leads us to the next premise, which we will formulate, for the time being, in general terms: the wondertale must be compared with the historical reality of the past, and its roots should be sought there. This premise contains the undeciphered concept of the historical past. If we understand it as did Vsevolod Miller, we may reach the same conclusions he did, claiming for instance that Dobrynja Nikitič's[1] combat with a dragon goes back to the conversion of Novgorod to Christianity. We have to decipher this concept and determine just which element of the past explains the wondertale.

The Wondertale and the Social Institutions of the Past

If the wondertale really has a certain economic basis, we must examine the forms of production reflected in it. Direct references to production occur rarely in wondertales. Agriculture plays a minimal role in them, whereas hunting is reflected somewhat more broadly. Plowing and sowing are usually mentioned only at the beginning of the story. (The beginning is especially prone to change.) Further on in the narrative, a large role is played by marksmen, royal and free huntsmen, and various animals.

However, a survey of the forms of production in the wondertale only from the point of view of its *object* and *technique* will not tell us too much about its sources, for not the production technique but the social conditions that correspond to it are important. Such an approach narrows down the concept of the historical past in relation to the wondertale: now we have to determine under what social conditions separate motifs and entire tales sprang up.

"Social conditions" is, however, a very general notion. We need less abstract entities, for instance, social institutions. We cannot compare the situation in the wondertale with the situations in tribal society, but we can investigate some wondertale motifs in light of certain institutions of that society insofar as the wondertale reflects them or is conditioned by them. The roots of the wondertale must be sought in the social institutions of the past; this important premise refines the concept of the historical past relevant for the origin of the wondertale. For example, we see that the wondertale contains forms of marriage different from those of today. The hero goes in quest of a bride far away, rather than to his own people. This practice may reflect exogamy: it could have been forbidden to take a bride from one's own kin. We must examine forms of marriage in the wondertale and find the system, stage, phase, or level of social development that these forms reflected. In another instance, we see that the hero occupies the throne not of his own father, but of his father-in-law, whom he very often kills. This raises the question of what forms of power succession are reflected in the wondertale. In short, we set out from the premise that the wondertale preserves traces of vanished forms of social life, that these survivals should be studied, and that such study will reveal the sources of many motifs.

Of course, some motifs reflect institutions that once existed, whereas others do not. Consequently, not everything can be explained by the existence of social institutions.

The Wondertale and Ritual

It has long been recognized that the wondertale has some connection with cults and religion. Strictly speaking, cults and religion can also be called institutions. However, just as social conditions are manifested in institutions, religion is manifested in certain cult activities. Each of these activities cannot be called an institution: and the connection of the wondertale with religion poses a special question. In his *Anti-Dühring,* Engels (1966, 344-45) formulated the essence of religion quite clearly:

> All religion, however, is nothing but the phantastic reflection in men's minds of those external forces which control their daily life, a reflection in which the terrestrial forces assume the form of supernatural forces. In the beginnings of history it was the forces of Nature which were at first so reflected, and in the course of further evolution they underwent the most manifold and varied personifications among the various peoples. . . . But it is not long before, side by side with the forces of Nature, social forces begin to be active; forces which present themselves to man as equally extraneous and at first equally inexplicable, dominating them with the same apparent necessity as the forces of Nature themselves. The phantastic personifications, which at first only reflected the mysterious forces of Nature, at this point acquire social attributes, become representatives of the forces of history.

Just as one should not compare social systems described in wondertales with existing social systems in life *in general,* one should not compare religion in general with the religion as we find it in wondertales; only concrete manifestations of religion should be compared. Engels stated that religion is a reflection of natural forces and social forces. This reflection may be twofold: it may be either cognitive and result in dogmas and teachings or volitional and result in actions intended to *influence* nature and subjugate it. We will call such actions rituals and customs.

Ritual and custom are not the same thing. If corpses are cremated, that is custom, not ritual. But custom is accompanied by ritual, and it is methodologically incorrect to separate them. The tale has preserved traces of numerous rituals and customs, and the origin of many motifs can be explained only by reference to rituals. For example, there is a tale that narrates how a maiden buries the bones of a cow in a garden and sprinkles them with water (Afanas'ev 1957, no. 100). Such a custom or ritual really existed: animal bones were for some reason not eaten or disposed of, but buried (Propp 1934). If we could demonstrate which motifs go back to which rituals, the origin of these motifs would find an explanation. But the wondertale is not a chronicle, and between the wondertale and ritual are various forms of relations and various forms of connection.

Direct Correlation Between the Wondertale and Ritual

The simplest case is the complete congruence of ritual and custom with the wondertale. This case is rare. For instance, in the wondertale there is an episode of how bones are buried, and the same practice was known in life; or a wondertale narrates that royal children are locked in a dungeon, kept in darkness, and fed in secret, and exactly the same thing was done in life. Discovery of such parallels is important for the folklorist; it may turn out that the motif goes back to some ritual or custom that will explain its genesis.

Reinterpretation of Ritual in the Wondertale

More common is reinterpretation of the ritual, i.e., the replacement in the wondertale of one or several elements of the ritual that have become superfluous or incomprehensible with another element that is easier to understand. Reinterpretation is usually concomitant with a change in form. Most often it is the motivation that undergoes change, but other components of the ritual may be changed as well. For instance, the hero of a wondertale sews himself into the skin of a cow or horse to escape from a hole or reach a faraway kingdom. He is then seized by a bird; the skin, with the hero inside, is taken to some place on a mountain or beyond the sea that the hero would not have been able to reach in any other way. There is a well-known custom of sewing corpses in a skin. Systematic study of the custom and the motif demonstrates an indubitable connection between them;

they are congruent both in form and content: the meaning of the motif in the story parallels the meaning of the ritual in life. Yet there is one difference: in the wonder-tale the hero sews himself into the skin alive, whereas in the ritual it is *a corpse* that is sewn into it. Such a discrepancy is a simple instance of reinterpretation: in the custom, sewing into a skin made it possible for the deceased to reach the kingdom of the dead; in the wondertale a similar action makes it possible for the hero to reach the faraway kingdom. In other cases the original basis has become so blurred that it no longer can be found.

The term *reinterpretation* conveniently indicates the process of change. The fact of reinterpretation proves that in the life of a people some changes have occurred that entail a change in the motif.

Inversion of the Ritual

In one special case of reinterpretation all the forms of the ritual are preserved in the wondertale but are given an opposite meaning. I will call such cases inversions. Let us look at some examples. Formerly it was customary to kill aged people, but the wondertale narrates how an old man was spared. During the time that this custom existed, a person who showed mercy to the old man would have been held up to ridicule, perhaps castigated, or even punished; in the wonder-tale, the person who shows mercy to the old man is depicted as a praiseworthy hero who acts wisely. Similarly, it was customary to sacrifice a virgin to the river whose flood ensured good crops. This would be done at the beginning of sowing and was supposed to facilitate the growth of vegetation. But in the wondertale the maiden is rescued from the monster by the hero. As long as the ritual existed, such a "liberator" would have been torn to pieces as the greatest of profaners, as one who jeopardized the well-being of the people, the crops. The plot, therefore, sometimes displays a negative attitude toward an earlier historical reality. Such a plot (or motif) could not have sprung up in a wondertale while the system requiring the sacrifice of virgins still existed. But with the decay of the once sacred system, the custom in which a virgin went (sometimes willingly) to her death became needless and repugnant, and the role of the protagonist switched to the former profaner who interfered with the sacrifice. This is a highly significant discovery. It shows that the plot arises not in an evolutionary fashion by direct reflection of reality but by a negation of it. The plot stands in reverse relation to reality. Thereby we have confirmed Lenin's juxtaposition of development as evolution with development as the unity of opposites. "The second *alone* furnishes the key to the 'self-movement' of everything that exists; it alone furnished the key to the 'leaps,' to the 'break in continuity,' to the 'transformation into the opposite,' the 'destruction of the old and emergence of the new' " (Lenin 1961b, 360).

All these ideas and preliminary observations allow us to put forth another premise: the wondertale should be compared with ritual and custom so that we may determine which motifs go back to which ritual and what their interrelation is.

A specific difficulty arises here. Ritual, which arises as a means of struggling with nature, does not die out when rational means of struggling with and influencing nature are developed; instead, it is also reinterpreted. It may happen that the folklorist, while tracing a motif to ritual, will find that the motif goes back to a reinterpreted ritual, which itself has to be explained. Sometimes the original foundation of a ritual is so blurred that it demands special study. But that is the business of the ethnographer, not the folklorist.

There is another difficulty. Like ritual life, folklore is composed of thousands and thousands of different elements. Is it necessary to find economic causes for every element? In this connection Engels (1942, 482) says:

> The low level of economic development in the prehistoric period is supplemented and also partially conditioned and even caused by the false conceptions of nature. And even though economic necessity was the main driving force of the increasing knowledge of nature and has become ever more so, yet it would be pedantic to try and find economic causes for all the primitive nonsense.

These words are clear enough. We may add that if the same motif can be traced to tribal society, to slavery (as in ancient Egypt), to antiquity (a very usual case), etc., and if we are tracing the development of the motif, we need not point out each instance when the motif has changed owing to a new historical situation, rather than from within. We will try to avoid both pedantic and overly abstract schemes.

To return to ritual: generally, if a link has been established between ritual and the wondertale, it is the ritual that serves as the explanation of the corresponding motif in the tale. An abstract scheme admits only this conclusion, but sometimes the opposite is true: although the wondertale goes back to ritual, the ritual may be obscure, whereas the wondertale may have preserved the past so fully and accurately that the ritual (or some other past phenomenon) can be understood in its true light only through the wondertale. In some cases, the wondertale, instead of requiring explanation, itself explains something, namely, it serves as a source for studying the ritual. "The folk narratives of various Siberian tribes have served as our main source for reconstructing ancient totemic beliefs," said D. K. Zelenin (1936, 232). Ethnographers often rely on wondertales, though they do not always know them. This applies particularly to Frazer: the grand edifice of *The Golden Bough*[2] was erected on premises taken from wondertales, which he neither knew well enough nor understood properly. A meticulous study of the wondertale will allow us to introduce a number of corrections to that work and even shake its foundations.

The Wondertale and Myth

If we examine ritual as a manifestation of religion, we cannot ignore its other manifestation—myth. There is an enormous literature on the relationship of the wondertale and myth, which I will pass over. For the moment we may simply propose to study the problem and to include myth among the possible sources of the wondertale.

The variety of existing interpretations of myth makes it necessary to define this concept in precise terms. By myth we mean a tale about divinities or divine beings in whose reality people believe. Faith is not a psychological but a historical factor. Tales about Herakles are very close to the wondertale, but Herakles was a divinity, the object of a cult. The wondertale hero, who, like Herakles, sets out in search of the golden apples, is the protagonist of a fictional work. Myth and the wondertale differ in social function, not in form (Tronskij 1934). The social function of myth itself is not always the same and depends upon the stage of culture in which it is current. The myths of peoples in tribal society are one thing; the myths of ancient civilizations, known to us through their literature, are something quite different. Myth cannot be formally distinguished from the wondertale. Wondertales and myths (particularly the myths of preclass societies) sometimes overlap so much that in ethnography and folklore myths are often called wondertales. There has even been a certain fashion for "the wondertales of primitives," and many anthologies of such tales have been published, both scholarly and popular. A study of these texts as endowed with a social function reveals that most of them are myths rather than wondertales. Contemporary bourgeois folklore ignores the *all-important message of these myths*. They are collected but hardly studied. Thus, in Bolte and Polívka's index (1913-32), the "wondertales of primitives" occupy a modest place. However, such myths are not "variants"; they are products of earlier stages of economic development, products that have not yet lost their connection with their economic base. What has been reinterpreted in the contemporary European wondertale is frequently contained in myth in its original form. Myths often provide a key to understanding the wondertale.

Some scholars realize the message of primitive myths, but the matter does not progress beyond declarations. The fundamental significance of these myths has not been understood because the scholars have a formal, rather than a historical, point of view. Myths have been ignored as a historical phenomenon, whereas particular instances of the reverse dependence (of the folklore of "savage" peoples on that of "civilized" ones) have been noted and investigated. Only in the most recent times has the idea of the social significance of myth surfaced somewhat in bourgeois scholarship, which is now beginning to acknowledge the close link between the spoken word, *myths*, and sacred tales with the social organization of the tribe, ritual, moral, and even practical actions. Still these observations have never been extended to European wondertales; such an idea seems too bold.

Unfortunately in most cases myths have been recorded in an unsatisfactory way. Usually only the texts are given and nothing more. Often editors do not even say whether they know the language and whether they recorded the texts directly or through an interpreter. Even in the texts collected by such an outstanding scholar as Franz Boas there undoubtedly are retellings; however, he does not specify the fact anywhere, though the smallest details, minutiae, nuances, even the intonation, are important. Still worse is the situation when indigenous people narrate their myths in English. A. L. Kroeber published a number of such recordings in this fashion: his collection *Gros Ventre Myths and Tales* (1907) contains fifty texts, of which forty-eight were narrated in English, but this is mentioned in the middle of the book, in a footnote, as if it were a point of minor importance.[3]

We have already said that myth has a social significance and that its significance is not the same everywhere. Anyone can see the difference between Greek and Polynesian myths. Even preclass societies vary in this respect and should not be lumped together. Myths of individual countries and peoples differ according to their stage of culture. It has so happened that for my purposes the most valuable data have come from America and partly from Oceania and Africa and not from Europe or Asia, as one might expect from their territorial proximity to Russia. Asiatic peoples as a whole were on a higher cultural level than the peoples of America and Oceania when European ethnographers and folklorists began to study them. Moreover, Asia is a continent of very ancient civilizations, a melting pot in which streams of peoples resettled, mixed, and displaced one another. On the expanse of this continent are all stages of culture, from the nearly tribal Ainu to the most highly civilized Chinese,[4] and at present it is also the home of the socialist culture of the USSR. For this reason, the Asiatic data constitute a mixture that makes research difficult. Thus, the Yakuts tell the tale of Il'já Múromec along with their probably authentic Yakut myths. In Vogúl folklore are mentions of horses, of which the Voguls are ignorant[5] (Černecov 1935, 18). These examples show how easy it is to take the imported and the foreign for the authentic. As we aim at studying not the *phenomenon itself*, not the *texts*, but the connections of myth with the soil that gave rise to them, we run the great risk of misconstruing a phenomenon borrowed from India, to cite one example, for a phenomenon from the hunting stage only because it is found among a hunting people.

The same is also true of Africa, but to a lesser degree. On this continent are peoples at the lowest level of development, like the Bushmen, as well as cattle-raising peoples like the Zulu, and farming peoples already familiar with forging; nevertheless, mutual cultural influences are not so strong as in Asia. Unfortunately, African tales have sometimes been recorded no better than American ones. But American scholars are immediate neighbors of the American Indians, whereas Africa has been studied by newcomers, colonizers, and missionaries—French,

English, German, and Dutch—who have taken little trouble to learn the languages, and when they have, their purpose has not been to record folklore. Leo Frobenius, one of the most distinguished African scholars, knew no African languages, which did not prevent him from publishing great lots of African data without as much as a mention of how he obtained them. His practice cannot but put us on our guard. Even though America is by no means free from extraneous influences, it is America that has yielded data unregistered elsewhere.

The myths of Greco-Roman antiquity, Babylon, Egypt, and, in part, India and China are quite different. We do not know these myths directly from their creators—the lower strata of society—but only through literature: the poems of Homer, the tragedies of Sophocles, the works of Vergil, Ovid, and so on. Wilamowitz (1925, 41-62) refused to see any connection between Greek literature and folk culture. He asserted that Greek literature is as unsuitable for the study of folk plots as the works of Hebbel, Geibel, and Wagner for the study of the Nibelungen legend.[6] This approach, which denies any folk quality to ancient myth, opens the way to all kinds of reactionary theories. We will recognize a genuine folk quality in these myths but will remember that they have not come down to us in their pure form and consequently should not be equated with recordings from genuine oral tradition. By and large, the same applies to Egyptian myths, which again have not been obtained first-hand. The ideas of the Egyptians are known through gravestone inscriptions, the *Book of the Dead*, and so on. For the most part we know only the official religion, cultivated by priests for political ends and supported by the court and nobility. The lower strata may have had different concepts and even different plots. Nonetheless, the myths of ancient civilizations form part of my subject. They are *indirect* sources, while the myths of preclass societies are *direct* sources. They *reflect* popular notions, without *representing* them. It may turn out that the Russian wondertale is, in a way, more archaic than the Greek myth.

The wondertale should be compared with the myths of ancient civilizations as well as with those of primitive, preclass societies. This is my next premise and the final clarification of the concept *historical past*, introduced earlier for the comparison and study of the wondertale. I am not interested in individual events from the past, which by themselves are usually meant as history and were meant as history by the Russian Historical school.

The Wondertale and Primitive Thought

As pointed out earlier, we are looking for the foundations of wondertale images and plots in the reality of the past. However, the wondertale also contains images and situations that do not hark directly back to any reality. Among such images are the winged serpent and the winged horse, the little hut on chicken legs, Koščej, etc.

It would be a great mistake to take a purely empirical position and view the wondertale as some sort of chronicle, as do those scholars who search prehistory for real winged serpents and assert that the wondertale preserves recollections of them. Winged serpents and huts on chicken legs have never existed. Yet they are historical—indeed, not *in themselves* but *in their origins*.

Ritual and myth are conditioned by economic interests. If, for example, people dance to bring on rain, this behavior is caused by a wish to influence nature; but it is not clear why they just dance, sometimes with live serpents (Warburg, 1938-39, 286). We could more easily understand them if they poured water (as is frequently done), for such an action would be no more than an instance of sympathetic magic. This example shows that the action is not caused *directly* by economic interests, but is a result of a certain *thought-process*, conditioned by the same factors as the action itself. Both ritual and myth are products of thought. Although it is sometimes difficult to explain and determine the forms of thought, the folklorist must not only take them into account but also find out what ideas underlie certain motifs. Primitive thought does not know abstractions; it manifests itself in behavior, forms of social organization, folklore, and language. Occasions arise when a wondertale motif cannot be explained by any of the premises adopted so far. For example, some motifs rest on an understanding of space, time, and number different from ours. It follows that the forms of primitive thought must also be considered if we wish to explain the genesis of the wondertale. Here I can only indicate this enormously complex question as supplying another premise of my research. If we recognize that thought is a historically determined category, we will not need to "interpret" myths, rituals, and wondertales. And indeed my objective is not to interpret them but to trace them to their historical antecedents. Myth has its own semantics, but fixed, absolute semantics divorced from history does not exist. The entire situation is fraught with great danger: one can easily mistake the reality of thought for the reality of actual life, and vice versa. If Baba Jaga threatens to eat the hero, it does not necessarily follow that we are dealing with a vestige of cannibalism. The figure of the ogress could well have arisen in another way—as the reflection of certain mental (and in that sense, historical) images, rather than of images borrowed from reality and everyday life.

Genesis and History

The present work aims at discovering the genesis of the wondertale. A genetic investigation, though always historical, is not the same thing as a historical investigation. Genetics attempts to discover the *origins* of things, whereas history concentrates on their development; genetics precedes history and paves the way for it. This book, too, concerns itself with the movement of phenomena, and all institutions to which the wondertale is traceable are examined in it as processes. For example, when I establish the connection between some wondertale motifs and notions of death, I view death as a developing, rather than an abstract, concept. The reader can even get the impression that he is presented with the history or prehistory of individual motifs, but, though I treat several processes in relatively great detail, the result is not history. It is also a common occurrence that the phenomenon to which the wondertale has been traced is clear in itself but cannot be developed into a process. This happens with some very early forms of social life, surprisingly well preserved in the wondertale—for example, the initiation rite. Their history requires a special historical and ethnographic investigation, which may be beyond the folklorist's means. Numerous attempts fail just for want of an exhaustive ethnographic analysis, and therefore, the historical treatment of many phenomena is not always equally profound and broad. Often, one can at best point out the existing connection. A certain disproportion is also caused by the different "specific weights" of wondertale motifs. The more important, "classical" motifs of the wondertale will be discussed in detail, while other, less important, ones will not.

Method and Material

Although the principles set forth here may seem simple, their realization presents serious difficulties. The greatest of them lies in mastering the data. Scholars often make the mistake of confining their material to one plot or one culture or of fixing some other arbitrary limits. A case in point is Hermann Usener (1965), who studied the plot, or myth, of the world flood only in ancient texts. Surely, a subject of this kind can be narrowed down, but all-embracing conclusions about genesis should not be drawn from limited data. Folklore is an international phenomenon. Granted this universality, the folklorist is at a great disadvantage in comparison with specialists in Indology, classics, Egyptology, and so on, who are complete masters of their fields. The folklorist only touches those fields as a guest or wanderer, to make a few observations and go on. One cannot have a full command of everything; but it is absolutely necessary to broaden the framework of folklore studies. One must risk errors, annoying misunderstandings, and inaccuracies. This is a dangerous practice but it is less so than methodologically incorrect premises based on perfect mastery of partial data. A similar broadening is necessary even for specialized research, which, too, must be illuminated by comparative data. So many preliminary works on individual cultures and peoples exist that we must at least try to use them, even though our knowledge is imperfect.

Thus, I believe that an investigation can begin even if the data have not been exhausted; this is my next premise. I defend my view not out of necessity; I really find it acceptable as a principle. Here I agree to differ with most scholars, but I find support for my position in the recurrence and inner organization of folklore facts. I am going to study the *recurring* elements of the wondertale, and it matters little whether I have considered all 200, 300, or 5,000 variants and versions of each existing element. The same applies to rituals, myth, and so on. "If one should wait until the material for a law was *in a pure form*," said Engels, "it would mean suspending the process of thought in an investigation until then and, if only for this reason, the law would never come into being" (1940, 159). All facts either require explanation—for us this is first and foremost the wondertale—or provide it. Everything else is only *test material*. A law always reveals itself gradually, and the initial choice of data is not predetermined. Therefore, the folklorist does not have to consider the entire mass of facts; if the law is true, it will be true everywhere.

The principle proposed here is at variance with current practice. Usually the first order of business is to exhaust the material. But even where this goal has been achieved, questions have been solved incorrectly, because they have been asked incorrectly. I believe that a question correctly asked will result in a correct method and the correct solution.

The Wondertale and Later Formations

It follows from the foregoing remarks that I consider rituals, myths, forms of primitive thought, and some social institutions as belonging to the wondertale world; I believe that they can explain the wondertale. But folklore comprises more than the wondertale. Related to the wondertale in plot and motif are the heroic epic and all sorts of tales and legends—for instance, the *Mahabharata*[7], the *Odyssey* and the *Iliad*, the *Elder Edda*, bylinas, the *Nibelungenlied,* etc. Generally these monuments will be disregarded, for they themselves can be explained by the wondertale and often hark back to it. True, it sometimes happens that epic poetry has preserved elements and features absent elsewhere. For example, in the *Nibelungenlied,* Siegfried, after killing the dragon, bathes in its blood and acquires invulnerability. This is an important episode; it explains something about the image of the dragon (serpent) that cannot be found in the wondertale. In such cases, for lack of other data, we may make use of the heroic epic as well.

Prospects

My premises are now clear, and so is the main task. What prospects will open to us through our comparison? Suppose we have found that in the wondertale children are thrown into a dungeon and that in historical reality this was also done. Or suppose we have found that a maiden preserves the bones of a slaughtered cow and that in reality this was also done. Can we conclude that in such cases the motif entered the wondertale from historical reality? Undoubtedly we can. But will we not then obtain an unusually fragmented picture? We do not know yet. It is usually believed that the wondertale has absorbed elements of primitive social and cultural life. We will see that they are, indeed, its very substance. As a result, we will obtain a picture of the sources of the wondertale.

The solution of this problem will advance us in our understanding of the wondertale but will leave us facing other equally difficult questions, for example, Why did people tell such stories? and, How did the wondertale take shape as a narrative genre? By discovering the source of individual motifs as plot components, I will lay bare the source of storytelling and of the wondertale as such. As regards the questions formulated above, I will try to answer them in the final chapter; here we have to consider a more special problem. It is impossible to separate the telling of wondertales from the telling of other tales, e.g., animal tales, and until other genres have been studied from a historical point of view, all our conclusions about the wondertale will be preliminary and hypothetical.

Obviously, a search like this can never be considered finished; the present book is only an *introduction* to the study of the wondertale. This work is like an exploratory expedition to lands yet unknown. We make note of the mineral deposits and draw outline maps, but a thorough mining of each deposit must wait until the future. The next step can consist of a detailed study of the individual motifs and plots in conjunction with the whole. At this stage it is more important to examine the connection of phenomena than to delve deeply into each of them. A last reservation is in order here. This study is based on the Russian wondertale, especially northern. As indicated above, the wondertale is international and its motifs are also largely international. Russian folklore is varied, highly artistic, and well preserved. For this reason it is only to be expected that a Soviet scholar should first turn to his native, rather than foreign, folklore. I have considered all the basic types of wondertale. These types are represented in the world repertoire by both Russian and foreign material. In comparative studies it makes no difference which examples of a given type are chosen. Where Russian data have proved insufficient I have used foreign examples, but my book is not research into the Russian wondertale. It examines comparative historical folklore, with Russian tales as its point of departure.

Chapter Eight.
Historical Roots
of the Wondertale:
The Wondertale as a Whole

The Unity of the Wondertale

We have examined the sequence of compositional elements in the wondertale. These elements are the same for various plots. They follow one another in a definite way and form a whole. We have also examined the sources of each motif, but we have not yet compared the sources and their interrelationships. To put it differently: although we know the sources of the individual motifs, we do not know the source of their sequence; we do not know the source of the wondertale as a whole.

A quick retrospective look at our sources will show that many wondertale motifs derive from social institutions, among which the rite of initiation occupies a special place. We also observe many ideas about the world beyond the grave and journeys to the other world. These two sequences yield the greatest number of motifs. Some motifs are traceable to other sources.

If we arrange our results according to sources or historical correspondences, the following picture will emerge. The initiation complex gives rise to these motifs: children led into or abandoned in the forest or abducted by a forest spirit; the hut; the provisional contract; the hero beaten by a witch; the cutting off of a finger; feigning death to the survivors; the witch's oven; hacking someone to pieces and resuscitating this person; the swallowing and spitting out of the hero; receiving a magic agent or help; disguise and changing one's sex; the forest teacher; sorcery. The period before the wedding and the moment of return are reflected in the motifs of the big house, the table set inside the big house, the hunters, the robbers, the little sister, a beautiful woman in her grave, a beautiful woman in the enchanted garden and castle (Psyche), the Unwashed One (*Neumójka*), the husband at his wife's wedding, the wife at her husband's wedding, the forbidden pantry, and several others. These correspondences show that initiation is the oldest basis of the wondertale. The motifs underlying the plot can be combined into countless tales.

The other sequence that corresponds to the wondertale is formed by ideas about death. This group of motifs includes maidens abducted by dragons; all kinds of miraculous births; the return from the dead and the setting off on a journey in iron shoes; the forest as the entrance to the other world; the hero's scent; sprinkling the doors of the hut; the witch's banquet; the ferryman; a long journey by eagle, horse, boat, etc.' combat with the guardian who watches over the entrance and tries to devour the newcomer; being weighed on scales; and otherworld journeys with all that accompanies arrival there.

Combinations of these two sequences yield *nearly* all the basic items of the wondertale. It is impossible to draw the line between the two, for the entire initiation rite was experienced as a visit to the land of death, and conversely, the deceased went through everything experienced by the initiate—he received a helper, encountered a swallower, and so forth.

If one envisions everything that happens to the initiate and narrates it in sequence, the result will be the compositional basis of the wondertale. If one narrates in sequence everything thought to happen to the deceased, the story will produce the same core, with the addition of some elements absent from the rites.

The compositional unity of the wondertale lies neither in the specific features of the human psyche nor in the peculiarities of artistic creation; rather, it lies in the reality of the past. What is now recounted as a story was once enacted or represented, and what was not enacted was imagined. Of the two sequences, the first (the initiation rite) was lost earlier than the second. The ritual was no longer performed, but old ideas about death survived, developed, and changed, even divorced from ritual. The disappearance of the ritual went hand in hand with the disappearance of hunting as the only, or main, source of livelihood.

From that point the plot developed as a kernel that absorbed new details from later reality. On the other hand, new ways of life created new genres, like the novella, but their soil was different from the soil that produced the composition and plot of the wondertale. The development proceeded by adding new layers by changes, reinterpretations, and so on, as well as by innovations. Thus, the motif of royal children locked in a dungeon derived from the custom of isolating kings, priests, magicians, and their children. The motif of the deceased father or grateful dead man who gives the hero a horse corresponds functionally to the motif of the witch making the same gift. Under the influence of ancestor worship, a later phenomenon, the character of the donor was reinterpreted and distorted, while his function was preserved. Consequently, the question of motifs unconnected to the sequences mentioned above should be solved on an individual basis. A case in point is the hero's marriage and ascending the throne. The princess is reminiscent of the independent woman of high birth who possesses totemic magic. She can also be compared to the widow or daughter of a king who has been killed and disposed of by his heir.

Especially problematic are the motifs connected with difficult tasks. It cannot be proved that the wondertale has preserved the custom of testing the heir's magic powers, but some evidence seems to point in this direction.

In later periods the law according to which the composition of the tale is preserved while its characters are changed remained stable, and the development of the wondertale proceeded in conformity with this law. Daily life and changing customs are the sources of many substitutions. Thus, the beggarwoman is the modified Baba Jaga; the two-story house with a balcony, the modified men's house, and so on.

This conclusion is at variance with current notions of the wondertale. It is usually believed that, though the wondertale contains elements from prehistory, as a whole it is the product of "free" artistic creation. Actually, the wondertale consists of elements deriving from phenomena and ideas of preclass society.

The Wondertale As a Genre

We have discovered the sources of the individual motifs. We have also discovered that their connection and sequence are not accidental. But none of this explains the origin of the wondertale as a genre. What is the most ancient stage of storytelling? During the rite of initiation the young man was told something. What was it?

The composition of myths and wondertales coincides with the sequence of events during initiation, which suggests that someone described to the young man the very thing that was happening to him, but with reference to an ancestor—the founder of the clan and its customs—who had been born in some miraculous fashion, had spent time in the kingdom of bears, wolves, etc., and had come back with fire and magic dances, the ones the elders were showing the young man. At first, these events were not so much recounted as portrayed in a conventional dramatic way. They also formed the subject matter of applied arts. The carving and ornaments of many peoples cannot be understood without knowledge of their legends and "wondertales." The initiate learned the meaning of the rites he passed through. The tales were part of the cult and were secret. This secrecy is another proof of the hypothesis that the narrative was directly connected with the rite.

Unfortunately, almost all collections of tales from so-called primitive peoples contain nothing but texts. We are ignorant about the situation and circumstances in which they were told. However, there are exceptions. In the introduction to his *Traditions of the Skidi-Pawnee*, George A. Dorsey (1904) provided a complete picture of how such tales function. He mentioned numerous ceremonies and dances, including the ceremony of transmitting the sacred bundles. These bundles are a sort of amulet, kept in the home and considered the home's holy protectors. Well-being, luck, success in the hunt, etc., depend upon them. Their contents vary; they can contain feathers, grain, tobacco leaves, and so on. In short, we recognize in them the prototype of "magic gifts." "Each bundle ceremony and each dance was accompanied, not only by its ritual, but by its tale of origin," said Dorsey (xxi). As the collector indicated, such a tale might include information about how the first owner of the bundle had gone off into the forest, met a buffalo, and had been led by him into the buffalo kingdom, where he received the amulet and was taught the dances. Then he returned, taught all this to his people, and became their chieftain. Each tale was "generally the personal property of the keeper or owner of the bundle or dance, and, as a rule, was related immediately after the recitation of the ritual or at the time of the transmission of the possession of the bundle or the ceremony to its next owner" (xxi-xxii). The tale is part of the ritual; it is attached to the rite and to the person who is to take possession of the amulet. It is a sort of verbal amulet, a magic agent to affect the surrounding world. "Thus, each of these tales was esoteric. . . . Hence it is that only with the greatest difficulty can anything like an origin-myth of the Skidi as a whole be obtained" (xxii).

Two things deserve special mention. First, as already indicated, tales exist alongside ritual and form an integral part of it. Second, we note the sources of a phenomenon that continues right up to the present—namely, the interdiction of storytelling. Storytelling was forbidden, and the ban was observed not for reasons of etiquette, but because of the magic functions inherent in the tale and in the act of narration. "As he [the storyteller] tells them, he gives out from himself a certain part of his life, levying a direct contribution upon its termination. Thus, as one middle-aged individual exclaimed, 'I cannot tell you all that I know, for I am not yet ready to die;' or as an old priest expressed it, 'I know that my days are short. My life is no longer of use. There is no reason why I should not tell you all that I know' " (xxii).

We will return to the interdictions later, but now let us again examine the tie between tales and ritual. Some people may object that the phenomenon noted by Dorsey is too local. Dorsey himself seems to have thought so, for he cited no comparative material. However, this objection is not valid. The link between the tale and rite cannot be *proved*, but it can be richly demonstrated. Consider Franz Boas's collection of Indian legends and his research into the social organization and secret societies of the Kwakiutl tribe (Boas 1895 and 1897). The collection contains only texts. From the point of view of traditional folklore, these are "Indian versions" or "variants" of wondertales and motifs known in Europe. At first blush they seem to be mere fiction. But everything changes the moment we look at the social organization of any one tribe. The texts suddenly appear in a completely new light. We begin to realize how closely they are connected with the entire way of life of the tribe—so much so that neither the rituals nor the tribe's institutions can be understood without the tales, the "legends" as Boas called them, while the tales themselves become comprehensible only from an analysis of social life. They are not simply a component part of social life; in the eyes of the tribe they are one of the prerequisites of life, on a par with tools and amulets, and they are protected and preserved as the Holy of Holies. "The myths are literally the most precious treasure of the tribe. They belong to the very core of what the tribe considers holy. The most important myths are known only to the old men, who jealously guard their secret. . . . The old preservers of this secret knowledge sit in the villages silent as sphinxes and decide to what degree they can without danger entrust the knowledge of the ancestors to the younger generation, and at what precise moment this transfer of the mysteries will be most fruitful" (Lévy-Bruhl 1937, 262). Myths are not only components of life; they are part of every individual person. To take away a man's tale is tantamount to taking away his life. Such myths have inherent economic and social functions, and this is not a local phenomenon, this is a law. Divulging a myth would deprive it of its sacral character and thereby of its magic or "mystical" (Lévy-Bruhl) force. Without its myths a tribe would not be able to perpetuate itself.

Unlike the wondertale, whose plot content is a relic, myth provides a living link between a tale and the entire reality of a people, their economic production, social structure, and beliefs. The animals encountered by the hero and by the initiate's ancestor were represented on totem poles; the objects mentioned in the legends were carried and worn during the dances, and the dances depicted bears, owls, crows, and other animals that give the initiate magic power.

The data and comments presented in this book explain how a certain category of myth comes into being, but they tell us nothing about the origin of the *wondertale*. In Chapter One I noted that the wondertale is not the product of the social order in which it is current. Now I can formulate this conclusion more precisely. The plot and composition of the wondertale are conditioned by a kinship system at the stage of development represented by the American tribes that Dorsey, Boas, and others have investigated. Basis and superstructure correspond directly in this case. The new social function of the plot and its purely *artistic* use are linked to the disappearance of the order that gave rise to them. Externally, the beginning of this process—the degeneration of myth into the wondertale—is manifested in the detaching of the plot and narrative from ritual. When this detachment takes place, the history of the wondertale begins, whereas the syncretism of the tale with the rite belongs to its prehistory. The rupture may have occurred naturally, as a historical necessity, or it may have been accelerated by the coming of the Europeans, the conversion of the Indians to Christianity and the forced resettlement of entire tribes to new, inferior lands, the change in their way of life, the change in their mode of production, and so on. Dorsey, too, observed this detachment. One should not forget that Europeans have been the masters of America for more than 500 years now, and we often see only the reflection of the original situation there; it has already begun to disintegrate and only its fragments, its more or less obliterated traces, are still visible. "Naturally, these myths about the origin of bundles and dances do not always remain the exclusive property of the priesthood; they find their way among the ordinary people, where, when told, they lose much of their original meaning. Thus, by a gradual process of deterioration, they come to be regarded as of no especial religious significance, and are told as tales are told" (Dorsey 1904, xxii). Dorsey called the process of detachment from the rite "deterioration." However, the wondertale devoid of its religious functions is not inferior to the myth from which it was derived. On the contrary, exempt from religious conventions, it finally emerges into the free air of artistic creation, now motivated by different social factors, and begins to live a life of its own.

I have been able to explain not only the origin of the plot in terms of its content but also the origin of the wondertale as an artistic narrative. I want to repeat that my reconstruction cannot be *proved*; it can only be demonstrated on copious data. But such a demonstration is not my objective.

One more point should be cleared up. I have discussed only wondertales. I thought it possible to separate them from other tales and to study them in isolation. After breaking the contact, I must now close it once more, for the study of other genres may change our idea of how the wondertale was formed.

I have examined the rites and myths of so-called primitive peoples and linked them to modern wondertales, but I have not studied the wondertales of these peoples, I have not taken into account a possible *early artistic tradition*. Although this work has not concerned itself with plots unrelated to the wondertale, I believe that many other tales, for example, animal tales, have the same origin. This common origin should be proved by special investigations, and I will mention only a few facts. American Indian tales seem to be of an entirely ritual nature, and the wondertale in our sense of the word is unknown to the aborigines. The folklorist will find such a thesis less convincing than the ethnographer, who is familiar with the texts and the circumstances of their functioning. Neuhauss observed this state of things in the former German colony of New Guinea. The indigenous population "knew only legends: they had no concept of either Märchen or fables. Stories that to us are fantastic fairytales are for them legends like any others" (Neuhauss 1911, 161). Lévy-Bruhl was of the same opinion (1937, 267). This view finds confirmation in animal tales. For example, in North America there is a cycle of tales about the coyote, humorous stories about the coyote's tricks. The Skidi Indians say of him, "Coyote is a wonderful fellow. He knows all things, and is virtually indestructible. Moreover, he is full of wild conceits and is very tricky and is overcome only with the greatest difficulty, and rarely ever finally vanquished" (Dorsey 1904, xxii). But these wondertales are narrated before some enterprise, when the coyote's wit must be transferred to the narrator. What is claimed here about American Indians, Bogoráz observed among some Paleo-Siberian tribes. "Korjak-Kamčadal folklore is cheerful and mocking. Many strange and funny stories are told about the crow Quth—how he did battle with the mischievous little mice-girls, how he set fire to his own house, and so on. Quth sometimes appears as a man and sometimes as a crow. Folklore treats him without any respect. At the same time, Quth is also the Demiurge-Crow who *created heaven and earth*. Quth created man, procured fire for him, and then presented him with beasts to hunt'' (Bogoraz 1936). What Bogoraz considered to be lack of respect may reflect admiration for the crow's shrewdness, as Dorsey pointed out. In any case, if the crow who is the hero of such funny tales is the creator of heaven and earth and if the tales are told before the hunt, here, too, the sacral character of the tale is beyond doubt, and the idea of the sacral character of various folktales gains additional support. After all, initiation was not the only rite; there were also seasonal hunting, sowing, and harvest rites and many, many others, each of which could have had its own origin-myth. The connection of these rites with myths and the connection of both rites and myths with the wondertale has never been studied. One would have to examine the entire corpus of preclass folklore to provide worthwhile insights.

The "profanation" of the sacral plot began very early; by "profanation" I mean the transformation of a sacral tale into a profane, artistic (not spiritual or "esoteric") one. This is the moment when the wondertale springs up. But it is impossible to draw an exact temporal line between the sacral story and the wondertale. As was shown by D. K. Zelénin (1934) the interdiction of storytelling and the practice of ascribing to tales a magic influence over the hunt persist to this day even among cultured peoples. This is true of Vogul and Mari[1] tales, for instance. But these are all relics, survivals, whereas among the Indians tales are almost all sacral, that is, myths, though even in this case they are becoming detached from rite and display rudiments of purely artistic tales, just like the modern wondertale.

The wondertale absorbed the social and ideological culture of earlier epochs. But the wondertale is certainly not the only successor to religion. Religion as such has also changed and itself contains extremely ancient traits. All the ideas about the world beyond the grave and the fate of the deceased that were developed in Egypt, Greece, and later in Christianity arose much earlier. Likewise, shamanism took over a great deal from prehistoric epochs, and much of it has been preserved in the wondertale. If we collect shamans' tales of their trances—how the shaman went to seek a soul in the other world, who helped him in this endeavor, how he was conveyed, and so forth—and compare these with the wanderings and flight of the wondertale hero, the correspondence will be obvious. I have traced this correspondence for individual elements, but it also exists at the level of the whole. Thus, I can account for the similarity in the composition of myth, the tale of a journey beyond the grave, the shaman's narrative, the wondertale, and later of the poem, the bylina, and the heroic song. With the rise of feudal culture, some elements of folklore become the property of the dominant class; cycles of heroic legends, such as *Tristan and Isolde* and the

Nibelungenlied, are based on this folklore. The movement proceeds from the bottom up and not in the other direction, as reactionary theoreticians assert.

I have offered a historical explanation of a phenomenon that has always been considered difficult, viz., the universal similarity of folklore plots. This similarity is much broader and deeper than it appears to the naked eye. Neither the theory of diffusion nor the theory of psychic unity put forth by the Anthropological school can solve this problem. The solution lies in the joint historical study of folklore and the production of material life.

The problem that seemed so complicated is not insoluble. But a problem once solved always gives rise to new problems. Folklore can proceed in two directions: it can study either the similarity or differences among phenomena. Folklore, particularly the wondertale, is both uniform and varied. The study of this variety and of individual plots is more difficult than the study of compositional similarity. If the solution proposed here is correct, it becomes possible to examine, interpret, and trace the origin of individual plots from an entirely new angle.[2]

Chapter Nine.
Ritual Laughter in Folklore
(A Propos of the Tale of the
Princess Who Would Not Laugh
[Nesmejána])

The Tale of the Princess Who Would Not Laugh (Nesmejana)

The tale of Nesmejana is not especially famous or popular. It is not "Little Red Riding Hood," "The Sleeping Beauty," "The Tale of the Fisherman and His Wife," or the like. It has not inspired poets; there are no operas or pictures based on it. In the inventory of Russian folktales it is represented by a total of five recordings (Andreev 1929, no. 559). Nevertheless, this modest folktale is of outstanding interest.

Like other folktales, "Nesmejana" cannot be easily forced into a definite plot scheme. Its features are rather diverse, and it partly overlaps other plots and types. The kernel of the situation is that for some reason a princess never laughs. The king promises his daughter's hand to him who will make her laugh. The task is solved in different ways, but there are three main variants. In one, the hero has helpers: grateful animals that he has bought, redeemed, etc. In front of the palace windows he falls into the mud or a puddle. The animals (a mouse, crab, beetle, catfish, etc.) tenderly clean him off with their paws and help him, and this evokes the princess's laughter. In another, the hero owns a golden goose, and everyone who touches it remains stuck. A chain is formed, and the spectacle of the procession makes the princess laugh (the index treats this case as a special type: Andreev 1929, no. 571). In the third variant the hero owns a magic pipe and causes three pigs to dance to its sounds under the princess's window. She laughs, and their marriage follows.

The folktale consists of elements that can occur elsewhere. Thus, the motif of people who cannot pry themselves loose is not uniquely characteristic of "Nesmejana." An unfaithful wife is exposed in the same way (Afanas'ev 1957, no. 256; Zelenin 1915, nos. 22, 55—punishing an unfaithful bride; Smirnov 1917, no. 44; Xudjakóv 1860-62, vol. 3, no. 99— exposing a priest's thieving daughter). The motif of the hero who falls into a puddle to make the princess laugh presents no problems: this is an ad hoc comic situation.

However, the motif of the dancing pigs is very important for understanding the history of "Nesmejana." More often this motif is part of another folktale, usually called "The Marks of the Princess" (Andreev 1929, no. 850). The two folktales are so closely related in form and, as will be shown below, in origin that one cannot be studied without the other. The plot of this tale is very simple. The hand of the princess is promised to him who will find out her marks. The hero accomplishes this task with the aid of the dancing pigs. In order to obtain a pig she shows the hero her marks. At first glance it seems that the affinity or similarity between the tales is not so great. This affinity will come to light gradually. We will note only that neither tale necessarily ends in marriage. In both, the marriage is followed by another very important and interesting concluding episode, the shaming of the rival.

The Main Problem and the Method for Its Solution

We intend to study the tale of "Nesmejana." What does "to study a folktale" mean? We can, for example, collect all the recorded variants and compare them. This work has been done for "Nesmejana" by Polívka (1904). We can also map the distribution of the plot and define different versions and redactions, the extent of their distribution, etc. This stage is indispensable, and without Polívka's work the present study would not have appeared. But this is only preliminary work, *Sichtung*, as Engels called it in *Anti-Dühring*. Such a *sifting* of the data permits only partial conclusions, and Polívka, a very cautious scholar, whose caution verged on agnosticism, did not draw even these partial conclusions.

The problem will not be solved by collecting and comparing data, because they are taken in isolation instead of in their interrelationships. Engels called the study of isolated phenomena "metaphysical thinking." Its opposite is a dialectical study. "An exact representation of the universe, of its evolution and that of mankind, as well as the reflection of this evolution in the human mind, can therefore only be built up in a dialectical way, taking constantly into account the general actions and reactions of becoming and ceasing to be, of progressive or retrogressive changes" (Engels 1966, 29). Engels is speaking about scholarship in general. The folklorist should apply these principles to folklore.

The folktale is an ideological phenomenon, a reflection of the world in men's minds. It is not a reflection of itself. We know what calls forth phenomena of the superstructure and what causes them: there is no need to go into the theory of basis and superstructure. If the folktale reflects the forms of production that existed at very early stages, one may speak about the paleontological analysis of a folktale motif. Each motif must be listed and examined in terms of socioeconomic stages and of the changes in the motif that correspond to them, rather than in terms of territorial distribution and formal differences ("variants"). Many folktales have preserved such unambiguous traces of tribal organization, hunting, and early forms of agriculture as the basic form of production, together with traces of the social institutions that went with them, early forms of thought, family relations and marriage, etc., that a careful comparison of the folktale and the past leaves no doubts about the historical roots of most folktale motifs.

The methodology for such an analysis can be elaborated in great detail, but one motif is hardly worth the effort, since the motif of the princess who does not laugh reflects only a few of the relationships known to the wondertale.

Where do we stand with "Nesmejana"? What are the historical roots of this motif? Usually the comparison of variants leads to certain initial suppositions and preliminary hypotheses and points the direction in which one can begin a historical search. This, however, is not the case with "Nesmejana." The motif under study contains no *direct* traces of the historical past. Tens, even hundreds of variants of this tale are just as enigmatic as each individual text.

The situation changes when we broaden the investigation. The content of this motif is related to *laughter*. Laughter had a definite religious, or ritual, significance, and if "Nesmejana" is connected with it, then the historical roots of this motif clear up somewhat. Consequently, we must digress from the folktale and discover the character of laughter in general, though not in the sense of abstract philosophical constructions, the way Bergson did in his book on laughter (1938) but as a historical entity. We must examine the phenomenon in its development and in its connections with the life of the peoples among whom we observe it. This extended examination of the data is the first step in studying the subject, but not yet an investigation as such. The study of laughter in general, and not only of "Nesmejana," will give a firm basis to the entire construction and show that the connection between the princess who does not laugh and the dancing pigs is not accidental.

It has long since been observed that laughter had a special meaning in the religious life of the past. Laughter was discussed by Usener (1913), Reinach (1912), and Fehrle (1930). Fluck's work (1934) is devoted to Paschal laughter, as is the older work by Müller (not noted by Fluck). Mercklin (1851) studied sardonic laughter. In addition, there are individual statements in the more general works of Mannhardt (1858, 1884), Norden (1924), Dieterich (1911), O. M. Freudenberg, and others. These works have been of great use to the present author, especially with regard to classical material. But they did not solve the problem. They are all brief essays containing a certain amount of data followed by attempts at explanations, or rather guesses.

Usener compared laughter accompanying death and funerals with laments and believed that laughter frees people from grief. Someone who is grieving must be made to laugh and, therefore, buffoons mix with mourners. Fehrle expressed approximately the same opinion, "Everyday experience shows that people who can go through life with a light heart, laughing, are in general healthier and better able to cope with reality than those who feel dejected. And thus people came to demand laughter as something vital in dire need and to establish it partially as a religious custom" (Fehrle 1930, 4-5).

For O. M. Freudenberg (1936, 100) "Laughter . . . is semanticized . . . as a new shining of the sun, as the birth of the sun." Reinach (1912, 111) believed that laughter expresses the intensity, or fullness of life: "That is why Homer speaks about the laughter of the greening earth" (*Iliad* XIX, 362). Explanations of Paschal laughter are no better. The term refers to the fact that in the Middle Ages at Easter the priest tried to make his congregation laugh by telling various jokes (frequently obscene) during the divine liturgy. Fluck thought that after the long fast of Lent merriment was needed.

We see that the scholars did not draw conclusions from their data but appealed to "everyday experience" and gave crudely rationalistic or abstract philosophical explanations. I will not discuss these works further. They could not give the desired results, because the authors did not observe the principle of affinity (their data were examined in isolation, and all folklore was left out) or the principle of development (data of different periods were lumped together, without any historical perspective, without any differentiation, and without any connection with the basis). Peoples at the preclass stage were ignored, among them the natives of America, Oceania, Africa, and Siberia, whose customs shed light on the problem. I have done the preliminary work in another manner.

Laughter is a special type of conditioned reflex, but it is a reflex that characterizes man alone and has its own history. To understand ritual laughter we must reject our ideas of the comic. We do not laugh now as people once laughed. Therefore, it is hardly possible to give a general philosophical definition of the comic and of laughter: such a definition can be only historical.

I have taken from the world's inventory of folklore, ritual, religion, and myth everything that relates to laughter. Rituals, beliefs, myths, folktales, and games also have been considered. I have noted for each fact which people it characterizes. A "people" is important to us not as an ethnic or racial unit but as a representative and example of a particular socioeconomic stage. This approach prepares the ground for a genuinely scientific explanation of the phenomenon and eliminates guesswork. The second phase of the research was distribution of the data, which could have proceeded in two directions: the data could have been distributed either by varieties of laughter (for example, laughter accompanying death, laughter accompanying sowing, etc.) or by peoples in accordance with the stage of their development. This is the most critical, the most exciting moment in the investigation. Something really remarkable emerged. It turned out that there were not two points of view or two possibilities for classification. It turned out that each category or type of laughter characterizes peoples at a certain stage in their economic and social development. The result was a historical sequence, rather than a rootless classification. It proved the connection between types of laughter and the stages and explained certain outwardly puzzling forms of material production in the past.

The folktale also took its place in this historical sequence; it proved to be the last link in it—a phenomenon characteristic of the last stage before socialism, that is, capitalism. The social functions of the folktale are different from those of myth and ritual.

Yet this research has a flaw unavoidable in small works, namely, artificial limitation of the phenomenon. Any phenomenon must be examined in all its interconnections. The very task of investigating one plot is incorrect for folklore. As pointed out earlier, "Nesmejana" cannot be studied without the folktale "The Marks of the Princess"; but "Nesmejana" contains other widespread folktale motifs, for example, difficult tasks connected with courtship or marriage, and making a princess laugh is only one of them. The nature of difficult tasks needs a wider framework than one plot. They must be examined in all plots where they occur, and this is something to be done in a much broader investigation. The same applies to the enthronement of the hero. Therefore, the tale of Nesmejana will receive only a partial solution here, a solution that deals with the content of the task, not its origin.

A difficulty of another sort arises. Although we have at our disposal more data than our predecessors had, facts relating to laughter remain scarce. They sometimes turn up quite unexpectedly where no one seeks or expects them and must be gleaned one by one. It is quite probable that further searches will give a clearer, more precise, and better substantiated picture for each type of laughter and uncover whole layers of material that I have missed. Nevertheless, this work can begin, even if its only value is an attempt to go beyond the limits of formalist comparativism and look at folklore as a type of ideological superstructure.

Interdiction of Laughter

Let us now present the data according to the principles set forth above.

First of all we note interdiction of laughter. I do not mean those situations in life when laughter is forbidden or awkward but the interdiction of laughter in plots describing the penetration of a living person into the kingdom of the dead. Such plots are numerous. Where they are original both their shamanistic basis and the type of production that underlies them can be reconstructed.

A living person penetrating into the kingdom of the dead must conceal the fact that he is alive; otherwise he will provoke the wrath of its inhabitants as a transgressor who has crossed the forbidden threshold. By laughing, he gives himself away as a living person. This idea is openly expressed in a North American Indian myth. The hero penetrates into the kingdom of the dead, which is zoomorphic: it is inhabited by animals. "Then the spring salmon said, 'Don't you see that he [the beaver] is dead?' But the Cohoe salmon did not believe it and said, 'Let's tickle him; then we will see whether he is alive or dead.' After this they began to nudge him in the side so that he barely kept from laughing" (Boas 1895, 43). The idea of wrath is especially clear among the Eskimo.

> The souls who go to the over-world have to pass the abode of a strange woman who dwells at the top of a high mountain. She is called *Erdlaverissok* (i.e. the disemboweller), and her properties are a trough and a bloody knife. She beats upon a drum, dances with her own shadow, and says nothing but 'My buttocks, etc.,' or else sings 'Ya, ha, ha, ha!' When she turns her back she displays huge hindquarters, from which dangles a lean sea-scorpion; and when she turns sideways her mouth is twisted utterly askew, so that her face becomes horizontally oblong. When she bends forwards she can lick her own hindquarters, and when she bends sideways she can strike her cheek, with a loud smack, against her thigh. If you can look at her without laughing you are in no danger; but as soon as anyone begins to smile she throws away her drum, seizes him, hurls him to the earth, takes her knife and rips him up, tears out his entrails, throws them into the trough, and then greedily devours them. (Nansen 1894, 257-58)

A variety of this old woman has also been found in Greenland, in the shaman legends recorded by Rasmussen (Rasmussen 1922, 38). The story is accompanied by an Eskimo drawing. When the intruder laughs, the old woman rips out his lungs. In another of Rasmussen's recordings she is the mistress of the rain.

In Russian folktales the equivalent of the old woman who guards the entrance to the other kingdom is Jaga. "Well, take care, when you go into the hut—don't laugh" (Zelenin 1915, no. 11). This motif is further elaborated in a Komi folktale. "At the entrance to the hut a girl says to her brother, 'Let's go in, but don't dare laugh. Don't be a fool. If you want to laugh, bite your lower lip. And if you should laugh, Baba Jaga will catch us both, and that will be the end of us' " (Novikov 1938, 134).

Such interdictions are given not only at the entrance to the other kingdom; inside that kingdom, it is forbidden to laugh in general. An especially good example, is provided by a Zuñi myth. The hero is married to an eagle. She forbids him to fly into the land beyond the mountains. But he breaks the interdiction. In the distant land he is met very hospitably, and he and all the eagles are invited to a festival. He returns to his eagle-wife and tells her this. His wife is grieved. She says, "Go with us tonight to the city you saw, the most fearful of all cities, for it is the city of the damned and wonderful things you will see; but do not laugh or even smile once." They fly off to the festival. There beautiful girls dance and shout, " 'Dead! dead! this! this! this!,' pointing at one another, and repeating this baleful expression, although so beautiful, full of life and joy and merriment." The contrast between this exclamation and the fact that those who pronounce it are alive strikes the hero and he laughs. The girls fall on him and entice him to their quarters, and in the morning he finds himself in the embrace of skeletons (Cushing 1931, 47).

Interdiction of laughter also occurs in ritual, namely, in the rite that represents the descent into the kindgom of death and the return from it, namely, the initiation of youths at the onset of puberty. In spite of a huge literature, data on initiation are very sparse, since this rite is a deep secret. Nevertheless, some things are known. In Boas's extensive study of the social organization and secret societies of the Kwakiutl tribe are two brief mentions of the fact that during the rites the initiates are forbidden to laugh (Boas 1897, 506, 642). P. W. Schmidt gave a more detailed picture for one of the islands of Oceania. The last act of the ceremony is an attempt to make the youths laugh. They line up in a row. "Now there appears a young woman dressed in men's clothing; she behaves and speaks like a man. She carries a spear with many spearheads and a burning torch, and she walks along the line of boys. If none of them laughs, she reaches the end of the line, but if someone laughs, she rejoices and goes away without finishing her walk. The boys have been warned of the man-woman and instructed not to laugh. If someone laughs, his father says to him, 'Now we won't receive any gifts' " (Schmidt 1907, 1052).

In light of the data given above, this case also becomes clear. It is forbidden to laugh in the kingdom of death. The whole rite of initiation is a simulation of death. The one who laughs discovers that he has not been fully cleansed of earthly things, just as a shaman in the kingdom of death gives himself away as alive by laughter. Note also that the one who laughs does not receive gifts: he is considered not to have passed the test (we cannot go into the phenomenon of travesty, although it is not accidental here).

This is the first category, the first series of facts. The interdiction of laughter on entering the kingdom of the dead is only one such in a large class. In myth and folktales, as well as in ritual, we can also observe the interdiction of sleep, yawning, speech, food, looking, etc. Consider just one example: in the Grimms' tale about twelve brothers, the girl is told, "For seven years you must be dumb, you must neither speak nor laugh" (Grimm 1956, no. 9). The connection of this tale with initiation was proved by S. Ja Lur'e (1932; see also my article "Men's House in the Russian Folktale" [Propp 1939a]). All these interdictions point to the opposition of life and death. They point to the fact that a differentiated concept of death had already been formed. This concept had not always existed and was preceded by the complete identification of the dead and the living. At the new stage death is experienced like life with a minus sign. The living see, talk, yawn, sleep, and laugh. The dead do not do these things. At the same time the differentiation is not yet so complete that a gulf can be placed between the dead and the living. In some cases (usually it is the shaman or the initiate; in the folktale it is the hero, and the kingdom of death is transformed into a separate, faraway kingdom), a living person can go there during life, but then he must simulate death: he is not supposed to sleep, speak, see, or laugh. All such cases cited above are early (their connection with the basis of production will be explained below), but they shed light on later survivals. Thus, the spirits who find themselves together with Holda in the Venusberg are forbidden to laugh (Mannhardt 1884, 100). According to western European notions, corpses, even when they visit people in human form, do not laugh: De resurgentibus dicitur, quod ridere non soleant (Mannhardt 1884, 99).

Laughter As the Giver of Life

The concepts discussed in the preceding section can be applied in reverse. If all laughter ceases and is forbidden upon entrance into the kingdom of death, then entrance into life is accompanied by laughter. Moreover, if there we saw the interdiction of laughter, here we observe the command to laugh, or laughter under compulsion. The thought goes still further: laughter is endowed not only with the power to accompany life but also with the power to call it forth.

As already mentioned, initiation rites are poorly known, since Europeans are not normally allowed to observe them. The very fact that a European can be admitted to an initiation points to the decline and degradation of the ritual. An indirect source for eking out our knowledge of initiation is myth. According to one of the forms of the rite, the initiate was supposed to be swallowed and then spat out by a monster. Numerous myths about swallowed and regurgitated people are known. They seem to indicate that if presence in the state of death was accompanied by the interdiction of laughter, the return to life, that is, the moment of a new birth, was accompanied by laughter, possibly obligatory laughter. In an American Indian myth two brothers are swallowed by a whale. The whale carried them to another land. It is so hot in the belly of the whale that they lose their hair and become bald. On leaving the whale, each sees the other's bald head and laughs (Boas 1895, 101). It is important that leaving the whale is accompanied by laughter, which the storyteller motivated by the loss of hair as an afterthought. An Arapaho myth tells of a boy swallowed by a fish. The man who taught him how to fish catches the fish and cuts the boy out of it. The boy comes out smiling (Dorsey and Kroeber 1903, 112). In this case laughter is weakened into a smile. Since it is the youth's teacher that cut him out of the fish and restored him to life, the connection with rite becomes clear.

Such instances are mere hints. The objection can be made that the ties of these myths with ritual have not been demonstrated. But the study of the myth as a whole and ritual as a whole leaves no doubt that these ties exist, and the detail of the loss of hair points in the same direction (cf. Propp 1939a). Consider also one of the episodes of the myth of Maui. Frobenius (1898, 183) said: "The original life-giver (*Hine-nui-te-po*) opens her mouth where the sky meets the earth. Maui decides to conquer her. He takes birds as his companions and warns them that when he crawls into the monster's mouth they must not laugh, but they *must* laugh when he comes out. In the first instance, he himself will perish, in the other the monster will die. They take off their clothes. . . . When he goes into the monster's maw, the little bird Tiwakawaka bursts into laughter. The monster wakes up and kills Maui. *If Maui's intention had been realized, men would not have to die.*" Of special interest is the interdiction of laughter while the hero is inside the beast, combined with the command to laugh at the moment he comes out of it. The moment of coming out of the swallower in myth corresponds to the moment of symbolic birth in ritual.

All this may help us to understand a genetically much later case, but one directly related to the phenomena touched upon here, namely, the ritual symbolic killing of two youths during the Roman festival of the Lupercalia. In the Arapaho myth the boy laughs on coming out of the fish because he passes from death into life, and this is what Fehrle (1930, 3) wrote about ancient Rome: "During the spring festival of the Lupercalia two Roman youths were subject to symbolic killing and resurrection. A knife dipped in sacrificial blood was touched to their foreheads, then the blood was wiped off with a piece of wool, and the youths, who thus were symbolically brought back to life, were supposed to laugh. This emphasized the opposition between life and death." Mannhardt described the rite in somewhat greater detail. According to him, the boys were cut in the forehead and, what is especially important, two goats were killed during the rite. "The laughter of the boys," said Mannhardt, "can be understood as the opposite of death, symbolizing their new birth" (1884, 99-100).

Whether the point is indeed only in the symbolism or emphasis of the opposition of life and death will become clear later. The data prove that laughter not only accompanies the transition to life but also calls it forth. In the ritual of the Lupercalia this is rather obvious. The boys were supposed to laugh on returning to life, and they were forbidden to laugh while in the state or kingdom of death.

Yakut folklore contains a story about two women shamans, who live apart from other people and obtain husbands for themselves by magic. Finally the time comes for them to have their children. "Both husbands ran out, killed two white foals, and spread the foal skins on the sleeping shelves for the goddess of birth. She tossed and turned on the shelves alongside one woman and then the other. The goddess of birth was anointed with oil and perspired heavily, and she spent three nights there continually laughing" (*Jakutskij fol'klor* 1936, 132). The goddess's name is Ijexsít (Jastremskij 1929, 198-200), and the myth reflects a Yakut ritual. Cf. the following description. "On the third day after birth women gather for seeing the goddess Ijexsit to the house of the new mother. During the ritual feast one of those present begins to laugh long and loudly, which evokes general joy since it foretells pregnancy and the future birth of a child to her who laughs. In this case people say: 'She has been visited by Ijexsit' '' (*Jakutskij fol'klor*

1936, 305). Modern man tries to understand which is the cause and which the effect. Does the goddess (directly or "having visited" the future mother) laugh because a child is being born, or do conception and birth occur because of the laughter? This question has no significance for earlier thought, which does not know or differentiate cause and effect. From Jastremskij's data it follows that "at first they laugh a forced laugh" (Jastremskij 1929, 199). "Finally, they are genuinely overcome with laughter." This means that laughter is primary and pregnancy secondary; that is, they laugh so as to cause pregnancy and not the other way around. This is what constitutes the magic of laughter. In the same Yakut myth a woman shaman brings back the soul of a dead man and sings:

> If I am permitted to wake the dead man to life,
> If I am able to bring back a living soul to this man—
> Having crossed over three laughing thresholds . . .
>
> (*Jakutskij fol'klor* 1936, 119)

or

> Having crossed over three laughing thresholds,
> I have brought back the living soul of your son.
>
> (*Jakutskij fol'klor* 1936, 120)

The threshold separating life from death is called the laughing threshold, or the threshold of laughter. That side of the threshold it is forbidden to laugh; this side it is necessary to laugh.

The image of a woman laughing during conception calls to mind the image of Sarah who laughed at the good news that she would be given a son. Usually this laughter is understood as sarcastic: Sarah is old and does not believe in the possibility of giving birth. However, such sarcasm before the face of God would be out of place. Probably, this is a reflection of the same magic laughter, again obscured and misunderstood in the new historical situation. It is all the more likely because, as suggested by Reinach, the name Isaac means 'laughing.' The Jews knew well that Yishak means 'he who laughs' " (Reinach 1912, 122). In later days Yishak was connected with Ishakel (God laughs). If the connection is valid, then Isaac laughs not only as one who was born, but also as a parent and progenitor.

However, Isaac's laughter is problematical. Reinach, Fehrle, and Norden cited clearer cases of a divinity who laughs while creating the world. According to a Greco-Egyptian treatise on the creation of the world, "Seven times god laughed, and seven gods embracing the world were born. The seventh time he laughed the laugh of joy and Psyche was born" (Norden 1924, 66; Fehrle 1930, 2). In the hexameter hymn of a certain Platonist on Helios we read: "Thy tears are the human race full of pain. While laughing, thou brought into the world the holy race of gods" (Norden 1924, 66). And finally in the Leiden papyrus of the third century A. D. it is written: "God laughed and gave birth to the seven gods who control the world. . . . When he burst out laughing, light appeared. . . . He laughed a second time, and everything turned to water. With the third burst of laughter Hermes appeared" (Reinach 1912, 112).

Thus a divinity creates the world laughing and the laughter of a divinity creates the world. On entering the world, the goddess of birth laughs, a mother or pregnant woman laughs, a youth symbolically returning to the world laughs, and the divinity that creates the world laughs. There are several other cases in which the one who is being born or created laughs, without any connection with ritual. In Africa, among the tribes living in Togo, God first creates man, then woman; they look at each other and laugh (Frazer 1918, 23). They laugh because they have been born, not because they are man and woman. He who is born or is created laughs on entering life. In *Rustem and Zorab*[1] we find, "The boy never cried; just born, he was already smiling" (Norden 1924, 65). Pliny maintains (*Natural History* VII, 72) that Zoroaster laughed at his birth. The same situation is to be found in the Fourth Eclogue of Vergil. This Eclogue praises the new political order and predicts the birth of a new god who will save the world. The boy-god laughs when he is born. It becomes understandable why the Greeks honored Gelos, the god of laughter, (γέλως 'laughter') and why among the Romans Risus (*risus* 'laughter') was honored as *deus sanctissimus* and *gratissimus* [the most sacred and beautiful god] (Fehrle 1930, 4).

If the facts set forth here are indeed based on one single concept of laughter, they can explain some other facts that at first glance seem baffling, for instance, laughter accompanying death, a classic example of which is so-called sardonic laughter. Among the very ancient people of Sardinia, who were called Sardi or Sardoni, it was customary to kill old people. While killing their old people, the Sardi laughed loudly. This is the origin of notorious sardonic laughter (Fehrle 1930, 3), now meaning cruel, malicious laughter. In light of our findings things begin to look different. Laughter accompanies the passage from death to life; it creates life and accompanies birth. Consequently, laughter accompanying killing transforms death into a new birth, nullifies murder as such, and is an act of piety that transforms death into a new birth.

Incidentally, this example of laughter accompanying death is not the only one, although it is the best known. Strabo (*Geography* 16, 776) reported that there were Egyptian nomads who buried their dead to constant laughter (Fehrle 1930, 2). Perhaps the rite that Usener reported is a distant echo of sardonic laughter. In Gallura, in the north of Sardinia, after a corpse has been carried away and the clergy has returned to the house of the bereaved, there appears a woman, a *buffona*, who with anecdotes and jokes tries to provoke laughter among those present (Usener 1913, 469-70). Comparing sardonic laughter with similar cases among other peoples, Reinach said, "The Sards laughed while sacrificing their old people; the Troglodytes, while stoning their corpses; the Phoenicians, when they put their children to death; the Thracians, when one of them was on the verge of death" (Reinach 1912, 124). Ludwig Mercklin discussed the Phoenicians in great detail; he even came up with a Phoenician theory of sardonic laughter (Mercklin 1851). We will not go into this; nor will we go into later cases of laughter during funerals in the Ukraine.

In all cases laughter emerges as a magic means for creating life. This unity in the basis of thought corresponds to a unity in the historical basis. The most ancient instances have been observed in tribal society and are connected with its social organization and institutions (especially with initiation) and continue into antiquity. With antiquity this line ceases and a new one begins. But, on the one hand, we know how strong the elements of tribal society were in Greece and Rome (Engels 1962, chapters 4, 5, and 6, 253-83), and on the other, classical data can be understood only in light of data from primitive societies. This is how Engels studied the Greek gens using data on the Iroquois tribe.

The basic means of existence in the early stages of tribal society was hunting. The entire purpose of initiation was to make a youth into a hunter by giving him power over animals and to make him a full-fledged member of the community. Laughter is not directly connected with hunting, though people are known to have laughed not only when killing or burying a man but when killing an animal. A case in point is again the Yakuts, among whom laughter accompanying birth is very widespread and occurs in myths and in rites at the birth of a child. "When they have brought in a trapped ermine," said Iónov (1916, 5), "they smear its nose with butter or cream, *roar with laughter,* and pronounce an incantation. When they see in the distance an elk felled by a crossbow, they jump up and down, leap, shout and *roar with laughter.*" The explanation that they laugh from joy must be left on Ionov's conscience: it fails to explain the fact of the incantations. But if they were not laughing from joy, why were they laughing?

The incident recorded by Ionov shows that hunters laugh *after* capturing an animal. Consequently, laughter is not a means for capturing it. However, the hunter's interests are naturally concentrated on the capture. We may suppose that the hunters laughed to resurrect the dead animal to a new life and to capture it a second time; that is, they were laughing "for the birth" of the animal, just as the Yakuts laughed "for the birth" of a child. That hunters tried to resurrect a slain animal by various means (in particular by burying its bones) for a second hunt is well known in ethnography (Propp 1934). Laughter is one of the means for the creation and recreation of life.

We may quote from Engels's letter to Conrad Schmidt of 27 October 1890, "As to the realms of ideology which soar still higher in the air, religion, philosophy, etc., these have a prehistoric stock, found already in existence and taken over in the historical period, of what we should to-day call bunk. These various false conceptions of nature, of man's own being, of spirits, magic forces, etc., have for the most part only a negative economic basis; but the low economic development of the prehistoric period is supplemented and also partially conditioned and even caused by the false conceptions of nature" (Engels 1942, 482).

We have just one instance of such an incorrect idea. Engels pointed out the reason for such incorrect notions of nature, man, and his characteristics. The reason lies in the low economic development of the prehistoric period. Laughter is directed at increasing the human tribe and animals. "According to the materialist conception," said Engels, "the determining factor in history is, in the last resort, the production and reproduction of immediate life. But this in itself is of twofold character. On the one hand, the production of the means of subsistence, of food, clothing, shelter and the tools requisite therefor; on the other, the production of human beings themselves, the propagation of the species" (Engels 1962, 170-71). It is the second type of production that we are dealing with here.

Characteristically enough, our sources are almost silent about the real causes of man's birth. At the center of the action stands a woman, a mother, a powerful shaman, a child-bearing woman, the goddess of birth, but nowhere do we see her spouse. If he is mentioned, his role is extremely insignificant. For example, he spreads a skin for the goddess of birth. The male divinity turns up much later and appears in the role of a woman: he creates, we may even say he gives birth to, people by the force of laughter. But nowhere do we see a human couple. Laughter is sexual, but for the time being it is not erotic. We will see that when a new phase of social development sets in, the situation changes radically. Such are the incorrect ideas of nature and man underlying the motifs at hand. They are based on incorrect ideas of the real causes of birth, on echoes of ancient matriarchal relations, when woman, the mother, the reproducer, was honored for her mysterious, as yet unclear ability to reproduce the species, which Engels called the "decisive moment in history." The role of the male has not yet been realized. This ancient and apparently matriarchal culture creates the husbandless mother. The old Eskimo woman mentioned above is of this type. She is markedly sexual but not erotic. She has no spouse. She is the mistress of the rain. Jaga, with her conspicuous attributes of female fertility, the mother and mistress of animals, is of the same type. Jaga has likewise never had and does not have a spouse.

If we now understand why life was not believed to be the creation of a human couple, the question still remains why this role was ascribed to laughter, rather than something else. This is the most difficult question of the entire cycle. Laughter can be compared with the dance. If people dance before a hunt, war, sowing, etc., they do it not for aesthetic gratification, but so as to influence nature, which they cannot yet influence by rational means. The dance is merely a convulsive effort. Convulsive fits are often the tool of a shaman, and at this stage laughter is just such a convulsive effort. In this sense laughter is a "magic," nonrational, means for creating life.

This exhausts the cases of laughter accompanying life and death. We will now turn to another group of phenomena, which are later and different in character. But before doing this, for the sake of completeness, we may mention the treatment the concept of laughter has undergone in Christianity. In Christianity it is death that laughs, the devils laughs, and mermaids laugh; the Christian God never laughs. "Christ never laughed," the artist A. A. Ivanov remarked to Turgenev, while painting his *Christ* (Turgenev 1967, 88).[2] We need not discuss this idea here, since it is a later phenomenon and does not help us understand the forms of laughter that Nesmejána leads to. Nesmejana does not laugh for other reasons.

Flowers That Bloom at Someone's Smile

We have not yet seen a couple as the reproducer of the human species; nor have we seen agriculture as a form of production. The shift to agriculture causes a sharp change in the forms of production, social relations, and thought.

Up to now human life practically alone was subject to the magic force of laughter. Now vegetation enters the orbit of laughter. But since vegetation also depends on the sun, the latter becomes connected with laughter as well. Thus, on the one hand, the Greek Ἥλιος τε γέλως 'the sun and laughter' arises, and on the other, the concept of the goddess or, in terms of the folktale, the princess whose smile causes flowers to bloom. Here we are already approaching Nesmejana.

Let us examine several cases of a laughing princess. A princess's laughter can cause flowers to grow. "The king learned that in a certain place there was a maiden whose laughter caused roses to appear and whose tears turned to pearls, and he wanted to marry her" (Afanas'ev 1957, no. 289). In a Turkish folktale the king overhears a conversation of three maidens. "I would bear him such children that when they laugh roses would appear and when they cry pearls would fall from their eyes" (Borovkov 1938, 121). In a modern Aramaic folktale a prince's son has the ability to cause flowers to bloom with his smile (Wesselski 1923, 186; Indian and Iranian parallels are also given there). More often, however, flowers are replaced with jewels. Gold and jewels have been substituted for the gifts of the earth. In a Baluchi folktale the hero is commanded to find a dish of gold and jewels. He meets an enchanted girl and frees her from the spell. "Now tell me something that will make me laugh." The hero spoke, the girl laughed, and the dish was filled with gold. The same thing happens with jewels (Zarubin 1932, 45-46). We may suppose that flowers and roses, in their turn, have replaced other gifts of the earth and that the origin of this motif should not be sought in the folktale. The capacity of laughter to cause life has been reinterpreted here as the capacity to evoke vegetable life. Inertia preserves the matriarchal tradition: flowers bloom at the smile of a maiden, not a woman. However, marriage has already been introduced: a smile is sometimes the condition for entering into marriage. Just such a girl will be selected as a bride. In these instances laughter or a smile is usually coupled with crying and tears. Crying is the same kind of magic means of help and even resurrection of the dead as laughter: "By crying and laments Isis and Nephthys resurrected Osiris: their cry was also life-giving for a dead person and was sometimes written on memorial papyruses" (Vikent'ev 1917, 81).

The Agricultural Conception of Laughter

The matter did not stop with the mechanical transference of the effect of laughter to vegetation. The farmer is well aware of how living things reproduce. This was also known before, but only now does marriage acquire a clearly expressed religious meaning. It crosses with the tradition of laughter, and together they form a single complex. If people laughed earlier when giving birth to a child or killing an animal so that it would be born again, now they laugh when sowing a field so that the earth will be fruitful; but something else has been added to this: while laughing in the fields they do what promotes reproduction—they copulate. Marriage and laughter become a "magic" means of increasing the harvest. Agriculture creates gods and goddesses. This is how the idea arose that for grass and grain to flourish it was necessary to make the goddess of the earth laugh and to give her a spouse.

We cannot go into the entire range of phallic agricultural rites. They extend from the classical period through the Middle Ages down to our days. We must keep to the data that lead us to the folktale. First of all we will briefly mention Paschal laughter. As noted earlier, on Easter the priest told jokes from the pulpit to induce laughter in his congregation. Easter is the holiday of the divinity's resurrection and at the same time the holiday of the resurrection of nature. Perhaps April Fool's jokes belong here too. Fehrle (1930, 4) reported a case from Germany when people laughed while planting vegetables. Fluck, who made a study of Paschal laughter, denied any mythic or magic origin for it and believed that it was a purely Christian phenomenon caused by the desire to cheer up a congregation after the gloomy days of Lent. However, Paschal laughter contained more than jokes. The priest went beyond stories and did things that recall the princess who showed her visible marks. Incidentally, the first person to write about Paschal laughter was the humanist Oecolampadius, whose treatise *De risu paschali epistola apologetica* [An apology for Paschal laughter] was published in Basel in 1518. But neither Oecolampadius nor Erasmus of Rotterdam (1535) told everything. Oecolampadius was silent about the things done outside the church, in the dark and in the fields, because they were *obsceniores* [obscene] (Fluck 1934, 193). It matters little what exactly was done; for we are interested in the character of the actions, which is clear even without details, and in the beliefs underlying them. The classical data show that cheering up a congregation tired from the Lenten fast is not the reason for Paschal laughter. Let us go over the few relevant points. First of all, the earth was thought of as a female being. "The farmer viewed the changes in the earth that produced the harvest as a birth, the release of the burden from the Earth's womb." (Bogaevskij 1916, 19). Plowing is interpreted in a similar way (Bogaevskij 1916, 91; Hahn 1896, 52).

We have no direct evidence that people laughed while sowing or plowing. But there is something else that corresponds to laughter, namely, the singing of obscene songs, the ritual use of obscenities (aeschrology), and gestures of exposing oneself. "In both Athens and Alexandria during the Thesmophoria women sang obscene songs while following Demeter's chariot. Aeschrology was also known during the sowing of caraway in Greece, so that it would grow well and in great quantity, during the sowing of barley on Cyprus, and the sowing of grain in Sicily" (Bogaevskij 1916, 59). In sowing grain the gesture of exposing oneself played a great role, the same gesture that the princess made when showing her visible marks, and that Iambe made in the presence of the unsmiling Demeter. "Greek farmers used obscenities ($\alpha \iota \sigma \chi \varrho o \lambda o \gamma \iota \alpha$) in agriculture and resorted to exposing themselves ($\dot{\alpha} \nu \dot{\alpha} \upsilon \varrho \mu \alpha$) to assure a good harvest" (Bogaevskij 1916, 57).

The Unsmiling Goddess

However, all these facts (and their number could be greatly increased) are of indirect significance; they characterize only the milieu that produced the goddess who must be made to laugh to ensure a better harvest. Of direct significance will be the image of this goddess.

The myth of Demeter and Persephone comes to mind first. In searching for her abducted daughter, Demeter does not laugh; she is called $\dot{\alpha} \gamma \dot{\epsilon} \lambda \alpha \sigma \tau o \varsigma$, "the one who does not laugh," which corresponds exactly to our Nesmejana. Only after the servant Iambe makes the same gesture as the princess who shows her visible marks does Demeter laugh. Here the agricultural aspect of the matter is important. Demeter is the goddess of fertility. When she laughs, spring returns to the earth (Fehrle 1930, 1). Fehrle noted a Japanese parallel: the goddess of the sun Ama-terasu was insulted by her brother, the god of the moon. She withdrew into a ravine and the earth became dark. She reappeared and the earth became light again only after Uzume, the goddess of joy, danced obscene dances in front of her.

Marriage is absent from all these cases. For magic, marriage is not required; performance of the appropriate gesture is sufficient. This accounts for the gesture of the princess who shows her visible marks, Iambe's gesture before Demeter, and one more gesture well known in world folklore and also necessary for our comparison, namely, the gesture of Loki before Skadi in *The Younger Edda*. According to *The Younger Edda*, the Æsir killed the father of the giantess Skadi. But Skadi made a bargain with them. Her first condition was that she might choose a spouse for herself. "A further condition was that the Æsir should make her laugh—which she thought would be impossible" (Snorri Sturluson 1964, 99). Loki assumed this task. He made a phallic gesture and Skadi laughed (Simrock 1882, 298, 299; Leyen 1899, 32-38). We need not prove that the gesture was phallic: see Simrock and Leyen, cited above.[3]

In this respect the case is clear, but it is unclear in that it contains no signs of agriculture. They have disappeared; only epic tradition itself has remained. Earlier instances (those going back to antiquity) give unmistakable indications of this, and so does the folktale. We will now turn to the folktale and will examine our data along the way. The folktale is specific in that it has two plots, one about the princess's visible marks and one about Nesmejana, but we have seen how closely they are related. They are not only related, there is an inseparable connection between the two axes of these folktales—laughter and gesture. Laughter is conditioned by gesture. Both folktales derive from one root.

The Princess's Visible Marks

The task of making the princess laugh is part of the task of learning what her visible marks are. The affinity between these tasks becomes obvious if only from the two following examples. "Who will guess what mark there is on my daughter, to him will I give her in marriage" (Afanas'ev 1957, no. 238). "Who will make my daughter laugh, to him will I give her in marriage" (Xudjakov 1860-62, vol. 3, no. 103). Both tasks are sometimes solved in a similar manner. Let us first examine how the princess's visible marks are learned.

This task can be formulated so: "Who will guess where my daughter has a birthmark, to him will I give her in marriage" (Zelenin 1915, no. 12). Nothing is said about what makes the king set such a task. "The king arrived and decided to give his daughter in marriage." How is this task solved? In Afanas'ev's version the hero spends some time at an old man's (he is the equivalent of Baba Jaga), and the old man gives him a self-playing *gusli* to whose sounds everyone must dance. He buys some pigs, comes to the princess's window, and the pigs dance to his gusli.[4] The princess asks him to sell them. " 'My pigs are not for sale, I'll only trade them for something.' 'What is it you want for them?' 'Well, princess, if you wish to have one of my pigs, show me your white body up to your knees.' The princess thought and thought . . . and raised her dress to her knees, and there was a little birthmark on her right leg." But when the pig was brought into the palace, it would not dance. After this there is an ellipsis in Afanas'ev's version. We may suppose that in the original the motif was tripled and that the matter did not stop with the princess's raising her dress to her knees. We might have supposed this even if there had been no note by Afanas'ev that this folktale is told with details inappropriate for printing. Afanas'ev knew Xudjakov's version and reported that even Xudjakov had printed his version "with significant omissions." In Xudjakov's version (no. 95), the mark is a golden hair under one of the princess's arms. In a Vjatka[5] folktale "under the right breast there is a birthmark, in the right groin a golden hair" (Zelenin 1915, no. 12). In a Low Saxon folktale the matter is told directly. The Bolte-Polívka version (vol. 2., no. 114, p. 528) gives it as follows: "The girl sees that the boy makes three handsome pigs dance to his pipe and talks him out of them one by one, but she must allow him to spend a night in her bed." The task, consequently, is to *take* the princess. In other words, the task about the visible marks can be understood thus: the one who will get the hand of the princess is the one who will find out her visible marks, that is, the one who will be her husband. This gradation is by no means artificial. There are folktales that say plainly: "The king proclaimed that he who would spend a night with his daughter would be given her in marriage" (Smirnov 1917, no. 142).

The question arises: Where is the task, what is the difficulty? In the folktale the difficulty is reduced to a riddle "where is the birthmark?" This is an obvious euphemism (cf. Ončukov 1909, no. 252). We might think of the dangers of the first night (this motif is well known in Russian folklore), but neither "Nesmejana" nor the folktale "The Princess's Visible Marks" contains this motif. What exactly is the difficulty is apparent from the second half of the folktale. Both "Nesmejana" and the folktale about the princess's visible marks have the same ending, thereby indirectly confirming their affinity. When the marks have been learned, a rival suddenly appears out of nowhere, *ex machina*. Sometimes he is a nobleman, a much more desirable husband than a shepherd. In Xudjakov's version, after the marks have been learned, the king devises the following plan: "Let me seat the boy and the nobleman at table: I will order various fruits to be served. Which of them will eat with better manners?" From other versions we know that the princess does not sit down with the rivals at the same table but lies with them in the same bed. Such cases also occur in the folktale about Nesmejana. In Xudjakov's story the nobleman and the shepherd lie with the princess in turn, and the nobleman persuades the shepherd "not to talk" with her and gives him a hundred rubles. "She embraces him, kisses him, but he keeps silent, just says nothing." In the morning her father comes into her bedroom and asks: "Well, is your bridegroom all right?" She answers through her teeth, "Yes" (Xudjakov 1860-62, no. 95). This case reveals the nature of the bridegroom's trial: he must make a preliminary demonstration of his potency.

The rival who appears at the end of the folktale may at one time have occurred at the beginning, so that the form "who will sleep with my daughter, to him will I give her in marriage" is the original form of this folktale. However, such a form of selecting a husband does not conform to later morality, and a riddle replaces it, while the contest of the suitors is removed to the background, transformed into sitting at the same table, etc. The gesture that the princess makes in order to get the handsome pigs is that of exposing herself. Iambe, or in other versions, Baubo, performs this gesture to make Demeter laugh. The meaning of the gesture has been subject to numerous different explanations in classical philology. Bogaévskij, Reinach, and Wehrli explain it as apotropeic (see Wehrli 1934, 81). However, absolutely nowhere, neither in the Homeric nor in the Orphic hymns, is there a word about danger. From whom or what was this gesture supposed to preserve or save? Karl Sittl (1890, 366) followed Clement of Alexandria: "Clement of Alexandria gives the correct motivation for Baubo's behavior. She is angered by Demeter's indifference." But it remains incomprehensible why lifting a dress should have aroused her from indifference.

The folktale admits the possiblity of another explanation. Iambe's gesture is one of invitation and challenge. In the more modest redactions of the folktale the curtain falls just after this gesture; in the less modest the matter is stated plainly. In the Homeric hymn a meeting of the spouses does not occur after Iambe's gesture, but something else happens: Demeter laughs, that is, she performs a more ancient magical act that promotes the creation of life. This more ancient form corresponds to another of Demeter's archaic characteristics. She has no husband, and, therefore, the only thing she does is laugh. Apparently, Demeter still reflects the ancient line of the mother without a spouse. Not having a spouse, she does not react to Iambe's gesture in the same way as do the human couple in the folktale; she reacts with laughter. However, there must have been attempts to provide a spouse for Demeter. This is evident if only because *coitus in argo* [copulation in the field] is transferred or attributed to Demeter. From Homer and Hesiod we know that Demeter came to Greece from the island of Crete, where she copulated on a thrice ploughed field with the hero-sower Iasion (Homer *Odyssey* 5.125; Hesiod *Theogony* 900). There are vague indications that Triptolemus and Dysaules were considered Demeter's spouses (Wehrli 1934, 93). Thus, Demeter was not completely husbandless. Historically, she is an underdeveloped spouse. The folktale shows a complete evolution of this line of thought and the fully developed life-giving spouse based on the image of the laughing life-giver. Nesmejana is connected with Demeter: she is a later stage of the Demeter idea.

Nesmejana in many respects, even in some details, displays a striking similarity to Demeter. First, the princess, like Demeter, does not laugh. But unlike the princess, who does not laugh for an obscure reason (only in one case—in Afanas'ev—she is enchanted), Demeter does not laugh for a quite definite reason: she has lost her daughter and longs for her. One does not have to be versed in mythology to realize that this motivation is secondary and that contamination is present here. The Russian folktale is much more consistent. No external reasons are given, but there are internal and historical reasons why she does not laugh: she does not laugh now so that she can laugh later, and people need her laughter. Second, it is said that the princess "walks for nine days, then sleeps for nine days like a bogatyr." Here we recall Kore, Demeter's daughter, who spends two thirds of the year on the earth (the wondertale's "walks") and one third under the earth (the wondertale's "sleeps"), which is what causes the change in seasons. Designation of periods of time, whatever the real time might be, is not at all characteristic of the wondertale. Such turns of speech as "two years passed," "in a month," and the like are quite impossible in the wondertale. "Whether late or soon," "not in days but in hours," "three days and three nights" or as here "nine days"—this is how the wondertale designates periods of time. Years and months do not figure in the wondertale at all. Therefore, one third of the year and two thirds of the year, the period of time that Kore spends under the earth and on the earth, respectively, are out of place here. Quite naturally, the wondertale prefers different time periods of sleep and life. Third, the wondertale princess is depicted as sitting under the ground on a throne and flying in a chariot. "After a short while, heaven and earth were illumined: a golden chariot flew through the air drawn by six fiery dragons; in the chariot sat Princess Elena the Wise of indescribable beauty. She descended from her chariot and sat on a golden throne; she began to call her doves in turn and to teach them all sorts of things" (Afanas'ev 1957, no. 236). Demeter, like Kore, is depicted as sitting in an underworld kingdom, on a throne (Bogaevskij 1916, 137).[6] Her attributes, sheaves and a torch, are naturally absent from the wondertale.

Demeter, too, is sometimes depicted in a chariot drawn by dragons. The princess teaches her doves various things, which reminds one of Demeter Thesmophora, the lawbearer or law giver. The chariot and the cart are also attributes of agriculture: the wheel as a tool of locomotion is unknown to hunters. The cart, on entering the sphere of mythic concepts, assimilated to the bird as did the horse, whence the flying or winged cart, the cart drawn by animals, etc.

The Agricultural Nature of the Princess

Even though we compare Demeter and the princess, it does not mean that our princess is a direct descendant of Demeter. It means only that features of the goddess of agriculture are characteristic of the princess. Her agricultural nature is clear even without comparison with Demeter.

We have already left the realm of one single plot. The princess is a definite type in the wondertale canon (like Baba Jaga, the horse, etc.) and can be examined as a type, independent of a concrete plot. This canonic princess displays very definite agricultural features.

The princess has preserved a connection with primal animal life better than Demeter. An example of this is the frog-princess. She is an animal, but at her wedding she dances. We easily recognize the ritual dance of the times of totemism. "She danced and danced, whirled and whirled, and everyone was amazed. She waved her right hand, and forests and lakes appeared; she waved her left hand, and all sorts of birds began to fly" (Afanas'ev 1957, no. 267). She is the creator, the designer of the forest and waters. This is a very ancient, still totemic hunting stage of the princess. It is at this stage that the world is created through dance. Later the forest and the dance will disappear. The princess is the giver of water, sometimes she herself is water. "And he noticed that wherever the princess went, wherever her horses stepped, springs appeared, and he followed her by the trail of springs she had left" (Afanas'ev 1957, no. 271, variant). Sometimes, as in the bylina about Sadko,[7] she turns into water and begins to flow. It is worthy of note that she creates springs and rivers, that is, water that the farmer needs, rather than seas. "The beautiful maiden lies, sleeping the sleep of a bogatyr, and from her hands and feet healing waters ooze." She gives the gift of water while asleep underground. This rather accurately reflects the idea of the earth as a woman. Later she also gives trees, but the trees are no longer wild. "Trees grow under the arms of Usón'ša the Bogatyr, and on these trees are apples of youth" (Xudjakov 1860-62, no. 41). It may be supposed that the name *Uson'ša* is connected with *son* 'sleep'; she has fallen asleep, died (*usópšaja*). That trees grow in another kingdom is an early agricultural idea, and its origin can be traced. The princess still connected with the forest and the animal world dances, while the agricultural princess only sleeps, sleeps magically, as it were, under the earth. The princess is connected not only with water, springs, lakes, trees, and fruits; she has a tie with grain and sowing, although such cases are very rare.

The princess in the other kingdom bids her husband farewell. "She says goodbye to her husband, gives him a small bag full of seed, and says, 'Whichever road you ride, scatter this seed on both sides; where it falls, trees will spring up at once, and on the trees wonderful fruits will begin to appear" (Afanas'ev 1957, no. 272). The seed produces trees, not grain; the wondertale princess has not reached the stage of grain. The wondertale contains a dead religion, its mere relic. Grain gave rise to its own religion among the peasants, a living religion of a later formation.

This princess offers to become the wife of him who will make her laugh or will learn her visible marks. She is not indifferent to who her husband will be. She offers herself to several suitors, which is a possible remnant of hieroporny (sacral prostitution). The hero is not an ordinary man. He owns a magic pipe or some other instrument and comes with a magic herd of dancing pigs.

The question of how the pipe is obtained and what it represents can be passed over here, although it is not without interest for understanding the phenomena under review. The magic pipe has its origin in the sacred pipes used during ritual dances. But the pigs require special attention. The pig is an unusual animal in the wondertale, in which wild animals predominate: wolves, bears, foxes, etc., and birds. Domestic animals also turn up: cows, goats, dogs, etc., but pigs occur much less often and rather sporadically. However, in the wondertale of the type "The Princess's Visible Marks" the pig is a stable, international fact; consequently, pigs are not accidental here.

We have already seen the close connection between the princess and Demeter, the goddess of fertility. The pig as an animal bringing fertility played a large role in the cult of Demeter. In Greek antiquity the pig was associated with married life. Pigs were thrown into the chasm where Demeter was supposed to live. After some time the putrefied remains were brought to the priest, who performed ritual plowing. They were placed on the altar, mixed with grain, and put into the furrow (Bogaevskij 1916, 182-83). Martin P. Nilsson (1935) noted a version according to which the earth swallowed up Kore and Eubuleus with his herd of pigs. He considered this story purely Orphic. But if it were purely Orphic, how did the swineherd with his herd of pigs turn up in the Russian folktale? The crux of the matter is that the pig is associated with the furrow and plowing. Incidentally, in a Vjatka folktale the pig is bought from a plowman. It follows the plowman behind the plow, that is, in the furrow. This is the pig that helps the hero overcome the princess (Zelenin 1915, no. 12).

The pig is associated not only with the furrow. As Bogaevskij pointed out, the word *porca* had yet another, more specific, sexual meaning. Hence the connection of the pig with Baubo's gesture, with the gesture of the princess showing her marks, and with laughter as a ritual agricultural act (Bogaevskij 1916, 175). It is absolutely clear why the man who leads a pig is the one to evoke the laughter of the princess. This man brings fertility with him, and the princess makes Iambe's gesture for him. The princess is not indifferent to who her spouse will be: she needs a spouse who will bring her fertility. He proves his potency by the fact that he brings pigs with him and later confirms that potency by his victory over his ordinary, human rival.

Several other details lead to the same conclusion. The biography of the hero who made the princess laugh is as follows in Afanas'ev's version. He works for a merchant three years and for each year of service takes only a kopeck. "Some people's crops dry up and wither, but his master's flourish; some people's horses have to be dragged down the mountain, but his master's cannot be held back" (Afanas'ev 1957, no. 297). This detail is somewhat simplified, as is the figure of the merchant. Other people's grain dries up while his ripens, not because he is a zealous servant, but because the hero of this wondertale, like the hero of other wondertales (cf. the task of sowing, harvesting, and threshing grain in one day), possesses the power of controlling plants and animals, and this is exactly the type of spouse for Nesmejana. Their union is what she and people need. "If I die," the hero says, "the flowers will fade, the apple trees will dry up" (Zelenin 1914, no. 10).

Conclusion

We can now say that the wondertale about Nesmejana reflects the magic of laughter. The early form of the magic of laughter is based on the idea that the dead do not laugh, only the living do. The dead people who have entered the realm of the dead cannot laugh, while the living people who have entered it must not laugh. On the contrary, each birth of a baby or a symbolic new birth in rites of initiation and other similar rites, is accompanied by laughter that is believed to possess the power not only of accompanying but also of creating life. Therefore, birth is accompanied by obligatory ritual laughter. The real causes of the appearance of life are not yet realized or reflected in rituals. With the emergence of agriculture laughter is believed to have the power of calling vegetation to life. On the one hand, the line of asexual creation of life is continued. A woman's smile causes flowers to bloom; her spouse does not participate in this. Demeter is a model of a husbandless goddess of fertility. Her laughter is connected with her agricultural character. On the other hand, the real cause of the origin of life and man is actively transferred to vegetation and is included in the ritual in which laughter and plowing and the meeting of spouses form a whole. In myths about Demeter we can find attempts to give her a spouse. The wondertale about Nesmejana and the princess's marks displays the full development of this line of thought. It is necessary simply to make the princess laugh, and she needs a magically potent husband. Both the princess and her bridegroom display an obvious agricultural character.

The remaining problems of "Nesmejana" cannot be solved without studying some other plots. But the facts we have cited clarify the historical roots of this wondertale. We can also give a more or less definite answer to the question why the princess does not laugh, why she must be made to laugh, what connection this has with marriage, and why this wondertale is overtly sexual. We now understand what is meant by the princess's marks and why these marks are learned with the help of pigs rather than some other animals. Nor is the episode of the two suitors' competition accidental. We understand both why the pig is taken from the plowed furrow and the origin of the agricultural features in the characters of the hero and the heroine. Although this does not exhaust all the problems of "Nesmejana," it advances our knowledge of this very interesting and historically significant wondertale.[8]

III. Heroic Poetry

Chapter Ten.
Russian Heroic Epic Poetry:
Introduction

General Definition of Heroic Epic Poetry

Each area of knowledge first defines the subject of its studies. We must do the same. What is epic poetry? At first glance this question seems unnecessary. Everyone understands that the Russian *bylína*, Karelo-Finnic *runes*, Yakut *olonxo*, Burjat-Mongol *uliger*, Uzbek *dastán*, Shor *kaj*, and other similar lays are epic poetry. However, to cite examples is not the same as to give a scholarly definition.

Epic poetry is not defined by any one feature that at once determines its nature. It possesses a number of features, and only all of them together provide a correct and complete idea of its essence. The most important feature of epic poetry is the *heroic character of its content*. Epic poetry shows whom people consider a hero and for what deeds. To define and study the character and inner content of heroism is our main task in relation to epic poetry. For the time being it will suffice to point out that the content of epic poetry is struggle and victory. We will see that in different historical periods the content of the struggle has been different, but there is one thing peculiar to the struggle at all stages of epic poetry: it is waged not for narrow, petty goals, not for personal interests, not for the well-being of the individual hero but for the people's highest ideals. The struggle is difficult; it demands the concentration of all the hero's powers and the ability to sacrifice himself, but in epic poetry it leads to success. The struggle is not personal but popular and national, and in later periods it also has a clearly pronounced class character.

However, this feature is not sufficient to assign a work to epic poetry. The *Lay of the Host of Igor* has heroic content; the chronicle accounts of the battle at Kulikóvo[1] and of the Mongol invasions of Moscow also have it. And so do Pushkin's *Poltáva*,[2] Tolstoy's *War and Peace*, and many works of contemporary

Soviet literature devoted to the struggle and deeds of the Soviet people. Therefore, heroic content is a decisive feature only if associated with others. One of the main features of Russian epic poetry is that it consists of lays intended not for reading but for musical performance. Unlike novels, heroic songs, legendary narratives, and so forth, epic poetry belongs to a genre of its own. Musical, vocal performance is so essential to it that works not meant to be sung do not qualify as epic. Musical performance of bylinas is inseparable from their content. The performance attests to the depth of the singers' personal involvement and their interest in the events described; it provides an outlet for their inspiration and expresses feelings aroused by the heroes and narrative. To eliminate the melody from a bylina, to perform it as a prose tale is to shift it to a completely different plane of expression. Like other properties of epic poetry, its music takes shape and develops gradually. It is always national and original. The singing of Russian bylinas was formerly accompanied by the national Russian instrument called the gusli.

Yet, from the point of view of music, epic poetry is inferior to the lyric song, which is deeper, more varied, and more expressive. Russian epic poetry possesses such musical qualities that the best Russian composers have time and again recorded bylina melodies and used them in their work (Jančuk 1919). Composers do not only adopt and harmonize folk melodies; they come away imbued with the spirit and style of this music. Rimskij-Korsakov (1909, 318) wrote about his opera *Sadko*, "What distinguishes my *Sadko* from all of my other operas and possibly not only my own operas but operas in general is the bylina recitative. . . . This recitative is not just speech but is, as it were, the conventional bylina narrative (*skaz*) or *raspev* ('slow singing'), the prototype of which can be found in the declamation of Rjabínin's bylinas.[3] Running through the entire opera, this recitative imparts to it the national, true-story character that can be fully appreciated only by a Russian." (See also the journal *Sovétskaja múzyka* 1948, no. 1, where statements of Russian classical composers on folk music are collected.)

All verse folklore is always *sung*. The form of oral verse is alien to folklore; it is possible only in literature. Therefore, when musical epic folklore becomes written literature, it first loses its musical form and sometimes its verse form as well. Examples are Irish sagas, the *Nibelungenlied,* and sixteenth and seventeenth century narratives of Il'já and Solovéj the Robber.[4] On the other hand, there exist heroic legends in prose that, even though they belong to narrative poetry, do not belong to heroic epics. In Russian, the stories of Stepán Rázin,[5] and in our time tales of Čapáev[6] may serve as examples. Usually such works are distinguished from epics by the lack of musical performance and by all the other stylistic devices.

Another important feature of epics is the verse form of the lays, which is closely connected with their melody. This form did not spring up at once but grew from prose and developed over centuries. Russian bylinas possess such a specific metric structure that even an uninitiated listener will recognize them at once by their verse, although alone this feature is not decisive. I will not investigate the forms and laws of bylina verse, since this has already been done (see Štokmar 1952). Suffice it to say that this verse is an inseparable property of Russian bylinas and that it accords with their content. Bylina verse is the product of a long cultural development. It was worked out over centuries and has reached its highest point.

Although bylina verse is one of the features of Russian heroic epics, it is not restricted to them; it is not their exclusive property. Bylina verse became so popular that it extended to works outside the sphere of epic poetry. In prerevolutionary scholarship versification was considered one of the chief epic features, and everything sung in bylina verse was included in collections of bylinas, irrespective of the content of the lays. Such a principle of selection is unacceptable.

Bylina verse is a broader phenomenon than heroic epic poetry. The latter always consists of lays in bylina verse meter, but the opposite will not necessarily be correct: not every song in the form of bylina verse can be considered epic. For example, religious epics can have the form of bylina verse. Most collectors distinguished religious poems from bylinas, but in collections of bylinas, one can come across such works as the lay of the *Golubínaja kníga*,[7] the lay of Aníka the Warrior,[8] and others that do not belong to bylinas. Religious poems cannot be considered epic since they appeal to people not for struggle but for submission and humility. They are, as was especially emphasized by Dobroljúbov, not of folk but of literary origin. ("Verse is not an original creation of the Russian people; it was brought to us from Greece and has remained foreign to the people." Dobroljubov 1934a, 219).

We will not classify lays of a ballad character as epic, however good and interesting they may be, even though such lays were included in collections of bylinas and performed in bylina verse. Thus the lay "Vasílij and Sóf'juška"[9] tells how two lovers meet in secret instead of going to church. The wicked mother gives them a potion, and they die. From their grave grow trees whose tops bend toward each other. This is a typical ballad. It concerns itself not with struggle, but with the tragic death of two innocent victims. The ballad, as well as other types of folk poetry, expresses certain popular ideals. For example, in the ballad cited above, there definitely is an anti-church tendency; but active struggle, the basic feature of epic poetry, is absent. The themes of the ballad are narrower than those of the bylina: they embrace primarily family and love relationships. The number of ballads in collections of bylinas is very great, but they do not belong to heroic epic poetry. (For more detail see Andreev and Černyšëv 1936.)

Similarly, we cannot classify jocular songs as epic. In the song about the guest named Teréntij, Terentij's unfaithful wife pretends to be sick and sends her husband to a distant city for medicine. On the way the husband meets *skomoróxi* (singers, jugglers, tumblers), who at once understand the situation. They suggest to Terentij that he crawl into a sack and return with them to his house. While sitting in the sack, the husband sees everything that is happening in his house and "cures" his wife with a club. Funny, humorous songs, very often with a satirical edge, are interesting in themselves and undoubtedly belong to *epic poetry* but not to *heroic epic poetry*.

Religious poems, the ballad, and tumblers' poems are genres different from the bylina, although close to it and sometimes merging with it.

Finally, there is one more genre close to the heroic song, namely, the historical song. The view that epics arise as historical songs, which over centuries come to be forgotten and distorted and are gradually transformed into bylinas, must be abandoned. The bylina is *older* than the historical song. The bylina and the historical song express in different forms the consciousness of the people at various stages in their development. Epic poetry portrays an ideal reality and ideal heroes. It generalizes the vast historical experience of the people in extremely powerful artistic images, and this generalization is one of its most essential features. Epic poetry possesses a certain dignity and solemnity, which, in the best examples, are combined with simplicity and artlessness. Heroic lays are usually based on fiction in which only the scholar can detect a historical basis. In historical songs the subject and plot are drawn directly from reality. Events related in historical songs are not invented (see the songs about the siege of Kazan and many others); only details are treated in a fantastic manner. The historical song is the product of a later epoch and of other forms of consciousness than the bylina. Historical songs cannot be classified as historical epics; they are unlike bylinas not only because they are not sung in bylina verse (although songs about Ivan the Terrible are still very close to this verse) but because their attitude toward reality is different from that in the bylina.

Indirectly connected with the bylina are some prose genres: first of all, the folktale and some types of the old narrative (*póvest'*).

As a rule, prose works are not included in collections of bylinas. However, the tale of the adventure of Il'ja Muromec with Solovej the Robber, for example, is sometimes told in the form of a folktale (see Afanas'ev 1957, no. 308).[10] According to the features discussed earlier, namely, musical performance and the types of verse, these works cannot be classified as epics. Close comparison of a folktale with a bylina on the same plot will always reveal that there are differences not only in the manner of performance but in the content itself: the folktale usually turns a heroic exploit into an amusing adventure.

The folktale is not the only form besides the bylina in which bylina plots appear. The bylina started to penetrate into old Russian literature. Beginning with the seventeenth century there are manuscript tales that have as their subject the exploits of bogatyrs (great warriors). The most popular were the tales of Il'ja and Solovej the Robber and of Mixajlo Potyk.[11] Such works were called tales, histories, or narratives. They told about the heroes and their feats in the literary language of that time and were intended not for singing but for reading. They are not the oldest recordings of bylinas as many scholars thought; they are just tales, which conformed to the tastes and needs of the literate population of thriving cities. (See editions of bylina tales: Tixonravov and Miller 1894; Sokolov 1926; Širjaeva and Kravčinskaja 1948; Golubev 1951; Malyšev 1956.)

The bylina that is sung, the folktale that is told, and the narrative (*póvest'*) that is read are different forms, since they express different *attitudes* toward narration. They all differ in their histories, their ideology, and their forms.

Such are the most general and most important features of Russian heroic epic poetry. But epic poetry is also characterized by its entire content, by its world of images and heroes, by the subject of its narrations, by the whole system of poetic devices inherent in it, and by its peculiar *style*.

Some Problems of Methodology

Correct methodology is the decisive factor in any science. A false method cannot lead to correct conclusions. Problems of methodology in the study of bylinas are complex. Here only the most general will be touched upon: those that determine the direction of the research. One of the basic requirements of contemporary scholarship is that all phenomena of human culture be studied in their historical development. The realization of the historical principle in the study of epic poetry is one of my basic objectives. However, this is a difficult objective to achieve. It depends, first, upon how we conceive the relationship of epic poetry to history and, second, upon what methods we will use for discovering the historical character and growth of epic poetry.

Attempts at the historical study of folk poetry were made even before the Revolution. We must know about these attempts in order to avoid mistakes made by bourgeois scholarship. In Russian academic scholarship of the nineteenth and twentieth centuries there were several trends.

Representatives of the Mythological school (Buslaev, Afanas'ev, Orest Miller, and others) believed that epic lays had originated as myths about deities; this is how they understood the connection between epic poetry and history. Lays were viewed as living monuments of ancient prehistory, and their importance to scholarship was limited to this. But since nothing was known about the real myths of primitive peoples, they were artifically reconstructed from the selfsame bylinas and folktales. The method of studying bylinas amounted to reconstructing myth from epic poetry. As a result of such reconstruction, Vladímir, called the beautiful sun (*krásnoe sólnyško*) in epic poetry, turned out to be an ancient sun god, Il'ja Muromec, a thunder god, etc. Heroes of folklore invariably proved to be relics of the gods of the wind, the thunderstorm, the sun, the windstorm, and the like. The political aspect of this trend was revealed by Dobroljúbov and Černyšévskij, who characterized the whole approach as uncritical, sterile, and divorced from life (Dobroljubov 1934b; Černyševskij 1950). In Soviet scholarship the influence of the Mythological school was felt in the teachings of Marr and his followers, who attempted to reconstruct primitive myth from modern folklore and who viewed this as their principal goal with respect to folk poetry.

The comparativists investigated folk poetry in an entirely different way. In their opinion, all epic poetry was ahistorical and completely fantastic. According to this school, epic poetry does not develop. Lays are allegedly composed in a definite place and at a definite time, and then plots begin to migrate from people to people; for the comparativists the history of these migrations and borrowings constituted the entire history of epic poetry. In studying Russian epic poetry, they traced it sometimes to the epic poetry of oriental, Asiatic peoples (Potánin), sometimes to borrowings from Byzantium or Western Europe (Veselovskij and his school). Comparisons of this type suggested that the Russian people had created nothing and that in its culture it had only followed other people.

Nor did the Historical school, headed by Vsevolod Miller, disclose the interrelationships between epic poetry and history. This school gave the whole problem short shrift. In its view, lays reflect or record events of the age in which they were composed. Epic poetry was treated as a kind of oral historical chronicle not unlike a written chronicle, only that a written chronicle is more or less reliable, whereas a bylina is not. Hence the method of this school, which amounts to verifying a bylina through a chronicle or other historical documents.

At first glance it may seem that this system contains a grain of truth. In collating a bylina with a chronicle, the Historical school seemingly traced art to reality. Perhaps it is for just this reason that the principles of this school have persisted so stubbornly in the Soviet period and have made their way into textbooks, courses, syllabi, and encyclopedias. However, the ideology and methods of this school, which does not warrant the name historical, are as unsound as those of the mythological and the comparativist schools. It is not only that the artistic aspect of epic poetry was completely ignored. According to Vsevolod Miller, heroic songs originate to glorify the princes who led military campaigns in the time of feudal strife. They were thought to be created not by the people, but by the ruling classes, by the feudal military leadership. "Having descended" to the people, these "historical" songs, through constant distortion among the ignorant peasantry, were transformed into bylinas. This is allegedly how epic poetry sprang up.

In Soviet scholarship A. P. Skaftýmov (1924) was the first to point out the fallacy of this school. He showed in minute detail that its premises were false, its arguments shaky, and its conclusions unconvincing. The antipopular nature of this school was exposed in 1936, when Dem'ján Bédnyj's play *The Bogatyrs* was withdrawn from the repertory. The decree to withdraw the play stated that it "calumniates the heroes (bogatyrs) of Russian bylinas, whose chief heroes are the bearers of heroic traits of the Russian people" (Decree of the Committee on the Arts, 14 November 1936). An extensive discussion laid bare the formalist, antihistorical attitude of this school toward history and folk poetry (see Dmitrakov, 1950).

I will not dwell on individual works written by representatives of many prerevolutionary schools. In the study of folk poetry, older Russian academic scholarship did not and could not have fundamental, major achievements, since its premises and methods were false. There could be and in fact there were only correct specific observations that we can use. The most progressive scholars collected masses of invaluable material, but this did not save their theories from total bankruptcy.

The search of Russian revolutionary democrats proceeded in a different direction. Bourgeois scholars studied texts without regard for the historical fortunes and aspirations of the people, whereas the revolutionary democrats concentrated on the people and the ways they expressed themselves in works of art. The founder of this school was Belinskij, and he deserves special attention, although this is no place for a full appraisal of Belinskij as an investigator of folk poetry.

Belinskij made the only attempt to explain the bylina not as an outcome of primitive mentality or as the product of other nations or the military aristocracy of the past, but as the creation of the Russian people itself determined by Russian history. He viewed epic poetry as an original creation of the Russian folk genius, in which the people expressed itself, its historic aspirations, and its national character.

First of all, Belinskij sought the *idea* underlying each lay. This idea expresses a certain *ideal* and is presented in artistic form. Therefore, scholarship, as he saw it, was expected not to look for parallels, but to state correctly the idea of the work. Since the idea is presented in artistic form, it can be determined only by analyzing the works' artistic message. For Belinskij the lay was first and foremost produced by the *artistic* genius of the people. Since art is generated by reality, by historical conditions, and by the struggle of social forces, the object of scholarship and criticism, as Belinskij understood it, was to explain a work of art in terms of the concrete historical conditions that called it to life. In this way Belinskij embarked on the path of a *scientific* and *historical* study of epic poetry. He taught that the artistic conception of a work is historical even when it is presented in a fantastic form.

Belinskij's principles laid the foundation of the modern science of folk poetry. He himself applied these principles most extensively to the study of his favorite Novgorod bylinas about Sadkó and Vasílij Busláevič.[12] He showed that the images of these heroes were the inevitable outcome of the social struggle, everyday life, and work experience of the inhabitants of ancient Novgorod. His method consisted of an artistic analysis of the lays; for this purpose he always *retold* the lays in detail. His retellings were meant to popularize epic poetry, and were the result of a certain *understanding* of bylinas. He examined all the details of the narrative, went over the heroes' actions, considered their words, their deeds, and the motives for these deeds, and finally deduced the general idea of the lay. The point was precisely in the details, in the scrupulous and sensitive examination of the work's entire fabric. Belinskij realized that abstract schemes never explain anything about the plot. In determining the idea, he showed what sort of reality gave rise to a particular idea in its particular form and thoroughly characterized the idea.

In 1841, when Belinskij wrote his main articles on folk poetry, the material was still inadequately known. In his conclusions about epic poetry he relied almost exclusively on the collection of Kírša Danílov.[13] For this reason, some of his judgments are correct with respect to the texts in this collection but incorrect with respect to the total corpus of epic poetry. For example, Belinskij claimed that the bylina about Dobrynja the dragon fighter does not make any sense; and indeed in Kirša Danilov's book the action is so confused that for this text Belinskij's opinion is correct.[14] On the whole, however, the lay about Dobrynja is among the best in Russian epic poetry. To be sure, Belinskij's mistakes came not only from a lack of material. He stood at the beginning of the Russian revolutionary movement and of Russian scholarship. He realized that the cause of liberating the people was in their own hands but did not see the social forces that could have brought about the revolution in the Russia of Nicholas I.

The study of folk poetry helped Belinskij free himself from Hegelianism, but some traces of it remained. He could not have a clear idea of the laws of history as we understand them. In several cases his judgments were abstract, contradictory, and subjective. Not only was Belinskij's material sometimes far from first-rate, it was also insufficient. We have thousands of texts, whereas in the collection of Kirša Danilov there are not more than twenty bylinas, and this was all that Belinskij had at his disposal. Yet despite some blunders, the lack of data, and their faulty character, Belinskij's genius, his love for the people and for folk poetry permitted him to set out on the *correct path*, to take the right *direction*, and this is the direction that a Soviet scholar must follow. Belinskij is the founder of the modern science of Russian epic poetry.

In the Sixties Belinskij's ideas were carried on and developed by Dobroljúbov and Černyšévskij. Neither wrote special contributions on the question of epic poetry, but their general works are important because of their approach to the study of folk poetry; certain statements about epic poetry scattered in their works are also important.

For Dobroljubov folk poetry was inseparable from the people itself, from the level of its historical development, from its contemporary life, its struggle, and its outlook. According to him, the task of scholarship is to know and understand one's own people better. Dobroljubov was guided not by an abstract ethnographic interest but by love for his people, who had to be helped, who lived in poverty and ignorance, and who had to be brought closer to civilization. Dobroljubov recognized as genuine only a scholarship that actually helps a people in its struggle. Study of a people's outlook through its poetry allowed Dobroljubov to solve a number of problems. For example, he saw clearly that Vladimir is a negative figure in epic poetry and that he is portrayed as a despot, like Byzantine emperors. He emphasized the fact that feudal wars were not reflected in epic poetry because they were not the people's wars, whereas the later Historical school treated the bogatyrs as heroes of feudal wars and tried to determine which wars and which military leaders were depicted in the bylinas (Dobroljubov 1934a, 215).

Černyševskij developed Belinskij's ideas of genuine and false *narodnost'*;[15] according to Belinskij genuine *narodnost'* always includes the best, the progressive ideals of mankind, and he studied folk poetry from this angle. Černyševskij's struggle came in the Sixties, i.e., at the time of the peasant reform.[16] He, like very few others, understood the true aspirations of the peasants, who were interested not in the reform but in the alienation of the property and power of the landowners. "Such revolutionary ideas could not but ferment in the minds of the serf peasants," wrote V. I. Lenin; " . . . even then there were revolutionaries in Russia who took the side of the peasantry, who saw how limited, how poverty-stricken was the over-advertized 'Peasant Reform,' and who recognized its true feudal nature. These revolutionaries of whom there were extremely few at that time were headed by N. G. Černyševskij" (Lenin 1963, 122). Černyševskij was a revolutionary and a patriot. He was ruthless toward everything that smacked of backwardness and stagnation in folk poetry, but he ranked folk poetry among the highest and best achievements of national culture. He said that epic poetry always reflects a heroic epoch in the life of a people and only those peoples have heroic epics that have waged an active struggle for their national independence. Therefore, epic poetry always expresses a people's vigor and will to victory (Černyševskij 1949, 291-317; 362-68).

The direct successor to the revolutionary democrats in the study of folk poetry was Gorky. His speech at the first All-Union Congress of Soviet Writers[17] signaled the beginning of a new epoch in the study of folklore—the Soviet period. Since he was a man of the people and possessed both artistic talent and the critical instinct of a genius, he was able to give methodological guidance in all branches of the science of folklore. Here it is not possible to set forth Gorky's teaching in its full breadth and significance, and only its most essential aspects will be highlighted. Gorky formulated the materialistic view of the origin of folk poetry from the struggle of man with nature and "two-legged enemies." He revealed the ever-present connection of folk poetry with history, and showed that in songs a people does not dispassionately record the facts of history, but expresses its will and judgment. According to Gorky, the content of folk poetry is always struggle, though the forms and direction of this struggle change; the creator of folk poetry is the people itself, the toiling masses. Finally, Gorky gave full credit to the high artistic achievements of folk poetry and of folk language. All the best that has been created in world poetry goes back to what has already been created by the people, said Gorky; genuine art is always based on the art of the people. Therefore, he called on young writers to learn from folk poetry.

Although a national and progressive tradition was developing in prerevolutionary Russia, the influence of bourgeois principles long persisted in Soviet scholarship, and the principles that the revolutionary democrats and Gorky set forth did not find concrete application. The first serious attempt to investigate folklore along new lines was made by the Institute of Russian Literature of the Academy of Sciences of the USSR (*RNPT*, 1953-56; see also *Očerki*, 1952). The authors of this collective book set out to study all folklore historically, using chronology as their point of departure. Soviet critics welcomed the effort but noted several shortcomings. Since methodology was not discussed in the book, many problems still need a thorough examination.

What lessons can be learned from the history of the science of folklore? How is the study of epic poetry to be conducted? After the Revolution the entire development of Russia has been exposed to new scrutiny. The periods in the history of the USSR have been established anew in conformity with historical materialism. Soviet scholars have given the correct picture and evaluation of the events in the past of their great motherland. The historical study of epic poetry must consist in revealing the connection between the development of epic poetry and Russian history and in determining the nature of this connection.

It is a difficult task, because lays often do not contain any external indications of belonging to one period or another. The features used by the old Historical school (personal names, place-names, nonessential details of the narrative, etc.) have proved irrevelant, since they are accidental and apt to change. According to Belinskij, one must begin by determining the *idea* of a work. The idea of all lays is connected with the struggle of the people at a definite time, and this provides a reliable criterion for dating them. The first thing to do is to discover the idea and the message of the lays. We must reread the bylina and understand what it is about. Prerevolutionary bourgeois scholarship ignored this stage, and only Belinskij took several steps in the necessary direction. Analysis should primarily deal with the *bylina itself*, its heroes, its narrative, and its idea. To understand a bylina means to understand what the narrators wished to express in it and what they valued in it; two or three texts of each will not tell us much: *all* the extant texts must be collated and compared.

This is the most difficult and most important part of the work. Bylinas were compared earlier too. For instance, Kireévskij[18] filled gaps in some texts with the corresponding passages from others, replacing less felicitous passages with more felicitous ones; that is, he produced a composite text, which was supposed to represent the most complete and perfect form of the lay. Needless to say, such an undertaking is useless. Soviet scholars must not avoid comparing the great number of lays available to them, but the aims and methods of comparison must be different from what they were in the past.

The Formalists compared folklore variants in another manner. They laid special emphasis on the most frequent variants of the narrative, whether they were bylinas, tales, or legends. Since in the legend about two great sinners, the main sinner is a robber in 34 out of 45 recorded variants, and in the others he is another type of criminal (a patricide or one who has committed incest, etc.) the conclusion was drawn that in the oldest form the main character was a robber (cf. Andreev 1924, 23, 59). The "archetype," or the "original form," that is, the oldest form of the plot, was determined statistically. Clearly, the method of determining the age of the tale by statistics is no good at all. The most archaic forms can prove to be precisely the rarest ones, or they can even disappear from the narrative, for new forms gradually displace old ones. This method, which flourished especially in Scandinavia and Finland, also had some adherents in the Soviet Union; it was exploded by A. I. Nikíforov (1934).[19]

In Soviet scholarship the study of variants must have a different aim in view. Bylinas have already been compared by Soviet folklorists to determine *regional* differences. Such a comparison is certainly justified. Indeed, the bylinas of the Pečóra region differ fundamentally from the Onéga bylinas, and the Onega bylinas differ from those of the Pínega and the Mezén'. Owing to the research of A. M. Astaxova, the impersonal North appears now divided into discrete regions, each possessing its own repertory and its own distinctive features. These regions are Pomor'e, that is, the coast of the White Sea; the Onega region—the shore of Lake Onega; then the shores of the Pinega, Kulój, Mezen', and Pečóra rivers.[20] Each of these regions can in turn be divided into subregions (Astaxova 1938, 44 ff.; see also Trautmann 1935).

Ultimately, however, this method is of subsidiary importance. If it is an end in itself, comparison leads the investigator to a special type of formalism, already condemned by Dobroljubov (1934c), who wrote in his review of Afanas'ev's collection, "To note that such and such a folktale was recorded in the Čerdýn' *uézd* and such and such in the Xar'kov *gubérnija* and to add variants from various locations is quite insufficient if we want to understand the meaning of tales for the Russian people. . . . What follows from the fact that in the Novogrúdok *uezd* there is a tale about Pokatigoróšek and in Novyj Toržók one about Seven Semeons?"[21] Dobroljubov condemned region-by-region comparison as an end in itself. Indeed, what follows from the fact that in the Onega tradition it is Dunáj who shows Vladimir his bride, while in the Mezen' tradition it is Dobrynja?[22] For Dobroljubov the folktale is "one means for determining the *stage of a people's development*." This is the crux of the matter, and it applies not only to folktales. If regional differences help in solving historical problems and in determining the stage of a people's development, they must be taken into account. If these differences are insignificant variations, they must be ignored.

Division of bylinas into regions is a form of *fragmenting* them. Further fragmentation will entail the study of epic poetry according to the narrators' individual features as well as the comparison of narrators in order to determine the degree and character of their individual mastery. This was a very popular approach in Russia at one time. Presumably, the main distinction of the "Russian" school consisted in studying epic poetry and folktales just according to their performers (see Bazanov 1949, 19 ff.). Some first-rate narrators certainly deserve special attention. The scholar must treat each variant critically and take into consideration by whom, when, where, and from which narrator the lay was recorded, but one should beware of evaluating the performer's mastery in terms of individual psychology divorced from the soil that raised him and from the general laws of folklore. Such a method would violate the axiom formulated by Gorky: "In myth and epic poetry as in language . . . it is the collective creativity of the whole people that comes to the foreground, not the personal thinking of one individual." Folk poetry is first of all *folk* poetry and must be studied as such. An individual singer is interesting insofar as he gives specific artistic expression to a folk idea.

We will not collate variants to produce composite texts or to ascertain regional and individual differences, but to determine their ideas. In collating variants not a single detail must be omitted. In monographic treatments of separate bylinas these details can be included in the edition, but in the description of epic poetry as a whole this is impossible. Clearly, *selection* is needed here. Since not all the material will be used, there is a danger that in the process of selection the scholar will show a bias and rely on subjective or arbitrary premises. However, the solution is facilitated by the great repetitiveness of the variants. Individual cases are easily and naturally grouped together, and these groups are quite manageable. Under such conditions selection will amount to choosing the illustrative material. The choice of examples will indeed be arbitrary, but the same conclusions would be reached with different data. We select the most striking, most expressive examples. The weak, uncharacteristic, artistically less felicitous ones are disregarded; they are cited only when their significance does not depend on their artistic merits.

The first step in comparing variants is to determine all the units of the narrative, to understand the course of action, and to find its beginning, development, and end. Thus, the bylina about Dobrynja the dragon fighter[23] contains the narrative of the death of Dobrynja's aged father and tells how his mother raises and teaches him. The narrative recounts how Dobrynja grows up. He then asks permission to leave home; his mother lets him go, but accompanies her permission with good advice or interdictions, for instance, not to bathe in the Pučáj river. The whole narrative should be examined in a similar fashion. None of the variants contains all the possible units: in some there is no mention of the death of Dobrynja's father, in others nothing is said about his good education;

Dobrynja's departure is not always accompanied by his mother's admonitions, etc. The sum total of the texts is always more complete than each of them taken separately. Can the picture thus obtained be of any scholarly value?

Strictly speaking, in presenting a *complete* picture of a plot the scholar produces something not corroborated (with rare exceptions) by any single version. Yet such a picture is absolutely necessary. It is not an "archetype," a "basic edition," or a "composite variant"; it is the discovery of the people's intention. Belinskij's statement, later taken up by Gorky, that folk creativity is collective, national creativity and that the creator of folk poetry is the entire nation, rather than individual people, predetermines the specific methodology of folklore: the object of study should be the intention of the people in all its manifestations; each individual version is only one realization of this intention.

The comparison of variants will reveal the laws of composition of each plot and the idea of the work, because the idea is expressed by the entire narrative. In most cases there is a single type of composition for each plot, despite the absence of certain units. But some bylinas lack single composition. Lays having the same subject but differing in the development of the action can be called *versions*; in belles lettres they would correspond to *redactions*. The bylina about Aljóša and Tugárin[24] occurs in two versions: in one of them the fight with the dragon takes place on Aljóša's way to Kiev, in the other, in Kiev, and the fight itself is also treated differently. The action of the bylina about Il'já and Ídolišče[25] is sometimes set in Kiev (the Kiev version), and sometimes in Car'grád (the Car'grad version); the narrative in these versions proceeds differently. The bylina about the fight of Il'ja with his son can have a tragic outcome (Il'ja kills his son) or a happy outcome (Il'ja is glad to meet his son and takes him to Kiev). A difference in versions usually presupposes a different message and a different treatment of the plot. When the plot varies, the work naturally lacks the unity of idea. One version can be old, another younger. In each case criteria are needed by which to distinguish an older version from a younger one.

After the patterns of composition have been determined, we must go on to the *texture*, that is, to the artistic aspect. Each element is possible in numerous variants. In the bylina about Sadko,[26] when Sadko goes down to the bottom of the sea, in some cases the Sea King summons him to hear him sing; in others, to punish him for not paying tribute; in still others, to resolve an argument with the Sea Queen about what is the most valuable thing in the world: steel or gold; sometimes the king wants to marry Sadko to his daughter; there are also variants in which the king calls Sadko to a chess match. Each variant occurs more or less often, but the numbers are finite. Study of these variants shows which forms are earlier and which are later and reveals some stages in the development of the plot.

Comparison of variants is important in yet another respect: it lifts the cover from the creative laboratory of the people. Some forms will prove aesthetically very successful, others less so. They will differ in imagery, give the images dissimilar meanings and new interpretations, or replace one set of images with another. Among the performers there are geniuses, mediocrities, and fumblers. All the depth and beauty of an idea and all the diversity of its artistic realization are revealed only through a detailed comparison of variants. Only total comparison of texts will yield a complete picture of the hero as he is represented by the people. This method discloses the motives of the heroes' actions; comparison of variants brings out the nature and development of the conflict that forms the basis of the narrative and lays bare details of the artistic design, which are thus thrown into sharp relief. And if each of the texts is poorer than the picture yielded by a comparative study, this is an argument for, rather than against, the method itself.

The high artistic qualities of the bylina are well known. Marian Jakóbiec (1955, iv) wrote, "Bylinas are the highest achievement of the rich literary activity of the Russian people and are among the most remarkable phenomena of world folklore."

Discovery of the idea is the first condition of the historical study of bylinas. A folk idea always expresses the ideals of the period in which they took shape and were active and is therefore the decisive criterion for determining the age of a lay. Analysis of the bylina as a work of art is inseparably connected with historical analysis. Here the scholar encounters many specific difficulties. The chief recordings were made during the nineteenth and twentieth centuries. Can a conclusion be drawn as to the state of epic poetry during previous centuries? *Exact* information has of course been lost, but the historical study of folk poetry is not made impossible by the fact that the texts are late. Lays preserve visible traces of past ages, sometimes so clear and concrete that they can have the force of historical evidence. In other cases, these traces have been obliterated, and the dating of such lays may have a conjectural, hypothetical character. Nor is this the only difficulty. According to the Russian Historical school, folklore arises like literature, that is, in a definite place and at a definite moment. For a certain part of folk poetry (e.g., for historical songs) this premise will be correct, just as it is correct for works of written literature, but for epic poetry, folktales, and certain other types of folk poetry, it is false. Epic poetry does not lie outside of time and space, but the question of the year, the city, or the locality in which a bylina arose cannot be asked. Bylinas reflect the people's greatest ideals, not isolated events. What past scholarship conceived as a one-time *act* of creation should be conceived as a long *process*.

A heroic lay never goes back to a single year or decade, but to all the centuries during which it was being composed, improved, and perfected, all the centuries between its emergence and eventual disappearance, right up to the present. For instance, some parts of the bylina about Djuk Stepánovič[27] contain elements of exceptionally remote, even pagan antiquity (a picket of serpents and monstrous birds ready to tear a stranger to pieces). Further, the bylina reflects Kievan Rus' (the court of Vladimir). In the description of details of buildings and in the picture of the city its reflects Muscovite Rus' of the sixteenth and seventeenth centuries. And, finally, in its basic idea (ridicule of the wealthy boyars) it reflects the class struggle of late feudal times. The power and brilliance of its satire directed against the ancient enemies of the toiling masses made this bylina live and popular when the class struggle assumed new forms but flared up even more intensely. The basic idea expressed in a bylina will have decisive significance for dating it. For "Djuk Stepanovič" such a decisive historical feature is the struggle with the boyars as it was waged in the sixteenth and seventeenth centuries. Therefore, despite the presence of disparate elements it can be traced to late feudalism.

If bylinas are studied in terms of their intention and idea, rather than according to mechanically selected components, they will reveal *age-old* ideals and aspirations of the people that go back not to one century, but to much longer periods and can be assigned to these periods with some degree of confidence and reliability. The people's aspiration for unity as a nation-state is characteristic of epic poetry during the feudal division. Lays reflecting the Tatar (Mongol) invasion took shape during the entire time of the dominion of the Tatars. Hatred of princes, boyars, merchants, and clergy permeates epic poetry from its early beginnings to modern times.

One of the axioms of the old Historical school was that epic poetry *reflected* history and did so passively. This point of view derives from the passive role that reactionary historiography attributed to the people in history and poetry: allegedly, the people "participated" in history and "reflected" it in its songs. From our point of view the people is not merely a participating but a *leading* force in history and in its poetry does not *reproduce* history as an impartial observer but expresses in it its historical *will*, its ancient aspirations, and ideals. Epic poetry does not lag behind history but expresses "the people's aspirations and expectations" as Lenin said of the folktale (see Bonč-Bruevič 1954, 116 ff.). These aspirations are ideals related to the future. In expressing its judgment and will, the people creates artistic works to *mobilize* its forces for the achievement of its aims. Epic poetry had always played an enormous educative role, and the scholar should determine the historical aspirations of the people expressed in it.

Consequently, we should study epic poetry in conjunction with the epochs, or periods, of its development, rather than with so many separate events. Initial distribution of the data is determined by the sequence of formations in Russian history: primitive-communal society, feudalism, capitalism, and socialism. The material for each period should be subjected to a detailed analysis and not arranged according to a predetermined chronological scheme. There is no knowing in advance which of the periods of feudalism will or will not be reflected in epic poetry; dating will come as the result of the work. My aim was to set the *direction* in which the investigation will proceed. If this direction is correct, the details can receive a correct interpretation. If the direction is wrong, the correct interpretation of some details will not save the scholar from erroneous conclusions regarding the main point.

Structure and Form: Reflections on a Work by Vladimir Propp
Claude Lévi-Strauss

The supporters of structural analysis in linguistics and anthropology are often accused of formalism. The accusers forget that structuralism exists as an independent doctrine which, indeed, owes a great deal to formalism but differs from formalism in the attitude it has adopted toward the concrete. Contrary to formalism, structuralism refuses to set the concrete against the abstract and to ascribe greater significance to the latter. *Form* is defined by opposition to content, an entity in its own right, but *structure* has no distinct content: it is content itself, and the logical organization in which it is arrested is conceived as property of the real.

This difference deserves some elaboration. We can now do so, thanks to the publication in English of an early work by Vladimir Propp, *Morphology of the Folktale*. Propp was one of the main representatives of the Russian Formalist school during the short period in which it flourished, roughly from 1915 to 1930.

The author of the introduction, Svatava Pirkova-Jakobson, the translator Laurence Scott, and the Research Center of Indiana University have rendered a tremendous service to the social sciences with the publication of this far too neglected work in a language accessible to new readers. In 1928, the date of the Russian edition, the Formalist school found itself in a crisis; it was officially condemned in the Soviet Union and lacked contacts with the outside world. In his subsequent works, Propp was obliged to give up formalism and morphological analysis and devote himself to historical and comparative research on the relationships of oral literature to myths, rituals, and institutions.

However, the message of the Russian Formalist school was not lost. In Europe, the Prague Linguistic Circle took it up and spread it; since about 1940 Roman

Jakobson's personal influence and teachings have carried it to the United States. I do not imply that structural linguistics and modern structuralism in and outside linguistics are only extensions of Russian Formalism. As I have already mentioned, they differ from it in the conviction that, if a little structuralism leads away from the concrete, too much structuralism leads back to it. But although his doctrine cannot in any way be called Formalist, Roman Jakobson has not lost sight of the historical role of the Russian School and its importance. In dealing with the antecedents of structuralism, he has always reserved a prominent place for it. Those who have listened to him since 1940 have felt indirectly this remote influence. If, as Pirkova-Jakobson writes, the author of these words seems to have "applied and even extended Propp's method" (p. vii, *p. xxi*)[1], it cannot have been done consciously, since he had no access to Propp's book until its appearance in English. But through Roman Jakobson some of its substance and inspiration had reached him. I am afraid that, even today, the form in which the English translation was published will do little to popularize Propp. I would like to add that printing mistakes make the book difficult reading, as do the obscurities that may perhaps exist in the original but seem rather to result from the translator's failure to render Propp's terminology and terse style. It will thus not be useless to follow the work closely while condensing its theses and conclusions along the way.

Propp begins with a brief history of the problem. Works on folktales consist mostly of collections of texts; generalizing studies are few and they are elementary. To justify this situation, some scholars complain of insufficient data. The author rejects this plea because in every other field of knowledge the problems of description and classification have been posed very early. In addition, there has been no lack of attempts to discuss the origin of folktales, even though one can speak about the origin of any phenomenon only after it has been described (p. 4, *p. 5*).

The existing classifications (Miller, Wundt, Aarne, Veselovskij) are of some practical use, but they shatter against the same obstacle: it is always possible to find tales in them that come under several categories at once. This remains true, whether the classification is based on the *types* of tales or on the *themes* brought into play. The assembling of themes is arbitrary with everybody and rests on the intuitions and theoretical creed of each author rather than on analysis (intuition being, as a general rule, more trustworthy than theory, as Propp remarks, pp. 5-6, 10; *pp. 5-6, 11*). Aarne's classification provides an inventory that is most helpful, but his assembling of themes is purely empirical, and tales are assigned to particular rubrics in an arbitrary way.

The discussion of Veselovskij's ideas is particularly interesting. Veselovskij split up themes into motifs, so that in his system, the theme adds only a unifying, creative dimension: it stands over motifs, which are treated as further irreducible elements. But in this case, Propp remarks, each sentence constitutes a motif, and the analysis of tales must be taken to a level that today would be called "molecular." However, no motif can be said to be indivisible, since an example as simple as "a dragon abducts the king's daughter" may be decomposed into as least four elements, each of which is commutable with others ("dragon" with "sorcerer," "whirlwind," "devil," "eagle," etc.; "abduction" with "vampirism," "putting to sleep," etc.; "daughter" with "sister," "bride," mother," etc.; and finally "king" with "prince," "peasants," "priest," etc.). Smaller units than motifs are thus obtained, which according to Propp, have no independent logical existence. I have dwelt so long on this point because Propp's statement, which is only half true, shows one of the main differences between formalism and structuralism. I will come back to it later.

Propp gives Joseph Bédier full credit for the distinction between variable and constant factors in folktales, with the invariants constituting elementary units. However, Bédier was unable to define what these are exactly.

If the morphological study of tales has made so little progress, it is because it has been neglected in favor of research into origins. Too often so-called morphological studies resolve into tautologies. The most recent one (at the time of Propp's writing), by the Russian R. M. Volkov (1924), demonstrated nothing except that "similar tales give similar schemes" (p. 13, *p. 15*). Yet a good morphological study is the basis of all scientific investigation. Moreover, "as long as no correct morphological study exists, there can also be no correct historical study" (p. 14, *p. 15*). According to Propp's formulation in the opening paragraphs of Chapter 2, his whole undertaking rests on the working hypothesis that wondertales make up a special category of folktales. At the beginning of the study, wondertales are empirically defined as numbers 300 to 749 in Aarne's index. The method is outlined in the following manner.

Consider the statements:

1. A king gives the hero an eagle that carries him to another kingdom.
2. An old man gives Sučenko a horse that carries him to another kingdom.
3. A sorcerer gives Ivan a little boat that takes him to another kingdom.
4. The princess gives Ivan a magic ring; young men appearing from out of the ring carry Ivan into another kingdom.

These statements contain both variables and constants. The dramatis personae and their attributes change, but the actions and the functions do not. Folktales attribute identical actions to various personages. It is the constant elements that will be used as a base if the number of these functions proves finite. Now, we see that they recur very often. It can be stated that "the number of functions is startlingly small, compared with the great number of dramatis personae. This explains the twofold quality of a folktale: it is amazingly multiform, picturesque, and colorful, and, to no less a degree, remarkably uniform and recurrent" (p. 19, *pp. 20-21*).

To define the functions, that is, the constituents of the tale, let us first disregard the dramatis personae, since their role is only to "support" the functions. A function is designated simply by the name of an action: "interdiction," "flight," and so forth. Second, in defining a function, we should consider its place in the narrative. A wedding, for instance, will have different functions depending on its role. Different meanings are given to identical acts and vice versa, and correct results can be determined only by putting the event among others, that is, in relation to preceding and succeeding ones. This operation presupposes that the *sequence of functions is constant* (p. 20, *p. 22*); as will be shown later, the sequence allows certain deviations of secondary importance, exceptions to a norm that can always be restored (pp. 97-98, *pp. 107-8*). The individual tale contains all the functions; however, their succession remains stable. Thus, the total system of functions—the empirical realization of which may well not exist—seems to present the character of what would be called today metastructure.

The preceding hypotheses lead to one last conclusion, although Propp admits that it seems at first glance "absurd or perhaps even savage": All wondertales are of one type in regard to their structure (p. 21, *p. 22*).

Finally, Propp poses the question whether the research needed to confirm or invalidate his theory must be exhaustive. If so, it will practically never be completed. Yet if the subject of the study is functions, the investigation will come to an end only when new functions stop turning up, provided, of course, that the sampling be random and as if "dictated from without" (p. 22, *p. 23*). Following Durkheim—no doubt unintentionally—Propp emphasizes that "we are not interested in the quantity of material but, rather, in the quality of the analyses of it" (p. 22, *p. 24*). Experience shows that a hundred tales constitute more than enough material. Consequently, the analysis will be confined to the tales 50 to 151 in Afanas'ev's collection.

We will skim more rapidly over the functions that form the subject matter of Chapter 3. Each function is summarily defined, reduced to a single term ("absence," "interdiction," "violation," etc.), and given a coded sign—a letter or symbol. For each function, Propp distinguishes the species from the genera, the former being sometimes subdivided into varieties. The overall scheme of the wondertale is as follows.

After the "initial situation" has been explained, a character goes away. This absence leads to some misfortune, either directly or indirectly (through the violation of an interdiction or obedience to an injunction). A villain enters the scene, obtains information about his victim, and deceives him to cause him harm.

Propp analyzes this sequence into seven functions coded with the first letters of the Greek alphabet to distinguish them from the subsequent functions (coded with capital Latin letters and many other symbols). These seven functions are indeed preliminary in two ways. They set the action going, and they are not universally present, as some tales start directly with the first main function, which is the action of the villain himself—abduction of a person, theft of a magic agent, bodily injury, the casting of a spell, substitution, or murder (pp. 29-32, *pp. 30-35*). A "lack" results from this "villainy," unless the initial situation links up directly with the state of lack. The lack is noticed, and the hero is asked to remedy it.

There are now two possible paths. The victim may become the hero (heroine) of the tale, or the hero may be distinct from the victim and come to his or her rescue. The hypothesis of the uniqueness of the tale is not thereby invalidated, because no tale follows both characters simultaneously. Consequently, there is only one "hero-function," which either character can "support." Nevertheless, a choice is offered between two sequences: (1) appeal to the seeker-hero, the hero's departure on a quest; or (2) dismissal of the victim-hero and perils to which he or she is exposed.

The hero (victim or seeker) meets a "benefactor," willing or unwilling, obliging or reserved, helpful or hostile at first. The benefactor tests the hero (in many varied ways, which can go as far as engaging the hero in combat). The hero reacts negatively or positively, on his own or by means of supernatural intervention (there are many intermediate forms). The acquisition of supernatural help (object, animal, person) is an essential feature of the function of the hero (p. 46, *p. 50*).

Transferred to the place of his intervention, the hero joins in combat with the villain (struggle, competition, game). The hero receives a mark of identification, physical or other; the villain is defeated, and the initial lack is liquidated. The hero starts home but is pursued by an enemy and escapes through help received or some stratagem. Several tales end with the hero's return and his subsequent marriage.

Other tales go on to what Propp calls another "move." Everything begins anew—villain, hero, benefactor, tests, supernatural help—after which the narrative follows another direction. So a series of "*bis*-functions" must be introduced (pp. 53-54, *p. 59*), which are followed by new actions. The hero comes back in disguise, and a difficult task is proposed, which he successfully accomplishes. He is then recognized, and the false hero (who has usurped his place) is exposed. At last, the hero receives his reward (bride, kingdom, etc.) and the tale ends.

The inventory summarized above leads Propp to several conclusions. First, the number of functions is very limited: thirty-one altogether. Second, the functions presuppose one another "with logical and artistic necessity"; they belong to the same axis so that no two functions are ever mutually exclusive (p. 58, *p. 64*). On the other hand, some functions can be grouped in pairs ("interdiction"—"violation"; "struggle"—"victory"; "persecution"—"rescue," etc.) and others in sequences (for instance, the group "villainy"—"appeal for help"—"decision for counteraction"—"departure from home"). Pairs of functions, sequences of functions, and independent functions make up an invariant system. This is a real touchstone, which allows us to evaluate each tale and find its place in a classification. Each tale is given a formula analogous to chemical formulae; it contains a string of letters (Greek or Latin) and symbols used to code the various functions. Letters and symbols can receive an exponent denoting a variety within a specific function. For instance, the formula for a simple tale summarized by Propp will be:

$$\beta^3\delta^1 A^1 B^1 C\uparrow H^1\text{-}I^1 K^4\downarrow w^0$$

The eleven symbols read so: "A king (father of) three daughters"—"the daughters go walking"—"stay late in the garden"—"a dragon abducts them"—"call for help"—"quest of three heroes"—"battles with the dragon"—"victory"—"rescue of the maidens"—"return"—"rewarding" (p. 114, *p. 128*).

Once he has defined the rules of classification, Propp devotes Chapters 4 and 5 to the solution of three difficulties. The first of these, already mentioned, refers to what seems to be an assimilation of one function to another. Thus, "the testing of the hero by the benefactor" may be told in a way that makes it indistinguishable from the "assigning of a difficult task." In such cases the identification is achieved not by the content of the function, which is ambiguous, but by its context, that is, by the place it occupies among the other functions. Conversely, a statement that appears to be equivalent to a single function can cover two really distinct functions, as, for instance, when the future victim allows himself or herself to be "deceived by the villain" and at the same time "breaks an interdiction" (pp. 61-63, *pp. 69-70*).

A second difficulty stems from the fact that, once the tale has been analyzed into functions, some residual material is left to which no function corresponds. This problems troubles Propp, who suggests dividing what is left into two nonfunctional categories: the connectives and the motivations.

The connectives most often consist of episodes explaining how character A learns what character B has just done, which he or she must know in order to take action. More generally, the connective serves to establish an immediate relation between two characters or between a character and an object, whereas circumstances in the story permit only an indirect relation. The theory of connectives is doubly important. It explains how the functions may seemingly be linked in the tale, even though they do not follow one another, and it reduces the phenomenon of trebling to a single function in spite of connectives, which do not have the nature of independent functions but serve to make trebling possible (pp. 64-68, *pp. 74-75*).

Motivations are "all reasons and aims of characters which give rise to their deeds" (p. 68, *p. 75*). But it often happens that the actions of the characters are not motivated. Propp concludes that when motivations exist, they may have an origin of their own. Indeed, the motivation for a state or for an action sometimes itself takes the form of a tale developing within the main tale and acquiring an almost independent existence. "The folktale, like any living thing, can only generate forms that resemble itself" (p. 70, *p. 78*).

We have seen that the thirty-one functions to which all wondertales can be reduced are "supported" by a certain number of dramatis personae. When the functions have been classified according to their "supports," each character will emerge performing several functions in the "sphere of action" that characterizes that person. Thus, the functions "villainy"—"struggle"—"pursuit" form the sphere of action of the villain. The functions "transference of the hero"—"liquidation of lack"—"rescue"—"solution of a difficult task"—"transfiguration of the hero" define that of the magic helper, and so forth. It follows that the dramatis personae of the tale, like the functions, are limited in number. Propp notes seven main characters: the villain, the donor, the magic helper, the sought-for person, the dispatcher, the hero, and the false hero (pp. 72-73, *pp. 79-80*). Other characters exist too, but they are part of "connectives." The correspondence between each of the seven characters and his or her sphere of action is rarely defined in a unique way. The same character can be active in several spheres and a single sphere can be shared among several characters. Thus, the hero can do without a magic helper if the hero has supernatural power; and in certain tales, the magic helper assumes functions that are elsewhere the attributes of the hero (pp. 74-75, *pp. 82-83*).

If the tale is looked upon as a whole, is it still possible to distinguish several parts of it? Reduced to its most abstract formula, the wondertale can be defined as a development that starts with villainy and ends with a wedding, a reward, and the liquidation of lack or harm, the transition being made by a series of intermediate functions. Propp designates such a whole by a term that the English translator renders as 'move' and that we prefer to call *partie* in French, which means both the principal division of a tale and a game of cards or chess.[2] We are indeed confronted with both things at once, since the tales containing several *parties* are characterized by the recurrence of the same functions at several intervals; in successive card games also one periodically shuffles, cuts, deals, calls, plays, and takes the tricks. In other words, *one repeats the same actions* in spite of *different deals.*

A tale can comprise several *parties.* But do these not constitute as many tales? This question can be answered only after the relations among the *parties* have been morphologically analyzed and defined. The *parties* may follow each other, or one may be inserted in another, interrupting its development, while it is itself subjected to the same type of interruption. Two *parties* may also be introduced simultaneously and one held over until the other is ended. Two successive *parties* may receive a single conclusion. Finally, it happens that certain dramatis personae are split into two, and they can be told apart only by some mark.

Without going into details, we will just note that Propp speaks of one single tale (in spite of several *parties*) when a functional relation exists among the *parties*, but, if those are logically disjointed, he analyzes the narrative as distinct tales (pp. 83-86, *pp. 92-96*).

After giving an example (pp. 86-87, *pp. 96-98*) Propp returns to the two problems formulated at the beginning of his book: the relationship between the wonder-tale and the folktale in general and the classification of wondertales regarded as an independent category.

The wondertale is a narrative containing a limited number of functions whose order is constant. The formal differences between several tales result from the choice made by each among the thirty-one functions and the possible repetition of some of them. However, nothing prevents the making up of tales in which wondertale personages have a role, but the narrative deviates from the previous norm. This is the case of the *Kunstmärchen* by such authors as Andersen, Brentano, and Goethe. Conversely, the norm may be respected in the absence of such characters. [. . .] For lack of a better definition and not without hesitation, Propp accepts the formula "tale with seven protagonists," as he feels he has shown that these seven protagonists form a system (pp. 89-90, *pp. 99-100*). But if one day we were able to give the investigation a historical dimension, the term "mythical tales" would be more suitable.

An ideal classification of tales would rest on a system of incompatibilities among functions. But Propp has recognized a principle of reciprocal implication (p. 58, *p. 64*), which presupposes an absolute compatibility. Now—with one of the second thoughts so frequent in his book—he reintroduces incompatibility restricted to two pairs of functions: "struggle with the villain"—"hero's victory" and the "assigning of a difficult task"—"solution." These two pairs are so rarely encountered within the same *partie* that the cases contrary to the rule can be viewed as exceptions. Four classes of tales emerge: those using the first pair, those using the second pair, those using them both, and those rejecting them both (pp. 91-92, *pp. 101-2*).

As the system reveals no other incompatibility, the classification continues according to the varieties of specific functions that are present everywhere. Only two functions are so universal: "villainy" and "lack." The tales will thus be distinguished according to the forms taken by these two functions within each of the four classes.

The problem becomes even more complex when one attempts to classify the tales into several *parties*. However, the privileged case of the tales in two *parties* makes it possible, according to Propp, to solve the apparent contradiction between the morphological unity of wondertales (postulated at the beginning of the work) and the incompatibility of the two pairs of functions (introduced at the end) as offering the only possible basis for a structural classification. In point of fact, when a tale comprises two *parties* (of which one includes the pair "struggle"—"victory," and the other "difficult task"—"solution"), these pairs are always in the order in which they have just been cited, that is, "struggle"—"victory" in the first *partie*, "difficult task"—"solution," in the second. Moreover, the two *parties* are linked by an initial function, common to both (pp. 93, *p. 103*).

Propp regards this structure as a certain archetype from which all the wonder-tales have been derived, at least in Russia.

By integrating all the typical formulae a canonical formula is obtained:

$$A\ B\ C\dagger D\ E\ F\ G\ \frac{H\ J\ I\ K\dagger Pr\text{-}Rs^0\ L}{L\ M\ J\ N\ K\dagger Pr\text{-}Rs}\ Q\ Ex\ T\ U\ W^*$$

from which the four fundamental categories are easily drawn, corresponding respectively to:

1. First group + upper group + last group.
2. First group + lower group + last group.
3. First group + upper group + lower group + last group.
4. First group + last group.

The principle of morphological unity remains intact (p. 95, *p. 105*). The principle of the invariable succession of functions also remains intact, though subject to the permutation of function L, "claims of a false hero" in the final or in the initial position, depending on the choice between two incompatible pairs: HI and MN. Propp accepts other permutations of isolated functions and even sequences. The typological unity and the morphological kinship of all wondertales is not brought into question by these permutations, since they imply no difference in the structure (p. 97-98, *p. 106*).

The most striking aspect of Propp's work is the power with which it anticipates further developments. Those among us who first approached the structural analysis of oral literature around 1950, without direct knowledge of Propp's attempts a quarter of a century earlier, recognize there, to their amazement, formulae—sometimes even whole sentences—that they know well enough they have not borrowed from him: the notion of an "initial situation"; the comparison of a mythological matrix with the rules of musical composition; the necessity of a reading that is at once "horizontal" and "vertical" (p. 107, *p. 119*); the constant use of the idea of a group of substitutions and of transformation in order to resolve the antinomy between the constancy of the form and the variability of content (*passim*); the effort—at least indicated by Propp—to reduce the specific functions to pairs of oppositions; the privileged case of myths in structural analysis (p. 82, *p. 90*); and, finally and above all, the essential hypothesis that there exists, strictly speaking, but a single tale (pp. 20-21, *p. 22*), that the collection of known tales must be treated as a series of variants of a unique type (p. 103, *p. 113*), with the result that one may discover through calculations vanished or unrecorded variants, exactly as one can infer the existence of invisible stars as functions of the laws of astronomy. These are so many intuitions, whose perspicacity and prophetic character arouse our admiration. They earn for Propp the devotion of all those who, unknown to themselves, were his followers.

If in my discussion I am led to formulate certain reservations and to offer some objections, they can neither diminish Propp's tremendous merit nor contest the priority of his discoveries.

This made clear, one can try to guess the reasons that made Propp choose wondertales, that is, a certain category of tales, to test his method. These tales should not be classified as separate from the rest of oral literature. Propp writes that, from a certain point of view ("historical" according to him, but we think also psychological and logical), "the fairy tale in its morphological bases amounts to a myth. We, of course, realize," he adds immediately, "that, from the point of view of contemporary science, we are stating a totally heretical idea" (p. 82, *p. 90*).

Propp is right: there is no serious reason to isolate tales from myths, although the difference between the two is subjectively felt by a great many societies, although this difference is objectively expressed by means of special terms to distinguish the two genres, and finally, although prescriptions and prohibitions are sometimes linked with one and not the other (recitation of myths at certain hours or during a season only, whereas tales, because of their "profane" nature, can be narrated any time).

These native distinctions are of great interest for the ethnographer, but it is not at all certain that they are based on the nature of things. On the contrary, folktales in one society are known to be myths in another, and vice versa. This is the first reason to beware of arbitrary classifications. Besides, the mythologist usually notices that in an identical or remolded form the same tales, the same characters, and the same motifs reappear in the tales and myths of a given community. Moreover, in attempting the complete series of transformations of a mythical theme one can seldom limit oneself to the myths (so qualified by the natives); some of these transformations must extend to the tales, although it is possible to infer their existence from the myths proper.

There is no doubt, however, that almost all societies regard the two genres as distinct and that the regularity of this distinction has some cause. I believe that such a cause exists but reduced to a difference of degree, which is twofold. Tales are constructed on weaker oppositions than those found in myths. The former are not cosmological, metaphysical, or natural, but, more often, local, social, and moral. In addition—precisely because the tale is a weakened transposition of the theme whose stronger realization is the property of myth—the former is less strictly subjected than the latter to the triple consideration of logical coherence, religious orthodoxy, and collective pressure. The tale offers more possibilities of play, its permutations are comparatively freer, and with time they acquire a certain arbitrary character. But if the tale works with reduced oppositions, these will be so much more difficult to identify. And the difficulty increases because, when the oppositions become very weak, they mark an instability that comes close to literary creation.

Propp saw this latter difficulty very clearly and said "that the purity of folktale construction"—indispensable for the application of his method—"is peculiar only to the peasantry—to a peasantry, moreover, little touched by civilization. All kinds of foreign influences alter and sometimes decompose a folktale." In this case, "it is impossible to make provision for all details" (p. 90, *p. 100*). Nonetheless, Propp admits that the narrator has relative freedom in the choice of certain characters, in the omission and repetition of certain functions, in determining the forms of the functions, and, finally, to a much greater degree, in the nomenclature and the attributes of the characters added to: "a tree may show the way, a crane may give a steed a gift, a chisel may spy, and so forth. This freedom is a peculiarity of the folktale alone" (pp. 101-2, *pp. 112-13*). Elsewhere, he mentions the attributes of these characters, such as "their age, sex, status, external appearance (and any peculiarities of same), and so forth," which are variable because they "provide the folktale with its brilliance, charm, and beauty." Thus, external causes alone can explain why in a tale one attribute is substituted for another; they are a transformation of real-life conditions, the influence of foreign epic literature, bookish culture, religion, and superstitions. "The folktale has gradually undergone a metamorphic process, and these transformations and metamorphoses are subject to certain laws. These processes create a multiformity which is difficult to analyze" (p. 79, *p. 87*).

All this really means that the tale lends itself imperfectly to structural analysis. This is no doubt true in a measure, but less so than Propp believes, and not exactly for the reasons he gives. I will return to this problem, but first we must find out why, given such conditions, it is the wondertale that Propp chose for testing his method. Should he not rather have used myths, the privileged value of which he recognizes several times?

The reasons for Propp's choice are many and are of varying importance. As he is not an ethnologist, one can suppose that he had no access to or control over mythological material collected by him and among peoples known to him. In addition, he started on a path on which others immediately preceded him. It is tales, rather than myths, that his predecessors discussed and that provided the ground where certain Russian scholars outlined the first plans of morphological studies. Propp takes up the problem where they left it, using the same material: Russian folktales.

I believe that Propp's choice can also be explained by his lack of knowledge of the true relationship between myth and the folktale. He has the great merit of seeing in them *species* of the same *genus*, but he remains faithful to the idea of the historical priority of the former over the latter. He writes that to be able to start studying myth, one would have to add to the morphological analysis "a historical study which, for the present, cannot enter into our task" (p. 82, *p. 90*). A little further on he suggests that "very archaic myths" constitute the realm in which folktales have their distant origin (p. 90, *p. 100*). He even says, "Everyday life and religion die away, while their contents turn into a folktale" (p. 96, *p. 106*).

The ethnologist will beware of such an interpretation because he knows that in present times myths and folktales exist side by side. One genre cannot then be held to be a survival of the other, unless it is postulated that tales preserve the memory of ancient myths, themselves fallen into oblivion. [For a discussion of such hypotheses, see Lévi-Strauss 1976, Chapters 9 and 14.] This proposition could not be demonstrated most of the time (since we are ignorant of all or almost all the ancient beliefs of the peoples we are studying and call them "primitive" precisely for this reason); besides, the usual ethnographic experience leads one to think that myth and the folktale use a common substance, each in its own way. Their relationship is not that of anterior to posterior, of primitive to derived. It is rather a complementary relationship. Tales are miniature myths, in which the same oppositions are transposed to a smaller scale, and this is what makes them difficult to study in the first place.

The preceding considerations certainly must not make one disregard the other difficulties Propp mentions, although one could formulate them in a slightly different manner. Even in our contemporary societies the tale is not a residual myth, but it certainly suffers from existing alone. The disappearance of myths has broken the balance. Like a satellite without a planet, the tale tends to get out of orbit, to let itself be caught by other poles of attraction.

Such are some additional reasons for turning to civilizations in which myth and the tale have coexisted until a recent period and sometimes continue to do so, in which the system of oral literature is whole and can be looked upon as a whole. The point is not to choose between the tale and myth but to realize that they are the two poles of a field that also includes all sorts of intermediate forms and that their morphological analysis must be the same, or else one may miss elements belonging to the same system of transformations.

Propp appears to be torn between his formalist vision and the obsession with historical explanations. One can, to some degree, understand the regret that made him give up the former in order to turn to the latter. As soon as he had settled on folktales, the antinomy became overpowering. Clearly, tales have history, but a practically inaccessible history, since we know very little about the prehistoric civilizations in which they originated. But is it really history that is lacking? The historical dimension appears rather as a negative factor resulting in the discrepancy between the tale as it exists and a missing ethnographic context. The opposition is resolved when one observes an oral tradition still in action, like those studied by ethnography. There the problem of history does not arise, or it arises only in exceptional cases, since the external references necessary for the interpretation of oral tradition belong to the same plane as the tradition itself.

Thus, Propp is the victim of a subjective illusion. He is not torn, as he thinks, between the demands of synchrony and diachrony. *It is not the past that he lacks, it is context.* Formalist dichotomy, which opposes form and matter and defines them by antithesis, is not forced on him by the nature of things but by the accidental choice he made in an area where only form survives, whereas matter is absent. Reluctantly he dissociates them and at the most decisive moments of his analysis he believes that what escapes him in fact has escaped him by right.

Except for certain passages, prophetic but very timid and hesitating, Propp divides oral literature in two: a form, which is of prime importance because it lends itself to morphological study, and an arbitrary content, which, just because it is arbitrary, he treats as less important. I would like to stress this point, since it sums up the difference between formalism and structuralism. For formalism, the two areas must be absolutely separate, as form alone is intelligible, and content is only a residual deprived of any significant value. For structuralism, this opposition does not exist; structuralism does not treat one as abstract and the other as concrete. Form and content are of the same nature, amenable to the same type of analysis. Content receives its reality from its structure, and what is called form is a way of organizing the local structures that make up this content.

The limitation, which we believe to be inherent in formalism, is particularly striking in the main chapter of Propp's work, the one on the characters' functions. The author categorizes them in genera and species. It is clear, however, that the former are defined exclusively and the latter only in part by morphological criteria; unwittingly Propp uses these criteria to reintroduce some aspects of content. The generic function "villainy"' is subdivided into twenty-two species and subspecies, such as: the villain "abducts a person," "steals a magic agent," "plunders or spoils the crops," "steals the daylight," "makes a threat of cannibalism," (pp. 29-32, *pp. 31-34*). The whole content of the tales is thus decomposed step by step, and the analysis oscillates between formal terms—so general that they can be indiscriminately applied to any tale (this is the generic level)— and a simple registration of the raw material, whose formal properties alone have been said at the beginning to possess an explanatory value.

The inconsistency is so flagrant that Propp desperately seeks a middle position. Instead of systematically cataloging what he maintains are species, he isolates some of them, putting together, pell-mell, in a single "specific" category all those not frequently encountered. "It is technically more useful," he writes, "to isolate several of its most important forms while, on the other hand, generalizing about those remaining" (pp. 29, 33, *pp. 31-32, 35*). But either one deals with specific forms and then one cannot formulate a coherent system without cataloging and classifying them all, or there is only content and—according to the rules set by Propp himself—one must exclude it from the morphological analysis. In any case, a drawer filled with unclassified forms does not constitute a species.

Why, then, should he rob Peter to pay Paul and feel happy about it? For a very simple reason, which explains another weakness of the formalist position.

Unless content is underhandedly reinterpreted as form, the latter will remain at so high a level of abstraction that it stops meaning anything and has no heuristic value. *Formalism destroys its object.* With Propp, it results in the discovery that there exists but one tale. In this way, the explanation is shifted elsewhere. We know what *the tale* is; however, since we observe not an archetypal tale but so many concrete tales, we are left without any resources of classifying them. Before the epoch of formalism we were indeed unaware of what these tales had in common. Now we are deprived of any means of understanding how they differ. We have passed from the concrete to the abstract but can no longer come down from the abstract to the concrete.

Concluding his work, Propp quotes an admirable page from Veselovskij:

> Is it permissible in this field also to consider the problem of typical schemes . . . schemes handed down from generations as readymade formulae capable of becoming animated with a new mood, giving rise to new formations? . . . The contemporary narrative literature, with its complicated thematic structure and photographic reproduction of reality, apparently eliminates the very possibility of such a question. But when this literature appears to future generations as distant as antiquity (from prehistoric to medieval times) seems to us at present—when the synthesis of time, that great simplifier, in passing over the complexity of phenomena, reduces them to the magnitude of points receding into the distance, then their lines will merge with those which we are now uncovering when we look back at the poetic traditions of the distant past—and the phenomena of schematism and repetition will then be established across the total expanse.'' (Quoted by Propp, p. 105, *p. 116*, from A. N. Veselovskij, *Poètika,* Vol. II.)

These views are profound but, at least in the passage given above, one cannot perceive on what basis the differentiation will take place when, looking beyond the unity of literary creation, one tries to determine the nature of and the reason for its variety.

Propp was aware of this difficulty and the last part of his work consists of an attempt, as feeble as it is ingenious, to reintroduce a principle of classification. There is but one tale, but this tale is an architale comprising four groups of logically connected functions. If we call them 1, 2, 3, 4, the concrete tales will be divided into four categories, depending on their use of all four groups or three groups (for logical reasons only 1, 2, 4 or 1, 3, 4 are possible), or two groups, which must then be 1, 4, (see p. 175 above).

Yet this classification into four categories leaves us as far from real tales as does the single category, since each category includes dozens or hundreds of different tales. Propp knows this so well that he continues: ''Further classification can also be made according to the varieties of this obligatory element. Thus at the heading of each class will come the folktales about the kidnapping of a person, then folktales about the stealing of a talisman, etc., on through all the varieties of element A (villainy). Folktales with *a* (i.e., folktales about the quest for a bride, for a talisman, etc.) appear thereafter'' (p. 92, *p. 102*). What does it mean if not that morphological categories do not exhaust reality and that the content of the tale after being rejected as an inappropriate basis for classification is admitted again because the morphological attempt has failed?

There is a more serious matter still. We saw that the fundamental tale, of which all tales offer an incomplete realization, is formed of two *parties* whose certain functions are recurrent—some being simple variants of others and some belonging specifically to each *partie* (see p. 173 above). These specific functions are, for the first *partie*, "struggle," "branding the hero," "victory," "liquidation of lack," "return," "pursuit of the hero," "rescue"; and for the second *partie* "the hero's unrecognized arrival," "assigning a difficult task," "success," "recognition of the hero," "exposure of the false hero," and "transfiguration of the hero."

How are these two series differentiated? Could they not be treated as two variants, so that the "assigning of a difficult task," would be a transformation of the "struggle" (or, rather, of the testing of the hero that takes place before); the false hero, a transformation of the "villain"; the "success," a transformation of the "victory"; and the "transfiguration," a transformation of the "branding"? In this case, the theory of the fundamental tale in two *parties* would collapse and, with it, the weak hope of a tentative morphological classification. There would then be, truly, a single tale. But it would be reduced to such a vague and general abstraction that nothing would be learned from it about the objective causes of a multitude of concrete tales.

The proof of the analysis is in the synthesis. If the synthesis appears to be impossible, it is because the analysis is incomplete. Nothing testifies more strongly to the inadequacy of formalism than its inability to reconstitute the empirical content that served as its starting point. What has it lost along the way? Precisely the content. To his great credit, Propp discovered that the content of tales is *permutable*. But he too often concluded that it is *arbitrary*, and this is the reason for his difficulties, since even permutations conform to rules. [For an attempt at joint synthesis of form and content see Lévi-Strauss 1976, Chapter 9.]

In the myths and tales of the Indians of North and South America the same actions are attributed—depending on the tales—to different animals. As an elementary example, let us consider birds: eagle, owl, crow. Shall we distinguish, as Propp does, between the function (constant) and the characters (variable)? No, because each character is not given in the form of an opaque element, confronted with which structural analysis should halt, telling itself to go no further. When, after the fashion of Propp, the narrative is treated as a closed system, just the opposite is true. The narrative does not contain any information about itself, and the character is comparable to a word occurring in a document but not registered by the dictionary—or even to a proper noun, that is, a term independent of context.

To understand the meaning of an element, we must always look at it in all its contexts. In oral literature, these contexts manifest themselves in numerous variants, that is, in a whole system of compatibilities and incompatibilities. That the eagle appears by day and the owl appears by night in the same function permits the definition of the former as a day owl and of the latter as a night eagle; consequently, the relevant opposition is that of day to night.

If the oral literature considered is of an ethnographic type, there are other contexts provided by the ritual, religious beliefs, superstitions, and factual knowledge. It turns out that the eagle and the owl together are put in opposition to the crow, as predators to scavenger, whereas they are opposed to each other at the level of day and night, and that the duck is in opposition to all three at the new level of the pairs sky-land and sky-water. Thus, step by step, we define a "universe of the tale," analyzable in pairs of oppositions interlocked within each character who—far from constituting a single entity—forms a bundle of distinctive features like the phoneme in Roman Jakobson's theory.

In the same manner, the American narratives sometimes mention trees, designating them, for example, as plum tree or apple tree. But it would be equally false to believe that only the concept *tree* is important and that its concrete realizations are arbitrary or that there exists one function of which the tree is only a "support." The inventory of contexts reveals that, philosophically speaking, what interests natives about the plum tree is its fecundity, while the apple tree attracts their attention because of the strength and depth of its roots. The one introduces a positive function, fecundity, the other a negative function, earth-sky transition, and both are related to vegetation. The apple tree, in its turn, is opposed to the wild turnip (removable plug between the two worlds), itself realizing the positive function of the sky-earth transition.

Conversely, by carefully examining the contexts, we can eliminate false distinctions. Among the Plains Indians, mythical narratives about eagle hunts refer to an animal species sometimes identified as wolverine, sometimes as bear. We can decide in favor of the former, for the natives, telling of the wolverine's habits, especially remember that it makes game of traps dug into the ground. The eagle hunters, however, hide in pits, and the opposition eagle-wolverine becomes that of "game in the sky" to a chthonic hunter, the strongest one conceivable in hunting. By the same token, this maximum amplitude between elements generally less remote explains why eagle hunting is subjected to a particularly exacting ritual (see Lévi-Strauss 1954-55, 25-27; 1959-60, 39-40, and 1962, 66-71).

To maintain, as I have done, that the permutability of contents is not arbitrary amounts to saying that, if the analysis is carried to a sufficiently deep level, behind diversity we will discover constancy. And, of course, the avowed constancy of form must not hide from us that functions are also permutable.

The structure of the folktale as it is illustrated by Propp presents a chronological succession of qualitatively distinct functions, each constituting an independent genre. One can wonder whether—as with dramatis personae and their attributes— Propp does not stop too soon, seeking the form too close to the level of empirical observation. Among the thirty-one functions that he distinguishes, several are reducible to the *same* function reappearing at *different* moments of the narrative but after undergoing one or a number of *transformations*. I have already suggested that this could be true of the false hero (a transformation of the villain), of assigning a difficult task (a transformation of the test), etc. (see p. 181 above), and that in this case the two *parties* constituting the fundamental tale would themselves be transformations of each other.

Nothing prevents pushing this reduction even further and analyzing each separate *partie* into a small number of recurrent functions, so that several of Propp's functions would constitute groups of transformations of one and the same function. We could treat the "violation" as the reverse of the prohibition" and the latter as a negative transformation of the "injunction." The "departure" of the hero and his "return" would appear as the negative and positive expressions of the same disjunctive function. The "quest" of the hero (hero pursues someone or something) would become the opposite of "pursuit" (hero is pursued by something or someone), etc. Thus, instead of Propp's chronological scheme, in which the order of succession of events is a feature of the structure

$$A, B, C, D, E, \ldots \ldots \ldots M, N, H, \ldots \ldots \ldots T, U, V, W, X$$

another scheme should be adopted, which would present a structural model defined as the group of transformations of a small number of elements. This scheme would appear as a matrix with two, three or more dimensions:

w	$-x$	$\dfrac{1}{y}$	$1-z$	$\ldots$
$-w$	$\dfrac{1}{x}$	$1-y$	z	$\ldots$
$\dfrac{1}{w}$	$1-x$	y	$-z$	$\ldots$
$1-w$	x	$-y$	$\dfrac{1}{z}$	$\ldots$

$$\ldots \ldots \ldots \ldots \ldots \ldots \ldots \ldots \ldots$$

Its system of operations would be closer to Boolean algebra.

In Vol. I of *Structural Anthropology*, p. 209, I have shown that this analysis alone can account for the double aspect of time representation in all mythical systems: the narrative is both "in time" (it consists of a succession of events) and "beyond" (its value is permanent). With regard to Propp's theories my analysis offers another advantage: I can reconcile much better than Propp himself his principle of a permanent order of wondertale elements with the fact that certain functions or groups of functions are shifted from one tale to the next (pp. 97-98, *p. 108*). If my view is accepted, the chronological succession will come to be absorbed into an atemporal matrix structure whose form is indeed constant. The shifting of functions is then no more than a mode of permutation (by vertical columns or fractions of columns).

These critical remarks are certainly valid for the method used by Propp and for his conclusions. However, it cannot be stressed enough that Propp envisioned them and in several places formulated with perfect clarity the solutions I have just suggested. Let us take up again from this viewpoint the two essential themes of our discussion: constancy of the content (in spite of its permutability) and permutability of functions (in spite of their constancy).

Chapter 8 of *Morphology of the Folktale* is entitled "On the Attributes of Dramatis Personae *and Their Meaning*" (italics added). In rather obscure terms (at least in the English translation) Propp reflects upon the variability of elements. This variability does not exclude repetition, and one can recognize some basic forms, as well as some derived, or heteronomous forms. Propp distinguishes an international model, national or regional models, and finally models characteristic of some social or professional groups. "By grouping the material of each heading, we are able to define all methods, or more precisely, all aspects of transformation" (p. 80, *p. 89*). But in reconstituting a typical tale from basic forms peculiar to each group one notices that this tale conceals certain abstract representations. The tests imposed by the benefactor on the hero can vary depending on the tale, and yet they imply a constant intention with regard to the dramatis personae. The same holds for the tasks imposed on the abducted princess. Among these intentions, which are expressible in formulae, we observe a common feature. In comparing "these formulae with other attributive elements, we unexpectedly come upon a connective link in both the logical and the artistic plans. . . . Even such details as the golden hair of the princess . . . acquire a completely special meaning and may be studied. The study of attributes makes possible a scientific interpretation of the folktale" (pp. 81-82, *p. 90*).

As Propp does not have at his disposal an ethnographic context (which, ideally, a historic and prehistoric inquiry could alone procure), he gives up this program as soon as he has formulated it or postpones it until better times (which explains his return to the search for survivals and to comparative studies). "Everything we state, however, is in the form of a supposition." Nevertheless, "the study of the attributes of dramatis personae, as we have outlined it, is of great importance (p. 82, *p. 90*). Even reduced for the time being to an inventory (of little interest in itself), the study may lead us to examine "the laws of transformation and the abstract notions which are reflected in the basic forms of these attributes" (p. 82, *p. 90*).

Here Propp gets to the bottom of the problem. Behind the attributes first dismissed as an arbitrary, irrelevant residue, he feels the presence of "abstract notions" and a "logical plan," whose existence (if it could be established) would allow us to treat the tale as a myth (p. 82, *p. 90*).

As far as the second theme is concerned, the examples gathered in Appendix II show that Propp does not hesitate at times to introduce notions such as the negative function or the reverse function. He even uses a special symbol for the latter (=). We have seen (p. 183 above), that certain functions are mutually exclusive. There are more that presuppose each other, such as "interdiction" and "violation," on the one hand, "deception" and "submission," on the other; these two pairs are most often incompatible (p. 98, *p. 108*). (The second system of incompatibilities pertains to functions that Propp called preparatory because of their contingent character. It should be remembered that for Propp the main functions have only one pair of incompatibilities.) Hence the problem explicitly stated by Propp: "Are the varieties of one function necessarily linked with the corresponding varieties of another function?" (p. 99, *p. 109*). Always in some cases ("interdiction" and "violation," "struggle" and "victory," "branding" and "recognition," etc.); occasionally in others. Certain correlations can be unilateral, others reciprocal (the act of throwing down a comb always appears in the context of flight, but the opposite is not true), so "unilaterally and bilaterally substitutable elements would appear to exist" (p. 99, *p. 110*).

In an earlier chapter, Propp studied permissible correlations between the different forms of "testing" of the hero by the benefactor and the forms of "transmitting the magic agent" to the hero. He concluded that two types of correlations exist, depending on whether bargaining does or does not characterize the transmission (pp. 42-43, *pp. 46-47*). In working with these rules and others like them, Propp foresaw the possibility of verifying his hypotheses experimentally. It would be sufficient to apply the system of compatible and incompatible functions, of implications and correlations (total or partial) to the making of synthetic tales. One would then see these creations "come alive and become folktales" (p. 101, *p. 112*).

Obviously, Propp adds, that would be possible only if the functions were distributed among the dramatis personae (borrowed from tradition or invented) and if no omission were made of motivations, connections, "and other auxiliary elements" (p. 102, *p.112*) whose creation is "absolutely free" (p. 102, *p. 112*). Let us repeat that it is not free; Propp's doubts show that his attempt first appeared (to him) unsuccessful.

The origin myths of the western Pueblo Indians start with the account of the first human beings' emergence from the depths of the earth where they lived at first. This emergence must be motivated, and it is indeed motivated in two ways:

either humanity becomes conscious of its miserable condition and wishes to escape from it, or the gods discover their own loneliness and call the people to the sur- face of the earth to have people pray to them and worship them. One recognizes Propp's "situation of lack" motivated either from the human viewpoint or from that of the gods. But this change of motivation from one variant to the other is so far from being arbitrary that it brings in its wake the transformation of a whole series of functions. In the last analysis, it is linked to different ways of posing the problem of the relationship between hunting and agriculture (see Lévi-Strauss 1976, Chapter 11, 1952-53, 19-21, 1953-54, 27-29). But it would be impossible to arrive at this conclusion if the rituals, technique, knowledge, and beliefs of the peoples concerned could not be studied sociologically and independently of their occurrence in myth. Without those data one would remain in a closed circle.

The error of formalism is thus twofold. By restricting itself exclusively to the rules that govern the arrangment of elements it loses sight of the fact that no language exists whose vocabulary can be deduced from its syntax. The study of any linguistic system requires the cooperation of the grammarian and the philologist. In regard to oral tradition it means that morphology is sterile until fertilized by direct or indirect ethnographic observation. Propp's idea that the two tasks can be separated, that the grammatical study can be undertaken first and the lexical study postponed until later will result only in the production of a lifeless grammar and a lexicon in which anecdotes replace definitions. In the end, neither will accomplish its purpose.

This first error of formalism is explained by its failure to understand the com- plementarity of signifier and signified, which has been recognized since Saussure in all linguistic systems. But to this error, formalism adds another; it treats oral tradition as a linguistic expression similar to all the others, that is, amenable to structural analysis in different measure, depending on the level.

It is now believed that language is structured at the phonological level. We are gradually becoming convinced that it is also structured at the level of gram- mar but less convinced about vocabulary. Except perhaps for certain privileged areas, we have not yet discovered the angle from which vocabulary would yield to structural analysis.

An analogous view of oral tradition explains Propp's distinction between a single truly morphological level—that of functions—and an amorphous level where characters, attributes, motivations, and connections all pile up and which is the exclusive area (as it is said about vocabulary) of historical investigation and literary criticism.

This view ignores the fact that myths and tales (each of them itself a language) are "hyperstructural"; they form a "metalanguage" in which structure operates at all levels. It is owing to this property that they are immediately recognized as folktales or myths and not as historical or romantic narratives. Like all discourses, they naturally employ grammatical rules and words. But another dimension is added to the usual one because rules and words in narratives build images and actions that are both "normal" signifiers, in relation to what is signified in the discourse, and elements of meaning, in relation to a supplementary system of meaning found at another level. To give just one example: in a tale a "king" is not only a king and a "shepherdess" not only a shepherdess; these words and what they signify become recognizable means of constructing a system formed by the oppositions *male/female* (with regard to *nature*) and *high/low* (with regard to *culture*), as well as by all possible permutations among the six terms.

Language and metalanguage, which, united, constitute folktales and myths, can have certain levels in common, though these levels are shifted in them. While remaining elements of the narrative, the words of myth function as bundles of distinctive features. From the point of view of classification these mythemes do not belong to the level of vocabulary but to the level of phonemes. The difference between them is that they do not operate on the same *continuum* (resources of sensuous experience in one case and of the phonatory apparatus in the other), and the similarity between them is that the *continuum* is decomposed and reassembled according to the binary and ternary rules of opposition and correlation.

The problem of vocabulary differs then, according to whether language or metalanguage is considered. Because in American tales and myths the function of the trickster can be "supported" sometimes by the coyote, sometimes by the mink, or sometimes by the crow, an ethnographic and historical problem is posed, comparable to a philological investigation of the modern form of a word. And yet it is altogether a different problem from that of discovering why a certain animal species is called *vison* in French and "mink" in English. In the second case, the result can be considered as due to chance, and it is only necessary to reconstruct the development that led to a definite verbal form. In the first case, the restrictions are much stronger because the constituent elements are few and their possible combinations are limited. The choice must be made among the existing possibilities.

However, if we look a little more closely, we notice that this seemingly quantitative difference is not related to the number of constituent units (this number is not of the same order of magnitude in dealing with phonemes and mythemes) but to the nature of the constituent units, qualitatively different in the two cases.

According to the classical definition, phonemes are elements that have no meaning but whose presence or absence serves to differentiate other units—words, which are endowed with a meaning of their own. If these words seem arbitrary in their phonetic form, it is not only because they are the random products (although possibly less so than it is believed) of numerous phonemic combinations allowed by every language. Verbal forms mostly owe their arbitrary character to the fact that their constituent units (phonemes) are themselves undetermined with regard to meaning. There is no reason why certain combinations of sounds should convey the meaning they do. As I have tried to show elsewhere (Lévi-Strauss 1967,

Chapter 5), the structuralization of vocabulary appears at another stage: a posteriori and not a priori.

It is a different matter with mythemes, since they result from a play of binary or ternary oppositions (which makes them comparable to phonemes). But the elements themselves are already meaningful at the level of language; they are the "abstract representation" of which Propp speaks and which can be expressed by words. Borrowing a neologism from the building technique, one could say that, unlike words, mythemes are "prestressed." Of course, they are still words but with a double meaning; they are *words of words*, operating simultaneously on two levels: that of language, where they retain their own meaning and that of metalanguage, where they participate as elements of a supermeaning, the fruit of their union.

If this is true, it follows that nothing in folktales and myths can remain alien or resistant to structure. Even vocabulary, that is, the content, emerges stripped of the character of "naturing nature" (*nature naturante*), in which one is ready (probably by mistake) to detect unpredictable and contingent entities. In tales and myths, vocabulary appears as "natured nature" (*nature naturée*). It is something given, with its laws, which impose a kind of grid upon the real and upon the mythical vision. For the latter it only remains to discover the permissible arrangements of the pieces of a mosaic whose number, meaning, and shapes have been determined beforehand.

We have denounced the error of formalism, namely, the belief that grammar can be tackled at once and vocabulary later. But what is true for some linguistic systems is even more so for myths and tales, because in this case grammar and vocabulary are not only closely linked while operating at distinct levels, but are inseparable and cover each other completely. In contradistinction to language with its problem of vocabulary, metalanguage has no level whose elements do not result from strict operations carried out according to the rules. In this sense everything in metalanguage is syntax. But in another sense everything in it is vocabulary, since the distinctive elements are words. Mythemes are also words; functions (mythemes raised to the second power) are designated by words, as Propp knows very well. And it is likely that languages exist in which an entire myth can be expressed in a single word.

Postscript

In the Italian edition of his work (Propp 1966a) Propp responded to my discussion with an offended harangue. Invited by the Italian publisher to answer but, concerned not to perpetuate what seemed to me to be a misunderstanding, I restricted myself to a brief comment. Not having kept the original, I can reconstruct the text approximately from the translation on page 164.

> All those who read the essay that I wrote in 1960 about Propp's prophetic work included in this volume by the Italian publisher cannot have failed to take it for what it was meant to be: a homage rendered to a great discovery that preceded by a quarter of a century all the attempts made by others and myself in the same direction.

> This is why I note with surprise and regret that the Russian scholar, to whose deserved fame I thought I had modestly contributed, saw something quite different in my words: not a courteous discussion of some theoretical and methodological aspects of his work but a perfidious attack.

> I do not wish to engage with him in a polemic on this subject. It is clear that treating me as a philosopher he shows that he ignores all my ethnological work, whereas a profitable exchange of views could have been based on our respective contributions to the study and interpretation of oral traditions.

> But whatever conclusions better informed readers can draw from this confrontation, Propp's work will, to them and to me, forever keep the merit of having been the first.

Notes

Notes

1. The Nature of Folklore

First published as Propp 1946b. Reprinted in Propp 1976a, 16-33.

1. Fjódor Ivánovič Busláev (1818-97) was an authority in folklore and linguistics. His works are devoted to epic poetry, early Russian literature, Old Russian art, and grammar.

2. Orést Fjódorovič Míller (1833-89): an advocate of the Mythological school. His main contribution is a book on Il'já Múromec (1869). His conclusions are, in principle, close to those drawn much later by Jan de Vries, Otto Höffler, and Georges Dumézil, who have attempted to discover mythic prototypes of epic heroes. O. F. Miller should not be confused with V. F. Miller (1848-1913), the founder of the Russian Historical school.

3. Aleksándr Nikoláevič Veselóvskij (1838-1906) was the author of numerous works on comparative literature; two of them—*Historical Poetics* and *The Poetics of Plots*—are often cited by modern scholars. See more of him in the Introduction. He should be distinguished from his brother Alekséj Nikoláevič Veselóvskij (1843-1918), also a professor of comparative literature.

4. Márfa Semjónovna Krjúkova (1876-1954), a singer of Russian bylinas, lived in a village on the White Sea. After the Revolution she found herself in the limelight and even became a member of the Writers' Union. A replica of a fairytale house was built for her on the shore (reportedly, she never lived in it). As was the case with several other singers, for example, the Kazakh *akýn* Djambúl Djabáev and the Lezgin *ašúg* Sulejmán Stál'skij, publicity ruined her art, and she produced a spate of spurious bylínas, *stárinas* 'old songs,' and *nóvinas* 'new songs,' many of them about Lenin and Stalin. Cf. Kaun 1943, 184-91.

5. Lermontov's "Sail": one of the most famous lyrics by Mixaíl Júr'jevič Lérmontov (1814-41). Countless songs have been written to this lyric; especially popular is the one by A. E. Varlámov (1801-48). The poem tells about a sail looming in a blue haze. The sail neither seeks happiness nor flees from it. A stream, lighter than azure, is beneath it; a golden sunray is high above, but the sail asks for a tempest, as though in a tempest there were peace. The poem was written in 1832 and published posthumously in 1841; there are close to twenty translations of it into English

6. The correct title of this lyric by Antón Antónovič Dél'vig (1798-1831) is "Russian Song" (published in 1826). Its heroine tells a nightingale about her grief: the man she loves has forgotten

her. Del'vig's lyric acquired tremendous popularity because of a song set to its text by A. A. Aljáb'ev (1787-1851). Aljab'ev's theme was later used by Glinka for a piano piece and by John Field in one of his nocturnes.

7. "The Black Shawl": a lyric by Aleksándr Sergéevič Pushkin (1799-1837), written in 1820 and published in 1821. It was inspired by a Moldavian song Pushkin heard in Kishinev. Its content is as follows: a young man is told that the Greek girl whom he loves is unfaithful to him; he kills her and her Armenian lover, and only her black shawl reminds him of his past happiness. This lyric became a "folk song" as early as the 1830s and was reprinted in dozens of song books. The music to this "folk song" was written by I. I. Géništa (1795-1853).

8. *The Peddlers*: a narrative poem by Nikoláj Alekséevič Nekrásov (1821-77). It begins with a love scene between a young peddler and a peasant girl. The finale of the poem is tragic, but the opening lines (*Oj polná, polná koróbuška*) are full of life and energy; they have long since become a folk song.

9. "Dubínuška" ('Cudgel'): a folksong that was current among workers and boatmen. All sources state that the song was published in 1889 by N. M. Lopátin and V. P. Prokúnin. The stanzas containing the words *Èx! dubínuška úxnem* were first used by V. I. Bogdánov (1865). The author of the universally known text (published in 1885) is A. A. Ol'xín, not L. N. Tréfolev.

10. "Íz-za óstrova na stréžen' ": a song about Stepán Rázin (see note 2 on No. 2) and a Persian princess. (Razin and his people sail along the Volga. Razin's friends complain that their leader has forgotten them because of the princess. Razin throws the woman into the water.) The author of the text is D. N. Sadóvnikov (1847-83); it was first published in 1883 and became a folksong soon after that. The same data are discussed in Rozánov 1975, 67-69; first published in 1935.

11. *The faraway kingdom* is a nonidiomatic translation of the Russian folktale formula *tridevjátoe cárstvo, tridesjátoe gosudárstvo*, literally 'three-ninth (or thrice-ninth) kingdom, three-tenth (or thrice-tenth) country.

12. The *Edda*, also called The *Elder Edda*, The *Poetic Edda*, and *Sæmund's Edda* (after the medieval Icelandic scholar to whom at one time it was erroneously attributed), is a collection of songs (lays) recorded in Iceland in the thirteenth century. It contains texts of a mythological and of a heroic character. Several plots from *The Edda* are also known from non-Scandinavian sources.

13. For a detailed analysis of the myth of Oedipus, see Propp 1944, reprinted in Propp 1976a, 258-99. The Italian translation is Propp 1975, the English translation is Propp 1983.

14. The Egyptian *Book of the Dead* is a kind of manual for use in the afterworld. It contains charms, spells, formulas, and speeches to be pronounced before the presiding gods. The earliest collection (the so-called Heliopolitan Recension) dates from the Eighteenth Dynasty.

15. *Gilgamesh* is a Sumerian epic of about 3,000 lines. Composed in the third millenium B.C., it tells of Gilgamesh, the king of Uruk in Mesopotamia. The poem concerns itself with the quest for immortality and is among the masterpieces of world literature.

16. Folklore as "a sunken cultural property": Hans Naumann's theory of *versunkenes Kulturgut*. This theory (according to which epic songs originate in the aristocratic milieu and are later only distorted by the common people) as well as its linguistic offshoot in the teachings of German dialectologists, remained a pet target of Soviet critics for several decades. The theory was rejected out of hand, practically without any discussion. The nearly formulaic abuse ran the gamut from the academic epithet "undemocratic" to the accusation of profascist sympathies (see also the Introduction).

17. This unexpected flourish can be accounted for by the appearance of the article very soon after the war in a special anniversary issue of the University transactions.

18. The Civil War in Russia (1918-20) followed the 1917 (October) Revolution and ended in the victory of the Bolsheviks. World War II began in the Soviet Union on June 22, 1941, and is always referred to as the Great Patriotic War (*Velíkaja Otéčestvennaja vojná*).

2. Folklore and Reality

First published as Propp 1963b. Reprinted in Propp 1976a, 83-115.

1. Kazán, a town in the middle reaches of the Volga, traces its history to the thirteenth century. In the fourteenth century it became the capital of the Kazan khanate and was annexed to Russia by Ivan IV in 1552, after a seven-year siege. This event gave rise to numerous songs; in some of them the historical perspective is totally displaced. An example of a song about the siege of Kazan is the one by Varlaám in Mussorgsky's opera *Boris Godunov*.

2. Stepán Timoféevič Rázin (executed on June 6, 1671): the leader of a massive uprising of peasants and Cossacks. His army marched through the south of Russia but was later stopped by regular troops. He is the hero of many historical songs (cf. note 10 on No. 1).

3. *Lay of the Host of Igor*, first published in 1800, is believed to be a late twelfth century text. It is an epic poem about an unhappy campaign of Prince Ígor' Svjatoslávič (1151-1202) against the Cumans. Several English translations of the poem have been made; the other English titles are *The Song of Igor's Campaign* [Nabokov] and *The Tale of Igor's Campaign* [Čižévskij]. Borodín's opera *Prince Igor (Knjaz' Igor')* is based on episodes from this epic.

4. Koščéj is the villain of several Russian wondertales. He steals the hero's bride or wife, and the hero sets off to rescue her. Koščej's life is usually hidden in an egg, which the hero obtains with the help of grateful animals, and breaks.

5. AT is the accepted abbreviation for Aarne-Thompson 1961.

6. Masuccio Salernitano (his real name was Tommaso Guardati; Masuccio is from Tomasuccio) lived at the Neapolitan court in the fifteenth century. Propp's dates are inexact; the last of them is closer to 1475-1480. Masuccio is known for the book *Il Novellino* (1476), a collection of short stories written in the spirit of Boccaccio.

7. "Typical people in a typical setting" is the formula of realism coined by Engels: "Realism presupposes, apart from being true to details, truth in depicting typical people in a typical setting."

8. "One cannot describe her beauty in a tale, nor write about it with a pen" is a literal translation of the Russian wondertale formula *ni v skázke skazát', ni peróm opisát'*.

9. Il'já Múromec is the most popular hero of Russian bylinas. He is usually represented as an old man riding a mighty horse. Little is told about his youth, which seems to be a variation on the "male Cinderella" theme. His place of birth is the village of Karačárovo or the town of Múrom (perhaps a back formation from the name Muromec; although the place-name Murom is well known, the etymology of the word Muromec is debated). Some illness paralyzes the future hero in his babyhood, and he lies on the stove, quite motionless, for thirty years. He is cured in a miraculous way by a group of strangers, who also give him a potion of strength. Healed of his disease, he behaves like "a young giant" (that is, goes to help his parents, who work in the field, and begins to uproot oak trees), and later sets out on a long journey. On his way to Kiev he sometimes liberates the town of Černígov and always kills his first monster, namely, Solovéj the Robber. *Solovej* means 'nightingale'; he sits in a tree and defeats his enemies by loud whistling. In another bylina, Il'ja conquers Ídolišče ('a huge idol'), a monster that has subjugated either Kiev or Car'grád (Constantinople). In a bylina containing a widespread motif, Il'ja comes to a place from which three paths proceed, and an inscription on the stone warns the traveler that if he chooses the first path, he will perish, while the second will bring him marriage, and the third, wealth. He takes each path in turn and triumphs all three times: he destroys the robbers, defeats a witch, and finds a treasure. Il'ja is one of the heroes serving Prince Vladimir, the unifying figure of the Kiev epic cycle. The historical Vladímir Svjatoslávič died in 1016, but in bylinas he is still a magnificent ruler at the time of the Mongol invasion (the Mongols are called Tatars in Russian folk poetry). Il'ja's relations with Vladimir are not always depicted as friendly. According to one plot, he is thrown into a pit by the Prince, while

all the other heroes are banished. When enemies besiege Kiev, some sort of reconciliation is achieved; Il'ja agrees to defend Russia and gains a decisive victory over the Tatar King Kálin. There is also a bylina about Il'ja's fight with his son, reminiscent of many other similar fights, but the situation is not typical of Il'ja, who is otherwise never represented as a family man.

10. Vasílij Busláevič is the hero of two Novgorod bylinas. He is the leader of a gang that strikes terror in the hearts of all law-abiding citizens. When Vasilij Buslaevič decides to assemble such a gang, he appeals to the Novgorod artisans and rabble but takes only those who can lift and empty a bowl that contains a bucket and a half of wine and in addition can survive a blow on the head with an elm tree. Potánjuška, the stoop-shouldered hunchback, is one of the survivors in spite of his disability. The testing of Potanjuška is an important episode in several bylinas.

11. Djuk Stepánovič is a guest of Prince Vladimir. He is a wealthy fop, and his clothes are described in minute detail. His name is obscure; the seemingly obvious origin from the Latin *dux* or Byzantine *dukas* 'duke' has been contested.

12. The boyars were the upper nobility in Russia from the tenth through the seventeenth century. Both Ivan III (1440-1505) and Ivan IV (1530-84) feared their influence, and Ivan IV was especially successful in weakening their power, but the rank and title of boyar was abolished only by Peter I.

13. Mikúla Seljanínovič, a legendary plowman, is known from a bylina about his encounter with the warrior Vól'ga. Although the encounter takes place in the field, Mikula Seljaninovič is represented as richly, even sumptuously dressed, with a beautiful plow to match (see also note 30 on No. 4).

14. The bylina about Dunáj is very dramatic. Prince Vladimir is looking for someone who will obtain a bride for him. After much deliberation this errand is entrusted to Dunaj. Sometimes Dunaj has to be brought to the palace from a pit, where he has spent many years (the causes for the punishment are obscure). Dunaj goes to Lithuania to fetch the King's younger daughter Evpráksija (Vladimir's "epic" wife). According to some versions, Dunaj at one time served the Lithuanian king and was a lover of his elder daughter Nastás'ja. When he arrives in Lithuania and explains his mission to the King, he receives a curt refusal: he is told that neither the suitor nor the envoy is good enough; another excuse is that Evpraksija cannot marry before Nastas'ja. Dunaj takes Evpraksija to Kiev by force. On the way home he encounters a mysterious hero whom he conquers and is about to kill. But at this moment the hero's identity is disclosed: the defeated enemy turns out to be his former love, the warrior maiden Nastas'ja. Dunaj takes both princesses along, and in some versions the bylina ends with a double wedding à la Siegfried-Gunther in the *Nibelungenlied*. But usually events take a different turn. At the feast in Kiev Dunaj boasts of his deed and declares that he is the best hero (or the best shot, or the strongest man) of all. Nastas'ja objects, saying that she shoots better, Aljóša Popóvič is braver, and Dobrýnja Nikítič is more courteous. And indeed, she vanquishes him in a shooting contest, whereupon the infuriated Dunaj kills Nastas'ja, even though she tells him that she is pregnant with a boy of fabulous beauty and that only three months are left before the baby is due. He rips open the corpse, sees that Nastas'ja did not lie to him, and immediately takes his own life. His blood gives rise to the River Dunaj (the Russian name of the Danube); Nastas'ja also becomes a river.

15. Dobrýnja Nikítič, a warrior from Rjazán', Il'já Múromec, and Aljóša Popóvič (see notes 9 and 16) form the main triumvirate of Russian epic heroes. Like Il'ja Muromec, Dobrynja is a dragon fighter: he kills the dragon and sets free Prince Vladimir's niece. One of his adversaries is Marínka, a Kiev witch, and his victory over her is hard won. He also is a personage in the plot "a husband at his wife's wedding." During Dobrynja's long absence Aljoša makes an attempt to marry Nastas'ja Nikitišna, Dobrynja's wife. Dobrynja comes at the last moment and puts Aljoša to shame. In the cycle of the anti-Tatar bylinas, Dobrynja ostensibly accompanies Vasílij Kazimírovič, who volunteers to take tribute from Vladimir to Batu Khan, but actually it is Dobrynja who performs the heroic role: he wins three contests against Batu and with little help from outside destroys the entire Mongol army. He is the most refined of the Russian epic warriors; his popularity is second only to to that of Il'ja Muromec.

16. Aljóša Popóvič, that is, Aljoša a priest's son (Aljoša is a pet name for Alekséj), the youngest, the merriest, and the most impulsive of the Russian warriors, is another dragon fighter. In the bylina about him, the monster's name is Tugárin, and Aljoša kills him either on his way to Kiev or in Kiev. Among his feats are the rescue of Dobrynja Nikitič from the Tatars and the destruction of the Tatar hordes at Kiev. Although he fails in his courtship of Dobrynja's wife (see the previous note), according to a late bylina, he succeeds in obtaining the beautiful Eléna Petróvična.

17. Emel'ján Ivánovič Pugačëv (ca. 1742-75) stood at the head of the greatest uprising in the history of Russian Cossacks and peasants (1773-74).

18. "Vasilij and Sofjuška": a ballad on a widespread international theme. The hero and the heroine are lovers, who perish by Vasílij's or Sófjuška's mother's hand (both versions have been recorded), and two intertwining plants grow on their graves.

19. Propp, it appears, means the villain of the ballad "Dmitrij and Domna"; however, this example is not very good: see the next note.

20. There are two main versions of the ballad "Dmitrij and Domna." Dómna, a young girl, is courted by Prince Dmítrij Vasíl'evič, who is extremely ugly. The heroine describes him as a hunchback; he has a squint, his eyes are like those of an owl, his legs are like those of a crane, etc. According to one version, the suitor, offended by this description, kills Domna; in another, Domna commits suicide so as to avoid marriage. The hero's ugliness plays a decisive role in the development of the ballad.

21. Vladímir is the prince (knjaz') who entertains the heroes of most Russian bylinas. He is sometimes described as generous and kind, sometimes as a capricious tyrant. See also notes 9, 14, 15, 50, and 51 on this chapter and notes 14, 18, 22, and 29 on Chapter 4.

22. Tugárin: Aljoša's fabulous antagonist. See note 16. Tugarin's role is ambiguous, because Vladimir's wife is very fond of the monstrous guest.

23. Černígov: a town in the Ukraine on the Desná River. On his way to Kiev, Il'já Múromec (see note 9) has to pass Černigov (it is not always, but usually, Černigov), but the town is beleaguered by enemies. He defeats the army single-handed and goes on with his journey. Soon he meets Solovéj the Robber. The Černigov episode is not a necessary part of the bylina about Il'ja Muromec and Solovej the Robber.

24. Solovéj the Robber: Il'ja's first fabulous adversary. See notes 9 and 23.

25. Trofím Grigór'evič Rjabínin (1791-1885): one of the most outstanding Russian "singers of tales." His son and his grandson were also active carriers of epic tradition. Most Russians know Rjabinin's name thanks to Arénskij's popular fantasy for piano and orchestra "On Rjabinin's Themes." In the text, as it was recorded by A. F. Gil'ferding, two bylinas about Dobrýnja partly merged.

26. See note 15 for a description of Vasílij Kazimírovič's mission to the Golden Horde.

27. Modern Soróčincy is a town in the Ukraine (not far from Poltáva) often mentioned by singers of bylinas in vague contexts. The action of Gogol's tale *The Soročincy Fair* is set there. However, as always in the bylinas, geographical identification is uncertain, and the Russian adjective *soročinskij* is grammatically ambiguous.

28. Butján Butjánovič is one of several distortions of Batu's name.

29. Kozárin's adventure is known from epic poetry and from songs that lean toward ballads. In all versions the hero Kozarin comes across a tent with a captive girl, sets her free and wants to marry her, but it turns out that she is his sister. The two do not know each other because Kozarin, hated by his parents, was brought up away from his family. Some narrators start with Kozarin's leaving home; others, with the girl's captivity.

30. Vixr', or Vixor' (the name means 'whirlwind') carries away the tsar's wife and is finally conquered by her youngest son. Afanas'ev 1957, nos. 129 and 559.

31. That characters in epic poetry, especially women, do not age with time is well known. Of interest is the following nontrivial comment made in 1939 but published almost forty years later: "[She is] called young not because she is young but because every woman possessing functions of fertility is 'young' and a Juno. . . . Not logic, not the fact that the girl is fifteen or sixteen makes her 'young'.

She is 'young' throughout the time of her female potency. It is a property of Juno, of woman's nature. Every girl is a Juno" (Freudenberg 1978, 41).

32. Space and time in myth and folklore are a popular subject in contemporary Soviet studies. Of the works available in English, see Gurevich 1969 and Steblin-Kamenskij 1982 (1976).

33. "Kolobok" is a variation on the "The Gingerbread Man" theme. The word *kolobók* means 'dumpling.'

34. Propp devoted a special study to the cumulative tale, mainly in Russian; see Propp 1976a, 241-57.

35. The ancient ballad of Prince Román's misdeed is known in a number of versions, but the motivation for the husband's cruelty remains the same in nearly all of them.

36. This is a widespread ballad. Pushkin heard one of its versions near Pskov.

37. Ermák Timoféevič (died in 1584) is famous for his conquest of Siberia. Thanks to his efforts, Khan Kučúm was defeated, and his lands were annexed by Ivan IV. He is the hero of many Russian historical songs, which attribute all kinds of fictitious deeds to him.

38. Mixájlo Vasíl'evič Skópin-Šújskij was a relative of Tsar Vasílij Šújskij (1606-10). He owed his popularity to the campaign of 1609-10, in which the Polish army was repelled. Skopin's supporters even planned to proclaim him tsar, but in 1610 Skopin died under mysterious circumstances. He came to the christening of Prince Iván Mixájlovič Vorotýnskij's son as the boy's godfather and suddenly took ill. According to historical songs, the wife of Dmítrij' Šújskij (the Tsar's brother) poisoned Skopin. The death of Skopin did not save Tsar Vasilij; he was deposed less than three months later. In songs, Skopin's downfall is precipitated by his boasting speech.

39. Razin: see note 2.

40. Peter, that is, Peter I (1672-1725). His victories are celebrated in many songs.

41. Ivan IV, usually known as Ivan the Terrible (1530-84; Grand Duke from 1533, Tsar from 1547), is the hero of numerous songs. In 1582, in one of his rages, he killed his twenty-eight-year-old son Ivan. Nastás'ja Románovna (died in 1560) was Ivan IV's first wife; Nikíta Románovič, her brother. Folklore presents the young prince as a supporter of Novgorod against his father (in fact, Ivan's punitive expedition against Novgorod took place in 1570, and the boy had nothing to do with it). Besides Ivan, Ivan IV had two more sons—Fjodor and Dmitrij—and songs are very uncertain about who fell victim to the Tsar's frenzy; it is usually Fjodor, who is denounced by his own brother. In a popular version, the Tsar intends to have Fjodor executed. When the news of the disaster is brought to Nastas'ja Romanovna, she begs Nikita Romanovič for help, and indeed the boy's uncle hastens to the place where Maljúta Skurátov, Ivan's hated counselor, is about to cut off Fjodor's head. He kills Maljuta, or a servant, or an animal (to show the Tsar his saber red with blood, or the felon's heart and liver) and saves Fjodor, much to Ivan IV's joy as it turns out. In another version the events are told differently, but Nikita Romanovič is again the savior of his nephew and godson. Nikita (or Mikita) Romanovič figures in many songs of the sixteenth century.

42. Alekséj Andréevič Arakčéev (1769-1834) was a favorite of two tsars: Pavel I and Alexander I. A cruel despot and martinet, he became a symbol of oppression in modern Russian history.

43. Several Dolgorúkovs are known to folklore. In one historical song the tsar allows the soldiers to try Dolgorukov, who has not paid them for a long time. Arakčéev is often accused of a similar crime: he starves his soldiers to death and with their money erects a palace for himself.

44. "Sadko": a fantastic bylina of the Novgorod cycle. In its full (rarely recorded) form the bylina has the following plot. Sadkó is a *gusljár*, that is, he plays the gusli, a five- or seven-string instrument. For some reason, rich merchants have stopped inviting him to their feasts, and, insulted by their indifference, he goes to the shore of Lake Il'men' and plays there. He is overheard by the Sea (or rather, Lake) King, who rewards him: he teaches him how to catch a gold-feathered fish. He advises Sadko to go to the merchants and declare that he has seen such a fish. The merchants do not believe him and bet their stores against his head that the gold-feathered fish does not exist and that Sadko will never catch it. Sadko wins the wager and becomes rich. In the next part of the bylina, Sadko, not necessarily the owner of the shops, makes another bet: he announces to the merchants

that he can buy up everything they have. Sometimes he succeeds, more often he fails, but in both cases he loads his ships with goods and sets off to foreign lands to sell what he has. On his way he is stopped by the Sea King, who orders him to come down. On the bottom of the sea he plays his gusli for the King: the King's dance causes a terrible storm, and later Sadko is offered the choice of a bride among many sea beauties, the King's daughters. He chooses Černávuška and falls asleep. The name Černavuška means 'a black one'. The function of this girl and the idea of the name are not clear. Sadko is told either by a saint or by the Sea Queen to choose just her, because otherwise he will never see the world above. He goes to sleep with Černavuška but does not touch her, and in the morning he awakens on the bank of the river, usually the River Vólxov; his ships come there, too. In a few versions he is met by his wife.

Note that the libretto of Rimskij-Korsakov's opera *Sadko*, written by the composer himself and V. I. Bél'skij, deviates greatly from the bylina. Note also that Repin's picture representing Sadko and a procession of brides is among this painter's least successful works.

45. Mamáj, Khan of the Golden Horde, was defeated by Prince Dmítrij Donskój on September 8, 1380, at Kulikóvo.

46. Khan Batu (died in 1255) invaded Rus' in the thirteenth century. Cf. also notes 15 and 28.

47. *Bogatýr'* is the Russian word applied to an epic hero. It has been retained in the text of this book partly because it cannot be translated into English without losses, partly for the sake of local coloring. The German noun *Recke* is very close in meaning to *bogatyr'*.

48. Propp means only Russian epic poetry, whose heroes, with very few exceptions, triumph over their enemies and survive battles. The situation is quite different in Greek, Romance, and Germanic poetry.

49. Dunaj: see note 14.

50. "Danilo Lovčanin" is a bylina based on the same motif as the Old Testament tale of David, Uriah, and Bath-sheba. Prince Vladímir intends to marry. His evil counselor Mišáta Putjátin suggests to him that there is no woman more beautiful than the wife of Danílo Lovčánin (*Lovčanin* probably means 'hunter'). On Mišata's advice Vladimir sends Danilo on what seems a hopeless hunt for the bird Whitethroat and some ferocious animal. However, and here the bylina differs from the Bible and follows the same path as the Russian folktale on this plot, Danilo succeeds and returns unscathed. Before he enters Kiev, he encounters several armed men to fight him. He is killed, and Vladimir goes to Danilo's widow or sends messengers to her. But she does not consent to marry Vladimir and stabs herself. The contrite or frustrated Vladimir has Mišata boiled alive in pitch. The conflict of this bylina resembles more than one episode from the life of Ivan IV.

51. The bylina about Sux(m)án(tij) [pronounce: Sookhmán] Dománt'evič starts, like many others, with a feast in Vladimir's hall. Everyone boasts of his achievements; only Suxman is silent. He explains that he has nothing to boast of and promises to go on a hunt and bring an unwounded female swan to the Prince. It seems an insignificant pledge for a great hero, but a female swan is probably a poetic synonym for a bride (cf. the motif of swan maidens and see note 14 on No. 4). The bylinas about Suxman and Dunaj share several peculiarities. Dunaj, who obtains a bride for Vladimir (see note 14), also commits suicide in the end. Neither Suxman nor Dunaj is known outside the one bylina devoted to each, and both heroes are on especially bad terms with Vladimir. However, the courtship motif can only be guessed in the bylina about Suxman, because he fails to find a swan for Vladimir, whereas Dunaj comes home with a daughter of the Lithuanian king. Instead of the swan, Suxman meets a Tatar army. He kills all the enemies but is himself wounded (an occurrence almost unique in a bylina). He stops the blood with three poppy petals and returns to Kiev. Vladimir is irritated that there is no swan (which is comprehensible only if he expects a bride) and disbelieves Suxman's account of his feat. He has him thrown into a pit, and Dobrýnja is sent to inspect the battlefield. Dobrynja comes back with the news that Suxman has told the truth, and Vladimir is eager to set free and reward the unfortunate hero. But Suxman refuses to be mollified. He removes the petals from the wound and bleeds to death before the disconsolate prince. The melodramatic finale resembles

the denouement of a ballad. However, if, as suggested above, the original motif of this bylina is the prince's courtship, rather than an unexpected fight with the Tatars (of whom no one has heard anything in Kiev, though their troops are about to cross the Nepra River), it may be that the ancient tale of Vladimir's wooing originally ended in the messenger's death and that the bylina about Suxman is a late echo of a forgotten plot. Cf. Tristan's perilous voyage to obtain Isolde.

52. D(i)mítrij Ivánovič Donskój (1350-89) fought against many internal and external enemies and is famous for his victory over Khan Mamáj in 1380 (see note 45). Aleksándr Jaroslávič Névskij (1220-63), Grand Duke of Novgorod and later of Kiev and Vladimir, received his appelation Nevskij (that is, of the Neva) after the victory of the Russians over the Swedes. In 1242 his army vanquished the Livonian Knights. He is a saint of the Russian Orthodox Church.

53. In Russian historiography the Reform means the abolition of serfdom by Alexand(e)r II in 1861.

54. Irína Andréevna Fedósova: the most renowned Russian *vóplenica*, that is, singer of laments. E. V. Bársov recorded over 30,000 verses from her and brought them out in three volumes (1872, 1882, 1886).

55. Local arbitrators (*mirovýe posrédniki*): government officials who were supposed to settle disputes between the former serfs (see note 53) and the landowners.

56. See Kolpakova (1962), who noted several themes of lyric songs [Propp's note].

57. See note 38.

58. The lament referred to falls into two parts. The first consists of formulas ("Blow, winds, shake the high mountains, shake the tall forests, destroy the Tsar's grave . . . Arise, our Tsar."). The second part is a complaint: "Look at your army, look how it has changed: the mustaches are all shaved off, the beards are all cut." Laments addressed to Ivan IV, Peter I, and Catherine II are usually about the pitiful state of the army. This particular lament by a sentry, though addressed to Ivan IV, contains a picture from a later epoch.

59. Ksénija (Xenia) Godunóva was the daughter of Borís Godunóv. Boris died in 1605 amid great social unrest, and his throne fell to the adventurer Grigórij Otrép'ev, known as False Dmitrij I. Before False Dmitrij arrived in Moscow, an uprising broke out in that city. Ksenija was made to take the veil. Her laments are about her sorrowful plight after the tsar's death and about her fear of the convent.

60. Matvéj Ivánovič Plátov (1751-1818) was a hero of the war against Napoleon. In a humorous song he pays a visit to a Frenchman, who says that he knows everybody of importance in Moscow but has never met the Cossack Platov. The Frenchman would very much like to kill this Cossack. Platov mocks his host and his host's daughter and escapes from his enemy alive.

61. It is usually believed that the song about Ščelkán goes back to the uprising of Tver' against Čol-khan. (Tver', since 1931 Kalínin, is a city northwest of Moscow; until the end of Ivan IV's reign it was a strong competitor of Moscow.) In the song Khan Uzbék (called Azvják Tavrúlovič) gives away towns to his relatives. Only Ščelkan receives nothing, because at the moment he is collecting tribute. The song contains the anthologized description: "He took a hundred rubles from each prince (*knjaz'*), fifty rubles from each boyar, five rubles from each peasant; from him who has no money he will take a child, from him who has no child he will take his wife; who has no wife, himself will be taken." He returns home and asks "Tsar Azvjak" for a town. Azvjak grants Ščelkan his request on the condition that he will kill his own son and drink a cup of the boy's blood. Ščelkan does so quite willingly and is given Tver'. His reign brings all sorts of misfortunes with it, and two brothers Borísoviče s (that is, Boris-sons), acting as the people's messengers, come to Ščelkan and kill him. One takes him by the hair, the other by the legs, and between them they tear him apart; Ščelkan dies, and his murderers are never found out.

62. The song about Avdót'ja Rjazánočka (Avdot'ja from Rjazán') is very old. The events narrated in it are as follows. The Turkish king Baxmét has destroyed Rjazan': the men have been killed, the women taken captive; Avdot'ja is the only survivor. One day she decides to go to Baxmet's palace and ask him to set free her next of kin. She overcomes all difficulties, touches the heart of the Turkish king, and returns home with her brother. Later she has her native town rebuilt. For some reason,

throughout the song the girl is called Avdot'ja *Rjazanočka*, but the town itself is called Kazan, not Rjazan'; this is probably a late contamination partly owing to the common rhyme Rjazan': Kazan.

63. The battle of Borodinó between the armies of Kutúzov and Napoleon took place on August 26, 1812. The village of Borodino is situated about seventy miles west of Moscow, and the battle is one of the most memorable events in Russian history. There is not a single song about Borodino, perhaps only one indirect description of it: the great battle mentioned in the song "Kak ne dve túčen'ki, ne dve gróznye" 'Not two clouds, but two armies clashed' takes place on St. Semjón's Day, that is, on September 1, which is very close to the historical date of the battle of Borodino. Smolénsk, a city on the Dniepr River, over 200 miles southwest of Moscow, was an important point of the 1812 campaign. (One song contains these words: "In the town of Smolénsk they stood knee-deep in blood.") Možájsk (west of Moscow on the Moskvá River) is usually mentioned in the phrase "The whole road from Moscow to Možajsk has been plundered." On the Berezná River a huge French army (about 30,000 people) retreating from Russia suffered a devastating defeat (November 1812).

64. The battle of Poltáva, in the east central Ukraine, between Peter I's Russian army and the Swedes under Charles (Karl) XII, took place on June 27, 1709. Charles was routed. His ally, the Ukrainian commander-in-chief Mazéppa (the hero of Byron's narrative poem) fled.

65. The Jaik River (pronounced Yáh-ik) was renamed by Catherine II, who tried to eradicate every trace of Pugačëv's memory (see note 17). The song describes an attack of Pugačëv's army on the town of Jaik.

66. Stephen Báthory (Polish: Stefan Batory), King of Poland (1575-86), invaded Russia in 1579, in the reign of Ivan IV, and in 1581 besieged Pskov, an important historical center southwest of Novgorod. The names of all the defenders of Pskov mentioned in the song are borrowed from other songs. Semjón Konstantínovič Karámyšev is a well-known personage of Cossack songs of the sixteenth and seventeenth centuries (in which he is mixed up with Ivan Konstantinovič Karamyšev). On M. V. Skópin-Šújskij, see note 38. On Nikíta Románovič Vol'xónskij, Ivan's brother-in-law, see note 41. Borís Petróvič Šeremétev (1652-1719) was one of Peter I's chief military commanders.

67. Azóv, a port on the sea of Azov, which belonged to Turkey in the seventeenth century, was captured by the Don Cossacks in 1637, soon lost, and regained by the regular army in 1696 under Peter I. There are a number of songs about both events. In folklore, the main stratagem used by the Russians at Azov appeared to be a kind of Trojan horse: the soldiers reportedly hid in carts, and the carts were smuggled into the town, after which the invaders made a quick job of vanquishing the enemy. But the sapping of the walls is occasionally mentioned too.

68. Oréšek, a fortress in the upper reaches of the Neva River, was built by the people of Novgorod in 1232 on the island Oréxovoj; hence the name Orešek, which means, 'a little nut'. In 1611 it was ceded by the Russians to the Swedes and renamed Nöteborg. In 1702 Peter I got it back and once more renamed it, this time Šlissel'burg, that is, Schlüsselburg 'Keytown'. The main force in the battle was artillery; the walls were not sapped. Šlissel'burg, called Petrokrépost' 'Peter's fortress' since 1944, is mainly remembered today as a famous prison.

69. Ríga, the capital of Latvia, was wrested from the Swedes by Peter I's army in 1710 after bombardment and a long siege. The entire historical song devoted to this event is made up of narrative and verbal formulas, sapping the walls among them.

70. In 1780 the King of Sweden was Charles (Karl) XIII.

71. *Častúški* (pl.) are folk songs, usually consisting of four-line rhyming stanzas; they are sometimes lyrical but very often humorous and satirical. See Lopatin 1951.

3. The Principles of Classifying Folklore Genres

First published as Propp 1964. Reprinted in Propp 1976a, 34-45.

1. *Pošexóncy* means 'backward people living in the most out-of-the-way places and doing stupid things'. Anecdotes about such fools are popular all over the world. The word was coined by the writer

M. E. Saltykóv-Ščedrín (1826-89), who at the very end of his life wrote a book about the town of Pošexón'e inhabited by *Pošexoncy*.

2. See note 18 on No. 2.

3. Sívka-Búrka (véščaja kaúrka) is the name of a magic horse in Russian wondertales; all the parts of the name except *veščaja* 'prophetic, endowed with second sight' denote different colors.

4. On the Historicity of Folklore

First published as Propp 1968b. Reprinted in Propp 1976a, 116-31, abridged.

1. The Viljúj is a tributary of the Lena in its middle reaches. The Kobjája region is situated to the south of the confluence of the Lena and Viljuj rivers. The best account of Yakut settlement in connection with their epic tradition is Èrgis 1974.

2. Stepán Rázin: see note 2 on No. 2; Peter I: see notes 40, 64, 67, 68, and 69 on No. 2; Pugačëv: see note 17 on No. 2. The Decembrists were a group of officers who refused to take an oath of allegiance to Tsar Nicholas (Nikoláj) I on December 14, 1825 (hence the name Decembrists). Five of their leaders were hanged; over a hundred, deported to Siberia.

3. Ermak: see note 37 on No. 2.

4. Platov: see note 60 on No. 2.

5. *Skomoróšina* means a production of *skomoróxs*, the Russian *jongleurs, Spielmanns*, that is, strolling actors. They were narrators, singers, musicians, the authors of farces, jugglers, and acrobats. Their role as transmitters and shapers of the bylinas must have been very great. Some records of skomoroxs go back to the eleventh century; later they became the target of cruel persecutions. The Russian word is of obscure origin (probably related to *Scaramouch*), and there is no stable English term for it. The popular "Skoromoxs' Dance" from Rimskij-Korsakov's opera *The Snow Maiden* is called "The Tumblers' Dance." The best account of *skomoroxs* in English is Zgusta 1978.

6. See note 1 on No. 2.

7. See note 61 on No. 2.

8. On January 9, 1905, many thousand people marched to the Winter Palace (the royal residence in St. Petersburg) with a petition to Tsar Nicholas (Nikoláj) II. The police opened fire and dispersed the demonstration. This day has become known as Bloody Sunday.

9. The Nívxi, usually called in English Gilyaks, live in the region of the Lower Amur basin and on Saxalin Island. The Čúkči (spelt Chukchi or Chukcee) live in northwestern Siberia.

10. The Néncy inhabit large areas in eastern Siberia. The English name Samoyeds covers the Nency and several related smaller peoples.

11. The Šórcy: a Turkic nation in southeastern Siberia.

12. Tugarin: see notes 16 and 22 on No. 2.

13. Idolišče: see note 9 on No. 2.

14. Mixájlo Ivánovič Pótyk, as narrated in the bylina about him, is sent away from Kiev by Prince Vladimir to collect tribute or conquer new lands, or bring game to the royal table. In the forest he meets a swan-maiden. She agrees to marry him on the condition that when one of them dies the other will die too. Potyk accepts the condition and takes his young wife Avdót'ja Lixodéevna to Kiev. Many singers stop here, but the bylina may go on. Soon after the wedding Avdot'ja Lixodeevna dies, and Potyk is buried alive. In the crypt or grave he sees a dragon, fights it, and uses its blood or poison to bring the dead woman to life. They return to the world above and live for some time without further adventures. Different versions again develop differently here. In some, a foreign king appears near Kiev and demands Potyk's wife, for rumors of her immortality have spread far and wide. Potyk meets the invaders in battle, but, while he is fighting, his wife and the foreign king elope. Potyk sets off on a long journey and finds Avdot'ja Lixodeevna, but she attempts to destroy him; for instance, she twice turns him to stone and then crucifies him in the cellar. Il'já Múromec and

Dobrýnja Nikítič (two great heroes) rescue Potyk. In their mission they are aided by Nastás'ja, the younger sister of Potyk's wife. Potyk kills Avdot'ja Lixodeevna and marries Nastas'ja. The origins of this bylina have been a matter of long debate. Propp (1958b, 109-26) classified it with the prestate bylinas about courtship: "Sadko" (see note 44 on No. 2), "Iván Godínovič" (see the next note), "Dunaj" (see note 14 on No. 2), "Kozarin" (see note 29 on No. 2), and "Solovéj Budimírovič" (see note 18, below). The least convincing item in this group is "Sadko," whose main motif is hardly courtship.

15. The bylina about Ivan Godinovič is not unlike the one about Potyk (see the previous note), but its plot is less complex. Ivan Godinovič, a hero from Kiev, sets off on a wooing expedition. He has chosen a wife from an alien "pagan" country. He carries off his bride (sometimes called Nastás'ja) against her father's will and is overtaken by a rival, the king of another pagan land. He gets the better of his adversary, but at the decisive moment, when the pagan king lies prostrate under him, he discovers that he has no knife with which to kill the enemy. Both Ivan Godinovič and the pagan king ask Nastas'ja for help. She chooses the pagan king, and the two succeed in tying Ivan Godinovič to an oak tree. To mock Ivan Godinovič, they make love in his presence. Ivan is saved by unexpected intervention. He kills his rival, hacks up Nastas'ja in the most brutal fashion, and returns to Kiev.

16. Sadko: see note 44 on No. 2.

17. Dobrynja: see note 15 on No. 2.

18. Solovéj Budimírovič, a bylina hero, comes to Kiev to court Prince Vladímir's niece Zabáva Putjátišna. He is rich and likeable, and Vladimir is impressed with his gifts. He allows his guest to build three houses in Zabava's garden, and Solovej's men build them overnight. When Zabava wakes up, she is indeed surprised and immediately offers herself to Solovej, somewhat to the young man's embarrassment. Later he himself asks for Zabava's hand, is accepted, and marries her.

19. Djuk: see note 11 on No. 2.

20. On Vol'ga, see note 30, below. Oleg Svjatosláv(ov)ič (died in 1115) was the ruler of Černígov and many other towns (not to be confused with the much more famous Kiev Prince Oleg who died in 912 or 922 and is usually called the Prophetic Oleg or Oleg the Seer; he is also mentioned in Propp's survey of older scholarship). Ol'ga (died in 969) was the wife of Prince Igor' (killed in 945; not the Igor' of the *Lay of the Host of Igor*). Vseslav Brjačeslávič (died in 1101) fought against several Russian princes, burned Novgorod in 1066, led a tempestuous life, and finally became sole ruler of Polock. *Volxv* means magus, wizard (see Acts 8:9-24). Ortnit (or Ortnid) is a personage of later German heroic poetry. He is the son of the dwarf Alberich and is an adventuresome knight. He woos the daughter of a pagan Oriental king and with the help of Alberich abducts her. The enraged king sends two dragon eggs to Ortnit's land (Lamparten); when the dragons hatch, they devastate the whole country and kill Ortnit. Ortnit's successor and avenger is Wolfdietrich. Certain unquestionable ties exist between the tales of Ortnit and Russian heroic poetry, and Ortnit's uncle Ilias von Riuzen has been compared with Il'ja Muromec by several scholars. Veselovskij (1890) examined the episode of Ortnit's obtaining his bride. Another epic name of Ortnit, Hertnid von Gardar, means Hertnid of Russia. Robert le Diable is a personage of French, not German, folklore.

21. The Church of Our Savior on the Nerédica (1198 or 1199), called *Spas na Nerédice* in Russian, is one of the most celebrated temples of ancient Novgorod. (Neredica is the name of a small river.) Jarosláv Vsévolodovič (1139-98) ruled in Černígov from 1174 to his death. He participated in several successful campaigns.

22. Borís and Gleb were sons of Grand Duke Vladímir, a possible prototype of the bylina prince. Immediately after Vladimir's death (July 15, 1015, Old Style), their brother (or cousin) Svjatopólk instigated the murder of the two princes. Boris was about 25, Gleb, almost 31 years old. Boris and Gleb were among the most popular saints in Old Russia. Many icons representing them are extant.

23. Andréj Rubljóv (ca. 1360-1430): a famous painter. His icons and frescoes mark the highest peak of Old Russian artistic achievement.

24. Il'já Efímovič Répin (1844-1930): the most popular representative of Russian realism in genre painting and portraiture.

25. Svjatogór figures in several bylinas. He is a hero, a giant endowed with supernatural strength. According to one plot, he travels all over the land and meets Il'já Múromec (see note 9 on No. 2). They continue their journey together and come across a coffin. This coffin is for the hero whom it will fit. It proves to be too big for Il'ja and just right for Svjatogor. Svjatogor tries to get out of the coffin but fails. He resigns himself to his fate and decides to transfer his strength to Il'ja. In those versions in which Il'ja agrees to receive the gift, Svjatogor transfers part of his strength through his breath or sweat.

26. Propp means Putílov and Dobrovól'skij 1960. This volume is very important because it gives multiple variants of each song. In other books of this type, for example, in Putilov 1962, variants are represented minimally.

27. Sadko: see note 44 on No. 2.

28. Dunaj: see note 14 on No. 2.

29. In 977, Grand Duke Vladimir (see note 22, above) returned from exile in Sweden and made a successful attempt to oust his brother Jaropólk from Novgorod. On his way, he sent Dobrýnja, his uncle on the distaff side and a namesake of the bylina hero, to the Cuman Prince Rogvol'd and declared that he was going to marry Rogvol'd's daughter Rognéda. But Rogneda had been betrothed to Jaropolk and reportedly turned down Vladimir in very unflattering terms on account of his low origin (his father was Prince [knjaz'] Svjatosláv, but his mother was a commoner). This answer insulted both Vladimir and Dobrynja. According to the Chronicle, Rogneda's refusal caused a war. Vladimir conquered Rogvol'd's town Velíkij Pólock (Cumans or Kumans is another name for Pólovcy), killed Rogvol'd and his two sons, and carried off Rogneda. This semilegendary episode has been compared with the bylina about Dunaj many times (see also note 14 on No. 2).

30. Mikúla Seljanínovič is the only bylina hero who is a peasant. In all versions, the main event of this bylina is a confrontation between him and Vól'ga. Vol'ga, a nephew of Prince Vladimir, has been granted three towns as fief. He sets off to inspect these towns (called by name) and collect tribute. On his way he meets a plowman who works at supernatural speed. His tilling is described in fantastic terms: mighty trees fall down cut by his plow, Vol'ga's retinue cannot catch up with him in a day, etc. This is Mikula Seljaninovič. His clothes are quite inappropriate for plowing but beautiful, for example, a sable fur coat (see note 13 on No. 2). According to one version, his plow is of maple and the various parts of the plow are made of steel, silver, and gold. Mikula Seljaninovič happens to know all three towns now belonging to Vol'ga very well: he has traveled there for salt and knows how dangerous the route is; on his recent trip he had to fight a whole army of robbers. Vol'ga invites Mikula Seljaninovič to accompany him. Mikula agrees. After they have started he remembers that he has not put his plow under a bush, but no one in Vol'ga's retinue can lift it, and Mikula Seljaninovič has to return and take care of the plow himself. Later Mikula's horse proves to be faster than Vol'ga's stately charger, and at this point the two protagonists usually part company, apparently forgetful of the initial plan. According to Propp (1958b, 382-83), the descriptions in the bylina reflect natural economy. With regard to Vol'ga's name, Propp (1958b, 375) supported the etymology that identifies Vol'ga with Volx (?=volxv 'magus'), the hero of another bylina, a hunter, warrior, and werewolf. Volx's greatest feat is a fantastic raid of India.

31. Kulák (literally, 'fist') means 'a well-to-do peasant'. The word always had negative connotations (tight-fisted exploiter) but acquired a truly ominous meaning in the years of collectivization, beginning with 1927, when millions of farmers were killed or deported as kulaks. In official Soviet historiography this disastrous period is called the liquidation of the kulaks as a class. Allegedly, after the collectivization, capitalism lost its strongest support in the USSR. The depth of the sociological analysis in folklore, when it was based on current slogans, emerges quite clearly from Propp's comment. In 1968 he could afford a mild stab at a 1923 article.

32. See note 4 on No. 2.

33. Končák is a Polovec (Cuman), not a Pečeneg.

5. The Structural and Historical Study of the Wondertale

First published as Propp 1966a (in Italian). Serge Shishkoff had Propp's Russian text at his disposal, and his translation appeared in 1976 (see Propp 1976c). At the same time the Russian version was published in the Soviet Union: Propp 1976a, 132-52. Our text is based on Shishkoff's translation.

1. As is customary, Propp gave no references to his epigraphs, which were, moreover, cited in Russian. All of them have been identified in Breymayer 1972a, 60. See Goethe 1887-1918: II-6:298-99, II-8:221-22, I-35, 16 and IV:8, 232-33. The works cited are: "Vorarbeiten zu einer Physiologie der Pflanzen," "Versuch einer allgemeinen Knochenlehre," *Tag- und Jahreshefte 1780,* and a letter to Charlotte von Stein 9 June 1787. Some titles of Goethe's works have been supplied by editors and vary slightly from edition to edition. In the present book all the epigraphs have been translated into English from German; the ellipses stand for lacunas in Propp's text. See Steiner and Davydov 1977 and the literature cited there, Cassirer 1945, 105-8, and Ivanov and Toporov 1976, 264-66, for a discussion of Goethe's morphological views and their role in modern structuralism and semiotics.

To the Foreword. [Morphology] has to achieve the status of a special science by choosing as its main subject what other sciences treat by chance and in passing, by collecting what is scattered in other sciences and establishing a new standpoint that would allow it to examine nature with convenience and ease. . . . It concerns itself with the phenomena that are very important; the procedures of the mind (*die Operationen des Geistes*) by which it juxtaposes phenomena are in keeping with human nature and pleasant, so even an unsuccessful attempt can combine utility and beauty.

To Chapter 1. The history of science always presents a nice picture from one's point of vantage. Indeed, we respect our predecessors and are, to a certain extent, grateful to them for the service they have rendered us, but no one likes to view them as martyrs irresistibly driven to dangerous, sometimes even desperate situations; and yet, our ancestors who have laid the foundation of our existence were often more earnest than the descendants who enjoy and usually fritter away their legacy.

To Chapter 2. I was quite convinced that a general type based on transformations goes through all organic creatures and that at certain middle stages of development it can be well observed in all its parts.

To Chapter 9. The protoplant will be the most wonderful thing in the world, which nature itself will envy me. With this model and a key to it, one can produce an infinite number of plants, all of which will be consistent; plants that, though they do not exist, could have existed. They are not just artistic or poetical shadows or illusions, for they possess an inner truth and necessity. The same law will be applicable to everything that lives.

2. The English text of this quotation has been taken from p. 178 of the present volume.

6. Transformations of the Wondertale

First published as Propp 1928b; reprinted in Propp 1976a, 153-73. Translated into English by C. H. Severens: Propp 1971a, reprinted in 1981. The text in this volume is a revised version of Severens's translation.

1. Antti A. Aarne (1913) warns against such an "error" [Propp's note].

2. See Propp 1928a; 1958a; 1968a; and cf. Propp 1927 [a modified note by Propp].

3. The ancient Egyptian tale of two brothers, recorded in the so-called Orbiney Papyrus, must have been current about the time of the Nineteenth Dynasty. Its content is as follows. Once there were two brothers. The elder brother owned a house and was married, and the younger brother lived with him. One day, when both were out in the field plowing, they ran out of grain, and the younger brother was sent home to fetch some. At home his sister-in-law tried in vain to seduce him. Fearing disclosure, she calumniated the young man and said to her husband that she had been attacked. AT 318.

4. "The Firebird," AT 550. In this tale a clever thief steals the king's apples. Two elder brothers

fail to catch the criminal. The younger brother discovers that the thief is a firebird. He is sent to capture it, and after many adventures he returns home with the bird and a bride.

5. "Morozko," AT 480: see p. 69 of the present volume.

6. "The Fisherman and the Fish," AT 555. A poor fisherman catches a magic fish and lets it go without a ransom. His wife is angry that the old man did not ask the fish for anything. She sends him back to the sea to beg for a new house. The fish gives them a new house and many more things, until the fisherman's wife decides that she wants to be God. Then she loses everything and finds herself in her old ramshackle hut.

7. Cf. Panzer (1905, 10), who says: "Seine Komposition ist eine Mosaikarbeit, die das schildernde Bild aus deutlich abgegrenzten Steinchen gefügt hat. Und diese Steinchen bleiben umso leichter *auswechselbar*, die einzelnen Motive können umso leichter variieren, als auch nirgends für eine Verbindung in die Tiefe gesorge ist" (Their composition is a mosaic that has fashioned the descriptive image out of separate pieces. And these pieces are the more readily *interchangeable*, the individual motifs can vary the more easily because at no point is there any provision made for their in-depth interconnection.) This is clearly a denial of the theory of stable combinations or permanent ties. The same thought is expressed even more dramatically and in greater detail by Spiess 1917. See also Krohn 1926. [Propp's note.]

8. *The Rig-Veda* is a collection of 1,028 hymns in Sanskrit. Propp gives no references, and it is not known which edition he used and in what language. The hymn cited in the article is addressed to Araṇyānī (Ṛg-Veda X, 146 [972]). The present translation has been made by Professor Bruce Lincoln from the Sanskrit original; cf. Geldner 1951, 379-80.

9. Afanas'ev 99: "Mare's Head." In this tale a bad girl molests her half-sister. The good girl's stepmother tells her husband to take his daughter to the forest and leave her there. He obeys and leaves the girl in the hut. Soon Mare's Head, the owner of the hut, appears, and the girl serves it well. She is rewarded by Mare's Head. The bad girl also goes to the hut but behaves badly and is eaten up. AT 480. Afanas'ev's tale is in Ukrainian.

10. Sívka-Búrka: see note 3 on No. 3.

11. The two lines cited by Propp are from the introduction to Pushkin's narrative poem *Ruslán and Ludmíla* (there is an English translation of the poem by Walter Arndt). Actually, Pushkin did not say that mermaids are met with in fairy tales. Although mermaids do not occur in wondertales, they abound in legends; see Pomeránceva 1975, 68-91.

12. *Eruslán Lázarevič*: a seventeenth-century tale, a variation on the theme "fight between father and son." It goes back to Firdausi's *Shah Namah* and was known to practically every literate and semiliterate Russian from chapbooks. Ruslan, the hero of Pushkin's poem (see note 11, above), got his name from Eruslán (Uruslán) Lazarevič.

13. *Schwank* (German): a farce in prose or in verse. This genre originated in Germany in the late Middle Ages.

7. Historical Roots of the Wondertale: Premises

Propp 1946a, 5-24.

1. Dobrynja Nikitič: see note 15 on No. 2.

2. *The Golden Bough:* the main work of the English anthropologist Sir James George Frazer. Its broad treatment of myth and ritual had a lasting influence on the study of folklore and religion, on psychology, and even on literature.

3. Propp's statement is not accurate. Kroeber mentions all his informants in the very first footnote on p. 59, where the myths and tales begin. He says, "The Gros Ventre myths and tales here recorded were obtained from seven informants. . . . Nos. 7 and 19 were obtained as texts in Gros Ventre. All the others were recorded in English."

4. Propp's book was written before the Communists took over in mainland China.

5. The Vogúls, now usually called Mansi, are a Paleo-Siberian people living in west central Siberia.

6. Christian Friedrich Hebbel (1813-63), a German dramatist, is the author of the trilogy *Die Nibelungen* (1882). Emanuel von Geibel (1815-84), a German poet, wrote a drama entitled *Brünhild* (1858). Richard Wagner's operas on the Nibelungen theme comprise the tetralogy *Der Ring des Nibelungen: Das Rheingold, Die Walküre, Siegfried,* and *Die Götterdämmerung.* The intrigue of the Nibelungen legend turns around the relations between the knight Siegfried (Scandinavian: Sigurthr) and two women: Krimhild (Scandinavian: Guthrun) and Prünhilde (or Brünhilde; Scandinavian: Brynhildr). Also important is the fate of the great treasure owned by Siegfried, for it brings death to each of its successive owners.

7. *The Mahabharata* is a Sanskrit epic of more than 90,000 couplets, composed probably between 200 B.C. and 200 A.D. Outside India the most popular part is a fabulous account of a dynastic war.

8. Historical Roots of the Wondertale: The Wondertale as a Whole

Propp 1946a, 329-337.

1. The Mari are a Finno-Ugric people living in the middle reaches of the Volga. The Voguls: see note 5 on No. 7.

2. Here is the table of contents of Propp's book, chapters 2-9. *Chapter 2. Complication* I. 1. Absentation. 2. Interdiction connected with absentation. 3. Frazer on the isolation of the king. 4. The isolation of the royal children in the wondertale. 5. The incarceration of the girl. 6. Motives for the incarceration. 7. Conclusions. II. Misfortune and counteraction. 8. Misfortune. 9. The hero prepares to leave home. *Chapter 3. The Mysterious Forest.* 1. The advance of the wondertale. The hero receives a magic tool. 2. The types of Baba Jaga. 3. Initiation. 4. The forest. 5. A hut on chicken legs. 6. Fu-fu-fu [fee-faw-fum]. 7. Feeding the hero. 8. The leg of bone. 9. Jaga's blindness. 10. The mistress of the forest. 11. Baba Jaga's tasks. 12. Trial by sleep. 13. Banished children and children left in the forest. 14. Abducted children. 15. Selling children. 16. Beating. 17. Frenzy. 18. A severed finger. 19. Marks of death. 20. A temporary death. 21. People cut up and brought to life. 22. Jaga's oven. 23. A unique skill. 24. A magic gift. 25. Jaga as a mother-in-law. 26. Travestism. 27. Conclusion. *Chapter 4. A Big House.* I. Fraternity in the forest. 1. A house in the forest. 2. A big house and a small hut. 3. A table set for the meal. 4. Brothers. 5. Hunters. 6. Robbers. 7. Division of labor. 8. The sister. 9. The birth of a baby. 10. A beauty in the coffin. 11. Cupid and Psyche. 12. The wife at her husband's wedding. 13. The Unwashed One (*Neumójka*). 14. The One Who Knows Nothing (*Neznájka*). 15. The bald ones and the covered ones. 16. The husband at his wife's wedding. 17. Interdiction of praise. 18. A locked closet. 19. Conclusion. II. Donors from the other world. 20. A dead father. 21. A dead mother. 22. A grateful dead man. 23. A dead head. 24. Conclusion. III. Donors as magic helpers. 25. Grateful animals. 26. The Iron Forehead. 27. Redeemed prisoners, debtors, etc. *Chapter 5. Magic Gifts.* 1. Helpers. 2. A transformed hero. 3. An eagle. 4. A winged horse. 5. Rearing a horse. 6. A horse from the other world. 7. A rejected and a bartered horse. 8. A horse in the cellar. 9. The horse's breed. 10. The horse's fiery nature. 11. The horse and the stars. 12. The horse and water. 13. Some other helpers. 14. Later concepts of the helper. II. A magic tool. 15. The tool and the helper. 16. Claws, hair, skins, and teeth. 17. Various implements. 18. Tools invoking spirits. 19. A flint. 20. A stick. 21. Tools securing constant abundance. 22. Live and dead water, strong and weak water. 23. Dolls. 24. Conclusion. *Chapter 6. Reaching the Other Kingdom.* 1. Reaching the other kingdom as an element of composition. 2. Reaching the other kingdom in animal guise. 3. Sewing into a skin. 4. A bird. 5. On horseback. 7. By ship. 8. By a tree. 9. By a ladder or straps. 9. With a guide. 10. Conclusion. *Chapter 7. The Fiery River.* I. A dragon in the wondertale. 1. The dragon's outward appearance. 2. His connection with water. 3. His connection with mountains. 4. The abductor. 5. The collector of tribute. 6. The guardian of the borders. 7. The swallower. 8. Danger of sleeping. 9. The initial adversary. 10. The combat. 11. Scholarly literature on the dragon. 12. Dissemination of the dragon-fighting motif. II. The dragon as swallower. 13. Ritual swallowing

and spitting out. 14. The sense and nature of this ritual. 15. Birds' language. 16. Diamonds. 17. The swallower as a vehicle. 17. Fighting the fish as the first step of dragon fighting. 19. Traces of swallowing in the late instances of dragon fighting. 20. Conclusion. III. The hero in a tub. 21. A boat. IV. The dragon as abductor. 24. The erotic element. 25. Abduction in myths. V. The Water Dragon. 26. Its water nature. 27. Collecting tribute. 28. Myths. VI. The dragon and the kingdom of the dead. 29. The dragon as guardian. 30. Cerberus. 31. The dragon transferred to the heavens. 32. The celestial dragon as guardian; the Yakuts. 33. The dragon in Egypt. 34. The weighing of souls (psychostasia). 35. The dragon and birth. 36. A dragon perishing from another dragon. 37. Conclusion. *Chapter 8. In a Faraway Kingdom.* 1. Its situation in space. 2. Its connection with the sun. 3. Gold. 4. Three kingdoms. 5. The theriomorphic nature of the faraway kingdom. I. The other world. 6. Its early forms. 7. The open mouth and the crushing mountains. 8. Crystal. 9. The land of plenty. 10. The solar kingdom. 11. Classical antiquity. *Chapter IX. The Bride.* I. The princess's stamp. 1. Two types of princess. 2. Branding the hero. II. Difficult tasks. A. The milieu. 3. Difficult tasks. 4. A call to everybody. 5. Tasks for a suitor. 6. The tasks of the princess who runs away and is found. 7. The tasks of the princess abducted by false heroes. 8. The tasks of the water sprite. 9. The tasks of the voodoo. 10. A hostile father-in-law. 11. Tasks for the old king. B. The content of difficult tasks. 12. Searching for things. 13. Palaces, gardens, and bridges. 14. Trial by bathing. 15. Trial by food. 16. Contests. 17. Blindman's buff. 18. Recognizing the person. III. The enthronement of the hero. 21. Frazer on the succession of kings. 22. Royal succession in the wondertale. 23. Old age. 24. Oracles. 25. Killing the king in the wondertale. 26. A false hero. 27. A rope bridge. 28. Boiling milk. 29. Conclusion. IV. Magic Flight. 30. Flight in the wondertale. 31. Throwing a comb, etc. 32. Transformations during the flight. 33. The dragon's kin becoming wells, apple trees, etc. 34. Flight and pursuit with successive transformations. 35. The decisive obstacle.

9. Ritual Laughter in Folklore

First published as Propp 1939b. Reprinted in Propp 1976a, 174-204.

1. The reference is to the narrative poem by Friedrich Rückert (1788-1866) *Rostem und Suhrab.* In his retelling of *Shah Namah* Rückert says: "Der Knabe weinte nie; er hatte neugeboren/Gelächelt schon, als sei er nicht zum Weh geboren" (II, 10, 9-10). Both Theodor Birt and Eduard Norden refer to this place (Propp's source was Norden), but the place is of no interest from the point of view of folklore, because it is absent from Firdausi's poem.

2. "Appearance of Christ to People" (Tretjakov Gallery, Moscow) is the masterpiece of the painter Aleksánd(e)r Andréevič Ivánov (1806-58).

3. Cf. a short account of episodes in which laughter has a ritual character in Schröder 1941, 11-12. Schröder also cites Usener and Fehrle and mentions a parallel from *Parzival* missed by Propp (the young Parzival and Kunneware de Lalant: the lady will not laugh until she has met the greatest hero in the world; Wolfram's Parzival III: 151, 11 ff.). See also Dumézil 1973, 32-33.

4. There is some confusion in the original. Propp first speaks about a gusli and in the next sentence about a pipe.

5. Vjátka, now called Kírov, is a town in east central Russia.

6. Propp errs in his citation. Bogaevskij refers to Persephone here, not Demeter.

7. Sadkó: see note 44 on No. 2.

8. For a very detailed discussion of laughter and humor, see Propp 1976b.

10. Russian Epic Poetry: Introduction

Propp 1958b, 5-28.

1. The Battle of Kulikóvo: see notes 45 and 52 on No. 2. The *Lay of the Host of Igor:* see note 3 on No. 2.

2. *Poltava* is Pushkin's long narrative poem about the battle of Poltáva (see note 64 on No. 2).

3. Rjabínin: see note 25 on No. 2.

4. Il'ja Muromec and Solvej the Robber: see notes 9, 23, and 24 on No. 2.

5. Stepan Razin: see note 2 on No. 2.

6. Vasílij Ivánovič Čapáev (1887-1919), a Red Army hero in the Civil War, enjoyed great popularity, which increased manifold after the publication of Dmítrij Fúrmanov's novel *Čapáev* (1923) and the release of a film about him (1934). At present, the hero of countless scurrilous anecdotes (the main uncensored genre of Soviet post-Stalin folklore).

7. *Golubínaja kníga* (from the word *glubina* 'depth', not from *golub'* 'dove') is a religious epic, containing questions of the fabulous Tsar Volotomán Volotománovič and the answers of the no less fabulous Tsar Davýd Ieséevič, which the latter has read in a huge book of heavenly origin. The questions and answers concern themselves with the beginning of the world and all things. *Golubinaja kniga* was probably written at the end of the fifteenth century. The title can be translated as *The Book of the Depths*. The confusion between *glub'* and *golub'* is due to folk etymology.

8. "Anika the Warrior" was a universally known religious ballad. Aníka, a mighty and cruel man, sets off to crush Jerusalem and the Holy Sepulcher, but on his way he meets Wonder, half beast, half man. This is Anika's death. Anika begs for mercy and promises to give away his riches to the poor, but Death refuses to listen, declines the money bought with blood, and cuts down Anika, who dies before he has had a chance to carry out his sacreligious plan. The appellation *Aníka Vóin* 'Anika the Warrior' has become proverbial and is used ironically about someone who wants to do the impossible and suffers dismal defeat.

9. "Vasilij and Sof'juška": see note 18 on No. 2.

10. See note 4 above.

11. Mixájlo Pótyk: see note 14 on No. 4.

12. Vasilij Buslaevič: see note 10 on No. 2.

13. The collection of Kírša Danílov, published by A. F. Jakubóvič in 1804, contained twenty-six texts of bylinas, as well as historical, religious, and humorous songs. However, the entire collection is almost three times larger (seventy-one texts). Nothing is known about Kirša Danilov himself, the man whose name allegedly stood on the first page of the manuscript and who either dictated his songs to someone or even recorded them himself. The book reflects Siberian epic tradition and goes back to the eighteenth century. It was the first window into the world of epic poetry in nineteenth century Russia. It still remains a great classic, not only because it antedates all other collections but because many of Kirša's texts are among the best from an artistic point of view.

14. In Kirša Danilov's book, Dobrýnja's fight with the dragon (cf. note 15 on No. 2) is described in a usual way: Dobrynja is warned by his mother not to swim in the Izráj River beyond "the first stream," but he swims much farther and is abducted by the dragon, whom he manages to deceive and kill. In the river he discovers the dragon's kin and kills all his children, and, surprisingly enough, in the same palace he meets his beloved aunt Márja Dívovna. They return home, but the house is empty: Dobrynja's mother is feasting with Prince Vladimir. Vladimir himself is very sad, and only the appearance of Dobrynja and later of Marja Divovna dispels his melancholy. Usually Dobrynja rescues Zabáva Putjátišna.

15. *Naródnost'* is a Russian noun that cannot be translated into English. Its root is *naród-* 'the people'; *-ost'* is a suffix forming abstract nouns (like *-hood, -ment, -ism*), so the whole means 'relatedness to the people', 'the being of the people's nature' and has patriotic connotations. Both the conservatives and the radicals appealed to narodnost' as the supreme criterion of the social truth, but the conservatives understood it as faithfulness to ancient traditions, including first and foremost monarchy, and freedom from the extraneous (West-European) influence, while the radicals emphasized revolutionary tendencies and associated narodnost' with the fight against the Tsar and serfdom. Hence the concept of "genuine narodnost'," which everybody interpreted in his or her own way.

16. The peasant reform: see note 53 on No. 2.

17. Gorky's speech at the first All-Union Congress of Soviet Writers (17 August 1934), entitled

"Soviet Literature" (Gorky 1953, 298-332), is a survey of world·literature from the point of view of class struggle. It is a landslide against "bourgeois culture," "bourgeois literature," and "bourgeois philosophy" (which included nearly everybody from Dostoevsky to Conan Doyle, Oscar Wilde, and Henri Bergson). It also contains several passages on mythology, epic poetry, and folktales (mainly about their connection with reality and their superior mastery). Quotations from this speech, together with similar quotations from Belinskij, Černyševskij, and Lenin, have become indispensable currency in Soviet folkloristics.

18. Pjotr Vasíl'evič Kireévskij (1808-56): an outstanding collector of folklore. Very famous is the three-volume set of Russian songs he published: Kireevskij 1860-74.

19. In this passage Propp attacks the Finnish school and uses the word formalism as a general term of abuse. A. I. Nikíforov was a pioneer in the study of folktale morphology (see Nikiforov 1928), and his opinion must have meant very much to Propp. Incidentally, the Finnish School was much less devoted to statistics than it is usually believed. Cf. Jason 1970.

20. The Pečóra, the Onéga, the Pínega, the Mezén', and the Kulój are rivers in the north of the USSR. All five flow through the Archangel region.

21. Čerdyn' is a town in the Urals, in the Perm' region; Xár'kov is a major city in the Ukraine. Novogrúdok is a town in the Grodno region of Byelorussia; Nóvyj Toržók is a town near Kalínin (Tver'). Uézd and gubérnija were administrative territorial units in prerevolutionary Russia (the gubernija was made up of uezds). Pokatigoróšek means 'roll-a-pea'. In this tale the brothers are working in the field. Their sister is going to take their dinner to the field but is abducted by a dragon along the way. The brothers fail to rescue her because they renounce the help of the shepherds and are also captured by the dragon. Meanwhile, their mother finds a magic pea that becomes her youngest son. His name is Roll-a-pea (Pokatigorošek). He kills the dragon and sets his family free. There are two Byelorussian versions of the tale (see Afanas'ev 1957, nos. 133 and 134). Of the three versions of the tale "Seven Simeons" (see Afanas'ev 1957, nos. 145-147), only no. 147 was recorded in the Novyj Toržok uezd. According to this tale, a man has seven sons; they were born on the same day, and each is called Simeon. Each possesses a unique skill. The tsar sends them to obtain a bride for himself. The youngest brother, who is a master thief, gives the prospective bride a beautiful cat and lives in her house three days. Later the brothers abduct the princess, and the tsar marries her.

22. In the Onéga tradition it is Dunaj who shows Prince Vladimir his bride, while in the Mezén' tradition it is Dobrynja. See note 14 on No. 2.

23. Dobrynja: see note 15 on No. 2.

24. Aljoša and Tugarin: see note 16 on No. 2.

25. Il'ja and Idolišče: see note 9 on No. 2.

26. Sadko: see note 44 on No. 2.

27. Djuk Stepanovič: see note 11 on No. 2.

Supplement

1. The page numbers in Prof. Lévi-Strauss's text refer to the first edition (1958). As the second edition (1968) is now more commonly used, we have added in italics the page references to this latter edition when it is cited in the text. [Translator's note]

2. The English word 'move' is closer to the Russian term xod than the French partie. In Monique Layton's translation partie is rendered as 'move', in accordance with the English text of Morphology, but it seems advisable to retain Lévi-Strauss's own word. The same has been done with bienfaiteur (it corresponds to 'donor' in the English text). Lévi-Strauss could have used donneur but preferred not to do so. This terminological distinction, as well as Lévi-Strauss's equation of 'plot' with thème, is discussed in Propp's rejoinder, and it is important not to smooth down the disagreement between the two scholars, even though 'move', 'donor', and 'plot' would be preferable to partie, 'benefactor', and 'theme'.

Bibliography

Bibliography

(Titles added by the editor, except for the works by Propp, are given with an asterisk)

Aarne, Antti. 1928. *The Types of the Folk-tale: A Classification and Bibliography. Antti Aarne's "Verzeichnis der Märchentypen." (Folklore Fellows Communications no. 3).* Translated and Enlarged by Stith Thompson. Folklore Fellows Communications no. 74. Helsinki: Suomalainen tiedeakatemia. (2nd revision. Folklore Fellows Communications no. 184, 1961.)

*Adams, John W. 1974. "Dialectics and Contingency in 'The Story of Asdiwal': An Ethnographic Note." In Rossi:170-78.

Afanas'ev, A. N. 1936-40. *Narodnye russkie skazki A. N. Afanas'eva* [Russian folktales]. Pod redakciej M. K. Azadovskogo, N. P. Andreeva, Ju. M. Sokolova. 3 vols. [Leningrad:] Academia.

———. 1957. *Narodnye russkie skazki A. N. Afanas'eva* [Russian folktales]. Podgotovka teksta, predislovie i primečanija V. Ja. Proppa. 3 vols. Moscow: Xudožestvennaja literatura.

Andreev, N. P., and Černyšëv, V. I. 1936. *Russkaja ballada* [The Russian ballad]. Biblioteka poèta. Moscow and Leningrad: Sovetskij pisatel'.

———. 1929. *Ukazatel' skazočnyx sjužetov po sisteme Aarne* [Index of folktale plots according to the Aarne classification]. Leningrad: Gosudarstvennoe russkoe geografičeskoe obščestvo.

Andreev, N. P., and Černyšëv, V. I. 1936. *Russkaja ballada* [The Russian ballad]. Biblioteka poèta. Moscow and Leningrad: Sovetskij pisatel'.

Anikin, V. P. 1959. *Russkaja narodnaja skazka: Posobie dlja učitelej* [The Russian folktale: handbook for teachers]. Moscow: Učpedgiz.

*———. 1979. "Sovetskaja istoričeskaja škola v bylinovedenii (sorokovye-šestidesjatye gody) i Vsevolod Miller" [The Soviet Historical school in the study of the bylinas (from the Forties to the Sixties) and Vsevolod Miller]. Russkij fol'klor 19. Voprosy teorii fol'klora, 84-112. Leningrad: Nauka.

*Anonymous. 1948/1. "Protiv buržuaznogo liberalizma v literaturovedenii. (Po povodu diskussii ob A. Veselovskom)" [Against bourgeois liberalism in the study of literature. (Apropos of the discussion about A. Veselovskij]. *Kul'tura i žizn'.* 11 March, No. 7 (62), p. 3.

*Anonymous. 1948/2. "Bol'ševistskaja partijnost'—osnova sovetskogo literaturovedenija" [Loyalty to the Bolshevik party-line is the basis of Soviet literary scholarship]. *Literaturnaja gazeta,* Saturday, 13 November, p. 1.

214 □ BIBLIOGRAPHY

*Anonymous. 1970. [Review] Propp 1969. *TLS*, 23 July, 807-8.

Astaxova, A. M. 1938. *Byliny severa, tom 1: Mezen' i Pečora* [Bylinas of the north: vol. 1: The Mezen' and the Pečora]. Moscow and Leningrad: Akademija nauk SSSR.

*———. 1966. *Byliny. Itogi i problemy izučenija* [Bylinas. The State of the Art]. Moscow, Leningrad: Nauka.

Aufhauser, Johann B. 1911. *Das Drachenwunder des heiligen Georg in der griechischen und lateinishcen Überlieferung*. Leipzig: B. G. Teubner.

*Avalle, d'Arco S. 1970. "Systems and Structures in the Folktale." *20th Century Studies* 3:67-75.

*Azadovskij, M. K. 1935. "Pamjati N. Ja. Marra" [N. Ja. Marr in memoriam]. *Sovetskij fol'klor* vol. 2/3, 5-20.

Azbelev, S. N. 1962. "Novgorodskie byliny i letopis' " [The Novgorod bylinas and the chronicle]. Russkij fol'klor, vol. 7. Materialy i issledovanija, 44-51. Moscow and Leningrad: Akademija nauk SSSR.

*———. 1982. Istorizm bylin i specifika fol'klora [The historicity of bylinas and the specific nature of folklore]. Leningrad: Nauka.

*Bǎrbulescu, Corneliu. 1971. Review of Propp 1970. *Revista de ethnografie şi folclor*. 1971:345-48.

*Barksdale, E[thelbert] C. 1974. *The Dacha and the Duchess. An application of Lévi-Strauss's theory of myth in human creativity to works of nineteenth-century Russian novelists*. New York: Philosophical Library.

Barsov, E. V. 1872, 1882, 1886. *Pričitan'ja Severnogo kraja* [Laments of the northern region]. Moscow: Sovremennik.

*Barthes, Roland. 1965. *Le Degré zéro de l'écriture. Suivi de: Éléments de sémiologie*. Paris: Gonthier.

Baumgartner, Walter. 1915. "Jephthas Gelübde." *Archiv für Religionswissenschaft* 18:240-49.

Bazanov, V. G. 1949. Introduction to *Onežskie byliny, zapisannye A. F. Gil'ferdingom letom 1871 goda* [Onega bylinas recorded in the summer of 1871 by A. F. Gil'ferding]. 4th ed. vol. 1. Moscow and Leningrad: Akademija nauk SSSR.

Bazanov, V. G., and Razumova, A. P. 1962. *Russkaja narodno-bytovaja lirika* [Russian lyric folk poetry of everyday life]. Moscow and Leningrad: Akademija nauk SSSR.

Belinskij, V. G. 1954. "Razdelenie poèzii na rody i vidy" [The division of poetry into genera and species]. In *Polnoe sobranie sočinenij* [Complete works], vol. 5, 7-65. Moscow: Akademija nauk SSSR.

———. 1955. "O žizni i sočinenijax Kol'cova" [On the life and works of Kol'cov]. In *Polnoe sobranie sočinenij* [Complete works], vol. 9, 497-542. Moscow: Akademija nauk SSSR.

Bergson, Henri. 1938. *Le rire. Essai sur la signification du comique*. 44th ed. Paris: Librairie Felix Alcan. (1st ed. 1901.)

*Berkov, P. N. 1966. "Metod issledovanija narodnogo tvorčestva v trudax V. Ja. Proppa (k semidesjatiletiju so dnja roždenija)" [Propp's folkloristic method. V. Ja. Propp septuagenarian]. *Vestnik Leningradskogo Universiteta*. 2. Serija istorii, jazyka i literatury 1, 111-16.

Boas, Franz. 1895. *Indianische Sagen von der nord-pacifischen Küste Amerikas*. Berlin: A. Asher & Co.

———. 1897. *The Social Organization and the Secret Societies of the Kwakiutl Indians*. Report of the U.S. National Museum for 1895, 311-737. Washington, D.C. Reprinted in 1970 (New York: Johnson Reprint Corp.).

Bogaevskij, B. L. 1916. *Zemledel'českaja religija Afin* [The agricultural religion of Athens]. Vol. 1. Zapiski istoriko-filologičeskogo fakul'teta, part 130. Petrograd: M. A. Aleksandrov.

*Bogatyrev, Pjotr, and Jakobson, Roman. [1929]. "Die Folklore als eine besondere Form des Schaffens. *Donum natalicum Schrijnen 3. Mei 1929*. Nijmegen, Utrecht: Dekker & Van de Gegt, 900-13; reprinted in Roman Jakobson, *Selected Writings*, vol. 4. *Slavic Epic Studies*. The Hague, Paris: Mouton (1966), 1-15, and in P. G. Bogatyryov, *Voprosy teorii narodnogo iskusstva* [Questions of theory of folk art], 369-83. Moscow: Iskusstvo (1971).

Bogoraz, V. G. 1936. "Osnovnye tipy fol'klora severnoj Evrazii i Severnoj Ameriki" [The basic types of folklore of northern Eurasia and North America]. Sovetskij fol'klor, vol. 4, 29-50.

Bolte, Johannes, and Polívka, Georg. 1913-1932. *Anmerkungen zu der Kinder- und Hausmärchen der Brüder Grimm.* 5 vols. Leipzig: Dieterich.

Bonč-Bruevič, V. D. 1954. "V. I. Lenin o narodnoj poèzii" [V. I. Lenin on folk poetry]. *Sovetskaja ètnografija* 4:117-31.

*Boon, James A. 1972. *From Symbolism to Structuralism. Lévi-Strauss in a Literary Tradition.* Oxford: Basil Blackwell.

*Borillo, A[ndrée]. 1975. "Analyse de texte/analyse linguistique." *Mélanges offerts à Georges Mounin pour son soixante-cinquième anniversaire.* Vol. 1: Mélanges de linguistique et de stylistique. Aix-en-Provence: Université de Provence. Cahiers de linguistique, d'orientalisme et de slavistique, vol. 5/6:43-56.

*Borillo, Andrée, and Borillo, Mario. 1976. "Analyse de texte/analyse linguistique." Informatique et Sciences Humaines. (Institut des sciences humaines appliquées. Paris), 28:31-62.

Borovkov, A. K. 1938. *Skazki narodov Vostoka* [Folktales of the Orient]. Moscow and Leningrad.

*Bravo, Gian L. 1967. "Morfologia della fiaba." *Problemi* 2:64-72. (Reprinted in Cirese, Alberto M., ed. *Folklore e antropologia tra storicismo e marxismo.* Palermo:Palumbo, 1972, pp. 45-77; second edition 1974).

*Bremond, Claude. Review of Propp 1969. *Pamiętnik literacki* 4:285-91.

*———. 1973. *Logique du récit.* Paris: Éditions du Seuil.

*Breymayer, Reinhard. 1972a. "Vladimir Jakovlevič Propp (1895-1970)—Leben, Wirken und Bedeutsamkeit." *Linguistica Biblica* 15/16:36-66.

*———. 1972b. "Bibliographie zum Werk Vladimir Jakovlevič Propps und zur strukturalen Erzählforschung." *Linguistica Biblica* 15/16:67-77.

*Buchler, Ira R., and Selby, Henry A. 1968. *A Formal Study of Myth.* Center for Intercultural Studies in Folklore and Oral History. Monograph Series No. 1. Austin: The University of Texas.

*Caldiron, Orio. 1975. *Claude Lévi-Strauss. I fondamenti teorici dell'antropologia strutturale.* Università di Padova. Pubblicazioni della Facoltà di lettere e filosofia 54. Florence: Olschki.

*Cassirer, Ernst A. 1945. "Structuralism in Modern Linguistics." *Word* 1:99-120.

Černecov, V. 1935. *Vogul'skie skazki. Sbornik fol'klora naroda mansi-(vogulov)* [Tales of the Voguls. A collection of the folklore of the Mansi (Vogul) people]. Leningrad: Xudožestvennaja literatura.

Černyševskij, N. G. 1949. "Recenzija na *Pesni raznyx narodov* N. Berga" [Review of N. Berg's *Songs of various peoples*]. In *Polnoe sobranie sočinenij* [Complete works], vol. 2, 291-317; 362-68. Moscow: Xudožestvennaja literatura.

———. 1950. "Polemičeskie krasoty" [The flower garden of polemics]. In *Polnoe sobranie sočinenij* [Complete works], vol. 7, 742-52. Moscow: Xudožestvennaja literatura.

———. 1958. "Èstetičeskie otnošenija iskusstva k dejstvitel'nosti" [The aesthetic relations of art and reality]. In *Èstetika* [Aesthetics]. Moscow: Xudožestvennaja literatura.

*Chomsky, Noam. 1968. *Language and Mind.* New York, Chicago, San Francisco, Atlanta: Harcourt, Brace and World.

Čičerov, V. I. 1947. "Ob ètapax razvitija russkogo istoričeskogo èposa" [On the stages in the development of Russian historical epic poetry]. In *Istoriko-literaturnyj sbornik,* 3-60. Moscow: Goslitizdat.

———. 1959. "K probleme istoričeskoj i žanrovoj specifiki russkix bylin i istoričeskix pesen" [On the historicity and genres of Russian bylinas and historical songs]. In *Voprosy teorii i istorii narodnogo tvorčestva* [Problems in the theory and history of folklore], 257-310. Moscow: Sovetskij pisatel'.

*Cirese, Alberte M. 1982. Introduction to the second (1972) edition of V. Ja. Propp, *La radici storiche dei racconti de fate.* Turin: Einaudi, 1972. In de Meijer 1982a, 33-44.

*Cocchiara, Giuseppe. 1981. *The History of Folklore in Europe.* Translated from the Italian by John N. McDaniel. Philadelphia: The Institute for the Study of Human Issues. (First published as *Storia del folklore in Europa.* Turin: Einaudi, 1952. Collezione di studi religiosi, etnologici e psicologici 20).

*Codère, Hélène. 1974. "La Geste du Chien d'Asdiwal: The Story of Mac." *American Anthropologist* 76:42-46.

*Croce, Benedetto, 1949. Review of Propp 1949. *Quaderni della "Critica"* 15:102-5.

Cushing, Frank H. 1931. *Zuñi Folk Tales.* 2nd ed. New York: A. A. Knopf.

Dégh, Linda; Glassie, Henry; and Oinas, Felix J., eds. 1976. *A Festschrift for Richard M. Dorson. Folklore Today.* Research Center for Language and Semiotic Studies. Bloomington: Indiana University.

*Dement'ev, A. G. 1948. "Za bol'ševistskuju partijnost' v literaturovedenii" [Toward the Bolshevist party line in the study of literature]. *Vestnik Leningradskogo universiteta* 4:78-86.

Dieterich, Albrecht. 1911. "Die Göttin Mise." In his *Kleine Schriften,* 125-35. Leipzig and Berlin: Teubner. (Originally published in *Philologus* 52 [1893]: 1 ff.).

Dmitrakov, I. P. 1950. "Teorija aristokratičeskogo proisxoždenija fol'klora i ee reakcionnaja suščnost' " [Theory of the aristocratic origin of folklore and its reactionary nature]. *Sovetskaja ètnografija* 1:155-69.

Dobroljubov, N. A. 1934a. "Narodnye skazki Afanas'eva" [Afanas'ev's Russian folktales]. In *Polnoe sobranie sočinenij* [Complete works], vol. 1, 429-34. Moscow: Xudožestvennaja literatura.

―――. 1934b. "O stepeni učastija narodnosti v razvitii russkoj literatury" [On the degree of the people's participation in the development of Russian literature]. In *Polnoe sobranie sočinenij* [Complete works], vol. 1, 203-45. Moscow: Xudožestvennaja literatura.

―――. 1934c. "Zametki i dopolnenija k sborniku russkix poslovic g. Buslaeva" [Notes and additions to Mr. Buslaev's collection of Russian proverbs]. In *Polnoe sobranie sočinenij,* vol. 1, 496-521. Moscow: Xudožestvennaja literatura.

Dorsey, G. A. 1904. *Traditions of the Skidi Pawnee.* Memoirs of the American folk-lore society, vol. 8. Boston and New York: Houghton, Mifflin and Company; London: D. Nutt.

Dorsey, G. A., and Kroeber, A. L. 1903. *Traditions of the Arapaho.* Field Columbian Museum Publication 81. Anthropological Series, vol. 5. Chicago.

*Dorson, Richard M. 1963. "Current Folklore Theories." *Current Anthropology* 4:93-112.

*Douglas, Mary. 1966. *Purity and Danger; an Analysis of Concepts of Pollution and Taboo.* New York and Washington: Praeger.

*Drobin, Ulf. 1969. "A Review of Structuralism." *Temenos* 5:203-12.

*―――. 1970. [Review] Vladimir Propp, *Morphologie du conte.* . . . Paris: Seuil, 1970 and Vladimir Ja. Propp, *Morphologie du conte.* . . . Paris: Gallimard, 1970. *Temenos* 6:164-71.

*Dumézil, Georges. 1973. *From Myth to Fiction. The Saga of Hadingus.* Translated by Derek Coltman. Chicago and London: The University of Chicago Press. (First published in 1970 by Presses Universitaires de France as *Du mythe au roman: La Saga de Hadingus et autres essais.*).

*Dundes, Alan. 1962. "From Etic to Emic Units in the Structural Study of Folktales." *Journal of American Folklore* 75:95-105.

*―――. 1964. *The Morphology of North American Indian Folktales.* Folklore Fellows Communications no. 195. Helsinki: Suomalainen tiedeakatemia.

*―――. 1966. "The American Concept of Folklore." *Journal of the Folklore Institute* (Indiana University) 3:226-49.

*―――. 1976. "Structuralism and Folklore." *Pentikainen* 1976:79-93.

*Eimermacher, Karl. 1972. "Nachwort des Herausgebers." In Propp 1972:215-25.

*Eliade, Mircea. 1963. *Myth and Reality.* Translated from the French by Willard R. Trask. New York: Harper and Row.

*Emel'janov, L. I. 1955. Review of Propp 1955. *Večernij Leningrad,* 24 November.

*———. 1964. "Neres̆ënnye problemy v izuc̆enii sovremennogo narodnogo tvorc̆estva" [Unresolved problems in the study of folk art]. Russkij fol'klor, vol. 9. Problemy sovremennogo narodnogo tvorc̆estva. Moscow and Leningrad: Nauka.

*———. 1976. "Metodologic̆eskie principy istoric̆eskoj s̆koly i ix kritika v sovetskoj fol'kloristike" [The methodological principles of the Historical school and their criticism in Soviet folkloristics]. Russkij fol'klor, vol. 16. Istoric̆eskaja z̆izn' narodnoj poèzii, 3-34. Leningrad: Nauka.

*———. 1979. "O granicax metoda i 'edinicax istorizma' " [On the limits of a method and on "units of historicity"]. Russkij fol'klor, vol. 19. Voprosy teorii fol'klora, 113-25. Leningrad: Nauka.

*Emonds, Joseph. 1971. "A Reformulation of Grimm's Law." In Michael K. Brame, Contributions to Generative Phonology, 108-22. Austin and London: University of Texas Press.

Engels, Friedrich. 1940. Dialectics of Nature. Translated and edited by Clemens Dutt with a preface and notes by J. B. S. Haldane. New York: International Publishers. Russian text: "Dialektika prirody." In Karl Marx and Friedrich Engels, Soc̆inenija [Works], 2nd ed. vol. 20, 343-626. Moscow: Gospolitizdat, 1961. German text: "Dialektik der Natur." In Karl Marx and Friedrich Engels, Werke, vol. 20, 305-568. Berlin: Dietz, 1973.

———. 1942. "Letter 214. Engels to Conrad Schmidt. 27 October 1890." In Karl Marx and Friedrich Engels, Selected Correspondence 1846-1895 with explanatory notes. Translated by Dona Torr, 477-84. New York: International Publishers. Russian text: "Pis'mo k Konradu S̆midtu." In Karl Marx and Friedrich Engels, Soc̆inenija [Works], 2nd ed. vol. 37, 414-22. Moscow: Gospolitizdat, 1965. German text: "Engels an Conrad Schmidt." In Karl Marx and Friedrich Engels, Werke, vol. 37, 388-95. Berlin: Dietz, 1974.

———. 1962. "The Origin of the Family, Private Property and the State." In Karl Marx and Friedrich Engels, Selected Works in Two Volumes, vol. 2. Fifth Impression, 170-327. Moscow: Foreign Languages Publishing House. Russian text: "Proisxoz̆denie sem'i, c̆astnoj sobstvennosti i gosudarstva v svjazi s issledovanijami L. G. Morgana" [The origin of the family, private property and the state in connection with the research of L. H. Morgan]. In Karl Marx and Friedrich Engels, Soc̆inenija [Works], 2nd ed. vol. 21, 23-178. Moscow: Gospolitizdat, 1961. German text: "Der Ursprung der Familie, des Privateigentums und des Staats: In Anschluss an Lewis H. Morgan's Forschungen." In Karl Marx and Friedrich Engels, Werke, vol. 21, 25-173. Berlin: Dietz, 1973.

———. 1966. Herr Eugen Dühring's Revolution in Science ("Anti-Dühring"). New York: International Publishers. Russian text: " 'Anti-Djuring.' Perevorot v nauke, proizvedjonnyj gospodinom Evgeniem Djuringom" [Anti-Dühring. Herr Eugen Dühring's revolution in science]. In Karl Marx and Friedrich Engels, Soc̆inenija [Works], 2nd ed. vol. 20, 1-338. Moscow: Gospolitizdat, 1961. German text: "Herr Eugen Dühring's Umwalzung der Wissenschaft ('Anti-Dühring')." In Karl Marx and Friedrich Engels, Werke, vol. 20, 1-303. Berlin: Dietz, 1973.

Erasmus, Desiderius. 1535. "Ecclesiastes sive concionator euangelicus." In Opera omnia emendatiora et auctiora, vol. 5, col. 769-1100. Lugduni Batavorum, cura et impensis Petri Vander Aa, 1704. (Reprinted London: Gregg Press, Ltd., 1962.)

Èrgis, G. U. 1960. Istoric̆eskie predanija i rasskazy jakutov [The historical legends and stories of the Yakuts], Part 1. Moscow and Leningrad: Akademija nauk SSSR.

*———. 1970. Oc̆erki po jakutskomu fol'kloru [Essays on Yakut folklore]. Moscow: Nauka.

*Erjomina, V. I. 1979. Review of Propp 1976a and Propp 1976b. Russkij fol'klor, vol. 19. Voprosy teorii fol'klora, 200-6. Leningrad: Nauka.

*Erlich, Victor. 1955. Russian Formalism: History, Doctrine. (Slavistic Printings and Reprintings IV). The Hague: Mouton. (2nd ed: 1965. 3rd ed: New Haven: Yale University Press, 1981.)

Fehrle, Eugen. 1930. "Das Lachen im Glauben der Völker." Zeitschrift für Volkskunde, n.s., vol. 2, 1-5.

*Fischer, J. L. 1963. "The Sociopsychological Analysis of Folktales." Current Anthropology 4:235-73, 285-95.

Fluck, Hans. 1934. "Der risus paschalis: Ein Beitrag zur religiösen Volkskunde." *Archiv für Religionswissenschaft* 31:188-212.

Frazer, James G. 1918. *Folk-lore in the Old Testament*. Studies in Comparative Religion, Legend and Law. London: Macmillan and Co.

*Freilich, Morris. 1977. "Lévi-Strauss' Myth of Method." In Jason/Segal, 223-49.

Freudenberg, O. M. 1936. *Poètika sjužeta i žanra. Period antičnoj literatury* [The poetics of plot and genre. Classical literature]. Leningrad: Xudožestvennaja literatura.

*———. 1978. *Mif i literatura drevnosti* [Ancient myth and literature]. Moscow: Nauka, Glavnaja redakcija vostočnoj literatury.

Frobenius, Leo. 1898. *Die Weltanschauung der Naturvölker*. Weimar: E. Felber.

———. 1904. *Das Zeitalter des Sonnengottes*. Berlin: G. Reiner.

Geldner, Karl F. 1951. *Der Rig-Veda aus dem Sanskrit ins Deutsche übersetzt und mit einem laufenden Kommentar versehen*. Part 3: *Neunter bis zehnter Liederkreis*. The Harvard Oriental Series 35. Cambridge, Mass.: Harvard University Press; London: Geoffrey Cumberlege, Oxford University Press; Weisbaden: Otto Harrassowitz.

*Gel'gardt, R. R. 1976. "Nekotorye obščelingvističeskie idei i fol'kloristčeskie interesy akad. N. Ja. Marra v osveščenii naučnoj kritiki" [Some linguistic ideas and folkloristic interests of Academician N. Ja. Marr as illuminated by scholarly criticism]. *Voprosy jazykoznanija* 3:118-30.

*Georges, Robert A. 1970. "Structure in Folktales: A Generative-Transformational Approach." *Conch* 2 (2):4-17.

*Glucksmann, Miriam. 1974. *Structuralist Analysis in Contemporary Social Thought. A Comparison of the Theories of Claude Lévi-Strauss and Louis Althusser*. London and Boston: Routledge and Kegan Paul.

*Goethe, Johann W. 1887-1918. *Werke*. Weimar: Böhlau.

Golubev, I. F. 1951. "Povest' ob Il'e Muromce i Solov'e-Razbojnike" [The tale of Il'ja Muromec and Solovej the Robber]. Slavjanskij fol'klor. Trudy Instituta ètnografii Akademii nauk SSSR, n.s. 13, 241-51.

*Gorelov, A. A. 1972. "Pamjati V. Ja. Proppa (1895-1970)" [V. Ja. Propp in memoriam]. Russkij fol'klor, vol. 13. Russkaja narodnaja proza, 253-57. Leningrad: Nauka.

Gorky, Maxim. 1953. "Sovetskaja literatura" [Soviet literature]. In his *Sobranie sočinenij v tridcati tomax* [Collected works in 30 vols.], vol. 27, 298-332. Moscow: Xudožestvennaja literatura.

*Greimas, A[lgirdas] J. 1966. *Sémantique structurale, recherche de méthode*. Paris: Librairie Larousse.

*Greverus, Ina-Maria. 1964. "Bericht zu Veröffentlichungs- und Katalogisierungsplänen aus dem Zentralarchiv der Volkserzählung." In Ortutay 111-28.

Grimm, [Jacob and Wilhelm]. [1956]. *Die Kinder- und Hausmärchen der Brüder Grimm*. Vollständige Ausgabe in der Urfassung. Herausgegeben von Friedrich Panzer. Wiesbaden: E. Vollmer.

Gubernatis, Angelo de. 1872. *Zoological Mythology or the Legends of Animals*. New York: Macmillan; London: Trübner.

*Guépin, J. P. 1972, 1973. "Propp kan niet en waarom." *Forum der letteren* 13:129-47; 14:30-51.

*Güttgemanns, Erhardt. 1977. "Fundamentals of a Grammar of Oral Literature." In Jason/Segal, 77-97.

*Gurevich, A. Ya. 1969. "Space and Time in the *Weltmodell* of the Old Scandinavian Peoples." *Mediaeval Scandinavia* 2:42-53.

Hahn, Eduard. 1896. *Demeter und Baubo: Versuch einer Theorie der Entstehung unseres Ackerbaus*. Lübeck: Selbstverlag des Verfassers, in Commission bei M. Schmidt.

*Halliday, W. R. 1933. *Indo-European Folk Tales and Greek Legend*. Cambridge: At the University Press.

*Haltsonen, S. 1963. Review of Propp 1963. *Virittäjä* 2:283-84.

*Hansen, Børge. 1971. *Folkeeventyr. Struktur og genre*. Copenhagen:Munksgaard.

*Hayes, Nelson E., and Hayes, Tanya, eds. 1970. *Claude Lévi-Strauss: The Anthropologist As Hero.* Cambridge, Mass., and London, England: The M.I.T. Press.

*Hendricks, William O. 1970. "Folklore and the Structural Analysis of Literary Texts." *Language and Style* 3:83-121. Reprinted in Hendricks 1973a.

*———. 1973a. *Essays on Semiolinguistics and Verbal Art.* Approaches to Semiotics 37. Research Center for the Language Sciences. Indiana University. Paris, The Hague:Mouton.

*———. 1973b. "Verbal Art and the Structural Synthesis." *Semiotica* 8:239-62.

*———. 1975. "The Work and Play Structures of Narrative." *Semiotica* 13:281-328.

Hesiod. 1964. "The Theogony." In *The Homeric Hymns and Homerica.* With an English translation by Hugh G. Evelyn-White, M. A., 144-45. [The Loeb Classical Library]. Cambridge, Mass. Harvard University Press; London: William Heinemann, Ltd.

*Holbek, Bengt. 1972. "Strukturalisme og folkloristik. I anledning af Børge Hansens eventyranalyse." *Folk og kultur*:51-64.

*———. 1978. "Formal and Structural Studies of Oral Narrative. A Bibliography." Compiled in Collaboration with Dan Ben-Amos and others. *Unifol.* Årsberetning 1977 (Institute for Folkemindevidenskab. Københavns Universitet). Copenhagen, 149-94.

Homer. 1960. *The Odyssey.* With an English translation by A. T. Murray. 2 vols. Vol. 1. [The Loeb Classical Library]. Cambridge, Mass.: Harvard University Press; London: William Heinemann, Ltd.

———. 1963. *The Iliad.* With an English translation by A. T. Murray. 2 vols. Vol. 2 [The Loeb Classical Library]. Cambridge, Mass.: Harvard University Press; London: William Heinemann, Ltd.

*Honti, Hans. 1939. "Märchenmorphologie und Märchentypologie." *Folk-Liv* 3:307-18.

*I. V. 1948. "Zasedanie Učёnogo soveta Filologičeskogo fakul'teta." [Meeting of the Academic Council of the Philological Faculty]. *Vestnik Leningradskogo Universiteta* 4:132-37.

Ionov, V. M. 1916. "Dux xozjaina lesa u jakutov" [The spirit-master of the forest among the Yakuts]. Sbornik Muzeja antropologii i ètnografii im. Petra Velikogo pri Imperatorskoj Akademii nauk, vol. 4, no. 1. Petrograd: Akademija nauk.

*Ivanov, Vjač. V. 1976. *Očerki po istorii semiotiki v SSSR* [Essays on the history of semiotics in the USSR]. Moscow: Nauka.

*Ivanov, Vjač. V., and Toporov, V. M. 1976. "The Invariant and Transformations in Folklore Texts." *Dispositio* 1:263-70.

*Jacobs, Melville. 1959. Review of Propp 1959. *Journal of American Folklore* 72:195-96.

*———. 1966. "A Look Ahead in Oral Literature Research." *Journal of American Folklore* 79:413-27.

Jakóbiec, Marian. 1955. *Byliny.* Biblioteka narodowa, no. 96, Seria 2. Wroclaw: Zakład nardowy im. Ossolińskich.

*Jakobson, Roman. 1979. "The Statue in Puškin's Poetic Mythology." In Roman Jakobson, *Selected Writings*, vol. 5. The Hague, Paris, New York: Mouton, 237-80. (First published as "Socha v symbolice Puškinově." *Slovo a slovesnost* 3 [1937]: 2-24.)

*Jakobson, Roman, and Jones, Lawrence G. 1970. *Shakespeare's Verbal Art in Th'expense of spirit.* De Proprietatibus Litterarum 35. The Hague, Paris: Mouton.

*Jakobson, Roman, and Lévi-Strauss, Claude. 1962. " 'Les Chats' de Charles Baudelaire." *L'Homme* 2:5-21. (In English: Michael Lane, *Structuralism: a Reader.* London: Cape, 1970, 202-21.)

Jakutskij fol'klor [Yakut folklore]. 1936. Teksty i perevody A. A. Popova. Literaturnaja obrabotka E. Tager, obščaja redakcija M. A. Sergeeva. Moscow and Leningrad: Sovetskij pisatel'.

Jančuk, N. Ja. 1919. "O muzyke bylin v svjazi s istoriej ix izučenija" [On the music of the bylinas in connection with the history of their study]. In *Byliny*, vol. 2, 527-63. Edited by M. Speranskij. Moscow: M. & S. Sabašnikovy.

*Janovič, Clara Strada. 1982. Introduction to V. Ja. Propp, *Edipo alla luce del folclore. Quattro studi di etnografia storico-stritturale.* Turin: Einaudi, 1975. In de Meijer, 1982a, 45-56.

*Jason, Heda. 1970. "The Russian Criticism of the Finnish School." *Norveg* 14:285-94.

*———. 1977. "Precursors of Propp: Formalist Theories of Narrative in Early Russian Ethnopoetics." *PTL: A Journal for Descriptive Poetics and Theory of Literature* 3:471-516.

*Jason, Heda, and Segal, Dimitri, eds. 1977. *Patterns in Oral Literature.* The Hague, Paris: Mouton.

Jastremskij, S. V. 1929. "Obrazcy narodnoj literatury jakutov" [Specimens of Yakut folklore]. Trudy Komissii po izučeniju jakutskoj ASSR, vol. 7. Leningrad.

*Jenkins, Alan. 1979. *The Social Theory of Claude Lévi-Strauss.* London and Basingstone: Macmillan.

Kahlo, Gerhard. 1954. *Die Wahrheit des Märchens.* Halle/Salle: M. Niemeyer.

Karnauxova, I. V. 1927. "Skazočniki i skazka v Zaonež'e" [Tellers of wondertales and the wondertale in the Trans-Onega]. In *Krest'janskoe iskusstvo SSSR,* vol. 1. Iskusstvo Severa. Zaonež'e [Peasant art of the USSR. The art of the North. The Trans-Onega], 104-20. Leningrad: Academia.

*Kaun, Alexander S. 1943. *Soviet Poets and Poetry.* Berkeley and Los Angeles: University of California Press.

*Kazanskij, B. V. 1932. "Antičnye aspekty sjužeta Tristana i Isol'dy' [Some aspects of the plot of Tristan and Isolda in classical antiquity]. In Marr 1932, 115-35.

Kireevskij, P. V. 1860-1874. *Pesni* [Songs]. (Three volumes, ten issues). Moscow: Obščestvo ljubitelej rossijskoj slovesnosti.

*Kirk, G. S. 1970. *Myth, Its Meaning and Function in Ancient and Other Cultures.* Sather Classical Lectures 40. Berkeley and Los Angeles: Cambridge University Press, University of California Press.

*Klein, Sheldon, et al. 1977. "Modeling Propp and Lévi-Strauss in a Metasymbolic Simulation System." In Jason/Segal, 141-220.

*Klymasz, Robert B. 1976. "Soviet Views of American Folklore and Folkloristics, 1950-1974." In Dégh, Linda et al. 1976, 305-12.

*———. 1978. Folklore Politics in the Soviet Ukraine: Perspectives on Some Recent Trends and Developments." In Oinas 1978b:97-108.

Kolpakova, N. P. 1962. *Russkaja narodnaja bytovaja pesnja* [The Russian folk song of everyday life]. Moscow and Leningrad: Akademija nauk SSSR.

Korobka, N. I. 1908. Skazanija ob uročiščax Ovručskogo uezda i byliny o Vol'ge Svjatoslavoviče [Legends about the boundaries of the Ovruč uezd and the bylinas about Vol'ga Svjatoslavovič]. Izvestija Otdelenija russkogo jazyka i slovesnosti Rossijskoj Akademii nauk. vol. 13, book 1, 292-328.

Kovács, Zoltán. 1956. Review of Propp 1955. *Ethnographia* 4, 669-71.

Kroeber, Alfred L. 1907. *Gros Ventre Myths and Tales.* Anthropological Papers of the American Museum of Natural History, vol. 1, part 3. New York: The Trustees.

Krohn, Kaarle L. 1926. Die folkloristische Arbeitsmethode, begründet von Julius Krohn und weitergeführt von nordischen Forschern. Instituttet for sammenlignende Kulturforskning. Serie B 5. Oslo: Aschehoug.

*———. 1971. *Folklore Methodology Formulated by Julius Krohn and Expanded by Nordic Researchers.* Translated by Roger L. Welsch. Publications of the American Folklore Society. Bibliographical and Special Series, 21. Austin and London: The University of Texas Press.

Kryvelev, I. 1961. "Važnaja storona byta" [An important aspect of everyday life]. *Kommunist* 8:65-72.

Kuprijanov, Z. N. 1965. *Èpičeskie pesni nencev* [Epic songs of the Nency]. Moscow: Nauka.

*Kurzweil, Edith. 1980. *The Age of Structuralism. Lévi-Strauss to Foucault.* New York: Columbia University Press.

*Kuznecov, M. [M.], and Dmitrakov, I. [P.] 1948. "Protiv buržuaznyx tradicij v fol'kloristike. (O knige prof. V. Ja. Proppa 'Istoričeskie korni volšebnoj skazki.')" [Against bourgeois traditions in folkloristics. (On Prof. V. Ja. Propp's book *Historical Roots of the Wondertale.*)]. *Sovetskaja ètnografija* 2:230-39.

*Lapointe, François H., and Lapointe, Claire C. 1977. *Claude Lévi-Strauss and His Critics. An International Bibliography of Criticism (1950-1976)*. Followed by a Bibliography of the Writings of Claude Lévi-Strauss. New York and London: Garland.

*Larivaille, Paul. 1974. "L'analyse (morpho)logique du récit." *Poétique* 5:368-88.

*Lazutin, S. 1947. "Restavracija otživšix teorij" [Restoration of dead theories]. *Literaturnaja gazeta*, no. 29 (2344), Saturday, 12 July 1947, p. 3.

*Leach, Edmund R., ed. 1967. *The Structural Study of Myth and Totemism*. London: Tavistock.

*———. 1970. *Levi-Strauss*. Fontana: Collins.

Lenin, V. I. 1961. "On the Question of Dialectics." English translation, V. I. Lenin, *Collected Works*. 4th ed. vol. 38: Philosophical Notebooks, 359-63. London: Lawrence & Wishart; Moscow: Foreign Languages Publishing House. Russian text: V. I. Lenin, *Polnoe sobranie sočinenij* [Collected works]. 5th ed. vol. 29, 316-322. Moscow: Političeskaja literatura, 1963.

———. 1962. "Sed'moj èkstrennyj s''ezd RKP(b) marta 1918" [The seventh extraordinary congress of the RCP(B) March 1918]. In his *Polnoe sobranie sočinenij* [Collected works]. 5th ed. vol. 36, 1-76. Moscow: Političeskaja literatura.

———. 1963. "The Peasant Reform and Proletarian-Peasant Revolution." English translation, V. I. Lenin, *Collected Works*. 4th ed. vol. 17, 119-28. Russian text: V. I. Lenin, *Polnoe sobranie sočinenij* [Collected Works]. 5th ed. vol. 20, 171-80.

Lerner, N. O. 1907. "Primečanija k 'Bove' " [Notes on 'Bova']. In A. S. Pushkin, *Sočinenija*, vol. 1, 202-6. St. Petersburg: Brokgaus-Èfron.

*Levin, Isidor. 1967. "Vladimir Propp: An Evaluation on His Seventieth Birthday." *Journal of the Folklore Institute* (Indiana University) 4:32-49.

Levi-Brjul, L. [The Russian translation of Lévy-Bruhl, Lucien, *Le supernaturel et la nature dans la mentalité primitive*, 1931]. 1937. *Sverx"estestvennoe v pervobytnom myšlenii*. [The supernatural in primitive thought]. Moscow.

Lévi-Strauss, Claude. 1952-53. "Recherches de mythologie américaine (1)." *Annuaire de l'École Pratique des Hautes Études* (Section des Sciences religieuses):19-21.

———. 1953-54. "Recherches de mythologie américaine (2)." *Annuaire de l'École Pratique des Hautes Études* (Section des Sciences religieuses):27-29.

———. 1954-55. "Rapports de la mythologie et du rituel." *Annuaire de l'École Pratique des Hautes Études* (Section des Sciences religieuses):25-28.

———. 1958. *Anthropologie structurale*. Paris: Plon.

———. 1959-60. "Le dualisme dans l'organisation et les représentations religieuses." *Annuaire de l'École Pratique des Hautes Études* (Section des Sciences religieuses):39-42.

———. 1960. "La structure et la forme. Reflexions sur un ouvrage de Vladimir Propp." *Cahiers de l'Institute de Science économique appliquée*. Serie M, No. 7, 1-36. Reprinted in *International Journal of Slavic Linguistics and Poetics* 3 (1960): 122-49, under the title "L'analyse morphologique des contes russes." Its English translation appeared in Claude Lévi-Strauss 1976, 115-45.

*———. 1962. *La Pensée sauvage*. Paris: Plon.

*———. 1964. *Mythologiques 1: Le cru et le cuit*. Paris: Plon.

*———. 1966a. *Mythologiques 2: Du miel aux cendres*. Paris: Plon.

*———. 1966b. *The Savage Mind*. London: Weidenfeld and Nicolson.

*———. 1967. *Structural Anthropology*. Translated from the French by Claire Jacobson and Brooke G. Schoepf. Garden City, New York: Anchor Books, Doubleday. (First published by Basic Books, 1963).

*———. 1968. *Mythologiques 3: L'Origine des Manières de Table*. Paris: Plon.

*———. 1969. *The Raw and the Cooked. Introduction to a Science of Mythology:1*. Translated from the French by John and Doreen Weightman. New York and Evanston: Harper and Row.

*———. 1971. *Mythologiques 4: L'Homme nu*. Paris: Plon.

*———. 1973a. *Anthropologie structurale II*. Paris: Plon.

*———. 1973b. *From Honey to Ashes. Introduction to a Science of Mythology: 2*. Translated from the French by John and Doreen Weightman. New York, Evanston, San Francisco: Harper and Row.

*———. 1976. *Structural Anthropology. Volume 2.* Translated from the French by Monique Layton. New York: Basic Books.

*———. 1978. *The Origin of Table Manners. Introduction to a Science of Mythology: 3.* Translated from the French by John and Doreen Weightman. New York, Hagerstown, San Francisco: Harper and Row.

*———. 1979. "Sur S/Z." In Raymond Bellour and Catherine Clément, eds., *Claude Lévi-Strauss. Textes de et sur Claude Lévi-Strauss*, 495-97. Paris: Gallimard.

———. 1981. *The Naked Man. Introduction to a Science of Mythology: 4.* Translated from the French by John and Doreen Weightman. New York: Harper and Row.

Lévy-Bruhl. *See* Levi-Brjul.

Leyen, Friedrich von der. 1899. *Das Märchen in der Göttersagen der Edda.* Berlin: G. Reimer.

*Liberman, A[natoly] S. 1968. [Review] S. D. Kacnel'son, *Sravnitel'naja akcentologija germanskix jazykov* [A comparative Germanic accentology]. *Voprosy jazykoznanija* 2:124-31.

*———. Forthcoming. "Between Myth and the Wondertale." *Papers from the Symposium "Myth in Literature" Held at New York University on November 13-15, 1981.* New York University.

Liljeblad, Sven. 1927. *Die Tobiasgechichte und andere Märchen mit toten Helfern.* Lund: P. Lindstedts Univ.-bokhandel.

*Lima, Luiz C. 1968. *O estruturalismo de Lévi-Strauss.* Coleção Nosso tempo 6. Petrópolis, RJ: Vozes.

Lixačëv, D. S. 1953. "Narodnoe poètičeskoe tvorčestvo vremeni rascveta drevnerusskogo rannefeodal'nogo gosudarstva" [Folk poetry at the height of the Old Russian early feudal state]. In V. P. Adrianova-Peretc, ed., *Russkoe narodnoe poètičeskoe tvorčestvo*, vol. 1: *Očerki po istorii russkogo narodnogo poètičeskogo tvorčestva X—načala XVIII veka*, 141-216. Leningrad: Akademija nauk SSSR.

———. 1958. *Čelovek v literature drevnej Rusi* [Man in the literature of ancient Rus']. Moscow and Leningrad: Akademija nauk SSSR.

*Lopatin, Ivan A. 1951. "What the People are Now Singing in a Russian Village." *Journal of American Folklore* 64:179-90.

Lotman, Ju. M. 1963. "O razgraničenii lingvističeskogo i literaturovedčeskogo ponjatija struktury" [On delimiting the linguistic and literary concepts of structure]. *Voprosy jazykoznanija* 3:44-52.

*———. 1968. *Lektsii po struktural'noi poètike. Vvedenie, teoriia stikha.* Brown University Slavic Reprint 5. Providence, Rhode Island: Brown University Press. (First published as Trudy po znakovym sistemam 1. Učenye zapiski Tartuskogo gosudarstvennogo universiteta, vol. 160, 1964.)

*———. 1976. "O. M. Freidenberg as a Student of Culture." In Henryk Baran, ed. *Semiotics and Structuralism. Readings from the Soviet Union.* White Plains, New York: International Arts and Sciences Press, 257-68. (First published in Russian in 1973; see Trudy po znakovym sistemam 6. Učenye zapiski Tartuskogo gosudarstvennogo universiteta, vol. 308, 482-87.)

*Lüthi, Max. 1973a. Review of Propp 1972. *Zeitschrift für Volkskunde* 69:290-93.

Lur'e, S. Ja. 1932. "Dom v lesu" [The house in the forest]. *Jazyk i literatura* 8:159-95.

*———. 1973b. "Morphologie des Volksmärchens." *Neue Züricher Zeitung.* Sunday, 21 October (1973), no. 488, p. 50.

*———. 1974. *Das europäische Volksmärchen. Form und Wesen.* 4th ed., pp. 115-21. Munich: Francke. The English version of this book is Max Lüthi, *The European Folktale: form and nature.* Translated by John D. Niles. Philadelphia: The Institute for the Study of Human Issues, 1982 (pp. 126-33: Supplement: Structural Folktale Scholarship. Value of the achievement of Vladimir Propp).

Mackensen, Lutz. 1923. *Der singende Knochen. Ein Beitrag zur vergleichenden Märchenforschung.* Folklore Fellows Communications no. 49. Helsinki: Suomalainen tiedeakatemia.

Majkov, L. N. 1863. *O bylinax Vladimirskogo cikla. Issledovanie.* [The bylinas of the Vladimir cycle. A study]. St. Petersburg.

*Makarius, Raoul and Laura. 1973. *Structuralisme ou ethnologie. Pour une critique radicale de l'anthropologie de Lévi-Strauss.* Paris: Anthropos.

Malyšev, V. I. 1956. *Povest' o Suxane. Iz istorii russkoj povesti XVII veka* [The Tale of Suxan. From the history of the Russian tale (*povest'*) in the seventeenth century]. Moscow and Leningrad: Akademija nauk SSSR.

Mannhardt, Wilhelm. 1858. *Germanische Mythen.* Berlin: Schneider.

——. 1884. *Mythologische Forschungen aus dem Nachlasse von Wilhelm Mannhardt.* Quellen und Forschungen zur Sprach- und Kulturgeschichte der Germanischen Völker, vol. 51. Strassburg: K. J. Trübner.

*Maranda, Pierre, ed. 1974. *Soviet Structural Folkloristics.* The Hague, Paris: Mouton.

*Marc-Lipiansky, Mireille. 1973. *Le structuralisme de Lévi-Strauss.* Paris: Payot.

*Marr, N. Ja. 1928. *Jafetičeskaja teorija. Programma obščego kursa ob jazyke* [Japhetic theory. Syllabus of a course in general linguistics]. Baku: Azgiz.

*——, ed. 1932. *Tristan i Isol'da. Ot geroini ljubvi feodal'noj Evropy do bogini matriarxal'noj Afrevrazii. Kollektivnyj trud Sektora semantiki mifa i fol'klora pod redakciej akademika N. Ja. Marra* [Tristan and Isolda. From the goddess of love in feudal Europe to a goddess of the matriarchal Afro-Eurasia. A collective work by the Sector of the semantics of myth and folklore. Academician N. Ja. Marr, editor]. Trudy Instituta jazyka i myšlenija Akademii nauk SSSR, 2. Leningrad: Akademija nauk SSSR.

Marx, Karl. 1962. Preface to ''The Critique of Political Economy.'' In Karl Marx and Friedrich Engels, *Selected Works in Two Volumes,* vol. 1. 5th impression. Moscow. Russian text ''Predislovie. K kritike političeskoj èkonomii.'' In K. Marx and F. Engels, *Sočinenija* [Works], 2nd ed. vol. 13, 5-9. Moscow: Političeskaja literatura, 1959. German text: ''Vorwort. Zur Kritik der politischen Oekonomie.'' In Karl Marx, Friedrich Engles, *Werke,* vol. 13, 7-11. Berlin: Dietz, 1974.

*Maybury-Lewis, David. 1970. ''Science or bricolage?'' In Hayes, E. Nelson, and Hayes, Tanya, 1970, 150-63. (Originally published in *American Anthropologist* 71 [1969]:114-21.)

Megas, G. A. 1964. ''Referat über Wesen und Einteilungssystem der griechischen Sagen.'' In Ortutay 93-95.

Meier, John. 1926. *Deutsche Volkskunde.* Berlin and Leipzig: W. de Gruyter.

*de Meijer, P. W. M. 1970. ''Eenvoudige vertelstructuren: Propp en Lévi-Strauss.'' *Forum der letteren* 11:145-59.

*——. ed. 1982a. *Russian Literature, XII-I. Special Issue. Developments of the Theory of Literature III. Propp in Italy.* Amsterdam: North-Holland Publishing Company.

*——. 1982b. ''Propp in Italy.'' In de Meijer 1982a, 1-10.

*Meletinskij, E. M. 1956. Review of Propp 1955. Izvestija Otdelenija literatury i jazyka Akademii nauk SSSR, vol. 15, 178-82.

*——. 1969. ''Strukturno-tipologičeskoe izučenie skazki'' [A structural-typological study of the wondertale]. Supplement to Propp 1969, 134-66. (In English in *Genre* 4 (1971):249-79. Translated by Robin Dietrich and in Maranda 1974, 19-51.)

*——. 1976a. *Poètika mifa* [The poetics of myth]. Moscow: Nauka, Glavnaja redakcija vostočnoj literatury.

*——. 1976b. ''Perspectives et limites de l'étude structurale du folklore.'' In Pentikäinen:94-102.

*Meletinskij, E. M., and Nekljudov, S. Ju., eds. 1975. *Tipologičeskie issledovanija po fol'kloru. Sbornik statej pamjati Vladimira Jakovleviča Proppa (1895-1970).* [Typological studies in folklore. V. Ja. Propp in memoriam]. Moscow: Nauka.

Mercklin, Ludwig. 1851. *Die Talos-Sage und das sardonische Lachen.* Sonderdruck aus Mémoires des savants étrangers de l'Academie des Sciences de St. Petersbourg, vol. 7. St. Petersburg: [Akademija nauk].

Mikušev, A. K. 1960. ''O vneobrjadovyx improvizacijax (na materiale trudovyx improvizacij naroda Komi)'' [Extraritual improvisations (on data from Komi improvisations at work)]. Russkij fol'klor, vol. 5. Materialy i issledovanija, 144-56. Moscow and Leningrad: Akademija nauk SSSR.

Miller, O. F. 1869. [1870]. *Sravnitel'no-kritičeskie nabljudenija nad sloevym sostavom narodnogo russkogo èposa: Il'ja Muromec i bogatyrstvo kievskoe* [Comparative-critical observations of the strata in Russian folk epic poetry: Ilja Muromec and the warriors of Kiev]. St. Petersburg.

*Moravia, Sergio. 1969. *La ragione nascosta. Scienza e filosofia nel pensiero di Claude Lévi-Strauss.* Florence: Sansoni.

*Mounin, Georges. 1970. *Introduction à la semiologie.* Paris: Minuit. (The chapter "Lévi-Strauss et la linguistique," pp. 199-214, written in 1969, was translated into English under the title "Lévi-Strauss' Use of Linguistics," in Rossi 1974, pp. 31-52, and published with comments by Marschal Durbin, pp. 53-59.)

Nagiškin, D. 1957. *Skazka i žizn': Pis'ma o skazke* [The folktale and life: letters about the folktale]. Moscow: Detgiz.

Nansen, Fridtjof. 1894. *Eskimo Life.* 2nd ed. London and New York: Longmans, Green. Norwegian title: *Eskimoliv.* Kristiania: H. Aschehoug & Co., 1891.

*Nathhorst, Bertel G. 1969a. "Reply to Ulf Drobin's Criticism." *Temenos* 5:213-19.

*———. 1969b. *Formal or Structural Studies of Traditional Tales. The Usefulness of Some Methodological Proposals Advanced by Vladimir Propp, Alan Dundes, Claude Lévi-Strauss and Edmund Leach.* Translated by Donald Burton. Stockholm Studies in Comparative Religion, 9. Stockholm: Almqvist and Wiksell.

Neuhauss, Richard. 1911. *Deutsch-Neu-Guinea,* vol. 3. *Beiträge der Missionäre* [*Ch.*] *Keysser, Stolz, Zahn, Lehner, Bamler . . .* Berlin: D. Reimer (E. Vohsen).

Nikiforov, A. I. 1926. Review of *Kaiser und Abt* by Walter Anderson. *Izvestija Otdelenija russkogo jazyka i slovesnosti Akademii nauk SSSR,* vol. 31, 353-61.

*———. 1928. "K voprosu o morfologičeskom izučenii narodnoj skazki" [Concerning a morphological study of the folktale]. *Sbornik statej v čest' akademika A. I. Sobolevskogo.* Sbornik Otdelenija russkogo jazyka i slovesnosti Akademii nauk SSSR, vol. 101 (3), 173-78. (In English in *Linguistica Biblica* 27/28 (1973):25-35, translated and with an introduction by Heda Jason, and in Oinas and Soudakoff 1975, 155-61.) See a photocopy of the *Sbornik*: Russian Reprint Series, 4. The Hague: Europe Printing (1965).

———. 1934. "Finskaja škola pered krizisom" [The crisis of the Finnish school]. *Sovetskaja ètnografija* 4, 141-44.

Nilsson, Martin P. 1935. "Die eleusinischen Gottheiten," *Archiv für Religionswissenschaft* 32:79-142.

Norden, Eduard. 1924. *Die Geburt des Kindes: Geschichte einer religiösen Idee.* Leipzig: B. G. Teubner. (Reprinted Stuttgart: B. G. Teubner, 1958.)

*Nosova, G[alina]. 1964a. Review of Propp 1963. *Sovetskaja ètnografija* 1:176-78.

*———. 1964b. Review of Propp 1963. *Deutsches Jahrbuch für Volkskunde* 10:196-99.

Novikov, I. N., ed. 1938. *Fol'klor naroda Komi* [Komi folklore], vol. 1. Predanija i skazki [Legends and folktales]. Arxangel'sk: Ogiz-Arxoblgiz.

Očerki narodno-poètičeskogo tvorčestva sovetskoj èpoxi 1952. [Studies of the folklore of the Soviet period]. Moscow and Leningrad: Akademija nauk SSSR.

Oecolampadius, Joannes. 1518. *De risu paschali, Oecolampadii, ad V. Capitonem theologum epistola apologetica.* Basel.

*Oinas, Felix J. 1961. "Folklore Activities in Russia." *Journal of American Folklore* 74:362-70.

*———. 1971a. V. Ja. Propp (1895-1970). *Journal of American Folklore* 84:338-40.

*———. 1971b. "The Problem of the Aristocratic Origin of Russian *Byliny.*" *Slavic Review* 30:513-22.

*———. 1973. "Folklore and Politics in the Soviet Union." *Slavic Review* 32:45-58.

*———. 1976. "The Problem of the Notion of Soviet Folklore." In Dégh, Linda et al. 1976, 379-97.

*———. 1978a. "The Political Uses and Themes of Folklore in the Soviet Union. In Oinasb:77-95.

———, ed. 1978b. *Folklore, Nationalism, and Politics.* Indiana University Folklore Institute Monograph Series 30. Columbus, Ohio: Slavica Publishers.

*Oinas, Felix J., and Soudakoff, Stephen, ed. and trans. 1975. *The Study of Russian Folklore.* Slavistic Printings and Reprintings. Indiana University Textbook Series 4. Indiana University Folklore Institute Monograph Series 25. The Hague, Paris: Mouton.

Oncukov, N. E. 1909. *Severnye skazki* [Northern folktales]. Zapiski Imperatorskogo russkogo geograficeskogo obscestva po otdeleniju ètnografii, vol. 33. St. Petersburg: A. S. Suvorin.

*Oppitz, Michael. 1975. Notwendige Beziehungen—Abriß der strukturalen Anthropologie. Wissenschaft 101. Frankfurt am Main: Suhrkamp.

Ortutay, Gyula, ed. 1964. Tagung der Sagenkommission der International Society for Folk-Narrative Research. Budapest, 14.-16. Oktober 1963. *Acta Ethnographica Academiae Scientarum Hungaricae* 13 (1-4):1-131.

Panzer, Friedrich W. 1905. *Märchen, Sage und Dichtung.* Munich: Beck.

*Parret, Herman. 1974. *Discussing Language. Dialogues with Wallace L. Chafe, Noam Chomsky, Algirdas J. Greimas, M. A. K. Halliday, Peter Hartmann, George Lakoff, Sydney M. Lamb, André Martinet, James McCawley, Sebastian K. Šaumjan, and Jacques Bouveress.* Janua Linguarum. Series Maior 93. The Hague and Paris:Mouton.

*Pasternak, Boris. 1981. *Perepiska s Ol'goj Freudenberg* [Correspondence with Olga Freidenberg]. Edited with a Commentary by Elliott Mossmann. An original Harvest/HBJ Book. A Helen and Kurt Wolff Book. New York and London: Harcourt Brace Jovanovich.

*Paz, Octavio. 1975. *Claude Lévi-Strauss o el nuevo festín de Esopo.* 4th ed. México: Mortiz. (First edition 1967.) (In English *Claude Lévi-Strauss; an introduction.* Tr. by J. S. and Maxine Bernstein. Ithaca: Cornell Univ. Press, 1970.)

*Pentikäinen—Pentikäinen, Juha, and Juurikka, Tuula, eds. 1976. *Folk Narrative Research. Some Papers Presented at the VI Congress of the International Society for Folk Narrative Research.* Studia Fennica 20. Helsinki: Suomalaisen Kirjallisuuden Seura.

*Peretc, Volodimir. 1930. "Nova metoda vivčati kazki" [A new method in the study of the folktale]. *Etnografičnij visnik* 9:187-95.

*Petrov, Viktor. 1936. "Buržuaznaja fol'kloristika i problema stadial'nosti" [Bourgeois folkloristics and the problem of stadialism]. *Sovetskij fol'klor* 2-3:31-49.

Pliny the Elder. 1947. *Natural History.* With an English translation by H. Rackham. Vol. 2. Books III-VII. [The Loeb Classical Library]. Cambridge, Mass.: Harvard University Press; London: William Heinemann, Ltd.

*Pliseckij, M. M. 1960. [Comments on V. Ja. Propp's paper at the Fourth International Congress of Slavicists]. Russkij fol'klor, vol. 5. Materialy i issledovanija, 319-21. Moscow and Leningrad: Akademija nauk SSSR.

———. 1962. *Istorizm russkix bylin* [The historicity of Russian bylinas]. Moscow: Vysšaja škola.

Polívka, Jiří. 1904. *Pohádkoslovné studie* [Folklore studies]. Narodopisný sborník československský, vol. 10, no. 2: 67-106. Prague: Nákladem Společnosti národopisného muzea československého.

———. 1924. "Čichám človččinu—ruský dech, ruskou 'kost' " Narodopisný sborník československský 17: 3-19. Prague: Nákladem Společnosti národopisného muzea československého.

*Pomeranceva, E. V. 1975. *Mifologičeskie personaži v russkom fol'klore* [Mythological personages in Russian folklore]. Moscow: Nauka.

*Poole, Roger. 1970. "Structures and Materials." *20th Century Studies* 3:6-30.

Potanin, G. N. 1899. *Vostočnye motivy v srednevekovom evropejskom èpose* [Oriental motifs in the European epic poetry of the Middle Ages]. Moscow: Geografičeskoe otdelenie Imperatorskogo obščestva ljubitelej estestvoznanija, antropologii i ètnografii.

Pourová, Libuše. 1963. "Die Katalogisierung der tschechischen Volksagen." *Demos* 325, cols. 234-37.

Propp, Vladimir. 1927. "Morfologija russkoj volšebnoj skazki" [Morphology of the Russian wondertale]. In S. F. Ol'denburg, ed. *Skazočnaja komissija v 1926 g. Obzor rabot.* Leningrad: Gosudarstvennoe russkoe geografičeskoe obščestvo. Otdelenie ètnografii, 48-49.

———. 1928a. *Morfologija skazki* [Morphology of the folktale]. Gosudarstvennyj Institut istorii iskusstv. Voprosy poètiki, vol. 12. Leningrad: Academia.

———. 1928b. "Transformacija volšebnyx skazok" [Transformations of the wondertale]. In *Poètika. Vremennik otdela slovesnyx iskusstv. Gosudarstvennogo instituta istorii iskusstv* 4, 70-89. Leningrad: Academia. (All five volumes of *Poètika* reprinted as Slavische Propyläen 104. Munich: Wilhelm Fink, 1970, with the original pagination.)

———. 1934. "K voprosu o proisxoždenii volšebnoj skazki. (Volšebnoe derevo na mogile)" [On the origin of the wondertale. (A magic tree on the grave)]. *Sovetskaja ètnografija* 1-2:128-51.

———. 1939a. "Mužskoj dom v russkoj skazke" [Men's house in the Russian wondertale]. Učenye zapiski Leningradskogo gosudarstvennogo universiteta, vol. 20. Serija filologičeskix nauk 1:174-98.

———. 1939b. "Ritual'nyj smex v fol'klore. (Po povodu skazki o Nesmejane)" [Ritual laughter in folklore. (A propos of the tale of the princess who would not laugh—Nesmejana)]. Učenye zapiski Leningradskogo gosudarstvennogo universiteta, vol. 46. Serija filologičeskix nauk 3:151-75.

———. 1941. "Motiv čudesnogo roždenija" [The motif of miraculous birth]. Učenye zapiski Leningradskogo gosudarstvennogo universiteta, vol. 81. Serija filologičeskix nauk 12:67-97.

———. 1944. "Èdip v svete fol'klora" [Oedipus in light of folklore]. Učenye zapiski Leningradskogo gosudarstvennogo universiteta, vol. 72. Serija filologičeskix nauk 9:138-75. (Reprinted in Propp 1976a, 258-99.)

———. 1946a. *Istoričeskie korni volšebnoj skazki* [Historical roots of the wondertale]. Leningrad: Leningradskij gosudarstvennyj universitet.

———. 1946b. "Specifika fol'klora" [The nature of folklore]. *Trudy jubilejnoj naučnoj sessii Leningradskogo gosudarstvennogo universiteta. Sekcija filologičeskix nauk*, 138-51. Leningrad: Leningradskij gosudarstvennyj universitet.

———. 1949. *Le radici storiche dei racconti di fate.* Turin: Einaudi. (2nd ed. Boringhiere, 1972).

———. 1955. *Russkij geroičeskij èpos* [Russian heroic epic poetry]. Leningrad: Leningradskij gosudarstvennyj universitet.

———. 1958a. *Morphology of the Folktale.* Edited with an introduction by Svatava Pirkova-Jakobson. Translated by Laurence Scott. Indiana University Research Center in Anthropology, Folklore, and Linguistics, Publication 10. Bloomington, Indiana. International Journal of American Linguistics 24 (4). Bibliographical and Special Series of the American Folklore Society 9. Philadelphia.

———. 1958b. *Russkij geroičeskij èpos* [Russian heroic epic poetry]. 2nd ed. Moscow: Xudožestvennaja literatura.

———. 1961. "O russkoj narodnoj liričeskoj pesne" [On the Russian lyric folksong]. In *Narodnye liričeskie pesni.* Leningrad: Sovetskij pisatel'.

———. 1963a. *Russkie agrarnye prazdniki* [Russian agrarian festivals]. Leningrad: Leningradskij gosudarstvennyj universitet.

———. 1963b. "Fol'klor i dejstvitel'nost'" [Folklore and reality]. *Russkaja literatura* 3:62-84.

———. 1963c. "Pjotr Dmitrievič Uxov. Nekrolog" [P. D. Uxov. An obituary]. *Naučnye doklady vysšej školy. Filologičeskie nauki* 2:241-42.

———. 1964. "Principy klassifikacii fol'klornyx žanrov" [The principles of classifying folklore genres]. *Sovetskaja ètnografija* 4:147-54.

———. 1966a. "Struttura e storia nello studio della favola." In *Morfologia della fiaba. Con un intervento di Claude Lévi-Strauss e una replica dell' autore.* 201-27. Turin: Einaudi.

———. 1966b. "Trudy akademika Iv. Iv. Tolstogo po fol'kloru" [The works of Academician I. I. Tolstoj on folklore]. In: I. I. Tolstoj, *Stat'i o fol'klore* [Papers on folklore]. 3-16. Moscow and Leningrad: Nauka.

———. 1968a. *Morphology of the Folktale.* 2nd ed., revised and edited with a preface by Louis A. Wagner. New Introduction by Alan Dundes. American Folklore Society. Bibliographical and Special Series 9. Austin and London: University of Texas Press, 1975: 4th printing.

———. 1968b. "Ob istorizme russkogo fol'klora i metodax ego izučenija" [On the historicity of Russian folklore and on the methods of folkloristics]. Učenye zapiski Leningradskogo gosudarstvennogo universiteta, vol. 339. Serija filologičeskix nauk 72:5-72.

——. 1969. *Morfologija skazki* [Morphology of the folktale]. 2nd ed. Moscow: Nauka, Glavnaja redakcija vostočnoj literatury.

——. 1970. Morfologia basmului. Translated by Radu Nicolau. Bucharest: Univers.

——. 1971a. "Fairy tale transformations". Translated by C. H. Severens. In Ladislav Matejka and Krystyna Pomorska, *Readings in Russian Poetics: Formalist and Structuralist views*, 99-114. Cambridge, Mass. M.I.T. Press. (Pierre Maranda included an abridged version of this article in his *Mythology. Selected Readings*, 139-50. Penguin Education 1972, which was translated from the 1965 French translation by Petra Morrison; the Russian title is reproduced with two mistakes.)

——. 1971b. "Generic Structures in Russian Folklore." Translated by Maria Zagorska Brooks. *Genre* 4:211-48.

——. 1972. *Morphologie des Märchens*. Translated by Christel Wendt, edited by Karl Eimermacher. Münich: Carl Hanser.

——. 1975a. See Propp 1968a. (A reprint.)

——. 1975b. See Reeder, Roberta 1975.

——. 1975c. *Edipo alla luce del folclore. Quattro studi di etnografia storico-strutturale*. (Nuovo politecnico 73.) Turin: Einaudi.

——. 1976a. *Fol'klor i dejstvitel'nost'. Izbrannye stat'i*. [Folklore and reality. Selected papers]. Moscow: Nauka, Glavnaja redakcija vostočnoj literatury.

——. 1976b. *Problemy komizma i smexa* [Problems of laughter and the comic]. Moscow: Iskusstvo.

——. 1976c. "Study of the Folktale: Structure and History." *Dispositio* 1: 277-92. (Preceded by Shishkoff 1976.)

——. 1983. "Oedipus in Light of Folklore." In Lowell Edmond and Alan Dundes, eds., *Oedipus: A Folklore Casebook*. New York: Garland, 76-121.

Putilov, B. N. 1956. "O nekotoryx problemax izučenija istoričeskoj pesni" [Several problems in the study of historical songs]. Russkij fol'klor, vol. 1. Materialy i issledovanija, 63-78. Moscow and Leningrad: Akademija nauk SSSR.

——. 1960. *Russkij istoriko-pesennyj fol'klor XIII—XVI vekov* [Russian historical folk songs of the thirteenth through sixteenth centuries]. Moscow and Leningrad: Akademija nauk SSSR.

——, ed. 1962. *Narodnye istoričeskie pesni* [Historical folk songs]. Biblioteka poèta. Bol'šaja serija. Moscow and Leningrad: Sovetskij pisatel'.

*——. 1966. "Ob istorizme russkix bylin" [On the historicity of Russian bylinas]. Russkij fol'klor, vol. 10. Specifika fol'klornyx žanrov, 103-26. Moscow and Leningrad: Nauka.

*——. 1971. "Vtoroe roždenie knigi" [The second birth of the book]. *Voprosy literatury* 3:201-206.

Putilov, B. N., and Dobrovol'skij, B. M. 1960. *Istoričeskie pesni XIII—XVI vekov* [Historical songs of the thirteenth through sixteenth centuries]. Moscow and Leningrad: Akademija nauk SSSR.

Radermacher, Ludwig. 1906. "Walfischmythen." *Archiv für Religionswissenschaft* 9:248-52.

Rădulescu, Nicolae. 1961. Summary of *Antologie folclorică din ţinutul Pădurenilor (Hunedoara)*. *Demos* 152, cols. 92-93.

Rasmussen, Knud. 1922. *Grönlandsagen*. Berlin: Gyldendal.

*Reaver, Russell J. 1959. [Review] Propp 1958a. *Midwest Folklore* 9, 115-16.

*Reeder, Roberta, trans. 1975. *Down Along the Mother Volga. An Anthology of Russian Folk Lyrics, With an Introductory Essay by V. Ja. Propp*. Philadelphia: University of Pennsylvania Press.

*Régnier, André. 1971. "De la morphologie selon V. I. Propp à la notion de système préinterprétatif." *L'homme et la société* 22:171-89. (Reprinted in Régnier 1974:211-34.)

*——. 1974. *La crise du langage scientifique*. Paris: Anthropos.

Reinach, Salomon. 1912. "Le rire rituel." In his *Cultes, Mythes et Religions*, vol. 4, 109-29. Paris: E. Leroux. (Reprinted from *Revue de l'Université du Bruxelles*, mai 1911, 585-602.)

*Revzin, I. I. 1975. "K obščesemiotičeskomu istolkovaniju trjox postulatov Proppa (analiz skazki i teorija svjaznosti teksta)'' [Toward a semiotic interpretation of three postulates of Propp (analysis of the wondertale and theory of the coherence of the text)]. In Meletinskij and Nekljudov 1975, 77-91.

*Ricœur, Paul. 1976. *Interpretation Theory: Discourse and the Surplus of Meaning*. Fort Worth, Texas: The Texas Christian University Press.

Rimskij-Korsakov, N. A. 1909. *Letopis' moej muzykal'noj žizni*. St. Petersburg: Glazunov. English translation: *My Musical Life*. New York: A. A. Knopf, 1942.

RNPT (Russkoe narodnoe poètičeskoe tvorčestvo). [Russian poetic folklore]. 1953-56. 2 vols. in 3 books. Moscow and Leningrad: Akademija nauk SSSR.

Robinson, A. N. 1951. ''Fol'klor'' [Folklore]. In Voronina, N. N., and Karger, M. K., eds. *Istorija kul'tury drevnej Rusi*, vol. 2. *Domongol'skij period. Obščestvennyj stroj i duxovnaja kul'tura*, 139-62. Moscow and Leningrad: Akademija nauk SSSR.

*Røder, Viggo. 1970. ''Om Propp's 'Morphology of the Folktale.' '' *Poetik* 3:21-33.

Röhrich, L. 1956. *Märchen und Wirklichkeit: Eine volkstümliche Untersuchung*. Wiesbaden: F. Steiner.

Rossi, Ino, ed. 1974. *The Unconscious in Culture. The Structuralism of Claude Lévi-Strauss in Perspective*. New York: Dutton.

*Rozanov, I. N. 1975. ''From Book to Folklore.'' In Oinas and Soudakoff, 65-75.

Rubcov, F. 1962. *Intonacionnye svjazi v pesennom tvorčestve slavjanskix narodov* [Intonational relations in Slavic folk songs]. Leningrad: Sovetskij kompozitor.

Rybakov, B. A. 1963. *Drevnjaja Rus': skazanija, byliny, letopisi*. [Ancient Rus': legends, byliny, chronicles]. Moscow: Akademija nauk SSSR.

Rybnikov, P. N. 1910. *Pesni, sobrannye P. N. Rybnikovym* [Songs collected by P. N. Rybnikov]. 2nd ed. vol. 2. Moscow: Sotrudnik škol.

*Saintyves, P. 1923. *Les contes de Perrault et les récits parallèles. Leur origines (coutumes primitives et liturgies populaires)*. Paris: Émile Nourry.

Šambinago, S. K. 1905. ''K bylinnoj istorii starin o Vo'lge-Volxe Vseslaviče'' [Concerning the bylina tale of Vol'ga-Volx Vseslavič.] *Žurnal Ministerstva narodnogo prosveščenija* 11 [vol. 362, November], section 2, 131-49.

*Šarypkin, D. M. 1973. 'Rek Bojan i Xodyna . . . ' ['Quoth Bojan and Xodyna . . . '] Skandinavskij sbornik 18, 195-201. Tallinn: Eesti raamat. (With summaries in Swedish and Estonian.)

*Schlauch, Margaret. 1944. ''Folklore in the Soviet Union.'' *Science and Society* 8:205-22.

Schmidt, J. P. 1847. *De risu paschali*. Rostock.

*Schmidt, Johannes. 1872. *Die Verwandtschaftsverhältnisse der indogermanischen Sprachen*. Weimar: Böhlau.

Schmidt, P. W. 1907. ''Die geheime Jünglingsweihe der Karesau Insulaner (Deutsch-Neuguinea): Nach den Mitteilungen des Karesau-Insulaners Bonifaz Tamatai Pritak.'' *Anthropos* 2, part 6.

*Scholte, Bob. 1969. ''Lévi-Strauss' Penelopean Effort: The Analysis of Myths.'' *Semiotica* 1:99-124.

*Schröder, Franz R. 1941. *Skadi und die Götter Skandinaviens*. Untersuchungen zur germanischen und vergleichenden Religionsgeschichte 2. Tübingen: J. C. B. Mohr.

Senkevič-Gudkova, V. V. 1960. ''Èlementy improvizacii i tradicionnost' na rannej stadii razvitija fol'klora (na materiale pesennoj liriki kol'skix saamov)'' [Improvisational and traditional elements at the early stage of the development of folklore (on data from the lyric songs of the Kola Lapps)]. Russkij fol'klor, vol. 5. Materialy i issledovanija, 127-45. Moscow and Leningrad: Akademija nauk SSSR.

*Serebrjanyj, S. D. 1966. ''Interpretacija 'formuly' V. Ja. Proppa'' [An interpretation of Propp's ''formula'']. *Tezisy dokladov vo vtoroj letnej škole po vtoričnym modelirujuščim sistemam, 16—29 avgusta 1966*, 92-95. Tartu: Tartuskij gosudarstvennyj universitet.

*———. 1975. ''Interpretacija formuly V. Ja. Proppa (v svjazi s ee priloženiem k indijskim skazkam)'' [An interpretation of Propp's formula (a propos of Indian fairy tales)]. In Meletinskij and Nekludov, pp. 293-302.

*Shalvey, Thomas. 1979. *Claude Lévi-Strauss. Social Psychotherapy and the Collective Unconscious.* Amherst: The University of Massachusetts Press.

*Shishkoff, Serge. 1976. "The Structure of Fairytales: Propp vs. Lévi-Strauss." *Dispositio* 1:271-76.

*Shukman, Ann. 1976. "The Legacy of Propp." *Essays in Poetics* (Keele, England) 1:82-94.

*———. 1977a. "Russian Formalism: A Bibliography of Translations and Commentaries. (Works in English, French, German and Italian.)" Russian Poetics in Translations 4. Formalist Theory. Oxford: University of Essex and Holdan Books, 100-8.

*———. 1977b. *Literature and Semiotics. A study of the writings of Ju. M. Lotman.* Meaning and Art. A series of books on poetics, theory of literature and related fields, vol. 1. Amsterdam, New York, Oxford: North-Holland Publishing Company.

*Simonis, Yvan. 1968. *Claude Lévi-Strauss ou La "Passion de L'Inceste": Introduction au structuralisme.* Paris: Aubier, Editions Montaigne.

Simonsuuri, Lauri. 1961. *Typen- und Motivverzeichnis der finnischen mythischen Sagen.* Folklore Fellows Communications no. 182. Helsinki: Suomalainen tiedeakatemia.

Simrock, Karl J. 1882. *Die Edda.* 8th edn. Stuttgart: J. G. Cotta.

Širjaeva, P. G., and Kravčinskaja, V. A. 1948. "Dve byliny v zapisjax konca XVII-XVIII vv." [Two bylinas in recordings from the end of the seventeenth and the beginning of the eighteenth centuries]. Trudy Otdela drevnerusskoj literatury Akademii nauk SSSR 6, 338-71.

Sirovátka, Oldřich. 1962. "Jak katalogisovat textové varianty lidových písní?" [How does one catalogue textual variants of folk songs?] Summary in *Demos* 126, cols. 89-90. (Originally published in *Radostná země* 10 [1960]: 47-107.)

———. 1964. "Zur Morphologie der Sage und Sagenkatalogisierung." In Ortutay 99-106.

Sittl, Karl. 1890. *Die Gebärden der Griechen und Römer.* Leipzig: Teubner. (Reprinted in 1970.)

Skaftymov, A. P. 1924. *Poètika i genezis bylin* [The poetics and genesis of bylinas]. Moscow and Saratov: V. Z. Jaksanov.

*Skeels, Dell. 1967. "Two Psychological Patterns Underlying the Morphologies of Propp and Dundes." *Southern Folklore Quarterly* 31:244-61.

Smirnov, A. M. 1917. *Sbornik velikorusskix skazok Arxiva Russkogo geografičeskogo obščestva* [Collection of Great Russian folktales in the archive of the Russian geographical society]. 2 parts. Zapiski Russkogo geografičeskogo obščestva po otdeleniju ètnografii, vol. 44.

*Snorri Sturluson. 1964. *The Prose Edda of Snorri Sturluson: Tales from Norse Mythology.* . . . Trans. Jean I. Young. Berkeley and Los Angeles: University of California Press.

Sobolevskij, A. I. 1895-1902. *Velikorusskie narodnye pesni* [Great Russian folk songs]. 7 vols. St. Petersburg: Gosudarstvennaja tipografija.

Sokolov, B. M. 1923. "Èpičeskie skazanija o ženit'be knjazja Vladimira (germano-russkie otnošenija v oblasti èposa)" [Epic legends of the marriage of Prince Vladimir (Germano-Russian relations in epic poetry)]. Učenye zapiski Saratovskogo universiteta 1, no. 3, 69-122.

———. 1926, 1927. "Byliny starinnoj zapisi" [Old recordings of bylinas]. *Ètnografija* 1926, no. 1-2; 1927.

*Sokolov, Ju. M. 1941. *Russkij fol'klor* [Russian folklore]. Moscow: Učpedgiz. (In English: Y. M. Sokolov, *Russian Folklore.* Translated by Catherine R. Smith. New York: Macmillan, 1950. Reprinted, with an introduction and bibliography by Felix J. Oinas. Hatboro, Pa.: Folklore Associates, 1966.)

*Sokolova, V. K. 1948. "Diskussii po voprosam fol'kloristiki na zasedanijax sektora fol'klora Instituta ètnografii" [Discussions of the problems of folkloristics in the Sector of Folklore at the Institute of Ethnography]. *Sovetskaja ètnografija* 3, 139-146.

*Šor, R. O. 1928. Review of Propp 1928. Pečat' i revoljucija 7:192-93.

Speranskij, M. N. 1917. *Russkaja ustnaja slovesnost'* [Russian oral literature]. Moscow: Mixajlov. (Reprinted as Slavistic Printings and Reprintings, 182. The Hague: Mouton, 1969).

Spiess, Karl. 1917. *Das deutsche Volksmärchen.* (Aus Natur und Geisteswelt 587). Leipzig and Berlin: Teubner.

*Steblin-Kamenskij, M. I. 1971. *Mir sagi* [The world of the saga]. Leningrad: Nauka. (In English:

The Saga Mind. Translated from the Russian by Kenneth H. Ober. Odense: Odense Universitetsforlag, 1973).

*———. 1976. *Mif.* Leningrad: Nauka. (In English: *Myth.* Ann Arbor, Mich.: Karoma, 1982).

*Steiner, Peter, and Davydov, Sergej. 1977. "The Biological Metaphor in Russian Formalism. The Concept of Morphology." *Sub-stance* 16:149-58.

Štokmar, M. P. 1952. *Issledovanija v oblasti russkogo narodnogo stixosloženija* [Studies in Russian folk versification]. Moscow: Akademija nauk SSSR.

Strabo. 1961. *The Geography of Strabo*. With an English translation by Horace Leonard Jones. Vol. 7. [The Loeb Classical Library]. Cambridge, Mass.: Harvard University Press; London: William Heinemann, Ltd.

*Struve, Gleb. 1949. "Witch-Hunt: Russian Style. The Soviets Purge Literary Scholarship." *The New Leader* 32 (14), April 2.

*———. 1951. *Soviet Russian Literature 1917-50.* Norman: University of Oklahoma Press.

*———. 1971. *Russian Literature under Lenin and Stalin.* Norman: University of Oklahoma Press.

*Sydow, Carl W. von. 1965. "Folktale Studies and Philology: Some Points of View." In Alan Dundes, *The Study of Folklore*. Englewood Cliffs, N.J.: Prentice-Hall.

*Tarasenkov, An. 1948. "Kosmopolity ot literaturovedenija" [Literary cosmopolitans]. *Novyj mir* 2:124-37.

*Taylor, Archer. 1964. "The Biographical Pattern in Traditional Narrative." *Journal of the Folklore Institute* (Indiana University) 1:114-29.

*Thomas, Lawrence L. 1957. *The Linguistic Theories of N. Ja. Marr*. University of California Publications in Linguistics 14. Berkeley and Los Angeles: University of California Press.

*Thomas, L. L., et al. 1976. "Asdiwal Crumbles: a critique of Lévi-Straussian myth analysis." *American Ethnologist* 3:147-73.

Tixonravov, N. S., and Miller, V. F. 1894. *Russkie byliny staroj i novoj zapisi* [Old and new recordings of Russian bylinas]. Moscow: T-vo Skoropečatni A. A. Levinson.

*Todorov, Tzvetan. 1971. *Poétique de la prose*. Paris: Sueil. (In English: *The Poetics of Prose*. Translated from the French by Richard Howard. Ithaca, N.Y.: Cornell University Press, 1977.)

Tolstoy, L. N. 1953. *Polnoe sobranie sočinenij* [Complete works], vol. 62

*Toschi, Paolo. 1949. "Le radici storiche dei racconti di fate." *Lares* 15:137-49. Reprinted in his *Rappresaglia di studi di letteratura popolare*. Florence: L. Olschki (1956). Biblioteca de Lares 1, 45-63.

*Trautmann, Reinhold. 1935. *Die Volksdichtung der Grossrussen 1. Das Heldenlied (Die Byline)*. Sammlung slavischer Lehr- und Handbücher. 3. Reihe: Texte und Untersuchungen 7. Heidelberg: Carl Winter.

Tronskij, I. M. 1934. "Antičnyj mif i sovremennaja skazka" [The ancient myth and the modern wondertale]. In *Sergeju Fjodoroviču Ol'denburgu. K pjatidesjatiletiju naučno-obščestvennoj dejatel'nosti 1882-1932. Sbornik statej* [Oldenburg *Festschrift*], 523-34. Leningrad: Akademija nauk SSSR. (Listed as *Trockij*.)

Tudorovskaja, E. A. 1955. "Volšebnaja skazka" [The wondertale] and "Skazka o životnyx" [The animal tale]. In *Russkoe narodnoe poètičeskoe tvorčestvo*, vol. 2, book 1, 312-34; 334-44.

*———. 1972. "O strukture volšebnoj skazki" [On the structure of the wondertale]. Russkij fol'klor, vol. 13. Russkaja narodnaja proza, 148-59. Leningrad: Nauka.

*Turbin, V. 1964. "Reportaž so svjatok" [A report from Yule]. *Molodaja Gvardija* 1:289-99.

Turgenev. I. S. 1967. "Poezdka v Al'bano i Fraskati: vospominanija ob A. A. Ivanove" [Journey to Albano and Frascati: recollections of A. A. Ivanov]. In *Polnoe sobranie sočinenij i pisem v dvadcati vos'mi tomax* [Collected works in 28 volumes], vol. 14, 85-96. Moscow and Leningrad: Nauka.

Usener, Hermann K. 1913. "Klagen und Lachen." In *Kleine Schriften* 4. Berlin and Leipzig: B. G. Teubner.

——. 1965. "Zu den Sintfluthsagen." In *Kleine Schriften*, vol. 4. Arbeiten zur Religionsgeshchichte, 382-396. Reprint of the 1912-1913 ed. Osnabrück: Otto Zeller. (Originally published in *Rheinisches Museum* 56 [1901]:481-96.)

*Uspenskij, B. A. 1976a. *The Semantics of the Russian Icon*. Lisse, the Netherlands: The Peter de Ridder Press. (PdR Press publications in semiotics of art 3.)

*——. 1976b. "The Language of Painting." *Dispositio* 1:219-46.

*Uxov, P. D. 1956. Review of Propp 1955. *Sovetskaja ètnografija* 2:147-50.

*Vehvilainen, P. 1970. "The Structure of the Folktale: A Linguistic Approach." *Actes du X Congrès International des linguistes. Bucarest, 28 août–2 septembre 1967. III*. Bucharest: L'Academie de la République socialiste de Roumanie: 427-31.

Vergil. 1967. "Eclogue IV." In *Virgil*. With an English translation by H. Rushton Fairclough. 2 vols. Vol. 1. Eclogues. Georgics. Aeneid I-VI. Revised ed., 28-33. [The Loeb Classical Library]. Cambridge, Mass.: Harvard University Press; London: William Heinemann, Ltd.

Veselovskij, A. N. 1890. "Melkie zamečanija k bylinam; XV. Kto takoj Bravlin v žitii sv. Stefana Surožskogo?" [Brief notes on the bylinas. XV. Who is Bravlin in the life of St. Stefan of Surož?]. *Žurnal Ministerstva narodnogo prosveščenija*, 3, 18-26.

*——. 1913. *Poètika sjužetov*. [The poetics of plots]. In *Sobranie sočinenij* [Works]. Ser. 1 (Poètika) vol. 2, part 1. Saint Petersburg: Akademija nauk.

——. 1938. "Sravnitel'naja mifologija i ee metod" [Comparative mythology and its method]. In *Sobranie sočinenij* [Works] 16. Stat'i o skazke, 1868-1890, 83-128. Leningrad: Akademija nauk SSSR.

Vikent'ev, V. M. 1917. "Drevneegipetskaja povest' o dvux brat'jax" [The ancient Egyptian tale of two brothers]. Kul'turno-istoričeskie pamjatniki vostoka, vol. 4. Moscow.

*Voigt, Vilmos. 1977. "Anordnungsprinzipien." Kurt Ranke, ed. *Enzyklopädie des Märchens. Handwörterbuch zur historischen und vergleichenden Erzählforschung*. 1. Berlin, New York: Walter de Gruyter, 565-76.

*Volkov, R. M. 1924. Skazka. Razyskanija po sjužetosloženiju narodnoj skazki. T. 1. Skazka velikorusskaja, ukrainskaja, belorusskaja [The wondertale. Studies on the structure of the plot of the folk wondertale. vol. 1. The great russian, ukrainian, belorussian wondertale]. Odessa: Gosizdat Ukrainy.

*Vološinov, V. N. 1973. *Marxism and the Philosophy of Language*. Translated by Ladislav Matejka and I. R. Titunik. University of Chicago: Studies in Language 1. New York and London: Seminar Press.

*Vries, Jan de. 1930. "Over het russische sprookjesonderzoek der laatste jaren." *Mens en Mantschappij* 6:330-41.

Warburg, Aby. 1939. "A Lecture on Serpent Ritual." *Journal of the Warburg Institute* 2:277-92.

Wehrli, Fritz R. 1934. "Die Mysterien von Eleusis." *Archiv für Religionswissenschaft* 31:77-104.

Wesselski, Albert. 1923. *Märchen des Mittelalters*. Berlin: H. Stubenrauch.

Wilamowitz-Moellendorf, U. von. 1925. "Die griechische Heldensage." Sitzungsberichte der Berlinischen Akademie der Wissenschaften. Philosophisch-historische Klasse, 41-62, 214-42.

*Wosien, Maria-Gabriele. 1969. *The Russian Folk-Tale. Some Structural and Thematic Aspects*. Slavistische Beiträge 41. Munich: Otto Sagner.

Xudjakov, I. A. 1860-62. *Velikorusskie skazki* [Great Russian folktales]. 3 vols. Moscow [vols. 1, 2]: V. Gračëv; St. Petersburg [vol. 3]: Voennaja tipografija. (Reprinted as *Velikorusskie skazki v zapisjax I. A. Xudjakova*. Izdanie podgotovili V. G. Bazanov i O. V. Alekseeva. Moscow: Nauka,

1964. The numbering of the tales in the 1974 reprint does not follow that of the original publication; a table correlating the two editions is on p. 293.)

Zarubin, I. I. 1932. *Beludžskie skazki, sobrannye I. I. Zarubinym* [Baluchi folktales]. Trudy Instituta vostokovedenija Akademii nauk SSSR 4.

Ždanov, I. N. 1895. *Russkij bylevoj èpos. Issledovanija i materialy.* [Russian traditional epic poetry. Research and material.] St. Petersburg: L. F. Panteleev.

Zelenin, D. K. 1914. *Velikorusskie skazki Permskoj gubernii* [Great Russian folktales of the Perm gubernija]. Zapiski Imperatorskogo Russkogo geografičeskogo obščestva po otdeleniju ètnografii, vol. 41. Petrograd: A. V. Orlov.

———. 1915. *Velikorusskie skazki Vjatskoj gubernii* [Great Russian folktales of the Vjatka gubernija]. Zapiski Imperatorskogo Russkogo geografičeskogo obščestva po otdeleniju ètnografii, vol. 42. Petrograd: A. V. Orlov.

*———. 1929. Review of Propp 1928. *Slavische Rundschau* 1: 286-87.

———. 1934. "Religiozno-magičeskaja funkcija fol'klornyx skazok" [The religious and magical function of folklore tales]. In *Sergeju Fjodoroviču Ol'denburgu. K pjatidesjatiletiju naučno-obščestvennoj dejatel'nosti 1882-1932. Sbornik statej*, 215-40. Leningrad: Akademija nauk SSSR.

———. 1936. *Kul't Ongonov v Sibiri; perežitki totemizma v ideologii sibirskix narodov* [The religion of the Ongons in Siberia; remnants of totemism in the ideology of Siberian peoples]. Trudy Instituta antropologii i ètnografii Akademii nauk SSSR, vol. 14. Etnografičeskaja serija, vyp. 3. Moscow: Akademija nauk SSSR.

———. 1940. "The Genesis of the Fairy Tale." *Ethnos* 5:54-58.

Zelinskij, F. F. 1896. "Zakon xronologičeskoj nesovmestimosti i kompozicija Iliady" [The law of chronological incompatibility and the composition of the *Iliad*]. In Χαριστηρια: *Sbornik statej po filologii i lingvistike v čest' F. E. Korša*, 101-21. Moscow.

*Zemljanova, L. M. 1975. *Sovremennaja amerikanskaja fol'kloristika. Teoretičeskie napravlenija i tendencii* [Contemporary American folkloristics. Trends and tendencies]. Moscow: Nauka.

*Zgusta, Russell. 1978. *Russian Minstrels. A History of the Skomorokhi.* University of Pennsylvania Press.

*Zinder, L. R. 1960. *Obščaja fonetika* [General phonetics]. Leningrad: Leningradskij gosudarstvennyj universitet.

*Žirmunskij, V. M. 1947. Review of Propp 1946. *Sovetskaja kniga* 5:97-103.

Indexes

General Index

Index of Foreign Terms

Born in St. Petersburg in 1895, **Vladimir Propp** joined the faculty of Leningrad University in 1932 as a language teacher and folklorist, and remained there till his death in 1970. His major works include *Morphology of the Folktale, Historical Roots of the Wondertale, Russian Heroic Epic Poetry, Russian Agrarian Festivals,* and the posthumously published *Problems of Laughter and the Comic.*

Anatoly Liberman, also a native of Leningrad, is a professor in the German and Scandinavian departments at the University of Minnesota. He is the author of *Germanic Accentology, Volume I. The Scandinavian Languages* and translator and editor of *Mikhail Lermontov: Major Poetical Works,* both published by the University of Minnesota Press.

Ariadna Martin is a philologist with a diploma in Russian from Leningrad University, where she studied under Propp. **Richard Martin** holds degrees in the Slavic languages from the University of Chicago and Columbia University.